South Africa – The Present as History

as History

From Mrs Ples to Mandela & Marikana

John S. Saul
Professor Emeritus at York University (Canada)

Patrick Bond
*Senior Professor of Development Studies
& Director of the Centre for Civil Society
at the University of KwaZulu-Natal (Durban)*

JAMES CURREY

James Currey
is an imprint of Boydell & Brewer Ltd
PO Box 9
Woodbridge, Suffolk IP12 3DF (GB)
www.jamescurrey.com

and of

Boydell & Brewer Inc.
668 Mt Hope Avenue
Rochester, NY 14620-2731 (US)
www.boydellandbrewer.com

Published in paperback in Southern Africa in 2014
(South Africa, Namibia, Lesotho, Swaziland & Botswana)
by Jacana Media (Pty) Ltd
Orange Street, Sunnyside
Auckland Park 2092
Johannesburg
South Africa

With funding from the German Federal Ministry for Economic Cooperation and Development
and the Rosa Luxemburg Stiftung

First published in cloth 2014
First published in paperback outside of southern Africa 2016

British Library Cataloguing in Publication Data
A catalogue record is available on request from the British Library

ISBN: 978-1-84701-135-0 (James Currey paperback)
ISBN: 978-1-4314-1066-8 (Jacana paperback)

Typeset in 10/11.5pt Photina MT by Avocet Typeset, Somerton, Somerset

Dedication

for Neville Alexander, 1936–2012
Robben Island 'graduate', exemplary activist
and intellectual inspiration, after a life
dedicated to the achievement of a genuinely liberated
South Africa

and

to the memory of the 34 workers massacred
at Marikana by the post-apartheid state
16 August 2012

Contents

Part III
Conclusions: The Future as History 211

6.

Uneven and Combined Resistance:
Marikana and The Trail to 'Tunisia Day' 2020   213
(Patrick Bond)

7.

Liberating Liberation:
The Struggle against Recolonization in South Africa   243
(John S. Saul)

Postscript
(John S. Saul and Patrick Bond)   271

Introduction:
South Africa in History

JOHN S. SAUL AND PATRICK BOND

The late-twentieth century's most obvious historical anomaly, the 'legalized' form of racial oppression that was apartheid, remained for many decades an on-going challenge to both activists and analysts engaged in the project of realizing social justice – knowing all the while that this deeply inequitable system should change, could change, would change, but not knowing when it would change, or how, or by whose efforts. Nonetheless, by the end of the new millennium's first decade, we had in fact witnessed South Africa's negotiated realization of a new colour-blind democratic constitution as well as several elections on this new roughly open and non-racial basis: that of 1994 bringing Nelson Mandela and his African National Congress (ANC) to office; that of 1999 reaffirming, with the election of Thabo Mbeki as Mandela's successor as President, both the democratic content of the transition and the ANC's overwhelming legitimacy as governing party; that of 2004 reconfirming the ANC in state power (notwithstanding Mbeki and his team's dramatically flawed leadership); that of 2009 which, in the wake of Mbeki's dismissal from office, did reaffirm in power the ANC, now under President Jacob Zuma's leadership – albeit without much sense that the latter's newly-restructured ruling coalition would transform the deeply inequitable and dependent country now under his sway. The national election sometime in 2014 has seemed likely merely further to cement Zuma's dominance, although even that can no longer merely be assumed.[1]

In short, the country was finally freed from the most obvious racial-political shackles of white and Western domination that had dogged its path for centuries. Nonetheless, fluidity, tension and severe inequality have characterized what should have been the end of that long period of waiting and uncertainty. The world wanted South Africa's true, liberated history – and the writing of it – to begin in 1994, but deep contradictions have quickly bubbled to the surface, revealing a society gripped in turmoil. The results of all this have been, of course, paradoxical: a series of elections since 1994 seemed to confirm the ANC's hold, both popular and legitimate, on power. Yet, simultaneously, South Africa has found itself with one of the world's highest rates of protest and dissent, expressed both in the work-place and on township streets, in universities and technikons (higher education institutions of technology), clinics and

[1] See, *inter alia*, Allister Sparks, 'ANC is Becoming Beatable', *The Mercury* (August 14, 2013) and Sparks, 'A shift in the political landscape', *Cape Times*, June 19, 2013.

1

central city squares. This is a paradox that requires explanation – underscored most recently by the South African Police Service's cold-blooded shooting of 34 striking Lonmin miners at Marikana on 16 August 2012. For Marikana stands not only as a telling sign of the precise character of the post-apartheid state but also as an index of the many deep complexities that the student of South Africa must continue to ponder. At the same time, the fact of dissent so graphically expressed is also a source of hope for those who sense that something better than the semi-liberation that the ANC has presided over in its country must not be long delayed. We will have to examine the roots of such hope – both within the ANC itself and within the broader society of South Africa – before drawing our book to a close.

* * *

In the first instance, however, the book will seek to capture the excitement of the transition so described, to explore the moment of genuine possibility that the 1990s and the new millennium seemed to open up for South Africans. Nonetheless, the 'pre-history' of a liberated South Africa must not be forgotten either. It is a complex story, this interpenetration of black and white that was launched with the first significant European land-fall by the Dutch captain Jan van Riebeeck in 1652. The fingerprints of the long centuries of European domination and exploitation ensuing from that fateful coming together of peoples are to be found all over present-day South Africa; we will have to carefully assess this legacy in these pages.

It is true that 'pre-history' of post-apartheid South Africa also goes much further back, to a period long antedating the arrival of Europeans in the territory that would eventually come to be defined as South Africa. This is the history of the indigenous inhabitants of the continent of Africa and their peopling of the southern part of that continent. Social patterns and cultural dynamics were set in motion through this 'African history' of South Africa that would never quite be submerged, however much they might be altered, by the ruthless European appropriation of the sub-continent.

Indeed, this counter-history had seemed to find a certain apotheosis in Nelson Mandela's election, after many decades of liberation struggle, as the first 'African' president of a multi-racial South Africa. Are not the overwhelming majority of South Africa's people who are black now free to exercise their democratic rights and make their voices heard? Has not this outcome, this dramatic transition from white minority rule to a democratic South Africa, been realized, at least in its latter stages, 'peacefully' through negotiations, rather than having to be fought out to the bitter end as a 'race war' of unimaginable proportions and grisly consequences?

It is, of course, an exciting story, one of the great dramas of the twentieth century, when told in such terms. In these pages we will explore both the historical processes that have given rise to this transition and the ways in which a 'non-racial' outcome has begun to be institutionalized (and, simultaneously, undermined) constitutionally, politically, and economically, in the current post-apartheid period. For the problem lies in determining just how 'new' the new South Africa really is. Against the undeniable drama of the transition from the formal structures of white minority rule that has occurred must be set the fact that South Africa today is a much more unequal society than during apartheid, one deeply stratified in class and gender terms, and also in racial terms ('class' still remaining so substantially 'raced' in the country). Moreover, it is facing the prospect of genuine economic and ecological calamities.

In consequence, in this book we will have to ask just how meaningful – in terms of genuine popular empowerment and real accountability – the institutions of multi-party democracy actually are, crafted as they are in the teeth both of the negative legacies of the country's troubled past and of such new contradictions as logically emerged from the way the transition unfolded. After all, the social and economic policies of the post-apartheid South African government can now be understood as a coherent project ('social democratic' in its proponents' views, 'neo-liberal plus tokenist-welfarist' in those of its critics), but also questioned as to just how appropriate they are for the transformation of South Africa from a situation of socio-economic degradation.

There are tough questions here, even more complex than those of the past when an anti-apartheid perspective seemed able to carry us quite a long way in making sense of South Africa. Nor is the evaluation of the contradictory nature of the recent transition in South Africa of merely analytical interest. Questions regarding such issues as the ANC's social and economic policy choices are hotly debated inside South Africa itself. Some observers – within the trade union movement, the popularly-based organizations, academia, journalism, the progressive churches and the general public – are highly critical of what they consider to be the ineffectual, even unjust and undemocratic, nature of the ANC government's response to the existence of deep-seated inequalities in the country.

These observers argue, in fact, that much of the radical promise of the party's long-term historical trajectory as a people's movement appears to have been lost. They see in the 'neo-liberal' cast of the ANC's controversial economic strategies (centred on 'international competitiveness' and the overwhelming drive to attract foreign investment) an uncritical capitulation to the global 'free market', one that is unlikely to yield any very great return in development terms. Indeed, in the jettisoning of the more radical planks of its original 1994 election platform (as presented in parts of the Reconstruction and Development Programme, for example) they find proof that ANC elites have made an accommodation with centres of white and capitalist power – at the expense of the interests of the mass of the party's followers who continue to languish in poverty and squalor. Thus they see the massacre at Marikana as merely the most graphic example of what South Africa's troubled history has produced.

Many, analysts and politicians alike, argue quite differently, of course. Some of them are convinced that the ANC's post-apartheid course, modest and 'pragmatic', does represent a promising economic programme with 'developmental state' prospects. Others state merely that the current realities of global and local power give the new government little choice ('TINA' – 'There Is No Alternative'

– as this point of view is epitomized in contemporary South African parlance) other than embracing the neo-liberal option. Ensure growth by the untroubled embrace of a vibrant global capitalism, the yea-sayers assert, and eventually a redistribution of the returns from such growth will begin to have their positive impact on the lives of the vast majority of South Africans. In any case, they continue, it is still far too soon to judge the true socio-economic impact of the profound political changes that have occurred.

We will begin to assess such debates below. There can, however, be no escaping the urgency of addressing successfully – by whatever means necessary – the challenges posed both by history and by the present for a post-apartheid South Africa: poverty and squalor breed desperation, crime, and violence. Take 'violence': the history of South Africa has, of course, been permeated with violence, most notably in the manner of European seizure of the land over several centuries and in the subordination of the indigenous population to the white population's demand for cheap black labour. It has been violent, as well, in the brutal methods used by the apartheid state in its attempts to ensure its power against the just claims of those who challenged it. It has also been violent in the ways in which the subordinated black population often found it necessary to struggle for its most basic rights. Healing such a tormented society, rendering it a community rather than an armed camp, redressing the damage done and moving on to higher ground – these are not simple or straightforward tasks. Much has been accomplished in recent years but the struggle, to ensure that broad-gauged development and the deepening of a profoundly participatory democracy outpace the negative potential for distemper and decay inherent in post-apartheid society, continues. This also is the kind of high drama that this book seeks to examine.[2]

* * *

This, then, is South Africa's present as history: challenging, charged and contradictory. But what of our book's subtitle, 'From Mrs Ples to Mandela and Marikana'? A long distance to travel in historical terms as the following chapters will testify – although not, as it happens, nearly so far geographically. In fact, Mandela's residences since the 1950s included a Soweto standard four-roomed house, his Houghton mansion in Johannesburg and the presidential residence in Pretoria during the late 1990s, and the homes of Mrs Ples and Marikana mineworkers are themselves only a short distance apart from each other as the crow flies, although two intervening mountains and a valley make the road trip longer (about 90 minutes, without breaking the speed limit). So, if you desire, a few hours of driving and walking on a sunny afternoon will acquaint you with the geography of our species' origins some two million years

---

[2] See, on the broad theme of failed 'liberation' in South Africa but also throughout the region, John S. Saul, 'Race, Class, Gender and Voice: Four Terrains of Liberation'; Chapter 1 of Saul's *Liberation Lite: The Roots of Recolonization in Southern Africa* (Delhi and Trenton, NJ: Three Essays Collective and Africa World Press, 2011); also John S. Saul, 'The Strange Death of Liberated Southern Africa', *Transformation*, 64, 2007.

ago at one extreme, and, at the other extreme, with the grim denouement of what South Africa had become, in August 2012, so many centuries later (and, as it happened, in the 100th anniversary year of the ANC itself).

You might be visiting this area after a flight into the OR Tambo Airport east of Johannesburg or, much closer, the Lanseria regional airport in the Magaliesberg mountain range. If the latter, your journey would last barely a half hour, along Route 540 through the fields of Sterkfontein where, at the Cradle of Humankind World Heritage Site, a reception centre run by the University of the Witwatersrand, and a cave climb await. The best-kept skull of *Australopithecus africanus* – humankind's common ancestor – was named *Plesianthropus transvaalensis*, 'near-human from the Transvaal' (reflecting an old term for 'across the Vaal,' in as much as the Vaal river, lying about 100 km (60 miles) away, was the border with the old Orange Free State republic). The river was forded by Afrikaner farmers in the 'Great Trek' of the 1830s, but no one halted here in the Witwatersrand to dig for gold (or the subsequently pursued platinum group metals) until a half-century later. This province is now called Gauteng, and the first of the Magaliesberg ranges, in which Mrs Ples's skeleton was found during digs for cement ingredients during the heady post-war gold boom in the nearby West Rand, is the border with North West Province in which Marikana lies.

After taking in the hilly environs of Mrs Ples and other 'hominids,' many of whom were perfectly preserved in limestone graves after they (like Mrs Ples) accidentally plunged into crevices or died in caves, your drive in a north-westerly direction brings you to Marikana via the Hartbeesport Dam. For more than half a century, this has been the elite recreational weekend retreat for the wealthy of Pretoria and Johannesburg, sufficiently high in elevation to permit an escape from the blistering summer heat. It is worth pausing here so as to reflect on the health of the society and its water – because, just off the main road to the east, lies Kosmos Village, a wealthy 'gated community' whose service workers live in a shack settlement just a stone's throw away. It is one of South Africa's most extreme back-to-back wealth/poverty sites, within the world's most unequal large society, and not far from the major city judged by the United Nations in 2012 as the world's most income-unequal, Johannesburg.

There are hundreds of thousands of such shacks across Gauteng and North West Provinces, nearly all constructed since the 1986–91 demise of Pass Laws and the Group Areas Act permitted faster rural-urban migration. The vast majority of the shacks have no formal sanitation system, and hence defecation is common in un-serviced latrines or even in the bare veld. Especially after rains, the run-off into the Crocodile, Jukskei and Hennops Rivers which feed Hartbeesport Dam, in turn, causes dangerous surges in E. coli counts. By 2010, these reached such high levels that the main elite department store, Woolworths, warned it would cease purchasing agricultural produce irrigated from the Hartbeesport Dam's huge canal system. The dam, famous for water sports, now often stinks, with excessive toxic algae, cyanobacteria and water hyacinth that destroy both its water's health and the site's aesthetic value. The water colour in the dam is often an eerie-looking bright green.

Nor would fixing this be easy – because the notorious municipality office nearby (Madibeng) is under investigation: from 2005 to 2010 more than 340 of the area's bureaucrats were illegally running businesses which had dealings with the municipality, this thanks to 'tenderpreneurship' (involving the granting, via a tender process, of small contracts to fledgling African entrepreneurs complementary to much larger economic undertakings), a ploy devised by the ruling party and big business during the late 1990s as their profit-friendly strategy for deracializing apartheid. Here blowback from this entire system manifests itself most obviously in Kosmos Village: for it is this mix of ecological and social degradation that fuels what is probably the world's highest per capita rate of sustained community street protests and labour unrest.

But now, after you have traversed the dam, the road to Marikana soon appears and eventually the lush green Magaliesberg resorts – still hosting hundreds of fancy weddings (mainly still of whites) each weekend – are left behind. For here the dusty, desolate platinum belt looms, with the old Bophuthatswana homeland – an apartheid geopolitical abomination which lasted from 1971–94 – stretching out across northern South Africa. ('Bop' took in much of this minerals-rich area well before discoveries of platinum and the co-optation of the local ethnic leaders permitted several multinational corporate mining houses to set up shop.)

A little further west of Marikana is the former farming town of Rustenburg, a locale that became a mining boom town albeit without any really visible evidence of local accumulation of capital (aside from a new highway link to Pretoria), while further along the road you can stop in at Sun City and the Lost City, the one-time sanctions-busting casino and entertainment complex run by Sol Kerzner. A huge controversy did emerge on this very road in 2012 – as well as on most of the Johannesburg and Pretoria highways – when pay tolls were imposed by a European road-management contractor (sheltered under the rubric of a 'Public-Private Partnership'); working-class and middle-class residents considered these extortionate and campaigned against the tolls vigorously, albeit (in achieving only a slight discount on previously announced rates) unsuccessfully. Yet the area's diverse socio-economic tensions were already at breaking-point by that time. As Chapter 6 recounts, in early 2012 the largest of the three huge platinum firms, Implats, suffered a debilitating strike; in mid-2012 the third largest platinum firm, Lonmin, hosted a massacre near its mine (Marikana); and, in early 2013, the second largest, Anglo American Platinum, announced the closure of shafts and the firing of 13,000 workers.

Visiting this tumultuous site is instructive, especially if you wander the main street of Marikana. Facing north, you can look up to your left at the imposing mining headgear or, by turning to either side, you will find more than a dozen 'pay-day lender' and '*mashonisa*' microfinance offices amidst a hodge-podge of low-level consumer-goods outlets. Then wandering about a kilometre (half a mile or so) to the right you soon stumble across the infamous 'mountain' – a rocky hillock or '*kopje*' – near Eskom's huge electricity substation, a structure which nearly blocks your sight of the main energy-guzzler nearby: Lonmin's platinum smelter. From here, looking north-east, just beyond the smaller 'killing kopje' where mineworkers unsuccessfully sought refuge shortly after the shooting began at around 4pm on 16 August 2012, you will see the Wonderkop shack settlement. Though women there have forged survival and mutual-aid politics (despite the terrible imbalances in gender power relations that labour migration tends to foster), Wonderkop's tin shacks are graced by no apparent state services and only a few trivial Corporate Social Responsibility (CSR) projects. Migrant labour prevails, replicating many of the harshest aspects of apartheid's underlying political economy. This within spitting distance of one of the world's richest mineral deposits and of Lonmin itself, which the World Bank considers to be one of the success stories of CSR outsourced investment – the Bank having authorized a US$150 million investment in 2007 (though with next to nothing to show for it aside from profits). Indeed by 2013, mass unemployment and worsened defaults and degradation are certain, thanks to Anglo American's own restructuring.

Fired workers' recourse to employment on nearby farms (mostly still Afrikaner-owned) is less of an option these days. One reason is that the area is increasingly subject to climate change. Here the irony is that Marikana's mining and smelting are dependent upon the imposing pylons which transmit electricity from Eskom's vast coal-fired generators. Those generators are, in fact, the African continent's main contribution to changing climate, and it was in the era of Mandela that any attempts to shift the pattern of accumulation away from its 'Minerals-Energy Complex' would be foiled, by virtue of the ANC's 'Faustian moment' in the thrall of big business (as Ronnie Kasrils termed the 1990s). Moreover, the further destruction of even irrigated agriculture east of Marikana has been hastened by the platinum industry's own unrelenting direct water and air pollution.

But this (as Chapters 6 and 7 will further argue) is merely one more of the ways in which South Africa's multi-faceted contradictions unfold before your eyes at Marikana. Indeed, the border area of Gauteng and North West Provinces illustrates a great many of the contemporary era's profound restructuring of class, race, gender and ecological politics, one site amongst many others in South Africa where progressive-minded activists must begin to grapple much more effectively than they have to date with the challenge of how best to connect the dots so as to create a truly progressive politics. In sum, Mrs Ples's relatives would have foraged in once-fertile plains here – precisely where the blood of massacre victims must now nourish whatever might yet grow in the dry fields of Marikana, and elsewhere across the country.

* * *

Finally, this introduction cannot fail to note another rather different kind of complexity to the writing of this book, one no student of South Africa can easily escape: the question of what is the most appropriate language to use in making our arguments. The most controversial problems arise regarding the issue of 'racial' distinctions. It is impossible to write South Africa's story without reference to such distinctions, yet doing so presents a veritable mine-field. Just what language is most appropriate here? The 'official' categories most often used are those frozen into place under the auspices of white domination: Europeans, Coloureds, Indians, Africans. In this lexicon the term 'Coloured' refers to the people of mixed race, descendants both of forebears of South African provenance, in particular the Khoisan peoples of the Cape region, and of slave populations brought in, most notably, during the period of direct Dutch control of the emergent colony; 'Indian' to descendants of indentured labourers brought to Natal from the Indian sub-continent in the latter part of the nineteenth century and early twentieth century and who have retained a certain communal identity; 'European' to the hitherto politically dominant white population, drawn, over a number of centuries, from many European countries but principally from The Netherlands and Great Britain; 'African' to those 'indigenous' South Africans, the vast majority, who speak mostly Bantu languages and whose most remote forebears are of continental origin.

The reification of such categories served well the purposes of the racially-motivated white governments that ruled South Africa for so long, rationalizing the terms of their rule and helping to divide and conquer, along community lines, those over whom they ruled. As we shall also see, even the African National Congress of South Africa felt constrained, for long periods of its history and in the name, paradoxically enough, of 'non-racialism', to accept this set of categories for strategic and tactical reasons, presenting itself as part of an alliance of different political organizations representing these various racial groups rather than, straightforwardly, as a non-racial organization. Other political actors – notably the Pan Africanist Congress – for many years wore as a badge of pride their adherence to an exclusively 'indigenous' and racially defined African identity as being central to their own 'Africanist' claim to power.

This kind of quadripartite categorization has been vigorously resisted at various points in South African history, of course: for example, by the Black Consciousness Movement of the 1960s and 1970s which chose to define 'so-called Coloureds', Indians and Africans as all being, positively, 'black' (in phraseology subsequently adopted by the ANC and its internal allies) – over and against the 'whites' who were in power. The ANC has itself slowly but surely moved to give more formal substance to its non-racial definition of South Africa, approving, while in exile, first non-African membership in the ANC itself (1969) and ultimately the incorporation of non-Africans into the movement's leadership (1985). More recently, ANC leaders – notably Thabo Mbeki – advanced a definition of 'African' (alongside their already colour-blind category of 'South African') that asserts itself as being non-racial, a self-definition available to any of whatever prior racial category who align themselves with the project of creating a deracialized, post-apartheid South Africa.

This shifting exercise of naming is important, encapsulating in its own right a complex history to which we will have to return in subsequent chapters. Suffice to say here that problems of terminology will continue to haunt us as we proceed in this book. We will find ourselves sometimes forced to use the old quadripartite language for example, and to do so without always placing the terms in parenthesis or attaching the often-used qualifier 'so-called' (as in 'so-called Coloureds') as often as we might. Self-evidently, these are terms and categories that have had historical resonance and ones that, in many cases, still have present-day effects. These can be seen, for example, in the on-going resonance of a specifically Coloured identity – as distinct from either black or African identity – that facilitated, even in the post-apartheid period and notably in the Western Cape, the mobilization of many members of that community to support the erstwhile party of apartheid, the National Party. Such effects are also evident in the language of 'black' and 'white' that continues, almost inevitably, to structure much debate in post-apartheid South Africa.

Nor are these the only problems we will have with naming in this volume: there is, for example, the troubled matter of 'ethnicity'. Cultural differences (not least linguistic differences) and diverse regional histories do have a bearing on intra-African politics: at the extreme, for example, Chief Gatsha Buthelezi who sought for many years to manipulate 'Zulu' identity for his own ends at least as aggressively as the apartheid regime once sought to manipulate 'tribal diversity' for purposes of its divide and rule agenda. Still, the ethnic terrain is formidably complex conceptually as well as in practice. So too are the terrains of class and gender – and the language that we will have to develop, quite self-consciously, in order to analyse them as our argument proceeds. We must invite the reader to remain alert to the full ramifications of such complexities, both terminological and substantive, as they read this book.

We must note too that South Africa has never been a country that could be understood in isolation from its broader geographical context. The initial movement of African peoples into the southern tip of the continent embedded South African history from the outset in the history of the continent as a whole. Under white domination South Africa was also deeply enmeshed in global networks of capitalist and imperialist control and calculation, while, vis-à-vis other territories and countries of southern Africa, South Africa's mineral wealth and relative economic advancement gave it an overbearing presence that, in one form or another, continues into the present period. Moreover, the regional fight for liberation that swept the sub-continent from the early 1960s and that affected such neighbouring theatres of war as Mozambique and Angola, Zimbabwe and Namibia (as well as a number of 'Front-line States' who were drawn into the struggle) lodged South Africa's own transition within a much wider territorial framework. We will have to pay careful attention to this larger history, and also to the implications for present and future trends in South Africa of the country's continuing and multi-dimensional links to on-going developments at the global, continental and regional levels.

* * *

This book seeks, then, to offer a consistent, cumulative argument about the direction of developments in South Africa as the country has moved from its apartheid past into its post-apartheid future. It should also be noted that to keep the book as succinct and focused as publication requirements demand we have sought to synthesize, principally, the literature of professional scholarship and a range of public documents in developing our argument – while also drawing on our own experiences over a number of years: in South Africa itself, in southern Africa more generally, and in anti-apartheid-related support work in North America. There has not been scope in these pages to introduce the full range of indigenous voices that would, ideally, serve as a complement to the materials we have drawn upon.

A reading of this book will therefore be enriched by exposure to the wide range of creative writing (much of it almost inevitably drawn to political themes) produced by South Africans, to the many autobiographies and biographies written by local protagonists, and to various invaluable collections of documents and speeches: Alison Drew's two-volume *South Africa's Radical Tradition* (Cape Town: University of Cape Town Press, 1996/1997) and the six-volume *From Protest to Challenge* series edited, variously, by Gwendolyn Carter, Thomas Karis, Gail Gerhart and Clive Glaser (Stanford and Bloomington: Hoover Institution Press and Indiana Press, variously from 1972 to 2010) are particularly useful in this regard. We also celebrate the new multi-volume history of *The Road To Democracy in South Africa* being produced in South Africa by the South African Democracy Education Trust of which a number of its extremely useful volumes – as well as attendant volumes on 'International Solidarity' and the first of a closely related series entitled 'South Africans telling their stories' – have appeared (Cape Town and Braamfontein: Zebra Press and Unisa Press, variously from 2004 to 2013). Nonetheless, our hope is that those readers who are South Africans will find our contribution to be a useful overview of the situation in their country as it continues on through the new millennium, one complementary both to their own on-going social-scientific work and to the telling of their own stories. We trust that other readers will find it illuminating as well.

It remains only to thank those who have helped, over the years, in the composition of this book. In Saul's case, this is far too large a task, and demands much too long a list, to be a practical undertaking, ranging as it must through a vast wealth of contact and friendship with South Africans during his periods of extended residence, since the 1960s, in London, in Dar es Salaam, Tanzania, in Maputo, Mozambique, in Toronto in his native Canada, and in South Africa itself (in the course of many visits there and of a period spent teaching in Johannesburg in 2001). Similarly he wishes to acknowledge the role played, over the years, by his students in Tanzania, Mozambique, Canada and South Africa, with whom many of the ideas present in several of these chapters were first sketched out. Of course, Saul feels, to single out individual names would be invidious, but he must nonetheless note his more immediate gratitude to both Tom Lodge and Dale McKinley for helpful comments on his own chapters. He also wishes to underscore here the fact that this volume is dedicated the memory of one particular friend, the recently-deceased Neville Alexander – as well as to the martyrs of Marikana.

Saul must also thank, particularly warmly, his comrades – both in the late-lamented Toronto Committee for the Liberation of Southern Africa (TCLSAC) and in the *Southern Africa Report* magazine collective – whose shared enthusiasm and commitment over many years helped to make the distance between Toronto and the front-lines in South Africa seem much less daunting and demo-bilizing than would otherwise have been the case. He thanks, too, Leo Panitch, Greg Albo and Vivek Chibber, editors of *The Socialist Register*, as well as his other fellow members of the *Register*'s team of 'Contributing Editors', who helped shape his essay on South Africa's transition and its context to the recent issue of that annual volume (2013); the prior writing of that essay helped structure – and even contributed to some of its specific formulations – of the more devel-oped argument to be found in Chapter 2 below.[3] Finally, of course, there is his family, of all generations, who have accompanied him on so many of his travels and have, more recently, supported him firmly through some personally difficult times – with thanks, especially, to Pat for careful proofreading of seemingly endless draft versions of text and for many other useful discussions.

As for Bond, heartfelt thanks are again offered to all who have nurtured me and my understanding of South Africa from the point in the early 1980s when I took up solidarity activism (like many thousands in North America, decisively influenced by Saul and by exiled poet Dennis Brutus); to my earliest visit in 1984 (especially my Durban teachers Patmanathan and Rajen Naidoo); to when I moved from Harare to Yeoville's tumultuous Rockey Street in early 1990 (thanks to Mark Swilling's professional generosity); and to the countless critical conjunctures that have ratcheted up my social awareness and intellectual insights ever since, as did my political-economic training under David Harvey's watch at Johns Hopkins, which concluded in 1992 with a doctorate about Zimbabwe's uneven development. I then was torn between further civil society support and joining academia; once again it was Saul who showed how scholar-activism could reduce, not close, that gap. In South Africa today, as the academy neo-liberalizes, there are very few employed by our universities who can avoid at least considering the worsening social and environmental context as inte-gral to our research interests. There are a great many South African models of engaged politico-intellectual activity (to illustrate, a list of books about this country by independent progressive authors since 2000 exceeds 100 entries), although for me perhaps none provided as forcefully as by my friends Ashwin Desai and Trevor Ngwane. In addition, every so often I have taken a break to regroup in wonderful academic communities – Baltimore in 1994–95 (Johns Hopkins' Public Health School), Toronto in 2003–04 (York University's Depart-ment of Political Science) and Berkeley in 2010–11 (the University of Cali-fornia's Department of Geography) – where inspiring efforts to foster praxis epistemologies were also underway.

But from the empirical standpoint of learning enough about this society to tackle Chapters 3 to 5, it was the greatest privilege to first serve the Jo'burg area's urban social movements of the early 1990s; then to assist the Recon-struction and Development Programme team in 1993–94 and the Pretoria policy machine numerous times thereafter up to 2000 (until frustration finally

---

[3]   See John S. Saul, 'On Taming a Revolution: The South African Case' in Leo Panitch et al., *The Socialist Register 2014* (London: The Merlin Press, 2013).

overflowed when I 'wrote left' in order for them to 'govern right'); and then to explore the society and economy again, alongside those who had begun fighting class apartheid from around 2000. My institutional homes – in Johannesburg, Planact (1990–94), the National Institute for Economic Policy (1995–97) and the Wits University Graduate School of Public and Development Management (1997–2004); and in Durban after 2004, the University of KwaZulu-Natal's Centre for Civil Society – were more generous than I had any right to expect. My family, especially Jan and Kati, and my dearest friends (including Samantha) were always my saviours and *raisons d'être* – especially when, as so often happens, social-change projects spluttered. It is these durable bonds that keep heart and soul hopeful for the better world we know is possible – even in times when a massacre and its aftermath unveil so much that, frankly, we did not really want to know.

Part I
What's Past is Prologue[1]:
From the Beginnings to 1994

---

[1] This title is drawn from William Shakespeare, *The Tempest*, Act II, Scene i.

1.

The Making of South Africa ... and Apartheid, to 1970

JOHN S. SAUL

Across the complex landscape of the southern part of the African continent, human beings have carved a conflictual history, one that in the last several hundred years has witnessed particularly dramatic scenes: heroic accomplishments set against cruel examples – the apartheid system itself being the principal case in point – of 'man's inhumanity to man [sic]'. The present chapter will sketch this experience, tracing the long arc of history of those peoples who would ultimately form the citizenry of present-day South Africa. It must be borne in mind, however, that for much of the period covered in this chapter, the lines on the map that eventually came to encompass 'South Africa' did not exist: only with the benefit of hindsight can we see, with any clarity, that country 'in the-making'.[2] Up until a very late date, a diversity of 'histories' cut across the territory that is now South Africa, these histories fatefully intersecting in ways that deeply affected and qualified their independent trajectories, even as they also retained and reflected something of their own semi-autonomous structure, dynamics and inner meaning.

This chapter will, in turn, set the stage for an initial focus in the succeeding one (Chapter 2) on the attempt to forge one kind of synthesis of these diversities: the extreme form of institutionalization of racial supremacy represented by the ascendancy, from 1948, of the National Party and its authoritarian apartheid state. But we will also begin to evoke the emerging effort to establish, through resistance to white minority rule, an alternative synthesis, one that, in subsequent chapters (2 and 3), will be seen to find at least partial fulfilment in the dramatic election – democratic and non-racial – of 1994 and in the current political centrality of the African National Congress (ANC). The succeeding two decades, scarred so deeply by what had gone before, will be our focus in Chapters 4 and 5 (by Patrick Bond), marking as they did a liberation only partially realized and, for the vast mass of the population, principally black, marking no very substantive liberation at all. Here, however, we must begin at the beginning, with an African history that long antedates the incursion of the white colonizers into South Africa. It is a history, as we will see, that continued to have its own weight and substance throughout the entire period of white overlordship and one that promises to find further expression in the present

---

[2] We will refrain from placing the term 'South Africa' within quotation marks every time we use it in this chapter, but it would be well for readers to remember the qualifications as to its appropriateness suggested in this paragraph and seek to avoid the temptation to think either teleologically or anachronistically when they see the term.

post-apartheid period, a situation of recolonization (by global capital and its now black in-country allies) ... and the attempt, as well, to revive an on-going struggle for a more meaningful liberation.

An African history

In the wake of the recent transition to majority rule in South Africa it is easy to forget how much of a political football the subject of the initial peopling of southern Africa once was. For many white supporters of apartheid a version of this history was used to ground their prior claim to continuing control over the territory that would eventually become South Africa. This claim – the 'myth of the empty land,' as historian Shula Marks has referred to it[3] – stated quite simply that whites had, beginning from the Dutch captain Jan van Riebeeck's landing at the Cape in 1652, 'got here first'. Interestingly, an alternative version of prior claim has been voiced by some black politicians of 'Africanist' persuasion who have, from time to time, presented their country's history as one of straightforward dispossession, over several centuries, of blacks – who were, after all, there first! – of their land by conquering whites. The descendants of those whites, it is then stated, could have no real claim to future consideration once power had been wrenched from their grasp.

There is, as we shall see, much more validity to this latter reading of South African history than there is to its polar opposite, the 'empty land' version mentioned above.[4] Even so, by the twentieth century, the complex interweaving of races in South Africa had produced a far more complex outcome than either of these two versions could easily encompass. It is no accident, therefore, that a majority of South Africans have chosen to accept neither of these conflicting views as dictating present-day outcomes, opting instead for a reading of the legacy of South African history that the ANC, in the Freedom Charter of 1955, summed up in the following terms: 'South Africa belongs to all who live in it, black and white ... .'[5] This chapter will trace the political processes that have strengthened such a non-racial[6] reading of the lessons of South African history

[3] Quoted in Paul Maylam, *A History of the African People of South Africa: From the Early Iron Age to the 1970s* (New York: St. Martin's Press, 1986), p. 17.

[4] There are also 'debates', though they are not much more rewarding, as to the relative historical priority of the 'indigenous' San and Khoi peoples of the land mass that would become South Africa and the in-coming 'immigrant' Bantu peoples, although the latter themselves 'arrived' many centuries ago.

[5] 'The Freedom Charter,' reproduced in Volume 3 of Thomas Karis and Gwendolyn Carter (eds), *From Protest to Challenge: A Documentary History of African Politics in South Africa, 1882–1964*, in multiple volumes (Stanford: Hoover Institution Press, 1977), p. 205.

[6] Without in any way obscuring the importance of racial (and so often 'racist') designations to the playing out of South Africa's complex history we have chosen to employ this term 'non-racial' as an overall characterization of the longer term outcome of the historical process we are examining, much preferring it to the concept 'multi-racial' – a term much abused by the architects of apartheid, for example.

– while noting that even had those whites who made the 'empty land' claim been reading history accurately, their appeal to the past could not have provided any moral rationale for racial dictatorship in the diverse South African society that emerged in the twentieth century.

The fact remains, in any case, that the claim was entirely inaccurate in terms of the historical record. Archaeologists have found extensive evidence of Stone Age and Iron Age presences in South Africa from very early times, Paul Maylam suggesting, for example, that the date AD 270 and the name Silver Lakes, site of an important archaeological dig, should more than counter-balance the significance of 1652 and of Table Bay, site of van Riebeeck's land-fall, in the history books. After all, he writes, this 270 date stands as 'the earliest ... approximate date, as yet recorded by archaeologists, for the occupation of South Africa by Iron Age people'.[7] Moreover, well in advance of this date Stone Age peoples, precursors of those Khoisan whom Europeans first encountered in the area of the Cape, were already present in South Africa. There is also the famous skull of 'Mrs Ples', honoured in this book's subtitle and unearthed in 1947 not far from Johannesburg. Said to be the skull of a 2.14 million year-old boy (in spite of its name), one of the oldest known forebears of the human species, it has earned the Sterkfontein area (about 70 kilometres southwest of Pretoria) where it was discovered the label of the 'cradle of humankind'.[8]

Setting the record straight in racial terms is far from being the most important reason for seeking in the past the roots of South Africa's present situation, however. So searing has been the impact of white domination and exploitation on the southern portion of the African continent, so shaping of the parameters of choice for black men and women, that it has sometimes been easy to forget that such men and women were making their own history long before van Riebeeck's land-fall. It has been tempting, in consequence, to underestimate the extent to which Africans remained historical actors in their own right even during the harshest periods of racially-driven oppression. Locating recent periods of South African history within the long arc of the sub-continent's African history may help safeguard us against doing so here.

We can return, for this purpose, to the peopling of South Africa, mentioned now not so much to settle the question of historic primacy as to learn from the complexities of the process itself. Broadly speaking, South Africa has been one frontier in that larger history of Africa evoked dramatically by John Iliffe: 'Africans have been and are the frontiersmen of history [!] who have colonized an especially hostile region of the world on behalf of the entire human race ... The central themes of African history are the peopling of the continent, the achievement of human coexistence with nature, the building up of enduring societies, and their defense against aggression from more favoured

[7]   Maylam, *A History*, p. 2.
[8]   For a picture of 'Mrs Ples' (short for Plesianthropus, meaning 'almost human') and a brief discussion of the find's significance see: 'Mrs Ples' on *Prominent People* – a website dedicated to famous people, celebrities, VIPs, etc., available from www.prominentpeople.co.za/mrs-ples.aspx, accessed 30 September 2013.

nations'.[9] Despite the absence of written sources and with only often uncertain oral traditions and archaeological evidence to go by, much is now known about this process.

Take, for example, the Khoisan (a unifying name for the San and the Khoi peoples). The San were hunter-gatherers, perhaps never more than 20,000 in number, and were only loosely organized in small bands. They did not adapt easily to the new settler society that was to spring up in their midst in the western Cape; harassed militarily, some of them did manage to retreat deeper into the interior and even to survive to the present day in small pockets throughout the region. However, other San communities had made a shift to pastoralism even before the arrival of Iron-Age peoples in southern Africa. These latter, the Khoikhoi as they were called, developed communities on a larger scale and with more complex political organization than did the hunter-gatherer San. Numbering somewhere between 100,000 and 200,000 at the time of the Dutch arrival at the Cape, they at first established trading relationships with the Dutch, especially through the supplying of cattle to the new colony. Yet 'the European advance eventually cost the Khoikhoi their land, their stock, and their trading role'.[10] Dispossessed, defeated militarily and devastated by disease, those who survived had been forced, by the early eighteenth century, into dependent economic roles as labourers within white society – while also losing, slowly but surely, much of their autonomous identity as they became merely one more element making up the emerging 'Coloured' community in the Cape.

More significant in the long run was the second wave of the peopling of southern Africa by groups indigenous to the continent. Historians have begun to piece together a picture of the occupation of southern Africa by cultivators speaking Bantu languages from the early centuries of the first millennium – with the emphasis for much of the succeeding centuries on the continuing movement of peoples and on what Iliffe terms 'a long and painful colonization of the land.'[11] Two dimensions of this process stand out. First are its common features. It is true (as Omer-Cooper writes) that the issue of 'whether the first iron-using communities came into southern Africa in one or two identifiable streams, or in a whole series of small groups over the whole front from the Indian Ocean to the Atlantic is a matter of current controversy'. But far more important is the fact that 'the groups that settled in South Africa ... either inherited or developed an essentially common culture'.[12]

[9] John Iliffe, *Africans: The History of a Continent* (Cambridge: Cambridge University Press, 1995), p. 1.

[10] T. R. H. Davenport, *South Africa: A Modern History*, Fourth Edition (Toronto and Buffalo: University of Toronto Press, 1991), p. 8.

[11] As noted, the peopling of Africa (the dramatic 'colonization' of Africa by the continent's own indigenous inhabitants), especially southern Africa, is the central theme of John Iliffe's important book *Africans*; on the Africans 'colonising' of southern Africa 'during the thousand years between the end of the early Iron Age and the outside world's first extensive penetration in the eighteenth century' (p. 97) see Iliffe's Chapter 6, 'Colonising society in eastern and southern Africa'.

[12] J. D. Omer-Cooper, *History of Southern Africa*, Second Edition (London: James Currey, 1994), p. 8.

A common culture ... and a common mode of economic production: besides their shared linguistic traits, these Bantu-speakers, unlike the Khoisan, practiced various forms of settled agriculture – even if for some, especially the southern Nguni-speaking Bantu, cattle-keeping was at least as significant an undertaking as was food crop production. But if the accumulation of cattle was important this was only one dimension of a production process in which economic overlordship was exercised on the basis of gender and generational inequality: central to these societies, as Jeff Guy has carefully argued, was the power married men/heads of households had to extract labour, especially for most tasks linked to cultivation, from women and children/young persons (including as yet unmarried young men) under their control.[13]

Socially and politically, this structure was linked in turn to complex networks of kinship and clanship, although virtually all societies, especially in the south, also had, beyond the local level, more centralized and hierarchically-defined chiefly institutions able to extract for their own purposes some surplus (or 'tribute') from the base. The degree of bottom-up control of these chieftaincies varied, as did their differing propensities to produce ever more large-scale (and generally even more hierarchical) kingdoms. It was these peoples that the Europeans were to encounter as they pushed eastward from the Cape to the more well-watered areas that sustained such societies.[14] The fact that they were both firmly settled in considerable numbers on the land and organized in effectively focused political communities also meant that the Bantu-speaking peoples could not be so relatively easily (and genocidally) shoved aside by European expansion as the Khoisan had been or, elsewhere, the indigenous population of North America. In consequence, the manner of their dispossession by, and integration into, an emergent white-dominated South Africa would be rather different from that experienced by the Khoisan.

There is a second dimension of this wave of African peopling of southern Africa, however. Omer-Cooper, in underscoring, above and in broad terms, the 'common culture' of the Bantu-speaking peoples entering southern Africa, qualified this characterization by marking the existence as well of 'recognizable linguistic and cultural sub-groupings' amongst them.[15] It is worth noting in this regard that the new post-apartheid Constitution acknowledges eleven official languages, these being, in addition to English and Afrikaans, the African languages of Ndebele, Pedi, Sotho, Swazi, Tsonga, Tswana, Venda, Xhosa and Zulu. This latter list gives some preliminary sense of the diversity Omer-Cooper is referring to, a linguistic diversity that also interpenetrates with differing

---

[13] Jeff Guy, 'Analysing Pre-capitalist Societies in Southern Africa', *Journal of Southern African Studies*, 14, 1, 1987.

[14] Leonard Thompson, in his *A History of South Africa* (New Haven and London: Yale University Press, 1990), suggests that 'rainfall has had a profound influence on the history of the region' and emphasizes the importance of a twenty inch per annum rainfall zone that marks a crucial boundary between the dry western areas (excepting the immediate zone around the Cape itself) and the eastern areas' more arable conditions (p. 4).

[15] Omer-Cooper, *History of Southern Africa*..

cultural traits and with quite specific regional and ethnic histories.

It must be emphasized that these lines of difference are far from sharp, and the making of the 'ethnic' distinctions that such diversity points towards is no straightforward matter. Moreover, successive white regimes have sought to manipulate such distinctions amongst Africans as part of a 'divide and rule' political strategy. Nor is it inevitable – despite various misleading stereotypes as to the all-pervasive threat of 'tribalism' in Africa – that these distinctions become politicized in negative and destructive ways. Nonetheless, the fact of ethnic diversity amongst Africans is real, its roots to be found deep in the African past we are now considering.

The starting-point of such analysis of intra-African diversity is most often a linguistic one, a central distinction being drawn between those speaking the Nguni family of languages and those speaking the Sotho family of languages, these two broad groups together making up the vast majority of South Africa's African population. The Nguni-speaking peoples came historically to locate themselves along the southern and eastern coast of southern Africa, between the central plateau and the Indian Ocean and, for purposes of rough classification, can be further sub-divided into a northern group – the Zulu and Swazi – and a southern group, comprised of Xhosa-speakers and other related peoples. Sotho-speakers came to occupy the interior plateau; as Maylam writes, 'they can be distinguished from the Nguni in a number of ways' and also 'sub-divided into three main groups: firstly, the western Sotho or Tswana; secondly, the southern Sotho, who comprise the Pedi and Lobedu; and thirdly, the southern Sotho, or Basotho, who occupy present-day Lesotho and adjacent areas'.[16]

Not that the people identified by using these categories have necessarily defined themselves, either exclusively or even principally, with reference to such distinctions: the counter-pull towards a more inclusive sense of African and/or South African nationalism has tended to be very strong, especially in the twentieth century – although even in earlier periods, the evocation of any deep sense of a larger community defined in strictly 'tribal' terms, often did require considerable political effort to achieve. Here the most dramatic case in point was the creation, from a very modest and quite localized starting-point, of the Zulu kingdom by Shaka and his successors during the nineteenth century.

Although influenced, some historians have argued (and the temperature of this particular scholarly controversy has been quite high), in its origins by the growing pressures from Europeans in the south-eastern part of the sub-continent, the indigenous roots of this particularly dramatic instance of African state formation cannot easily be denied.[17] Even more controversial is the question of

---

[16] Maylam, *A History*, p. 21. In addition, two other groups – the Venda and Lemba – stand somewhat apart from this dual classification, although, as Maylam suggests, the Venda in particular do show 'elements of Sotho language and culture' (p. 52).

[17] The *Mfecane*, its causes and consequences as well as the actual extent of its importance, is the well-trodden ground of scholarly controversy. See, in particular, Carolyn Hamilton (ed.), *The Mfecane Aftermath* (Johannesburg: Witwatersrand University Press, 1995); also Julian Cobbing, 'The Mfecane as Alibi: Thoughts on Dithakong and Mbolompo', *Journal of African History*, 29, 1988; Cobbing, 'Political Mythology and

the exact impact of the Zulus' subsequent outward march and of the waves of political and social disruption that accompanied it throughout the region, although it does seem to have been not inconsiderable. For the militarily-inspired turbulence, or *Mfecane*, did devastate some peoples, notably the Tswana, leaving them more vulnerable to further European advance. It also encouraged others to organize themselves politically in ways that, in several cases (the Sotho kingdom of Moshoeshoe and the Swazi kingdom of Sobhuza, for example) helped them to resist successfully direct political incorporation into an emergent white-dominated South Africa.[18] At the same time, the '*Mfecane* question' seems likely to remain a controversial topic of discussion amongst historians for some time to come.

Conquest

The 'African' history of what was to become South Africa did not come to an end in 1652 when Jan van Riebeck first landed at the Cape, but it was to be dramatically shaped by the growing presence of Europeans that this land-fall foreshadowed. As Thompson writes, 'the seventeenth century was the Golden Age of the Dutch Republic, its merchants were the most successful in Europe, their Dutch East India Company was the world's greatest trading operation'.[19] Within the larger framework of unprecedented global capitalist expansion, van Riebeck's mission was merely to establish a way station at the Cape for provisioning the Dutch ships sailing to and from the far more lucrative East Indies. Fatefully, however, the decision was soon made to permit a measure of white settlement by 'free burghers', released, in the first instance, from their company contracts in order to grow and supply agricultural produce. From this seed a white settler-based colony began to grow, although these new farmers soon found better prospects in herding sheep and cattle over large tracts of land than

(*cont*) the Making of Natal's Mfecane', *Canadian Journal of African Studies*, 23, 2, 1989, J. D. Omer-Cooper, 'Has the Mfecane a Future? A Response to the Cobbing Critique', *Journal of Southern African Studies*, 19, 2, 1993, and John Wright, 'Mfecane Debates', *SARoB* (Double Issue), 39–40, 1995.

[18] Both Moshoeshoe's Sotho kingdom and Sobhuza's Swazi kingdom, although badly battered by the process of European conquest that would ultimately create South Africa, were, along with a Tswana kingdom in the north-west, ultimately to become High Commission Territories (as Basutoland, Swaziland and Bechuanaland respectively) under direct British colonial rule, winning their independence (as Lesotho, Swaziland and Botswana) in the 1960s. For a succinct account of the political fortunes of these kingdoms, see Omer-Cooper, *History of Southern Africa*, 'Appendix 1: The enclave states, Lesotho, Swaziland & Botswana'. Despite their quasi-autonomy, however, it is important to note Omer-Cooper's conclusion that there was 'no sense of commitment on the part of the British administration to develop the territories in any other way than as an addition to the South African economy' (p. 274). Note also, as part of this *Mfecane*-driven exodus, the settlement of the Ndebele people in what would become Southern Rhodesia and subsequently Zimbabwe.

[19] Thompson, *A History of South Africa*, p. 33.

in market gardening. As noted above, the indigenous Khoisan people whom the Dutch encountered in this part of southern Africa were particularly vulnerable to such settler expansion, more so than densely settled and politically well-organized Bantu-speaking populations further east would ultimately prove to be.

Slowly but surely over the next century and a half these peoples were subordinated both militarily and, with their land and herds expropriated, as dependent labourers. Slavery, too, was very much a building block of the new colony, additional labour requirements being met by the importation by the Dutch of slaves from elsewhere in Africa and from Asia. The lines of colour were not absolute in this context: miscegenation did occur and there were some 'free blacks'. But racism was clearly part of the equation. In the long run this complex milieu at the Cape would also produce a group of people of mixed race – the so-called 'Cape Coloureds' – who would develop a certain sense of their own multi-faceted identity, one distinct from both whites and Africans.

Meanwhile, the white community itself was also forging a distinct identity of its own. In Freund's words, 'through the seventeenth and eighteenth century the Cape settlers, a melange of Dutch, French, Scandinavians and Germans, evolved an African (or Afrikaner) society of their own with a distinctive dialect [Afrikaans] that moved away from standard Dutch'.[20] It was these Afrikaners, also called Boers, who were soon pressing out from the Cape, both to the north and to the east, in search of the new land their expansive form of agricultural activity demanded. This pattern of movement also meant there were tensions within the colony from early on, notably between company officials and these settlers. Dependent though the latter might be 'on the imperial economy to sell their produce and on imperial arms for the possibilities of further expansion' they became increasingly difficult to control and discipline the further afield their frontier moved; they were inclined to ignore unpopular regulations laid down in Cape Town and to develop their own local military institutions, termed 'commandos'.

In the east, as well, this frontier was increasingly extending itself into territories already occupied by more settled Xhosa-speaking populations. As land was clawed away from the latter, the tensions inherent in this process of ongoing expropriation became a defining feature of the colonial enterprise in South Africa. At first it was the Dutch East India Company that had to take responsibility for policing this outward movement of the colony, entering into the first of a series of wars with the Xhosa at the Fish River in 1781. An important shift in the geo-politics of South Africa was about to occur, however. For a period during the Napoleonic War (1795–1803) and more permanently afterwards (from 1806) the Cape passed out of Dutch colonial hands and into those of the increasingly more powerful British Empire.

It was the British army that would now engage – even more ruthlessly and successfully than it had been possible for the Dutch to do – in a steadily escalating series of 'Xhosa Wars' on the Eastern frontier in the first half of the

[20] Bill Freund, *The Making of Contemporary Africa* (Boulder: Lynne Rienner, 1998), p. 48.

century. The Europeans were able, on occasion, to play off various African groups against one other and also to take advantage of the social and cultural disarray amongst Africans these Europeans created through their remorseless advance (for example, the disastrous killing, in the 1850s, of their own cattle by one Xhosa group in support of a prophetic vision of deliverance being one example of this[21]). But most often the whites relied on their superior fire-power to overcome, across a broad frontier, spirited Xhosa resistance to the dispossession of their lands. Moreover, the British began to bring in settlers of their own to shore up their grip on the territory, notably, in the 1820s, to Albany and Grahamstown in the Eastern Cape and later, in the 1840s, to Natal.

As Tim Keegan has argued, the military muscle and entrepreneurial drive of the British imperial presence would now be the most crucial element in the on-going conquest and subordination of African peoples.[22] But Afrikaners, too, were on the move, the pace of their expansion north-eastwards across the sub-continent accelerated both by continuing Xhosa resistance to easy movement due east and by the difficulties many Afrikaners had in adapting to the new fact of British overlordship. There were early rebellions against the British, ruth-lessly repressed. Moreover, the British now sought their profits – wool was soon to become an important commodity to them, for example – under a more liberal, free-market dispensation than anything the insular Afrikaner community was accustomed to. Disconcertingly for many Afrikaners, slaves were freed and, under Ordinance 50 of 1828, the Khoikhoi were emancipated from many of the legal constraints that had been placed upon them. To be sure, a supply of cheap and docile labour was soon to be guaranteed by a series of legal controls that were, in many ways, as coercive of non-whites as slavery had been (the Masters and Servants Ordinance of 1841 providing a particularly draconian case in point). Moreover, many Afrikaners, some grown quite wealthy, remained quite willingly in the Cape, to become with time a formidable presence in white poli-tics there, particularly as a measure of local self-government was devolved, gradually, to the colony by the British.[23]

But others began to leave the Cape Colony for the interior. They did so singly, but, as in the case of the dramatic 'Great Trek' from the colony of the 1830s that later would become the stuff of Afrikaner legend, they also moved out in larger groups that quite self-consciously rejected the British rule from which

---

[21] The most dramatic instance was the massive cattle-killing inspired by Nongqawuse amongst the Xhosa in the 1850s; see Jeff Peires, '"Soft" believers and "hard" unbe-lievers in the Xhosa cattle-killing', *Journal of African History*, 27, 1986, and Peires, 'The central beliefs of the Xhosa cattle-killing', *Journal of African History*, 28, 1987.

[22] Tim Keegan, *Colonial South Africa and the Origins of the Racial Order* (Charlottesville: University Press of Virginia. 1996).

[23] Note as well that such devolution of authority to the local population as did occur even came to include some provision for a non-white franchise, albeit one that was to be severely restricted by high property qualifications. None of the other parts of South Africa were to follow this precedent, however, and even in the Cape itself (as we will see) this 'Cape Franchise' was to be eroded in the twentieth century.

they had become estranged. They began to settle, as Omer-Cooper notes, in 'the three areas of Transorangia, Natal and the Transvaal that the wars of the mfecane has particularly devastated'.[24] Military engagements with the African populations of the interior were part and parcel of this process, as was the establishment of complex patterns of economic interaction between invading whites and the black populations already on the land.

There were also hostilities with the British who oscillated for decades in deciding just how much control to attempt to exercise over expanding Afrikaner populations (whom they persisted in seeing as British subjects) in the interior. In Natal, where the trekkers skirted the Drakensburg mountains to enter from the north, the British feared the Afrikaners gaining strategic advantage as well as an outlet to the sea; as a result, they moved hurriedly, in the 1840s, to challenge the Afrikaners' nascent colony there and to establish, instead, a colony of their own. In the interior, however, the British proved more willing to recognize the establishment by settlers of 'Boer Republics', the Orange Free State and the Transvaal (also called the South African Republic) – albeit under a constantly shifting degree of imperial oversight.

What of African response to this process of European expansion? This is not an entirely straightforward matter. It is the case that some Africans were attracted by the opportunities – exemplified, for example, by the availability of novel commodities – that interaction through trade and employment with Europeans offered. Indeed, it would be difficult in this respect to overstate the cultural impact that the conquest was to have upon Africans, and especially the more educated and more assertive in terms of their offering community leadership. For, at its most negative, this impact underpinned the kind of consumerism and 'possessive individualism' encouraged (however unevenly) by the growing centrality of the market economy. In turn, this came to counter-balance the 'proto-socialist' claims of collectivity and of cultural resistance that mutual subordination to oppression (economic and political, local as well as global) might otherwise have encouraged. In fact, as Ibbo Mandaza, writing of neighbouring Rhodesia/Zimbabwe, has commented,

> [A]s the African petty bourgeoisie began gradually to find access to the same economic and social status as their white counterparts so, too, did it become increasingly unable to respond to the aspirations of the workers and peasants ... It became imperative, as the new state, to put a rein on its mass base [and eventually] political principles and ideological commitment appeared mortgaged on the altar of private property.[25]

Of course, both the impermeability of the racial hierarchy in an emergent apartheid South Africa and the mind-set of white racism tended to blur the grim logic of this polarizing tendency within the black community itself. Its malignant costs would only become fully apparent with the overthrow of apartheid,

---

[24] Omer-Cooper, *History of Southern Africa'*, p. 73.
[25] Ibbo Mandaza (ed.), *Zimbabwe: The Political Economy of Transition, 1980–1986* (Dakar: CODESRIA, 1986), p. 51.

made manifest in the truncated meaning, social and economic, given to liberation in a post-apartheid South Africa.[26]

Another cultural dimension of considerable importance was to be found in
the sphere of religion. For religious zealotry underpinned an effort, launched by
the Europeans, to convert the African to a full range of Christian messages and
meanings. Of course, the intention behind this effort, however paternalistic in
motivation, was not entirely malign, but its effect ran very deep in the society
that was to become South Africa – and this for both good and ill. For example,
a particularly arrogant Eurocentric reading of the gospels came to underpin,
as embodied in the teachings of the Dutch Reformed Church, the racist and
authoritarian Afrikaner polity. Amongst Africans (said, by 2001, to be 80 per
cent Christian), the effect of Christian teachings was to have particularly diverse
effects however, ranging from a passive quietism vis-à-vis authoritarian rule
and impoverishment to, on another reading of Christianity, a far more liberatory consciousness.

Meanwhile some Africans did find scope for realizing their immediate political goals – vis-à-vis African rivals for example – in diverse alliances, even at
times with the white invaders themselves (one upshot of the troubled relations
between Fingo and Xhosa on the 'Eastern Frontier', for example). At the same
time, there can be no blurring the fact that the conquest of the sub-continent
by Europeans and the subordination of the indigenous population to European
purposes set the overall terms of such interactions. In consequence, it was resistance that stood closest to the heart of the African response during much of the
nineteenth century, resistance that was both impressive and sustained.

We have already mentioned, in this regard, the long years of the Xhosa Wars.
But there were other African peoples who also resisted strenuously. The Tswana
on the Highveld rebelled repeatedly against the on-going seizure of their territories (not least after diamonds were discovered there). The Sotho under
Moshoeshoe battled both the Afrikaners of the Orange Free State and the
soldiers of the Cape administration and, despite being forced to cede a great deal
of territory, were able to safeguard some measure of autonomy from the emergent white-ruled South Africa (albeit, eventually, by becoming a British protec-
torate). The Pedi under Sekhukhune defended their land with great success over
a long period against Afrikaner encroachments in the northern Transvaal until
finally crushed by the British army in the 1870s.[27] The Zulu, perhaps southern
Africa's most powerful kingdom, inflicted dramatic defeats on both Afrikaners
and the British – crushing an imperial army at Isandlhwana in 1879, for
example – before succumbing to imperial might at Ulundi later that same year.

In this drama of 'primary resistance' – the term having come to refer to the
initial wave of indigenous resistance, however ethnically diffuse and under-
powered, to European conquest – more than enough heroism could be found

---

[26] John S. Saul, 'Race, Class, Gender and Voice: Four Terrains of Liberation', being
Chapter 1 in Saul, *Liberation Lite: The Roots of Recolonization in Southern Africa* (Delhi
and Trenton, NJ: Three Essays Collective and Africa World Press, 2011).

[27] See Peter Delius, *The Land Belongs to Us: The Pedi polity, the Boers and the British in the
Nineteenth Century Transvaal* (Johannesburg: Ravan, 1983).

to serve as a point of pride for future generations of Africans. Yet, when looking back at the grim balance-sheet of the nineteenth century, all these events still added up to a century of dispossession: slowly but surely, as whites took over the land for their own purposes, Africans were being pushed to the margins. True, some Africans remained on the ground that Europeans were staking their claim to, allowing, at least for a period, a wide range of economic relationships to exist between the new white 'owners' and blacks – notably various share-cropping and labour tenancy arrangements (Africans being granted tenancy on 'white-land' in return for labour services, for example).

The twentieth-century fate of Africans domiciled in the so-called 'white areas' of rural South Africa will concern us in subsequent sections. Even more immediately crucial, however, were the vast numbers of Africans now consigned to an ever smaller and more marginal proportion of South Africa territory as Europeans appropriated enormous stretches of the best land. Here, in conquest, lay the nineteenth-century origins of the 'reserve' system, reserves being those areas of exclusive African occupancy whose boundaries and links to the broader system of white power were ultimately to be formalized in the starkest of legal terms – notably by the Natives Land Act of 1913 that restricted African ownership or lease of land outside the reserves, while defining the African reserves themselves to comprise only 7 per cent of the land area of the country (a figure raised to a still meagre 11.7 per cent by 1939). Finally, there were those Africans who had also begun to enter the fledgling urban areas and who found themselves, from very early on, consigned to segregated living areas, this representing an important step towards the ever more systematically enforced township system that would so blight the South African cityscape in the following century.[28]

Once again, there were Africans who continued to seek, from a base in the reserves or in the new urban locations, to enter into South Africa's emergent modern market economy on their own terms, and a stratum of successful African farmers and fledgling professionals did begin to surface from the mid-nineteenth century. Nonetheless even the limited scope opened up by colonialism elsewhere in Africa for the beginnings of a vibrant smallholder-based peasant economy was not readily allowed to Africans in South Africa.[29] This was to be, in effect, 'white man's country', with Africans, having been pushed off the land, now viewed primarily as a potential labour-pool for the white-controlled economy (and certainly not as potential competitors in the agricultural market place or elsewhere).

But what, in the decades before and after the turn of the twentieth century, of those Africans who, as aspirant workers in the new world that confronted them, actively sought the opportunity to gain an income in the wider economy beyond the reserves? They, too, found themselves hemmed in by laws and social

[28] Jennifer Robinson, *The Power of Apartheid: State, Power and Space in South African cities* (Oxford and Boston: Butterworth-Heinemann, 1996).
[29] Colin Bundy, *The Rise and Fall of the South African Peasantry* (London: Heinemann, 1979).

barriers that restricted their freedom of movement, their upward mobility and their collective self-assertion. More broadly, then, the emerging system revealed itself as en route to becoming a massive engine for the gestation of migrant labour at low cost. Africans (largely male) were in the main to be forced, by penury and legal compulsion, to leave the increasingly overcrowded and unproductive reserves for various lengths of time to provide the cheap labour that would be so central to the development of South Africa's capitalist economy.

Much later, in the 1950s and 1960s, the reserves would also become the building blocks for the apartheid government's attempt to divide (in order to rule) the conquered African population by defining such territories as 'homelands', even 'independent Bantustans', and attempting to legitimate them in 'tribal' terms. But even in this early period the nascent reserves and separate locations allotted to Africans were central to a strategy of maintaining political control, whatever their growing significance in domiciling a mass of potential labourers may also have been. Concerned as he was about questions both of social order and of labour supply, the tenure of Theophilus Shepstone as Secretary of Native Affairs in Natal from 1845 to 1876 is often taken to be particularly illuminating.

In the various African locations in Natal, Shepstone structured a segregated system of 'indirect rule' of Africans through the closely-supervised role of local headmen and chiefs and of quasi-traditional 'Native Law' – while also devising a series of pass laws for tightly controlling the movement of Africans out from these locations. Moreover, as the still potent Zulus were soon after brought to heel by British troops on the very borders of the Natal colony, a variant on indirect rule – involving the devolution of formal authority to a multiplicity of chiefs – was used there by the British general Wolseley to help finesse Zululand's transition from independent kingdom to subordinated reserve under British overlordship. There, as elsewhere in South Africa, the foundations of racial segregation as a politics of order were being laid down just as firmly as were the foundations of a cheap labour system.

Racial segregation? Cheap labour? Some historians would argue that the South African story is one of racial oppression springing from the dictates of a racist ideology, pure and simple. Certainly it would be difficult to underestimate the effects of the racist premises secreted by the white population in the slave-based society of the old Cape Colony and further nurtured by the ideology of cultural superiority that helped to rationalize imperial conquest and settler frontier expansion during the first two-thirds of the nineteenth century. Precedents were being created here that would weigh heavily on the future South Africa, providing a touchstone for the segregated society of the twentieth century in which the institutionalization of white domination (culminating in apartheid) would easily overwhelm any counter-tendencies towards more liberal, colour-blind outcomes.

However, other historians argue that the long-term effects of these earlier episodes in the structuring of a hierarchical set of race relations between whites and 'people of colour' (as the white power structure liked to think of the people they were oppressing) could easily be overstated. They suggest instead that the drive to sustain an economic system based on a plentiful supply of cheap (black) labour – the beginnings of which were also sketched above – have been even more important in producing an apartheid society in South Africa than has been the theory and practice of racism in and of itself. We will see in subsequent chapters why such differences of interpretation are important. But the terms of this debate amongst historians may become clearer as we turn to one of the most defining moments in South Africa history: the 'mineral revolution' spawned, in the latter part of nineteenth century, by the discovery of diamond fields and gold deposits of staggering proportions.

The mineral revolution

The situation of South Africa-in-the-making was now to be transformed dramatically. Discovered in 1867, diamonds drove the first phases of the resultant 'mineral revolution'. The subsequent discovery of gold on the Witwatersrand in 1886 was to have an even more profound impact. As one historian has summarized the broad pattern of socio-economic change now set afoot, this mineral revolution (and in particular the impact of gold production) produced the shift 'from a patchwork of agricultural and pastoral communities to a predominantly industrial urban society'.[30] 'Whereas at the beginning of the period,' Marks and Trapido add, 'the region was still composed of a cluster of British colonies, Afrikaner republics, African protectorates and kingdoms, by 1910 the entire area ... was under British rule and the societies of the sub-continent were being increasingly meshed into a single political economy.'[31] These changes affected crucially the nature of the territory's overall economic development, the substance of certain important interactions within the white community and the evolving relationship between white and black. We will mention each of these three dimensions in turn.

As noted, it was on the basis of these mineral deposits that the industrialization of the southern tip of Africa, so far in advance of economic developments elsewhere on the continent, was to be realized. As more capital was required to dig deeper for diamonds, the multitude of small-scale miners gave way to the dominance of large companies, triggering, by the beginning of the 1890s, their amalgamation into a single monopoly, De Beers Consolidated Mines. The gold-mining industry experienced even more frenzied competition with the rise and fall of numerous mining houses. But in the end the pressing need for large amounts of capital to access the deep-running gold seams also narrowed the field of competitors dramatically.

The pattern of a few large firms, often linked to overseas financing and standing at the centre of the modern South African economy, was thus set very early on, and would have important implications for the future. Thus, in time

[30] Omer-Cooper, *History of Southern Africa*, p. 126.
[31] Shula Marks and Stanley Trapido, 'Lord Milner and the South African State', *History Workshop Journal*, 2, 1950.

and in the context of a further restructuring of the industry after World War I, one of the firms first spawned in these early mining days, Ernest Oppenheimer's Anglo American Corporation, would come to dominate the Johannesburg Stock Exchange, while also diversifying into a broad range of economic activities at home and abroad. More generally the broadening of the reach of such capital towards the servicing of its own needs and those of the larger settler population meant that it was encouraged to develop a more nationally-based and 'patriotic' bourgeois thrust than often characterized the fall-out of vast mineral investments elsewhere in the world.[32]

Mining thus shaped the structure of South Africa's developing economy in other essential ways. For example, even when considered merely in terms of economic structure there are some ambiguities attached to this legacy. Recent research has suggested the extent to which the subsequent growth of the economy has remained skewed towards servicing the mining industry, both in terms of the development of energy sources and of the kind of manufacturing sector created. The continuing centrality of the 'minerals-energy complex' may thus have rendered the South African economy somewhat more dangerously one-dimensional than the gross statistical indicators suggest.[33] Moreover, despite the substantial growth of the economy, the crucial importance to its health of the export of primary products (minerals not least amongst them) continued to render the country vulnerable to both the ups and downs in world market for its exports and to varying shifts in the terms of trade for necessary manufactured goods and technological inputs.

These are themes to which we will also have to return in later chapters, not least for purposes of assessing the economic prospects of a post-apartheid South Africa. Here, however, we must address the socio-political impact of the economic revolution set in train in this earlier period. As we will soon see, its most important impact was further to deepen the contradiction, so central to South Africa's twentieth-century history, between an oppressive and exploitative white population on the one hand and an oppressed and exploited black population on the other. But it was also to heighten greatly the tensions amongst the whites living in the region. The British imperial power, sometimes content to give Boer trekkers considerable room for economic and political manoeuvre in the interior, began to eye enviously those territories: territories claimed by the trekkers but ones where much of the new mineral wealth was now to be found.

In the case of diamonds it was decided merely to annex to the Crown – and against claims to the contrary by the Orange Free State and the Transvaal, as well as by the indigenous Tswana people and the Griqua (a people of mixed race) – the areas where the diamond-diggings were located. The issue of how, in the long run, to deal with the established Afrikaner states themselves was more

[32] Duncan Innes, *Anglo American and the Rise of Modern South Africa* (Johannesburg: Ravan, 1984).
[33] Ben Fine and Zavareh Rustomjee, *The Political Economy of South Africa: From Minerals-Energy Complex to Industrialization* (Boulder: Westview, 1996).

complicated. In 1870, for a range of reasons, both economic and strategic, the British actually moved to incorporate them into a larger confederation under direct imperial control. But the imperial power already felt itself overstretched in South Africa by its on-going wars to bring various African states (the Pedi, the Zulu) to heel. Settler rebellion in the Transvaal, including a spectacular Afrikaner military victory at Majuba Hill in 1881, convinced imperial politicians to back away, at least for the moment, from their earlier incorporation of the Boer Republics.

Once gold findings of vast potential were made in the Transvaal, however, the wheels of imperial expansion began to turn again.[34] The trigger was the growing tension between mining capitalists, largely of English origin, and Afrikaner politicians (crusty Transvaal President Paul Kruger, for example). The former complained of the inefficiency of the Afrikaner government (especially its failures to streamline the system of (African) labour supply and labour control), its corruption, and the punitive nature of its tax policies and some even tried to overturn the Kruger government by themselves (the infamous Jameson Raid of 1895). There is controversy amongst historians here too as Bill Nasson, in particular, has noted in his writing, some writers resisting any too economistic, mineral-centric reading of motives for war. But here Nasson is surely correct in noting, wryly, that 'had the Witwatersrand become famous for asparagus, there surely would have been no war crisis'.[35] In any case, the fact remains that the British government and the imperial army ultimately were drawn into the fray, the new governor at the Cape, Sir Alfred Milner, working closely with the mining magnates to lean heavily on the Transvaal, thereby provoking both it and the Orange River Colony into hostilities. An extremely bloody war ensued (1899–1902), one ably fought against overwhelming odds by the Boer commandos but won by the British whose cruel practices – as part of 'counter-insurgency' against the rural guerrillas (featuring scorched earth tactics and concentration camps where many women and children died) – have since become twentieth-century commonplaces.

The grisly nature of the Boers' defeat helped feed a sense of grievance that later politicians would draw on in mobilizing a particularly militant Afrikaner nationalist movement. Not that this was an inevitable outcome. Afrikaner politicians in the Cape had developed political organizations of their own, in particular the Afrikaner Bond. At first the Bond (as inaugurated by S. J. du Toit) did

[34] Ian Phimister, 'Unscrambling the Scramble: Africa's Partition Reconsidered', paper presented to the African Studies Institute, University of Witwatersrand, Johannesburg (17 August 1992), argues that, in the context of the overall 'Scramble for Africa' of the late-nineteenth century, the push for further expansion in southern Africa reflected, more generally, a dramatic over-accumulation of capital in Britain and a consequent taste for speculative commercial adventures, not least in the mining sphere.

[35] I owe this quotation from Bill Nasson to Tom Lodge but see too Nasson's *The South African War, 1899–1902* (London: Edward Arnold, 1999) for an extremely rich account both of the war itself and of the scholarly controversy that swirls around the unravelling of its causes and its consequences.

have a proto-Afrikaner nationalist and anti-British edge to it. But the further devolution of responsible government to the Cape Colony – and the close, often even dependent, financial links (loans and the like) with 'English' banks – would also find the Bond cooperating with English-speaking politicians, notably the diamond magnate (and Cape Colony premier) Cecil Rhodes, for many shared purposes. True, the latter link was severed after Rhodes' implication in the Jameson Raid. Yet, in the wake of the war, the British government of occupation was also able to cut a deal of mutual benefit with senior military leaders-cum-politicians of the recently defeated Boers (Generals Louis Botha and Jan Smuts of the Transvaal, most centrally). Self-government followed for the former rebel states, new Afrikaner-dominated governments acceding to power in 1907 in both the Orange Free State and the Transvaal. Shortly thereafter, with British blessing,[36] the four existing 'colonies' – the Cape, Natal, the Orange Free State and the Transvaal – negotiated a union, the Act of Union of 1910, amongst themselves, and also independence within the British Commonwealth.

The chief casualty of this process was the African population itself. Africans, too, had suffered greatly from the war, some in concentration camps.[37] But to win their support the British had also hinted at a prospective betterment of their condition, implying some reclamation of their land and expansion of political rights. After all, in the Cape Colony there had emerged, with the on-going devolution of responsible government in the latter part of the nineteenth century, one promising precedent, insisted upon by the British government: the granting of certain franchise rights on a colour-blind basis (albeit with stiff property qualifications attached) that gave an earnest of possible further political evolution in a non-racial direction. In the event, any hopes that the emancipatory spirit, however limited, of this 'Cape franchise' might be extended to the rest of now British-controlled South Africa were to be cruelly disappointed. The Peace of Vereeniging itself had made the 'momentous commitment' (in Thompson's words) of ceding to 'the white inhabitants in the defeated Transvaal and Orange River Colony' the decision as to whether or not 'to enfranchise their fellow black subjects'.[38]

---

[36] See Alexander Brady, *Democracy in the Dominions: A Comparative Study in Institutions* (Toronto: University of Toronto Press, 1947), especially 'Part 4: South Africa'. Also of importance in class terms was what Stanley Trapido once termed to be an apparent 'alliance of gold and maize', notably in the Transvaal; British authorities may have thought that this would re-emerge to help bridge any Afrikaner-English gap, this providing the basis (alongside shared class interests between Afrikaner and British economic actors in the Cape) for a sustained class alliance, and agreed racial and developmental strategies. See Stanley Trapido, 'South Africa in a Comparative Study of Industrialization', *Journal of Development Studies*, 7, 3, 1971, but also Robert Morrell, 'The Disintegration of the Gold and Maize Alliance in South Africa in the 1920s', *The International Journal of African Historical Studies*, 21, 4,1988.

[37] See P. Warwick, *Black People and the South African War, 1899–1902* (Johannesburg: Ravan, 1983).

[38] As Thompson (*A History of South Africa*, p. 144) continues: 'It was a foregone conclusion that they would exclude Blacks, since the [Boer] republics had never allowed Blacks to vote'.

As seen, the imperial government now assisted the four colonies towards a union and independence, with little more to be heard of the Cape franchise. Leaving such rights in place only in the Cape (where they were later to be whittled away), the British connived uncritically with local politicians to consolidate a 'whites-only' political system that, by incorporating the Afrikaner elites, was designed to produce the stability mining interests (non-Afrikaner in the main) required. As Shula Marks writes:

> African and Coloured opposition to the 'colour bar' provisions in the draft Act of Union was immediate and clear. A joint delegation was despatched to London in an attempt to get the British government to veto the discriminatory constitution. It availed them little. Most British politicians were convinced of the need for unification in the interests of economic development, and euphoric about the great reconciliation which had taken place between the white races. The few lonely voices raised against the dangers of a constitution which excluded the vast majority of the population from the political community were ignored in the atmosphere of mutual congratulation.[39]

This outcome, however cruel, was not surprising. After all, the British had, by 1910, realized much of what it had hoped to achieve in the post-war Transvaal by way of making it safe and profitable for mining capital. The precedents for their programme had been established in 'the Shepstone system' in Natal with its profitable blend of social and political segregation and aggressive recruitment of African labour. Other alternatives were not implausible. Natal itself had built its successful sugar industry from the 1860s onwards through the importation of indentured estate-workers from India (this group originating the substantial Indian population still living in South Africa). In 1904 a particularly severe labour shortage on the mines would lead to a parallel recruitment of poorly paid workers from northern China. Protests, especially from white workers, led to the latter's repatriation to China in 1908. But the low-grade ore of the Witwatersrand, difficult to access and costly to mine, demanded an inexpensive labour force. To complement white workers and, indeed, to undercut their wage demands, African labour would have to be used.

This had already begun to be the case before the war, of course, with recent experience in the diamond fields providing an even more forceful precedent for the Transvaal than did the practices of the Cape and of Natal. At Kimberley, white diggers had worked to limit black competition from a very early date and, as the larger companies took control, they too moved to squeeze black workers. Thus 'registration passes and fixed contract terms were enforced to limit the ability of labourers to play off one employer against another. In practice these were enforced for black workers rather than white.'[40] A closed compound

---

[39] Shula Marks, 'Southern and Central Africa, 1886–1910', in Roland Oliver and G. N. Sanderson (eds), *The Cambridge History of Africa* Volume 8 (Cambridge University Press, 1985) p. 491.

[40] Nigel Worden, *The Making of Modern South Africa: Conquest, Segregation and Apartheid* (Oxford: Blackwell, 1994), p. 38, and p. 40 (quoted below in this paragraph), provides a useful summary of these developments upon which I draw here. For the experience

system for domiciling black workers (but not for white workers, who vigorously resisted the possibility) was also introduced, ostensibly to prevent smuggling but also to realize other sorts of control over the black workforce. Contracts, compounds, company-stores and passes: these elements were to be carried forward to the more complex terrain of Johannesburg and its gold mines. Both before and after the war, Worden continues, 'the gold mines followed the example of Kimberley in using African unskilled migrant workers, housed in compounds, because they could be employed at low wages, sufficient only for the subsistence of single men'.

What was happening – as befitted the emergence of a more fully formed capitalist system in South Africa – was a systematic proletarianization of the African population beyond anything that had existed in South Africa before (and also on a scale unprecedented for Africa as a whole). It was, however, to be proletarianization of a quite specific kind. In this period 'fierce African resistance to the alienation of the land was a major factor in persuading colonial authorities and employers that industry would, in the first instance, have to be based on migrant labour. Yet if Africans could not simply be divorced from the means of production, these years saw a network of laws to push them onto the labour market, and to keep them on the treadmill for as long as possible.'[41] Moreover, with time, employers would come to see not just the necessity of a migrant labour system but the distinctive economic advantages that it offered them. Under this system, it became clear, the reserves could be expected to provide for the subsistence needs of women, children, the lame and the old, that a wage would have to cover if African workers were to relocate to the city.[42]

In short, the reserve system subsidized the wage, keeping African labour cheap. Small wonder that a Witwatersrand Native Wage Commission could still be found to be arguing, as late as 1944, that,

> it is clearly to the advantage of the mines that native labourers should be encouraged to return to their homes after the completion of the ordinary period of service. The maintenance of the system under which the mines are able to obtain unskilled labour at a rate less than ordinarily paid in industry depends upon this, for otherwise the subsidiary means of subsistence would disappear and the labourer would tend to become a permanent resident upon the Witwatersrand, with increased requirements.

Here, then, lay the logic underlying South Africa's coercive labour regime. With time the pass procedures on the Rand would merely be tightened up – making it so difficult for Africans to stay for any length of time in the urban areas that

[cont] of the diamond-fields he references, see in particular the important work of Rob Turrell, *Capital and Labour on the Kimberley Diamond Fields* (Cambridge: Cambridge University Press, 1987).

[41] Marks, 'Southern and Central Africa', p. 466.

[42] The male-centric nature of this overall structure, while not absolutely exclusive and determinant, did tend to reinforce such negative patterns of male dominance as already existed in the country settings from which migrant labour was drawn, thereby further exacerbating the challenges that South African feminists would face, as. with time, they became more vocal.

they would be forced to accept almost any terms and conditions offered them –
as were the rigours of the ever more restrictive contract and compound systems.
More broadly, the introduction of taxes payable in money was used, along with
other means, to force Africans to seek cash income through sale of their labour
(the Glen Grey Act of 1894 was introduced by Rhodes in the Cape in precisely
these terms, for example).

Complementing this, agreements on non-competitive recruitment practices
were being reached by the member companies of the Chamber of Mines in the
1890s that helped force down the wages Africans could actually expect to earn.
When Milner and his reconstruction team took over administration of the
Transvaal after the war, he sought merely further to streamline and reinforce
this kind of labour system. True, Milner was suspicious of the Boers and eager
to encourage (unsuccessfully) much higher levels of British immigration to
South Africa. His commitment to the hegemony of whites in a now united
South Africa was crystal clear, however: 'The ultimate end,' he wrote in 1899,
'is a self-governing white Community, supported by well-treated and justly-
governed black labour from Cape Town to Zambesi.'[43] So, too, was his commitment to the hegemony of the mining companies: the system he further locked
into place was to guarantee that, on the mines and in agriculture, the cost of
African labour would not much change for many years.

In analysing this period, historians have also taken note of the tensions
between white workers and black, and clearly these were of importance. Little
working-class solidarity across the colour line existed since white workers could
easily come to view Africans (as they also viewed those Chinese immigrants
who had been imported to complement the labour force) as rivals who, because
they were could readily be paid less than themselves, threatened their jobs while
also pulling the overall level of wages down. Under such circumstances the twin
factors of racial prejudice and material self-interest easily merged for white
workers. Having successfully resisted compounds and passes and strip searches
in Kimberley, such workers would now use any economic and political clout
they possessed to demand and defend a 'job colour bar' in the gold fields and
other sectors, a colour bar that reserved certain jobs, and higher levels of pay,
for whites.

Because of this pattern, one that continued for decades, many liberal historians have felt free to present these workers as having forced racism upon mine-
owners and other capitalists who would otherwise have applied the colour-blind
laws of the market equally to all comers. Yet the 'job colour bar,' while significant in the inequalities it helped reinforce, was scarcely at the core of the system.
The evidence suggests that far more importance must be attached to the existence of the 'exploitation colour bar' – the overall structure of racial oppression that forced Africans to work for less and also allowed them virtually none
of the rights that might have enabled them to seek redress of their grievances.
This 'exploitation colour bar' served, most heavily, the interests not of white
workers but of white capitalists who could, under South African circumstances,

[43] Quoted in Thompson, *A History of South Africa*, p. 144.

avail themselves of a cheap supply of black labour in order to increase their profits.[44]

Here also lay the main reason why, despite both the recent war and Milner's own suspicions of the Boers, his successors – colonial bureaucrats and mining magnates alike – could enter, whatever their prejudices, into an on-going process of accommodation with the Afrikaner elite. In the end, neither side had any real reason to question the fit between segregation and the emerging structure of racial oppression, on the one hand, and capitalism, the emerging structure of class exploitation, on the other. They were, unequivocally, to be two sides of the same coin in the new South Africa. Indeed, many Afrikaner farmers, especially in the Transvaal, had come to see 'their future as inextricably linked with the mining industry and imperial markets.'[45] And they were beginning to move in an ever more unequivocally capitalist direction within their own immediate economic enterprises as well. The melange of pre-capitalist (or, at best, quasi-capitalist) production relations that we have seen in the previous section to have existed on the white farms of the Highveld would have to give way to a more 'advanced' system of increasingly straightforward wage relations.

This development, too, was actively encouraged by the occupying power, Milner and the companies judging that it would 'free' many erstwhile rural dwellers, coerced off the land by such a 'rationalization' of production on the white farms, to become mineworkers. Note, as well, that the infamous Native Land Act of 1913 – one of the first legislative initiatives taken by South Africa's newly independent government – did more than formalize legally the racist division of South Africa's land mass. In fact, it now permitted Africans only to remain legally – the law was not always very strictly enforced, of course[46] – on 'white' land as farm labourers and labour tenants and not as 'sharecroppers'. The devastation such disruption of the established pattern of their lives promised to inflict on thousands of Africans was of no concern to the emerging 'alliance between maize and gold' that now drove South African policy-making.[47] It was this alliance, forged by entrepreneurs across the Afrikaner-English ethnic divide and at the expense of the African population, that sealed the Union of 1910.

[44] A distinction brilliantly argued and sustained in Frederick Johnstone, *Class, Race and Gold: A Study of Class Relations and Racial Discrimination in South Africa* (London: Routledge and Kegan Paul, 1976).

[45] Marks, 'Southern and Central Africa', p. 490. Moreover, the encouragement that the mining companies now felt to draw a growing percentage of its supply of workers from other territories in the southern African region also helped relieve some of the competition for labour between the two sectors that might otherwise have been more divisive.

[46] On many of these themes, see Charles van Onselen, *The Seed is Mine: The Life of Kas Maine, a South African Sharecropper, 1894–1985* (New York: Hill & Wang, 1997).

[47] See Trapido, 'South Africa in a Comparative Study of Industrialization'.

'White politics': from segregation to apartheid

After the Act of Union of 1910, politics within the dominant white community came to reflect, first and foremost, the vested interests that whites of all classes now had in defending a system that guaranteed their privileges and exclusive claim to power – while also producing a cheap supply of black labour. The theoretical possibility of the emergence of an integrated, colour-blind capitalist economy had been foregone in favour of an alternative that might best be termed 'racial capitalism'. We have seen above that the British moved, in the wake of the Boer War, to guarantee their economic interests by locking into place the system of segregation that had been so long foreshadowed in South African history. For decades, successor governments would define variations upon this system, up to and including the regime established after 1948 by the National Party – which offered its own particularly merciless brand of segregation in the form of apartheid.

What must be emphasized in this section is that the segregation project of the post-independence period sustained a dual mandate.[48] Driven by the pursuit of profit (cheap labour), the oppression of the black population that segregation sanctioned was also rooted in racist modes of thinking and in political concerns about white security in the face of a large and growing black population that had come to be thought of as a potentially dangerous 'other'.[49] The day might eventually come when profit-making and racial oppression would cease to be seen as quite so complementary to each other. But this was never really the case in the period here under review. We must also bear in mind that the implementation of segregation was not carried out by the white community without uneasy reference to the ebb and flow of significant black resistance, a key strand of the story and one that gives voice to the deepest of all contradictions in South African history.

We will return to an examination of the growth of such resistance across the full length of twentieth-century South African history in the following section. For the moment, however, the focus must be on the white polity and on the socio-economic roots both of its unity and of some very real tensions that existed within it. The latter tensions, rooted in class, ethnic/national and ideological differences amongst whites, would have significant effects of their own

---

[48] On this subject see, *inter alia*, Saul Dubow, *Racial Segregation and the Origins of Apartheid in South Africa, 1919–36* (Basingstoke: Macmillan, 1989) and William Beinart and Saul Dubow (eds), *Segregation and Apartheid in Twentieth Century South Africa* (London: Routledge, 1995).

[49] There was also a handful of observers and practitioners during this period who saw segregation as having more positive virtues, serving in some part to defend Africans in their traditional settings from the ravages of the modern world. This view, generally quite paternalistic in its articulation, was also naïve at best as to how far the subordination of African 'traditions' to external forces had already actually proceeded.

on the pattern of change in South Africa. The South African Party (SAP) of former Boer generals Louis Botha – the first Prime Minister of a united South Africa – and his close colleague and ultimate successor (in 1919) Jan Smuts was, with independence, the chief protagonist of 'the alliance of maize and gold' in the political realm. Other Afrikaners would prove far less enthusiastic about the kind of elite-pacting they felt this 'reconciliation' between Afrikaner and English represented. Because of this, internecine conflict within the Afrikaner community would prove to be one key component of white South African politics during the inter-war period. But so too would be the rise of a radical form of Afrikaner nationalism.

Thus, as early as 1913, a key cabinet member, Barry Hertzog (from the Orange Free State), had broken away to form a new National Party in opposition. This party was committed, in Thompson's description, 'to protecting the cultural and economic interests of Afrikaners and dissociating South Africa from the [British] empire': 'Hertzog's support came mainly from lower-class Afrikaners – marginal farmers who resented exploitation by rich landholders and people who had been dislodged from the land and who were hard put to make ends meet in the towns'[50] – with all as victims of Standard Bank usury too. But some middle-class Afrikaners – professionals, businessmen and farmers, many from the Western Cape – joined as well, their number overlapping with an emergent group of articulate, nationalist-minded intellectuals. The most militant of these petty-bourgeois elements also worked through the secretive Afrikaner Broederbond (a nationalist organization that was to become a major player deep within Afrikaner political and economic circles) to advance their goals.

Here was a seed that would grow. In 1933, Hertzog, by then himself Prime Minister, felt constrained to welcome Smuts and his colleagues into a joint 'Fusion' government (and soon into a National Party/SAP merger to form the United Party) in order to weather the severe impact of the world-wide depression on South Africa. At that point a number of the more militant Afrikaners, led by D. F. Malan, broke with Hertzog to form the Purified National Party (soon, once again, the National Party). The Fusion government did continue to hold majority support within the white community during the 1930s, amongst both English and Afrikaners: in the 1939 election, for example, it won 111 seats to the Purified Nationalists' 27. Yet by the time of the 1943 election, and despite the United Party once again winning a large majority, the National Party was clearly on the rise. Then in 1948, more quickly than anyone could easily have predicted at the time of its formation, Malan's organization became the party of government ... and the party of apartheid.

We will need to explore further the rise of Afrikaner nationalism between the wars. In 1910, however, Botha and Smuts were firmly in charge and they moved briskly to advance the interests of the employers whom they chiefly represented. Certainly, they moved when necessary to crush white labour unrest – as when, dramatically in 1922, white workers acted out against a mine-

---

[50] Thompson, *A History of South Africa*, p. 158.

owners' move to whittle down some of their privileges in order to further the use of cheaper black labour. Some of the tensions between 'capital logic' and 'race logic' were apparent in this 'Rand Revolt' as it came to be widely known and in the ruthless military means used to smash it. After all, white workers showed no inclination whatsoever to explore the possibility of working-class-based action across racial lines, actually going on strike under the banner 'Workers of the world unite and fight in defence of a White South Africa,' and physically attacking Africans who were chiefly seen as 'competitors' for their jobs. Strongly assertive of their own rights both in class and racial terms however, they had, when their activities culminated after a decade of widespread turmoil in virtual insurrection (the Rand Revolt of 1922), to be smashed by the most heavy-handed of military means and with marked loss of life.

Still, it was soon

> recognized that such clashes were to the disadvantage of all concerned. The period of confrontation gave way to a long compromise, to the mutual benefit of the mining companies, their white workers and the state itself, [and] at the expense of the mass of black mineworkers.[51]

For however dramatic might be the tensions that did surface from time to time between capital and labour within the white community, in the end both sides could live with the trade-offs they had to make with each other. For these compromises meant both the availability of cheap African labour to the mining magnates on the one hand and the advantage of some measure of 'white-skin privilege' (in terms of wages and supervisory positions) for the white workers on the other. In addition, there was also such spartan legislation as the Mines and Works Act of 1911 and the Industrial Conciliation Act of 1924, crafted to service capital along more familiarly racist lines both by containing the wage levels of black workers and by narrowing the legal space available to them for their self-organization into strong unions. Thus, when African workers themselves resisted (as in their own dramatic strike in 1920) they were themselves savagely repressed.

The Native Land Act of 1913 also helped deepen the reach of capitalist relations of production in the new South Africa, as we have seen. Nonetheless, like other legislation of the time, it was as much about consolidating political control over the black population as it was about profits. In its stark formalization of the unequal division between white and 'Native' areas, John Cell writes, this Act was 'the centrepiece of the segregationist program' more broadly defined, and a direct forerunner of the draconian Group Areas Act of 1950.[52] Other legislation reinforced this pattern. Thus, the Native Affairs Act of 1920 established a distinct Department of Native Affairs to oversee further consolidation of a dense network, separate and self-contained within the African reserves, of hierarchical political structures. Even more importantly,

---

[51] Robert Ross, *A Concise History of South Africa* (Cambridge: Cambridge University Press, 1999), p. 105.

[52] John Cell, *The Highest Stage of White Supremacy: The Origins of Segregation in South Africa and the American South* (Cambridge: Cambridge University Press, 1982), p. 216.

legislation was proposed which rested on the principle that the towns were the preserve of the white man, that Africans should only be permitted to live in the towns so long as they served the needs of the white man and that they should be removed from the towns when they ceased so to serve. The Native (Urban Areas) Act of 1923 laid down the principle of residential segregation in urban areas and reinforced the doctrine that Africans had no permanent rights in the town and no justification for being there unless needed by the whites as units of labour. Though implementing these measures fully was to take many years, the basis had been laid for the exercise of rigid control over African urban populations. Indeed in adopting this legislation, together with the 1913 Land Act, the South African Party government had established two of the key pillars of segregation.[53]

As Cell concludes, 'the principal architect of segregation was not General Hertzog. It was General Smuts.'[54] This observation underscores just how much was shared of the racial-capitalist agenda so vigorously implemented by white politicians in the inter-war period. In many ways, Hertzog was merely to deepen the pattern, even if his programme had an even more overtly racist edge (as witnessed in the passage of the notorious Immorality Act of 1927 that outlawed inter-racial marital and sexual relations, for example). Yet, charging Smuts with half-heartedness in the face of the 'Black Peril,' Herzog now ran up a substantial segregationist legislative track record of his own. The Native Administration Act of 1927 gave greater punch to the premise that Africans were 'to be retribalized under a distinct system of law and government' with absolutely no hope of future political assimilation into the Union: '[The Act's] conscious revival of tribalism, although bearing no resemblance to any pre-colonial structure, was to be crucially important to the development of diverse African ethnicities which were brought to full fruition in the homelands policy of the 1960s.'[55]

A pendant to this was Hertzog's dogged determination to claw back from Africans the political rights a handful of them still held through the availability of the Cape franchise, something he finally managed to achieve, after Fusion, with his Representation of Natives Act of 1936.[56] Meanwhile, the Native Trust and Land Act (1936) did add some lands for Africans to the territorial division formalized by the Native Lands Act of 1913, but was much more important in its now extending the terms of that earlier law to the Cape and in sustaining the assault on black tenants' rights on white-owned land. The Native Laws Amendment Act of 1937 further tightened up the urban pass law system.

In two important particulars Hertzog did also bend the pattern of South Africa's racial capitalism in ways that serviced the interests of the white underclasses his programme had come in part to represent. We noted, in a previous

---

[53] Omer-Cooper, *History of Southern Africa*, p. 169.
[54] Cell, *The Highest Stage of White Supremacy*.
[55] Worden, *The Making of Modern South Africa*, p. 75.
[56] Some trace of African representation was established to replace the franchise: three whites elected to represent Africans in parliament and a (very weak) Natives Representative Council; moreover, the Cape franchise remained in place for some Cape Coloureds. These remaining 'anomalies' were among the casualties of the legislative assault by Malan's National Party after 1948.

section, the debate as to the precise role of the white working class in the articulation of South Africa's racial-capitalist system. The Botha/Smuts legislation weakening the bargaining position of black labour might have been of some consolation to white workers. But it was also something of a two-edged sword. With the price of black labour kept low by such measures, white workers continued to see fresh evidence that their worst fears of capitalists' substituting black labour for white coming true. As we have noted above, a series of strikes (including the explosive Rand Revolt of 1922) that aimed, among other things, to defend white workers' relatively privileged position vis-à-vis African workers had been ruthlessly repressed by the Smuts government in the interests of the Randlords (entrepreneurs who controlled the diamond and gold mining industries in South Africa in its pioneer phase).

Small wonder that the workers' own increasingly influential Labour Party was prepared to ally with the National Party to overturn Smuts in the 1924 election and to form the 'Pact' government that first brought Hertzog to power. The reward to white workers, but also to the many unemployed Afrikaner 'poor whites' of the period whose fate was one of Hertzog's chief preoccupations, was the Colour Bar Bill of 1926. This further expanded the number of semi-skilled industrial jobs to be reserved exclusively for whites. Here was a concession that the captains of industry, who, in any case, could ride comfortably on the profitable cushion of the 'exploitation colour bar,' would just have to learn to live with. Moreover, the availability of such jobs, when added to those created for Afrikaners in an expanded state sector, helped weaken the dangerous possibility that 'poor whites' might, in their desperation, be tempted to link up with blacks in order to seek redress of shared grievances.[57]

'An expanded state sector?' Another important outcome of the nationalist thrust of Hertzog and his colleagues remains to be mentioned. Emboldened by its constituency's suspicion of British capital, the National Party was prepared to use the state to significantly qualify, if not more fundamentally contest, the prerogatives of big capital and to redirect the use of mining surpluses to purposes of more national (read: white and Afrikaner) economic development. Freund writes:

> If elsewhere in Africa colonial mining appeared to stand in the way of the emergence of any form of economic reorientation, in South Africa it was effectively harnessed as the motor force of a wider ranging capital accumulation process ... Under the Pact a battle was successfully waged for the establishment of the Iron and Steel Corporation (ISCOR), the state steel monopoly. In the teeth of mining opposition [protective] tariffs were raised and, most significantly, the mines began to be taxed more stiffly in order to benefit other sectors of the economy.[58]

It is also true, of course, that taxed surpluses would, to a significant degree, be used to deepen the long-standing policy of subsidizing white commercial

---

[57] Solly Sachs demonstrated the promise/danger here by his success, in the 1930s and 1940s, in organizing white, black and coloured female garment workers, for example.

[58] Freund, *The Making of Contemporary Africa*, p. 160.

farmers. But in the cases of ISCOR and its state-run nationalist twin, the Electricity Supply Commission (Eskom), there was also a broader economic logic at work: for any expanded economic development that South African politicians and planners might now have in mind would require the steel and electricity that the private sector could not, on its own, supply. Of course it is also (as some critics have argued) the case that in the absence of a coherent national industrial strategy and despite appreciable growth in the manufacturing sector, less transformation and diversification of the structure of the South African industry occurred than the state's increased access to mining surpluses might otherwise have seemed to suggest likely. As Fine and Rustomjee state of the 1918–39 period, a key determinant here was the lack of a precise fit 'between Afrikaner political and English economic power which impeded industrial diversification'.[59]

Perhaps, too, there was less empowerment of Afrikaner business interests than might have been anticipated: it was often the mining companies themselves who, after some initial suspicion, were those most able to avail themselves of the protected environment to diversify into a new range of economic activities. Still, state action to stimulate a national capitalism was only part of a broader movement by Afrikaners to advance within the economy. A strong Afrikaner nationalist bourgeoisie had grown in the western Cape from early in the century, driving the development of large publishing, trust and insurance companies (Nasionale Pers, Santam, Sanlam) in the 1910s. In the late 1930s such interests linked with the Broederbond to fund a national economic movement (the '*reddingsdaadbeweging*' or 'rescue action movement') designed to further stimulate the advance of Afrikaner entrepreneurs against 'foreign-dominated monopolies'. This was an initiative that, as O'Meara's fine-grained account of its growth and evolution shows, was to continue to gather speed in the 1940s, with important political repercussions.[60]

In the meantime, the Fusion government broke apart over the question of support for Britain in World War II. Smuts was prepared to follow Britain's lead in declaring war against Germany. But Hertzog, who from the beginning of his Prime Ministership had wrestled for more South African autonomy within the British Empire, now opted for neutrality – thus offering an eerie reminder of a much earlier group of Afrikaners who had actively rebelled against the Botha/Smuts government when it carried South Africa into World War I on the side of the British. Losing a parliamentary vote on the issue, Hertzog resigned and Smuts once again became Prime Minister. The war did serve, however, to enflame the passions of anti-British right-wing Afrikaners, some of whom had pro-Nazi sympathies in any case. Indeed, it was necessary

[59] Fine & Rustomjee, *The Political Economy of South Africa*, especially ch. 7, 'The Political Economy of the Inter-War Period'.

[60] Dan O'Meara, *Volkskapitalisme: Class, Capital and Ideology in the Development of Afrikaner Nationalism, 1934–1948* (Cambridge: Cambridge University Press, 1983). In this connection, O'Meara sees the Sanlam-Broederbond-sponsored '*Ekonomiese Volkscongres*' ('Peoples' congress on the economy') of October, 1939 as 'a great turning point in Afrikaner nationalism'.

for Malan's National Party to move vigorously during the war to outflank the even-more virulent, extra-parliamentary Ossewa Brandweg organization in order to retain leadership of the extremist camp of Afrikaner nationalism. From even before the war this camp had been on the rise, fuelled by decades of cultural campaigns (around language claims and initiatives in the sphere of 'Christian-National' education, for example) and by such symbolic events as the 1938 one-hundredth anniversary commemoration of victory over the Zulu at Blood River, accompanied by a massive re-enactment of the Great Trek.

Something more than mere nostalgia was a stake here, however. On the day of the Blood river celebration, for example, Malan had also 'proclaimed that the Afrikaner was engaged in a new Great Trek to the towns where he faced a new Blood river in competition for employment with Africans'.[61] Material interests were to prove at least as important as symbolic gestures and nationalist ideology in driving the victory for the advocates of apartheid that occurred in 1948. Crucial to opening the way for right-wing forces were deep changes in South Africa's underlying socio-economic structure. The economy, that had already begun to recover well before the war, entered into a boom period, not least in the manufacturing sector, during the war itself. This meant an escalating demand for African labour in the cities. Moreover, that was occurring at a point where further overcrowding in the reserves had weakened their capacity to provide that hidden subsidy that had once helped keep African men's wages low and their families in the rural areas. The consequent acceleration of what was, in any case, a long-standing trend of significant African settlement in the cities proved extremely difficult to control, prompting Smuts himself to admit in 1942 that 'segregation has fallen on evil days'.[62]

In addition, a massive 1946 strike of African mineworkers, although once again brutally beaten back by Smuts, suggested a new volatility and mass potential to African resistance. In this context the crucial link between capitalist profit-making and racial oppression appeared, momentarily, to again be stretched a bit thin. The government's Fagan Commission of 1948 recommended some easing of the pass laws, for example, and even introduced some social welfare measures (including a notionally universal state pension scheme![63]) to help smooth a process of urbanization now increasingly deemed to be inevitable. Certain actions by government and business also showed a flicker of willingness to redress African workers' disadvantages. That said, the United Party commitment to any real measure of liberalization remained, like that of the companies themselves, half-hearted at best. In fact, going into the 1948 election, the party merely managed to look confused.

---

[61] Quoted in Omer-Cooper, *History of Southern Africa*, p. 177.
[62] Quoted in Thompson, *A History of South Africa*, p. 181.
[63] See Jeremy Seekings, 'Visions, Hopes and Views about the Future: The Radical Moment of South African Welfare Reform' in Saul Dubow and Alan Jeeves (eds), *South Africa's 1940s: Worlds of Possibilities* (Cape Town: Double Storey, 2005).

Meanwhile, there was:

- the sustained impact of diverse communal affirmations as underwritten by the nationalist brains-trust active within the shadowy Afrikaner Broeder-bond;
- the continuing cultural resonance of such events as the 1938 ox-wagon treks to mark the 100th anniversary of a celebrated Afrikaner victory over the Zulu at Blood River;
- the cumulative impact from the early years of the century of the movement for Afrikaner economic empowerment (the development of major investment houses like Sanlam and Santam, for example);
- the active mobilization of the Afrikaner working class for nationalist purposes.

Such varied assertions had genuine resonance in the unifying of a decisive country-wide force[64] (and this despite the diversity along provincial lines of competing nationalist claims and aspirations).

Not that Malan's National Party won the 1948 election very decisively that first time. Nonetheless, in sharp contrast to the United Party's tentativeness in the face of the crisis of segregation, Malan and his colleagues did offer the clarity of a hard-line and the self-righteousness of a mission deemed, through the close association of the Dutch Reformed Church with the most extreme forms of nationalism, to be religiously sanctioned.[65] The party's own Sauer Commission on the racial problem (1946) recommended a severe tightening up, not relaxing, of the system of segregation – an increased formalization of 'apartness' (apartheid), directed, in the name of white supremacy and racial purity, not only against Africans but also against Indians and Coloureds. Inevitably, there was also a familiar contradiction running through Sauer's report. The theoretical goal of 'apartness' would have to accommodate itself to the demand for the cheap black labour so crucial to white agriculture and manufacturing. The migrant labour system would be fine-tuned, with pass laws policed more rigorously and, through the increased use of labour bureaus, rendered more effective in directing workers from the reserves to appropriate employers. But it would not be abolished.

For Malan may have been seen by many as the saviour of the Afrikaner *volk* and white civilization, but Afrikanerdom nonetheless remained a congeries of diverse interests, class and regional. The growing strength of the National Party reflected not only a triumph for the nationalist intelligentsia but also its ability to stitch together a complex coalition of such interests behind its ever more ambitiously xenophobic and racist project. Thus the support of many Afrikaner workers, assiduously weaned away from multi-ethnic trade unions and towards Afrikaner Christian-Nationalist ones in the 1930s, would now be consolidated

---

[64] O'Meara, *Volkscapitalisme*.
[65] On this subject, see T. Dunbar Moodie, *The Rise of Afrikanerdom* (Berkeley, CA and Los Angeles, CA: University of California Press, 1975).

by visions of further job colour bars and enhanced (white) welfare provisions. Afrikaner farmers, especially those in the Transvaal and Orange Free State who had previously voted United Party, were promised not merely more favourable pricing policies but also the kind of tightening up of influx and other controls over African workers that would stem the latter's movement off the farms and into the urban areas and the higher-paying industrial sector. Fledgling Afrikaner entrepreneurs, whose increasing ambitions we saw to be taking organized expression in the late 1930s, would not only benefit from the ever more efficient and rigorous channelling of labour throughout the economy as need arose but would also have their competitive positions enhanced by state intervention on their behalf and against the 'British monopolies'.

We must not overstate the case. The National Party did not merely sweep into power: in fact it had fewer votes than Smuts' United Party in that first 1948 election, with only the long-time skewing of the distribution of parliamentary constituencies in favour of white rural areas helping them to win enough seats to form a government (through an alliance with the small Afrikaner Party). After that first cliff-hanger, however, the National Party would proceed to win overwhelming victories in the ten additional all-white elections that would occur during the next 46 years (to 1994) of National Party power. Nor, even in the short run, was anything going to stop them from proceeding with the mandate they now claimed for themselves, that of implementing, as rigorously as possible, *baaskap* – white supremacy. Here too we must avoid overstatement. Writers like Deborah Posel have sensibly warned against presenting the apartheid government as being possessed of some 'grand design' which it then implemented absolutely logically and ineluctably. Stops and starts, cross pressures and contradictions, both in the realms of intention and of implementation, certainly existed, as Posel herself demonstrates to be the case with regard to the new influx laws she chiefly studies.[66] Yet, at the same time, the coherence of the project undertaken by apartheid's social engineers remains drearily impressive.

Once again, as so often in South African history, the goals of (class) exploitation and (racial) oppression intersected in complex ways within the policy package that emerged. The above-mentioned labour bureaus, and rural structures of control more generally, were indeed designed to move labour to a range of workplaces as efficiently as possible. Moreover, it would now be made even more difficult for Africans to organize themselves into effective trade union bargaining units of their own in order to seek to better the terms of their employment. Yet the firming up of institutionalized racism, pure and simple, was also a clear goal. Unbending distinctions were made between Whites, Coloureds, Indians and Africans and the Population Registration Act of 1950 set in motion the process of officially categorizing every South African along these racial lines. The Reservation of Separate Amenities Act, the Prohibition of Mixed Marriages Act and the Immorality Act all sought, as their names

---

[66] Deborah Posel, *The Making of Apartheid, 1948–1961: Conflict and Compromise* (Oxford: Clarendon Press, 1991).

suggest, to draw ever more thick and uncrossable lines between white and black.

It is, in fact, impossible to list here the full range of fronts across which the government moved to deepen segregation in the 1950s and 1960s: expanding their control over education at all levels for this purpose (while also under-funding African schools dramatically); packing the courts in 1956 to push through a contested bill to remove the last remnant of the Coloured vote, the Cape franchise; and, particularly important, passing the Group Areas Act of 1950 that formalized the urban segregation of racial groups and thus gave carte blanche to the forced removal of people to soulless townships constructed as far from the city centres as possible. But enforced removals would also take place, eventually in vast numbers, to the ever more impoverished rural reserves/Bantustans as well, these increasingly designated as the only place to which Africans could legitimately claim to belong. Thompson cites a 1967 circular from the Department of Bantu Administration and Development that captures the flavour of things – the purpose of the pass laws and of influx controls as well as of the emerging Bantustan policy – quite clearly, if, to the student of South African history, in an all too familiar way:

> It is accepted Government policy that the Bantu are only temporarily resident in the European areas of the Republic for as long as they offer their labour there. As soon as they become, for one reason or another, no longer fit for work or superfluous in the labour market, they are expected to return to their country of origin or the territory of the national unit where they fit ethnically if they were not born or bred in their homeland.[67]

What was the response of capital – whom some might have considered as the potential protagonist, in the name of the free market, of liberal reform – to such developments? In the event, investors, both those of British South African background and a growing number from overseas, were prepared to forego the theoretical advantages of any such liberalizing possibility in return for the heightened profitability that apartheid's intensified controls over the African population now offered. After all, 'the average wages for Africans in secondary industry (the highest paying sector) which had risen under pressure of working-class action by more than 50 percent in real terms between 1939/40 and 1947/8, actually declined for some years after 1948 and were still stagnating around the 1947/8 level at the end of the first phases [to 1963] of the apartheid period'.[68] It was also quickly apparent that the Nationalists' stated hostility to 'monopolies' and to 'English-speaking' big business was as much rhetorical as real: a 1948 election promise to nationalize the gold-mining industry was reined in by the government's obvious reluctance to kill the goose that lays the golden eggs, for example. Soon most captains of industry found they could live comfortably enough not only with apartheid but with such relatively minor irri-tants as the continued existence of jobs unprofitably reserved for whites and

---

[67] Quoted in Thompson, *A History of South Africa*, p. 181.
[68] Robert Davies, Dan O'Meara and Sipho Dlamini, *The Struggle for South Africa: A Reference Guide*, New Edition (London: Zed Books, 1988), pp. 21–22.

the granting of heightened competitive advantages to Afrikaner business groups that the new government was keen to foster.

Job reservation was rendered increasingly flexible in any case, by the emergence of practices like the 'floating colour bar' that allowed much less well-paid Africans to take over a new range of jobs as whites moved in numbers into supervisory and other intermediate employment categories. Moreover, Afrikaners were finding work elsewhere for themselves, favoured for the excellent employment opportunities provided within the expanding and increasingly Afrikanerized institutions of the state, for example. Facilitating the rising Afrikaner bourgeoisie, one of the National Party's major constituents as we have seen, was another particular preoccupation of the new government. Policy on this front came to involve 'handing over "plum" government contracts to Afrikaner firms, transferring the bank accounts of government departments, local authorities and state corporation to Afrikaner financial institutions, and appointing leading Afrikaner businessmen to a range of official boards where they were able to influence administrative decisions'. Key recipients of this largesse, identified by Davies and his co-authors, were Sanlam, Rembrandt (to become a tobacco and liquor giant) and the Volkskas bank, all relatively modest concerns in 1948 which are 'today [in the 1980s] respectively the second, fourth and fifth largest conglomerates in South Africa'.[69]

This transformation was not to be without its ironies: Afrikaner businessmen, as they elbowed their way closer to the commanding heights of the economy, would eventually find that they had far more in common with their English bourgeois counterparts than they had with their less successful Afrikaner brethren. This would have implications, under changed circumstances, of considerable future significance. For the moment, however, all shared in the bounty of *baaskap*. Small wonder that the apartheid government was prepared to use the might of the state to defend its accomplishments against dissenters even more aggressively than had its predecessors. But this intensification of repression was also necessary because the very ruthlessness of the Nationalists' assault on the black population, as well as the on-going impact of broader socio-economic changes in South Africa, had begun to stimulate a dramatic intensification of resistance (albeit, throughout the 1950s, one that was largely peaceful) to the structures of segregation and apartheid.

The state used this resistance as a further excuse in the next decades to introduce a vast array of new repressive legislation, notably, but by no means exclusively, the Suppression of Communism Act of 1950 that employed a very expansive definition of 'communism' to grant the police broad powers to restrict, by 'banning orders' and the like, the public activities of many individuals and groups. Judicial harassment, as exemplified by the massive Treason Trial of the mid-1950s, was employed to exhaust the energies of the opposition forces, while the organizational apparatus of a police-state-in-the-making was further streamlined and equipped to control centres of significant dissent. True, some other more innovative tactics were also used, heralded as we shall see by

[69] Davies, et al., *The Struggle for South Africa*, p. 23.

the entry into the Prime Ministership of Professor Hendrik Verwoerd in 1957. Long one of the staunchest ideologues of racial purity within the party, Verwoerd sought, through cultivation of a presumption of African 'ethnicity' and a further elaboration of the reserve/'homeland'/Bantustan system, to shift the centre of gravity in party discourse from *baaskap* to the presentation of apartheid as facilitating the beneficial 'separate development' of diverse peoples. As will be seen, under Verwoerd an even more dramatic programme of social engineering than anything the National Party had yet attempted was set in motion. More immediately, however, he would preside over the shooting of 69 unarmed blacks demonstrating against the pass laws at Sharpeville on March 21, 1960 and the brutal crack-down of the proclaimed Emergency that followed, declaring illegal the principal vehicles of majority dissent, the African National Congress and Pan Africanist Congress.

Resistance, to the 1960s

The resistance to white minority rule that reached this initial high water mark in 1960, and that would further escalate in later decades, had been building for decades. As we will see, the Act of Union of 1910, and subsequent legislation by the new united white government, were especially important in fuelling the transition to a more 'modern' brand of oppositional politics on the part of the African population in South Africa. Some have argued that echoes of 'primary resistance' – of the kind that stoked the fires of the Xhosa, Zulu, Pedi and Sotho wars throughout the nineteenth century – could still be heard as late as 1906 in the Natal's Bambatha rebellion where a chiefly-led uprising against the imposition of new taxes was brutally crushed by the British. Others have seen this rebellion more as an anticipation of the pattern of peasant-based resistance that would never quite disappear in twentieth-century South Africa, one that culminated in a country-wide wave of rural upheaval during the turbulent 1950s and, most notably, in the Pondoland uprising of 1960. Nonetheless, the centre of gravity of resistance politics had begun, even before the turn of the century, to swing towards the urban areas.[70] It also took on a novel character in class terms, with the emergence of new strata within the African population, both urban and rural, who felt there was now no alternative to acceptance of the fact of conquest but who hoped, nonetheless, to bend the new situation to African advantage.

Central was a rising 'middle class' of Africans, mission educated many of them and now stepping forward as teachers, lawyers, ministers and small-scale entrepreneurs. Often highly articulate and enormously active (John Tengo Jabavu, editor of such important newspapers as *Isigidimi samaXhosa*, 'The Xhosa Messenger', and *Imvo Zabantsundu*, 'Black Opinion', was a notable early exemplar), this group also had little inclination towards mass-based politics.

[70] See Govan Mbeki, *South Africa: The Peasants Revolt* (Harmondsworth: Penguin, 1964), especially Chapter 9, 'Resistance and Rebellion: The Peasants Rise'.

Their commitment to moderation was grounded in the precedent of the colour-blind 'Cape franchise,' a touchstone, they argued, for the realization of further reform along liberal, multi-racial lines. After all, as Peter Walshe reminds us, 'it is surprising how many people do not realize that by the 1880s there were 12,000 Africans on the common voters roll', with this group making up almost half the electorate in five Eastern Cape constituencies in 1886 and, together with qualified Coloureds voters, 16 per cent of the overall Cape electorate by the early 1900s.[71] At the same time, white efforts further to chip away at the African voting rights (as in the punitive Franchise and Ballot Act of 1892 that raised property and educational qualifications dramatically) and also at any remaining African economic autonomy (the Glen Grey Act of 1894, mentioned above) were on-going. Indeed, it was in response to such developments in the white polity that, from the 1880s, Africans in the Cape founded such organizations as *Imbumba yama Nyama* (1882), and the South African Native Congress (1892) in an effort to help defend both the African franchise and African access to land. Independent Native Congresses also emerged in Natal, the Free State, and the Transvaal in the years before union as part of a drive to sustain a claim to equality in the teeth of a white backlash against it.

Govan Mbeki also cites, as part of this ferment, the inauguration from the 1890s of various independent African churches (he mentions the Ethiopian Movement and the Bantu Presbyterian Church, in particular).[72] But these breakaway churches, though destined to be important actors in South African social and cultural life, exemplified a separatist response to the fact of white domination. For liberal-minded Africans of the period the problem was different, demanding resistance to their ever more systematic exclusion from the promise of an integrated and colour-blind future. For such Africans the British decision to facilitate, with the Act of Union, the virtual burial of the Cape franchise under the weight of the more racist practices of the other constituent provinces of the new South Africa came as an especially stark wake-up call. Despite some disunity, a strong showing of African delegates from the four colonies came together in Bloemfontein in 1909 as the 'South African Native Convention' to protest (however unsuccessfully) the constitution-making process then underway. The shock caused by the initial pieces of legislation produced by the new Union government (notably the Native Land Act of 1913) served to keep a sense of the need for united action alive. Indeed, the Convention had by now, in any case, transformed itself – in 1912, at a second Bloemfontein conference – into the South African Native National Congress, later renamed the African National Congress (ANC).

In retrospect, the emergence of the ANC represented an important step in consolidating the shift from localized and often ethnically-defined resistance towards the kind of nation-wide politics most relevant to confronting the dominant whites on the terrain of a newly united South Africa. In the words of one

---

[71] Peter Walshe, *Black Nationalism in South Africa* (Johannesburg: Ravan, 1973), p. 5.
[72] Govan Mbeki, *The Struggle for Liberation in South Africa: A Short History* (Cape Town: David Philip, 1992), p. 7.

of these early leaders, Pixley ka I. Seme: 'The demon of racialism, the aberrations of the Xhosa-Fingo feud, the animosities that exist between Zulus and Tsongas, between the Basuto and every other Native must be buried and forgotten ... We are one people.'[73] There was also an initial flurry of political activity directed against the Land Act and related legislation, including the despatching, in 1914, of a second delegation (one had also gone in 1909 to protest the Act of Union) to lobby the British government. But too little was done to reach out to the larger mass of impoverished and oppressed African people and when protest politics at home and abroad proved ineffectual the ANC merely receded, with various ups and downs, into a rather desultory existence over much of the period between the two world wars. As Thompson writes: 'Down to 1939 and beyond, the ANC remained under the control of lawyers, clergy, and journalists, who tried to elicit white support to redress African grievances "by constitutional means". Most of the time they adhered scrupulously to those cautious methods and modest objectives, lobbying sympathetic white missionaries, journalists and politicians.'[74]

The same could largely be said, Thompson adds, for 'the Coloured and Indian organizations [which] were under similar middle-class leadership and pursued corresponding goals for their people'. Initiatives taken in these latter communities do deserve some mention, however. In the Coloured community, the African People's Organization (APO), long led by the redoubtable Adullah Abdurahman, played a prominent role in protest politics from its founding in 1902 through to the 1940s (when its demise set the stage for the emergence of, amongst other successor initiatives, the more radical and racially inclusive Non-European Unity Movement). Amongst Indians, the figure of Mahatma Gandhi stands out: Gandhi spent some twenty years in South Africa (1893–1914) pioneering, in the anti-pass campaigns waged by his own Indian community, the techniques of 'passive resistance' that he would carry with him back to India and that would also become part of the repertoire of the broader South African resistance movement in the 1950s. Moreover, the provincial-based organizations that Gandhi and others had first helped organize did eventually jell (in 1923) into a South African Indian Congress. Gandhi himself, in his South Africa years, would move only slowly, if at all, from being a middle-class elitist rooted primarily in the Indian community to one of more non-racial and democratic persuasion. More generally, however, the Congress itself would later, under its more radical leaders in the 1940s, both reintroduce the tactic of passive resistance to the emerging struggles of that decade and also move to ally itself with a resurgent ANC.

The immediate claims of such organizations remained moderate, by and large non-confrontational and, in the end, ineffectual, as we have seen Thompson to suggest. The Hertzog Bills of the 1930s – embodying the further systematization of the segregation system – did succeed in focusing the attention of the varied organizations and individuals in the 'non-European' commu-

---

[73] Quoted in Mbeki, *The Struggle for Liberation*, p. 25.
[74] Thompson, *A History of South Africa*, p. 175.

nities, however. In 1936, the ANC called together a wide range of existing African organizations and individuals to meet as the All-African Convention (AAC) and embrace a protest agenda. As Karis writes, such activities of the period 'were in vain, but the heightened political agitation of 1935–1937 shaped the organizational and tactical issues of subsequent African politics'.[75] The AAC initiative itself was eventually to peter out but from the late 1930s the ANC, though slow to break from familiar tactics and demands, did begin to reorganize itself. Moreover, this was a period of great change in the South African social landscape, as pre-war economic recovery and war-time boom brought a fresh wave of Africans into the urban areas, thereby raising expectations and providing new recruits for the movement. The townships were in ferment in the 1940s, with rising discontent marked by direct action (bus boycotts, squatter movements and the like) and increased labour unrest. This was the milieu within which the revival of the ANC would continue throughout that decade.

Paralleling the rise of communal-cum-nationalist politics during the first half of the century were political assertions that highlighted the class demands of the most directly exploited of the racially oppressed, the workers themselves. We have mentioned the African mineworkers' strike in 1920 as one important avatar of rising working-class consciousness in an increasingly urbanized South Africa, and we might note as well other important strikes, such as those by Johannesburg municipal workers in 1917 and Cape Town dockworkers in 1919. The ANC made some effort to link up with these and other working-class initiatives in its earliest days. Nonetheless, on this front the Industrial and Commercial Workers' Union (ICU), under the colourful if erratic leadership of the former Nyasalander Clements Kadalie (himself sprung from the struggles on the Cape Town docks), became far more prominent during the 1920s. More quasi-nationalist political organization than effective trade union, and in any case more successful in mobilizing rural unrest than in driving industrial action, the ICU eventually played itself out in organizational chaos and political disarray. Nonetheless, it left behind a heightened sense of the potential for mass black involvement in politics, one that served both to focus the nervous attention of whites at the time as well as to provide a valuable point of reference for future black activists.

In the short run, however, efforts at working-class self-expression came to centre on the more mundane process of trade union organization. As Dan O'Meara has observed, the 1930–45 period witnessed, both in terms of numbers and in terms of militancy, a 'steady growth of trade unionism in the 1930s and its mushrooming during the war'.[76] Emphasizing the importance of

---

[75] Thomas Karis (ed.), 'Hope and Challenge, 1935–1952', in Volume 2 of Karis & Carter, *From Protest to Challenge*, p. 3. Karis adds: 'More important, the loss of special status for Africans in Cape Province [Hertzog's removal of Cape African voters from the common voters' roll] laid the basis for more effective cooperation in the future among Africans nationally.'

[76] Dan O'Meara, 'The 1946 African Mine Workers Strike and the Political Economy of South Africa', as reprinted in Martin J. Murray's valuable edited collection of articles entitled *South African Capitalism and Black Political Opposition* (Cambridge, MA: Schenkman, 1982), p. 370.

the emergent Council of Non-European Trade Unions (CNETU) to this development, O'Meara concludes that by 1945 at least 40 per cent of the some
400,000 Africans working in commerce and private industry were unionized.
Farm labourers and mineworkers – who were very often migrant workers and
who also lived on farms and in mining compounds easily isolated off from
would-be union organizers – were slower to make advances along these lines.
Nonetheless, efforts to organize amongst the miners did, ultimately, produce
results in the 1940s and culminated in the massive 1946 strike of upwards of
70,000 miners. Although ruthlessly crushed by the Smuts government, the
strike further exemplified the heightened level of social tensions in South Africa
that made the ANC's turn to mass action in the 1950s seem both plausible and
imperative.

It bears noting that members, black and white, of South Africa's Communist
Party were amongst those most active in many of these working-class initiatives. The Communist Party, as it emerged in South Africa in the 1920s and
1930s, had come to reject the racist preoccupations of most whites (including
white workers) in the interests of the recruitment of African members and of
dealing realistically with the racial contradictions so evident in South Africa. As
time went on it would also overcome its initial suspicions of the ANC's 'petty-
bourgeois' nationalist character in order to forge closer links with that movement, becoming an important source of the continuing radicalization (in class
terms) of the broader movement against the segregation/apartheid system; it
was also a key voice in persuading the ANC to adopt a strategy of armed struggle
and a major presence within the liberation movement's armed wing, Umkhonto
weSizwe (MK) itself. More immediately, however, the demand by many African
activists of the 1940s that a much stronger mass base be found for pressing
African claims was not driven principally by class analysis – and the Communist Party never did find a way to wed the socialist and nationalist causes
entirely persuasively. Certainly, the central criticisms of the time made by
younger African recruits to the ANC regarding the impotence of the movement's leadership were much more likely to produce a radical version of the
theory and practice of African nationalism itself rather than anything very
much further to the left.

In part this reflected world-wide developments: colonized people everywhere
found in the rhetoric of freedom employed in the 1940s by many of the European colonial powers to promote their own war against the Axis a language
that was also at least equally appropriate for stating firmly their own anti-colo-
nial demands. In South Africa this mood found expression in the 1943 adoption
by the ANC of its 'African Claims in South Africa', a document that drew on
Roosevelt and Churchill's Atlantic Charter to stake a more aggressive and
unambiguous claim to full citizenship rights, including franchise rights, than
had been demanded before. Even more important, however, was the nationalist
ferment that had begun to sweep across the continent of Africa itself and that
found its most pointed expression in South African terms in the writings of a
young recruit to the ANC, Anton Lembede. No doubt the visible hardening of
attitudes in the white community that was evidenced in the election of Malan's

apartheid government in 1948 was also important to such radicalization. Crucial, in any case, was the unmistakable existence of a fresh sense of urgency in pressing for more effective resistance to white minority rule.

Prominent in driving the renaissance of resistance that followed was the ANC Youth League which, in the first instance, found a range of rising leaders – Lembede himself, A. P. Mda, Nelson Mandela, Walter Sisulu, Oliver Tambo – radicalized behind a militant, even exclusivist, brand of Africanism, one that was, among other things, suspicious of whites, including both 'white liberals' and 'white communists'. Soon some of this group (notably Mandela, Sisulu and Tambo) would adopt more inclusive, multi-racial definitions of what an effective and morally defensible South African nationalism should entail. It was also the case that others continued to distance themselves from this kind of shift and indeed, by the end of the 1950s, many such 'Africanists' would break away from the parent organization in order to establish the Pan Africanist Congress (PAC). More immediately, however, the Youth League was an important force in pushing the Congress itself towards adopting bolder and more mass-based forms of resistance to racial oppression. The League developed a document that, when adopted by its parent organization in 1949 as its 'Programme of Action', established the framework for the escalation of such resistance during the 1950s. As Worden writes,

> this document marked a decisive break with the conciliatory politics of the previous decades. It called for 'national freedom' and political independence from white domination, a sign of the influence of Lembede's Africanism, together with rejection of all forms of segregation and the use of weapons of boycott, civil disobedience and strike. These tactics reflected the changing membership of the Congress and the final recognition that segregation had to be counteracted at the popular level and by more drastic means than those used previously.[77]

Debate continues amongst historians as to just how effective the ANC actually proved to be in mobilizing mass energies during the succeeding decade. Freund, for example, notes the extent to which developments like the murderous race riots of Zulus against the Indian population in Durban in 1949 and the further movement of large numbers of Africans into independent churches of the period marked a rejection, by Africans, 'of [a] political conceptualization of their lives' as a response to their frustrations. In the 1950s, he concludes, 'political organizations failed to come up with programmes and, more crucially, association and action that could counter the pressures felt by black South Africans'.[78] Others have also argued that an elitist cast continued to mark the politics of ANC-led resistance even during this period. This, they suggest, helps explain the fact that the considerable political energy so evident on a wide range of fronts throughout the decade never quite found effective focus as a real threat to those in power.

Of course, the 'failure' of the democratic movement in the fifties reflected, in

[77] Worden, *The Making of Modern South Africa*, p. 87.
[78] Freund, *The Making of Contemporary Africa*, pp. 224–225.

considerable part, the sheer ruthlessness of the government itself; we must not understate just how far the ruling Nationalist Party was determined to go in order to ensure, even deepen, white control. Criticisms of the movement may also underestimate just how much was actually accomplished during this period. For the 1950s were to become, in the much leaner years ahead, an important reference point for many who sought, subsequently, to revive resistance. Moreover, the historical memory of the campaigns of the decade would also help to consolidate the reputation of the ANC as a political actor of unique legitimacy as later it began to revive its own fortunes. As for the events themselves, the Programme of Action almost immediately gave rise to a series of concrete initiatives designed to focus mass energies against the newly minted apartheid state. Thus, a series of strikes and stay-aways at the turn of the decade laid the ground work for the celebrated Defiance Campaign of 1952, an initiative highlighted by the deliberate breaking of 'unjust laws' and the conscious courting of arrest. The campaign was uneven in its geographical spread (being most successful in the Eastern Cape) and also revealed various organizational weaknesses. Nonetheless, it represented one of the real high water marks of resistance in the 1950s.

In addition, behind such high-profile national campaigns was a range of other, more localized, actions that, momentarily at least, also seemed to give promise of producing a genuinely mass-based challenge to established authority. There was, for example, the real, if too sporadic, challenge to enforced township removals such as that which accompanied the destruction of the historic location of Sofiatown in central Johannesburg. There were the parents' school boycotts in the Eastern Cape and the East Rand townships of the mid-1950s and also the bus boycotts of 1955–57 in such places as Evaton and Alexandra. And there was also the continuing pulse of worker unrest, carried over from the previous decade, one given a renewed focus in the organizational activities of the Southern African Congress of Trade Unions/SACTU, the ANC affiliated union of the time that was active in a range of strikes and organizational drives but also in high-profile, quasi-political activities like the campaign for a 'pound-a-day' national minimum wage and the stay-aways of 1957 and 1958 linked to that and other demands.

Reflecting on this kind of campaign, critics of SACTU's role have suggested that the union may have sought to direct working-class energies too quickly and too exclusively towards national-level political undertakings without finding the means simultaneously to firm up workers' own organizational capacities to sustain labour militancy on the shop floor. When the working class re-emerged as an important force for resistance in the 1970s more attention would be paid to laying just such a firm local foundation for action. But this is merely one instance of a more general phenomenon of the time: the difficulty the ANC had in striking an effective balance between broadly national political objectives and organizational initiatives on the one hand and the generation of local self-confidence and self-empowerment on the other. For this reason Tom Lodge is led, like Freund, to conclude his own careful survey of the period with the observation that, 'despite promising objective conditions, mass response to

African political organization was uneven and often disappointing'.[79]

Yet, in retrospect, the sheer range of resistances remains impressive. The various urban struggles surveyed above had strong echo in (although more often than not quite minimal organizational linkages to) unrest in the countryside, for example. In these rural areas a generalized African hostility to the government produced many dramatic instances of rebellion. Lodge has itemized the range of relevant rural actions – from Sekhukuneland, Witzieshoek and the Marico reserve through Natal to the Mpondo and Tembu districts of the Transkei – while Govan Mbeki, writing closer to the time, has dramatized the extent to which such actions were capable, well into the 1960s, of spilling over into violent confrontation with the state.[80] There was also during this period the increased political role played by women. Indeed, the ANC-sponsored assembly of some 20,000 of them at the Union Buildings in Pretoria in 1956 to protest the extension of pass laws to African women was one of the most dramatic manifestations of the relative vigour of the anti-apartheid movement in the 1950s. True, there were some ambiguities to such assertions, linked as they were to the use by the ANC Women's League in its mobilizational efforts of conservative notions of 'motherhood' and its celebration of a quite traditional definition of women's role now felt to be under governmental attack.[81] Nonetheless, the long-term implications of women finding space to articulate a political voice of their own right probably far outweigh any such qualifications.

Suffice it to say that the movement created across these various fronts was a broad one. In 'racial' terms, for example, the ANC chose to retain its commitment to having an exclusively African membership. But it now linked itself in an overarching 'alliance' of parallel organizations in the other communities, as racially defined: the Indian National Congress, the South African Coloured People's Organization and, for whites, the Congress of Democrats. Here the terms of the ANC's commitment to the vision of a multi-racial future for South Africa was beginning to be consolidated. But there remained a range of ideological diversity within the alliance on this and other issues. Amongst African nationalists, for example, some were far more suspicious than others of the steps being taken in the direction of an ever more multi-racial politics of resistance. In addition, cutting across racial lines, there were those of liberal persuasion who sought some kind of democratic redress to the country's racist system but

---

[79] Tom Lodge, *Black Politics in South Africa since 1945* (New York and London: Longman, 1983, p. 153; Lodge's study provides a particularly helpful survey and analysis of the range of resistances during this period.

[80] Mbeki, *South Africa*; Lodge, *Black Politics in South Africa*, ch. 11, 'Resistance in the Countryside'. It is, however, Lodge's conclusion (p. 290) that 'only intermittently was there contact between the rebellion in the countryside and the political movements of the town ... [D]espite the evidence of a degree of sensitivity to rural tensions, Congress during the 1950s could do little to exploit them. Its organizational vulnerability apart, its social and ideological orientation during the 1950s helped to distance it from rural culture.'

[81] Cheryl Walker, *Women and Resistance in South Africa*, Second Edition (New York: Monthly Review Press, 1991), including her remarkable new 'Preface to the Second Edition' (pp. ix–ix).

did so without questioning the capitalist structures that many, further to the left, saw as underpinning that system. The latter, Communists (in effect banned as a party in 1950 but with many still very active within alliance structures) and others, looked towards a deepening of working-class politics in order to drive the struggle forward and, increasingly, in a socialist direction.

Not surprisingly, when the Congress Alliance came together in 1955 at Kliptown in a widely attended Congress of the People, the foundational document it produced – the historic Freedom Charter – reflected a compromise between these various currents. True, the Charter did embrace non-racialism (recall its key formulation, 'South Africa belongs to all who live in it, black and white,' highlighted at the very outset of this chapter), and it was also clear in its demand for a democracy that by now was defined, unequivocally, as meaning 'one-person, one-vote'. The Charter's projection of South Africa's future socio-economic structures was more ambiguous, however, the document being framed at its core by a wide range of eminently liberal demands regarding the guarantee of certain basic rights and freedoms for all. Of course, such demands could sound quite radical when articulated in the face of the apartheid state. But there were also more socialist ideas to be found within the document, regarding land redistribution, for example, and in support of the principle that 'the mineral wealth beneath the soil, the banks and monopoly industry shall be transferred to the ownership of the people as a whole'! The debate amongst 'Charterists' (as those supportive of both the document and the ANC-led alliance that produced it came to be called) over what choice of ideological direction the Freedom Charter actually called for would continue to the present day.

At the time there were certainly those on the left who found the Freedom Charter to be a mild document, one not sufficiently assertive in its attack upon capitalism. Many such critics also saw in the kind of 'multi-racialism' embodied in alliance politics, embracing as it still did the division between four racially defined peoples ('national groups' as they were referred to in the Charter), far too much of a concession to the regime's own segregationist principles.[82] In sharp contrast, however, were those within the ANC who found even this degree of multi-racialism to mark a betrayal of the principle that Africans must liberate themselves. Moreover, these 'Africanists' also thought they detected in the leftism (however mild) of the Freedom Charter the intrusive hand of the Communists whom they despised. Charging that the ANC had failed, as well, to act sufficiently aggressively in confronting the apartheid state, a number of them broke away to establish the Pan Africanist Congress (PAC) in 1958.

Although the PAC would more or less self-destruct in the long years of exile after 1960, the organization did serve briefly to help reenergize resistance at the end of the decade. It was at a PAC-sponsored pass-burning rally in Sharpeville, for example, that police shot and killed 69 demonstrators. This event, in turn, threw the country into chaos. Yet, to many observers, the imme-

---

[82] For an eloquent statement of this critique, see No Sizwe, *One Azania, One Nation: The National Question in South Africa* (London: Zed Press, 1979).

diate aftermath of 1960's Sharpeville Massacre[83] has come to seem another positive opportunity that was lost during this period. The apartheid regime did falter momentarily, support for it in the international community wavered, and spontaneous mass actions of considerable revolutionary potential broke out. But events were moving too quickly: neither the ANC nor the PAC were well prepared to seize the moment and the government soon recaptured the initiative, banning both movements (who each now went underground) and confirming – for international consumption – its ability to keep things under control. In short, the alliance between racism and capitalism still held ... and, at first and during the 'apartheid boom' of the 1960s very profitably so.

The 1960s: The apartheid boom

Some critics have questioned the nationalist movements' decision to now accept the government's own brutal terms and make the turn, as did both the ANC and the PAC, to underground action, increasingly planned and orchestrated from outside the country.[84] Certainly any transition to other, even more assertive, forms of resistance within South Africa itself was neither easy to conceive nor to mount, and yet the initial efforts by the ANC and PAC to mount the kind of armed confrontation that was now felt to be necessary also met with little success. A first brief sabotage campaign by the ANC led to the arrest of key cadres at the Rivonia Farm, for example, and the capture, while underground, of Nelson Mandela. Mandela's stirring address from the dock during his trial would become a ringing point of reference for future resistance, as would the symbolism that came to be attached to the heroic serving of his sentence, mainly in the bleak surroundings of Robben Island, for 27 years. For the moment, however, the relatively simple sidelining of Mandela and the liberation movements-in-the-making as they now passed into exile signalled smooth sailing for racial capitalism and apartheid.

   The international response to Sharpeville (1960) flashed signals of a related kind. True, South Africa was to take its leave from an increasingly critical Commonwealth in 1961. But the establishment of a republic had long been a cherished goal of Afrikaner nationalists, one recently sanctioned by a referendum, so this move could easily be presented as a triumph rather than a defeat. Other diplomatic rebuffs (at the United Nations, for example) were ones the apartheid regime felt it could also field quite comfortably, so long as they had no economic teeth to them. For it did seem initially that international reaction might prove more damaging on the economic front. The first response to

[83] Phillip Frankel, *An Ordinary Atrocity: Sharpeville and Its Massacre* (Johannesburg: Witwatersrand University Press, 2001; Tom Lodge, Sharpeville: *An Apartheid Massacre and Its Consequences* (Oxford: Oxford University Press, 2011).

[84] See the excellent discussion in Martin Legassick, *Armed Struggle and Democracy: The Case of South Africa* (Uppsala: Nordiska Afrikainstitutet, 2002), both Part 1, 'A Strategy of Rural Guerillaism, 1961–75' and Part II, 'What Strategy for Armed Struggle, 1976–87.'

Sharpeville was one of panic in world markets and, as capital began to flood out of the country, the government was forced to impose currency controls. Yet, as soon as brute force proved capable of carrying the day, international economic actors rallied to bail out the momentarily faltering economy in whose stability they had so much invested. In the long run, of course, economic sanctions and the international pressure for them would make a difference, complementing growing internal resistances, but this was still far from being the case in the 1960s.

In fact, such things as credits from the US-dominated IMF and World Bank, as well as from American banks, were particularly critical to restoring confidence in the wake of Sharpeville. Moreover,

> direct investment also bolstered the economy. Long-established firms like General Motors and Ford made no moves to withdraw. Companies new to South Africa, like Dow Chemical, Kaiser Aluminum, and Firestone made decisions to start up operations there. In 1962 US companies earned $72 million in profits in South Africa, at a rate twice their worldwide average. US direct investment increased $23 million in 1961 and $44 million the following year. One prominent South African politician, talking to visiting American theologian Henry P. Van Dusen in 1963, commented aptly, "So long as United States banks and business back us, we can go ahead."[85]

International involvement in South Africa's modern capitalist economy was not new, of course, dating back to the very first days of the mineral revolution. Moreover, it had been an important factor in driving the growth of the manufacturing sector from the 1930s on, its influx accelerating during the 1950s. Now it was to surge forward once again.

Small wonder: through its various measures of the 1960s, and its crushing of all opposition,

> the ruling class created the conditions for nearly a decade of uninterrupted boom from 1963 to 1972. This period was the golden age of apartheid for those class forces that benefitted from the system. It saw real growth rates of from 6 percent to 8 percent per annum. Based on the maintenance of a consistently high level of repression which kept the wage levels of black workers at a constant low level, the period also saw record profit rates well above the world average.[86]

It bears noting as well that, even at those moments when international investor confidence may have faltered, South Africa's domestic bourgeoisie continued to push forward. The 1960s were a period of great growth and diversification for giants like Anglo American for example, but this was also a period in which the lines between so-called 'English' capital on the one hand and 'Afrikaner' capital on the other began to fade.

The important ceding by Anglo American of one of its mining companies, Gencor, to Sanlam has been seen as a tactical concession to Afrikaner capital, one made in order to 'produce a moderating effect on some of the "extremist"

[85] William Minter, *King Solomon's Mines Revisited: Western Interests and the Burdened History of Southern Africa* (New York: Basic Books, 1986), p. 190.
[86] Davies et al., *The Struggle for South Africa*, p. 28.

policies of the [National] Party'.[87] But it was also part of a more general merging of financial, mining and energy-related entrepreneurial activities across the white ethnic divide, one further stimulated by a continuation of active state participation in certain key sectors of the economy. It is true, as noted above, that critics have seen this kind of merging of capitals as reinforcing a negative tendency to focus too narrowly on the elaboration of the 'mineral-energy complex' at the core of the economy at the expense of a more imaginative kind of economic diversification that would have been economically healthier for South Africa in the long run. It is also true that activities in such spheres as coal, armaments and chemical production had begun to emerge, to become sites of continuing dynamism during the 1970s and 1980s even after the overall importance of minerals had begun to decline. But this is a story we will pick up again. For the moment, however, these were sweet days indeed for capitalists in South Africa.

Nonetheless, if 'business as usual' summed up much of what was happening in South Africa in the 1960s, there were also significant changes occurring in the apartheid system. Yet, be it noted, these were 'changes' that merely reinforced the system, leading some to label the period after 1963 as a second, and even more ruthless, phase of apartheid. For this second phase meant a further reinforcement, rather than relaxation, of the parameters of segregation. Not that this went uncontested within the politically dominant Afrikaner community, of course. Indeed, there had been a simmering tension within the National Party between the two main provincial branches, that of the Cape and of the Transvaal, over this and other such matters.[88]

However Malan could not resist the rise of Hans Strijdom, a Transvaal hardliner, to be his successor in 1954–55. Strijdom's own death shortly thereafter (1957) brought into his Prime-Ministerial ascendancy the quintessential truebeliever in racial purity, the cold, determined and cunning idealogue, Hendrik Verwoerd. Verwoerd was to soon realize a fond nationalist ambition by carrying South Africa to the status of a republic outside the Commonwealth. He also oversaw some tightening up along familiar lines, with the General Laws Amendment Act of 1963 expanding police powers of detention without charge, for example. But the looseness of regulation and enforcement in the sphere of influx controls was also to be corrected – in order to make it more, not less, difficult for Africans to justify their being in the cities.

Moreover, conscious of the threat posed by the emergence of successful 'independence' movements elsewhere on the continent, Verwoerd now plotted a new 'grand design' for apartheid in order to consolidate and further 'legitimize' Afrikaner hegemony and racial dominance in a new Africa. In doing so he was apparently also driven by his stated faith in God's purpose, something reaffirmed, in his mind, by his own survival of a 1960 assassination attempt on his own life.[89] In any case, Verwoerd now saw the South African solution to

[87] Davies et al., *The Struggle for South Africa.*
[88] See, *inter alia*, Posel, *The Making of Apartheid.*
[89] In 1966, a second assassination attempt, this time in Parliament itself, was successful.

the unrest that threatened white supremacy to lie, more than ever, in the reserves (Bantustans), these now presented by him as being, potentially, en route to becoming 'independent states' themselves. As indicated earlier, this development was to be rationalized by assigning a new centrality to the notion of 'separate development' in the state's official discourse: all Africans were now to be defined as the 'ethnic' other, identified in their 'tribal diversity' as being 'merely' different, nationally, from 'South Africans' (who were, of course, white).

As suggested, this was essentially a tactical gesture in any case, one made in the teeth of the 'winds of change' that was bringing about decolonization elsewhere in Africa and throughout the world. For this purpose the ploy remained unconvincing, since few outside South Africa could fail to see the arbitrariness of the ethnic discourse here being invoked, the shallowness of the prospective Bantustan independence that was on offer ... and the reality that Africans were in fact being stripped of any claim to citizenship in the greater South Africa. No doubt the government's intention was also to sow division amongst an otherwise restive black population, encouraging 'tribal' consciousness and the creation of a stratum of privileged middle-class African politicians, bureaucrats and businessman within the confines of these statelets-in-the-making who would then have a vested interest in linking their fortunes to the overarching apartheid system.[90]

Yet, whatever the other calculations that lay behind this macabre experiment in social engineering, the chief role of such Bantustans was all too clear: to serve, more than ever, as 'dumping grounds' for the 'discarded people' of South Africa. For thousands upon thousands of South Africans – their brutal treatment rationalized in the name of 'repatriation' – now became fresh victims of Verwoerd's grand design: of ever more rigid pass-law enforcement, of forced removal from urban areas (where many of the unskilled had been rendered 'unemployable' as increased mechanization hit both industry and agriculture), and of the cleansing of the 'black spots' of African settlement that still dotted the 'white' countryside.[91]

As O'Meara states, the Nationalists' sweeping triumph in the 1961 election was a 'personal vindication of Verwoerd'. Indeed, a 'general climate of fear infected the entire society', paving the way for a decade that was to be 'perhaps the bleakest period in South Africa's dismal history': thus

> [t]he relentless, paranoid witch hunt for perceived enemies, the morally-blind and fanatical implementation of the smallest details of apartheid, the mother Grundy

[90] The Bantustan ploy, with its new public emphasis on cultural, rather than racial, differences can also be seen as part of a move away from relying on the thrust of Afrikaner nationalism per se as the vital motor force for framing and driving the racist project. It was now yielding pride of place to a more generalized appeal to the white community: certainly a larger number of English-speaking whites were voting for the National Party as the years wore on.

[91] An essential point of reference here is Cosmas Desmond, *The Discarded People* (Harmondsworth: Penguin, 1971).

censorship, and the imposition of fundamentalist Calvinist values on the broader society, all conspired to reinforce the most mean-spirited, petty-minded and ignorant political philistinism in public and intellectual life.[92]

Indeed, the election had made quite clear that 'most white South Africans were more than ready for [Verwoerd's] promised walls of granite around their privileges'.

But was this racist side of 'racial capitalism' – as exemplified by such a crystallization of the Verwoerdian vision – becoming a bit too extreme for capital's liking? Not yet noticeably so, certainly. To be sure and as we will see below, the requirements of a booming, rapidly changing, capitalist system for more skilled labour and a wider consumer market than the mere super-exploitation of the black population could readily deliver would eventually cause some problems. Nonetheless, as will become equally clear, the principal ingredient of the deepening crisis to come for the apartheid system would not lie in any such difficulties in fine-tuning the precise fit between the requirements of capital and the imperatives of racial oppression. Rather, it was the renewed political challenge from the dominated black population that would prove to be the system's real Achilles heel. In any case, this still lay in the future. For the moment, the mounting of such a challenge was difficult to foresee, given the defeat, marked above, of the mass movements and the continuing 'onslaught on dissent' by the apartheid state that scarred the decade.[93]

Some principled whites did act, through student organizations (NUSAS, the National Union of South African Students) and in church circles (the University Christian Movement and the Christian Institute) and they did have black allies. Nonetheless, for the moment, much of the black population itself had a defeated air. For black workers, for example, the sixties were (as David Lewis has termed them) mere 'survival years,' characterized by 'official repression and comprehensive legal discrimination, employer hostility, weak organization, and by quiescence on the factory floor'.[94] Not that this 'defeat' was purchased easily by the white regime and the dominant classes, even in the rural areas where there were indeed notable manifestations of dramatic resistance throughout in the 1950s and early-1960s, these well chronicled by Govan Mbeki, Peter Delius and others. But these assertions too were beaten down. Indeed, as Paul Nugent succinctly concludes, 'the crushing [of the rural revolt] the state put paid for all time to the thesis that South Africa was a country ripe for guerilla warfare. The liberation movements thereafter

[92] See Dan O'Meara's magisterial portrait of intra-Afrikaner politics, *Forty Lost Years; The apartheid state and the politics of the National Party, 1948–1994* (Athens, OH and Randberg, S.A.: Ohio University Press and Ravan Press, 1996), especially, as quoted here, pp. 109–10.

[93] The phrase is that of Thomas Karis and Gail Gerhart in the extended introduction to their compendium, monumental and essential, *From Protest to Challenge: A Documentary history of African Politics in South Africa, 1882–1990, Volume 5: Nadir and Resurgence, 1964–1979* (Bloomington, IN: Indiana University Press, 1997) p. 62.

[94] David Lewis, 'Black Workers and Trade Unions,' being his chapter in Karis & Gerhart, *From Protest to Challenge*, p. 189.

concentrated more of their energy on mobilizing an urban constituency.'[95]

True, Nugent continues, with nationalist organizations like the ANC and the PAC now banned and with 'the efflorescence of rural resistance in the 1950s' stilled, 'the following decade ushered in a period of relative acquiescence, born of a combination of exhaustion and fear'. Indeed, as Tom Lodge has suggested more generally in offering 'a tentative explanation of the relative tranquility of the 1960s' the 'most obvious cause' of the overall set-back that popular resistance now experienced was 'the suppression of the nationalist movements and the imprisonment, banning or exile of an entire generation of politicians and trade unionists' on the one hand and the 'unlimited powers of arrest and detention as well as the increasingly lavish budgets' granted the police on the other. This, plus 'an army of informers, ... fresh restrictions on political discussion,' further controls over population movement and settlement, and 'a limited degree of cooption'![96]

Despite all this, however, resistance was by no means dead. Yet it is important to note that its rebirth was not to be the exclusive achievement of any 'mobilizing' efforts undertaken by 'the liberation movements', themselves now principally in exile (or in jail on Robben Island). For a new set of actors inside the country were to begin to make their voices of resistance heard, voices not indifferent to the liberation movements but, as the product of fresh contradictions within the country, not reducible to them either. This fact was soon signalled (as we will see in the next chapter) by both the inspiring strikes of 1971 in South African-occupied Namibia and, most dramatically, by the 1973 Durban strikes inside South Africa itself. Even more urgently, however, the most promising signs of future broad-based possibilities for the struggle lay with a new generation of black students, smarting from the defeat of their parents' generation and also from their own consignment to inferior educational settings (to the so-called 'bush' universities, for example) by the state's system of Bantu Education. Reacting against white rule (and even the 'white leadership' of otherwise progressive organizations like NUSAS) they developed a philosophy of 'Black Consciousness' – influenced in part by parallel 'Black Power' assertions in the United States – and instituted autonomous organizations like the South African Students' Organization (SASO) to focus their hostility to the system.

The fate of such race-sensitive psychological rearmament by blacks would be a complex one in the coming decades. But certainly the kind of renewed confidence amongst the oppressed population that the Black Consciousness Movement sought to build would feed into the dramatic student-driven uprising of Soweto in 1976, as well as having further impact beyond it. At the time some within the regime thought the separatist implications of 'Black Consciousness' might actually service their long-term goal of reinforcing the 'apartness' that the architects of the apartheid system had dreamed of. For, in the context of the previous decade's boom and the apparent impregnability of their racist

---

[95] Paul Nugent, *Africa since Independence* (Basingstoke: Palgrave Macmillan, 2004), p. 133
[96] Lodge, *Black Politics in South Africa*, pp. 321–22.

fortress, it was difficult for most whites at the beginning of the 1970s to imagine the scope of the crisis that awaited apartheid and, indeed, the system of racial capitalism as a whole. Yet we will, in the following two chapters, have to proceed precisely to an analysis of the nature of the system's underlying crisis, of the variety of attempts made to resolve it, and of the dramatic series of events that would, ultimately, find Nelson Mandela moving from prison to the Presidency.

2.
The Transition:
The Players Assemble, 1970–1990

JOHN S. SAUL

The present chapter, and the briefer but complementary one that follows it, tell a complex story. On the one hand, they chart the slow but ineluctable struggle on the part of the vast majority of the population, who were, by and large, not white, to overcome the cruel 'pigmentocracy' – as finally epitomized by the apartheid regime – that had come to dominate their lives and stunt their human potential. At the same time, however, the enemies of promise were many more than those embedded in the fact of racial rule itself. For, as seen in the previous chapter, there was also, linked to and interpenetrating with white rule, the grim fact of capitalist domination. Indeed, for many South Africans, the struggle for racial freedom and equality was simultaneously a struggle for freedom from class and external economic domination – and also one for gender equality, environmental security and the institutionalization of democratic structures within which the voices of all could be heard and heeded. Yet the fact remains that the struggle for racial equality – in part eminently successful – has been far more fully realized than have been any struggles for class, gender and environmental justice and for the guaranteeing of any meaningful and effective democratic 'voice' for all citizens.[1]

In short, there can be no question that the victory over the grim system of apartheid, recorded in this chapter, was dramatic. But there has also been a graphic and readily identifiable shortfall with respect to liberation more expansively defined, this having determined, to put it quite baldly, a failure to realize 'freedom' on very many diverse fronts. Indeed, there can be no doubt that such 'failure' has severely qualified any easy sense of achieved victory, the primary victors of the South African struggle being, as we will see, global capitalism on the one hand and the relatively thin layer of ANC-linked black elites that slipped into power on the other. True, many will claim that the ANC cohort that obtained power in 1994 did all that could be done and achieved all that could have been achieved under the circumstances that confronted it; such observers float the argument that what was realized – formal democracy in a colour-blind capitalist order – represented the exact limit of what was possible.

This would, of course, be an easier case to accept had the incoming ANC-

---

[1] See, for the southern Africa region more generally and the implications (both real and imagined) of the region's experience, John S. Saul, 'Socialism and Southern Africa', being Chapter 8 of Michelle Williams and Vishwas Satgar (eds), *New Approaches to Marxism: Critique and Struggle* (Johannesburg: Wits University Press forthcoming).

linked elite not passed quite so comfortably into positions of privilege, while also simultaneously encouraging the vast majority of the population to passively accept 'mere' national liberation as a perfectly adequate, even worthy, return for the sacrifices they had made and the struggles they had engaged in. It is also true that many commentators who do adopt the conventional line of analysis being criticized here nonetheless feel forced to admit to the anti-climactic character of much of the outcome so achieved – even as they argue that the story historians now tell should chiefly be about 'the limits of the possible' during the period of transition in South Africa and also about the judicious approach taken by the ANC in the light of such limits. But this latter is not an easy account to swallow in light of what has actually befallen post-apartheid South Africa on the ANC's continuing watch. As will be seen, in fact, it is a very different reading of 'the art of the possible' under South African circumstances and in light of the country's own history that these two chapters seek to offer.

* * *

Let us, then, return to our history and to our chronology. As witnessed at the end of the preceding chapter, there was in the 1960s an apparently successful culmination of the white population's locking into place a closed, all-embracing system of racist colonialism and 'racial capitalism', a system that we have shown to have emerged in South Africa out of the preceding several centuries of white and capitalist domination. In this chapter we turn the page, however, in order to survey the dramatic and relatively rapid waning of that system's viability and credibility over the next two decades: first in the 1970s in the crucial 'moments' epitomized by their familiar short-hand code-names: 'Durban' and 'Soweto'; then, with the beat of resistance now resonating and swelling into the 1980s, new code-words came into prominence to signal a very different possible future: COSATU (Congress of South African Trade Unions, the UDF (the United Democratic Front) and the MDM (the Mass Democratic Movement), for example. We will also have to countenance the renewed prominence of an older 'code-word' as well: the ANC.

The reactions of both capital and the 'white community' more generally to these new assertions from below will then be discussed in this chapter, as will the role these two sets of players would then take in the transition to a novel post-apartheid dispensation. Together with the feverish rearrangement of the white power structure in the 1980s and with 'negotiations' afoot, came – as is recounted in Chapter 3 – the last manoeuvrings of the early 1990s and finally the election, on a one-person, one-vote basis within a unified South Africa, of the ANC to power in 1994. Here was, apparently, that dramatic victory of the heretofore visibly oppressed in the country referred to above, and a genuine cause for celebration for all those, in South Africa and beyond, who had embraced the anti-apartheid cause.

But, celebrating what exactly? Though most definitely a victory, just how much of a victory was it? For, as noted, we will also have to emphasize its partial nature, the victory's limitations already visible – in spite of (or was it because of) the consolidation of the ANC ascension to formal positions of mass electoral legitimacy and power – by the time of the 1994 elections. For what did such a 'consolidation' in power of the ANC – and, by implication, of the black majority – actually mean? What, to repeat, did it mean in terms of any significant beginning in the overcoming of contradictions still visible with respect to racial inequalities, for example, but also in terms of class and gender disparities, of environmental concerns, and in the meeting of the requirements of genuine popular-democratic empowerment? 'Not enough' is the short answer. Here, of course, we begin to broach issues that will be explored much more fully by Patrick Bond in Chapters 4 and 5. In this chapter, however, my principal task will be to underline the main features of recent and long-term history that have helped define the very unevenness of the transition beyond apartheid. Moreover, we will begin to see that a clear focus on such features will help us to comprehend the grip that the country's complex and contradictory history has continued to have upon a now ostensibly liberated South Africa.

To begin with, it was quite clear by the 1970s that the enforced political calm of the 1960s was not to last. True, as witnessed at the end of the previous chapter, that decade had seen the triumph of repression domestically and the further consolidation of the apartheid system. Moreover, Western countries and corporations locked in behind the South African leadership, confirmed in their high profit margins and still relatively untroubled by the exiled nationalist movements' on-going efforts to find the means to launch a different kind of resistance to apartheid. Indeed, the smug nature of Western response was perhaps best summarized at the very dawn of the 1970s in an important American report of the time written by the National Security Council Interdepartmental Group for Africa and entitled the 'Study in Response to National Security Study Memorandum 39: Southern Africa' (also known as the *Kissinger Study on Southern Africa*). There the 'option' ultimately chosen by decision-makers was frankly stated: 'The whites are here to stay and the only way that constructive change can come about is through them. There is no hope for the blacks to gain the political rights they seek through violence, which will only lead to chaos and increased opportunities for the communists ... Our tangible interests form a basis for our contacts in the region, and these can be maintained at an acceptable political cost.'[2] Equally smug were the white leaders in South Africa's state and business spheres themselves. As Younis writes of the moment:

> In the decades since 1948, apartheid-driven economic growth had proven both rapid and supremely profitable. [In fact,] under the state's patronage, Afrikaner capital had [even] succeeded in penetrating the heights of historically English-dominated monopoly capital. A confident Afrikaner bourgeoisie was now well ensconced in all sectors.[3]

---

[2] National Security Council (USA), *The Kissinger Study of Southern Africa* (Nottingham: Spokesman Books, 1975), p. 66.
[3] Mona Younis, *Liberation and Democratization: The South African and Palestinian National Movements* (Minneapolis: University of Minnesota Press, 2000), p. 124.

Yet there were already signs that such rulers were beginning to live on borrowed time and that the apartheid system was far more vulnerable than, momentarily, it had appeared to be. There were economic vulnerabilities to be sure, although these would, as we shall see, have to share the stage with some very real vulnerabilities of a more immediately political nature. Moreover, the paradoxical effects of the apartheid boom must also be underscored. For this 'boom' brought many more, and not fewer, Africans to the cities. By the mid-1960s as well industrial capital was ascendant, with manufacturing contributing a greater share of the GDP (Gross domestic Product) than mining and agriculture combined. In addition, mechanization, introduced in these boom years, made a skilled and stable workforce increasingly necessary even in mining and agriculture. Now, in fact, apartheid began to present impediments to further growth: acute shortages of skilled labour despite an abundance of work-seekers, a relatively small domestic market despite a substantial population lacking all types of goods, and massive pressures to enter the industrializing centres by the victims of apartheid's underdevelopment in the rural periphery.

Apartheid, in sum, kept African labour poor and unskilled and was increasingly doing so at some real economic cost. Thus, for capital, the system of inclusion of African labour came, increasingly, to demand modification. But even more important was the fact that escalating black resistance now also made such modification seem imperative. As in 1946 and 1960 – moments that saw massive worker unrest – employers touted reforms, even if behind the scenes they still looked primarily for the government to restore order. This time, however, stability would be elusive, and black resistance (and an ever expanding black presence, both 'legal' and 'illegal', in the urban areas) would considerably raise the stakes.

For such a growing black population increasingly posed a grave political threat to apartheid and to racial capitalism – a threat even more dramatic in its potential political consequences than were those contradictions already visible in the economic sphere. Indeed, in the 1970s, two main constituencies within the black population – the urban workers and the urban poor – would make themselves heard ever more assertively and in quite dramatic ways. On the one hand, the working class was, with industrial expansion, a much larger and increasingly strategically placed grouping within the country. Here was a class, in fact, that was well aware of both its political rights and its economic grievances and, as the decade wore on, becoming better organized to do something about them. The second constituency was best epitomized, at least at first, by the youth, especially as they found themselves grouped together for potential action in schools and universities. In addition, however, there were their families and other adult members of the urban poor – some working class, some not quite as easily categorized in such terms – who would, with time, themselves be moved to action by the student example and become ever more prepared to act out as a political force, a force that can defined by its very urban-ness and can best be labelled a 'precariat' – although (as we will suggest below) a 'precariat' in a broader and more expansive sense than the manner in which this term is sometimes used elsewhere.[4] As protagonists of popular mass politics this latter 'class' thus came to complement in crucial ways more strictly proletarian driven assertions. The key flash-point for the re-emergence of the proletariat as it stepped ever more forcefully onto the South Africa political stage were the Durban strikes of 1972–73; the comparable flash-point for the students – and, in the longer run, for the precariat, the community of urban-dwellers as a whole – was the Soweto uprising of 1976. To these two flash-points and their crucial fall-out across the country in the following decade we now turn.

The 1970s and the 1980s: Socio-economic contradictions and the rebirth of resistance

The politics of the proletariat: Durban, COSATU and the resurgent working class

As suggested, it is not surprising that in such a context as defined the 1970s there did surface a novel and distinctly working-class-centred mode of thinking and action in the form of a newly emergent trade union movement. Here was a movement that was destined to grow and mature as a crucial component of COSATU as that vitally important overarching union federation emerged in the 1980s. Of course, there already existed the Southern African Congress of Trade Unions (SACTU), a trade union grouping quite closely affiliated historically with the ANC/SACP (South African Communist Party) nexus of resistance, but now, like the latter, in exile; indeed, by the 1970s SACTU had become a much more distant voice coming from well beyond the border, more real outside South Africa than in. It was fresh working-class voices that were now being heard, with fledgling organizations beginning to step forward. Indeed, one of the seminal moments in the rebirth of resistance, the aforementioned Durban strikes, reflected this reality, as did the emergence of such trade union initiatives as that represented by the Federation of South African Trade Unions/FOSATU and others. The new unions continued to intertwine in some important ways with organizational echoes of SACTU influence, especially in

4   The 'precariat,' is a term that I use in a very different sense from the way in which it is employed by Guy Standing in his *The Precariat: The New Dangerous Class* (London: Bloomsbury Academic, 2011) – and by Ronaldo Munck, who, in his 'The Precariat: A View from the South', *Third World Quarterly*, 34, 5, 2013, defines, with Standing, the 'precariat,' much too simply in my opinion, as a 'precarious proletariat'. On this see the section of the present chapter, below, entitled 'The Politics of the Precariat: Soweto, the Townships and the UDF', but also John S. Saul, 'What Working-Class? Non-Transformative Global Capitalism and the African Case' in Baris Karagaac and Yasin Kaya (eds), *Capital and Labour in Contemporary Capitalism* (forthcoming). This latter article has, in turn, been recast in a more developed form, as 'Resistance Redefined: Proletariat, Precariat and the Terms of Possible Revival in Africa', which is ch. 5 of John S. Saul, *A Flawed Freedom: Rethinking Southern African Liberation* (Delhi, London and Toronto: Three Essays Collective, Pluto Books and Between-the-Lines, 2014).

the Eastern Cape, as they moved towards the formation of an even more potent union central, the aforementioned COSATU, in the early 1980s. But this was still, overall, a distinctively novel and progressive voice, one that demanded to be heard – although, as we will see, COSATU itself was, by the 1990s, to be swept up into the emergent ANC-led coalition, becoming a partner within the ruling Tripartite Alliance (comprised of the ANC, the SACP and COSATU), albeit a rather junior partner and an increasingly uneasy one as the ANC itself carried the country into the maw of neo-liberalism.[5]

Here, of course, it bears emphasizing that it was precisely such fresh working-class action that, in the first instance, surfaced to revive resistance within the country in the 1970s. True, as we shall see, this new assertion was just too class-based (rather than 'merely' racially-based) and class-conscious to be unqualifiedly approved of by those, to be discussed below, who were of the increasingly popular 'Black Consciousness' persuasion. But it was also much more specific and responsive in its orientation to the immediate grievances of workers on the shop floor than had been SACTU – this organization's leadership now banned in any case and itself existing largely in exile as an international lobby group both within the global trade union network and as part of the ANC's own established alliance of organizations. SACTU's slant had been and continued to be (albeit now largely from exile rather than on the ground) the mobilization of workers for the broader purposes of 'national liberation struggle'.

But why did Durban – and what has been labelled 'the Durban moment' – become, at least, briefly the epicentre of working-class action in South Africa? Grievances aplenty existed for workers everywhere in South Africa in the early-1970s of course, for reasons alluded to above. Meanwhile, dramatic worker action (the so-called 'Ovambo strikes' that occurred between 1971 and 1973) in Namibia – South-West Africa, illegally occupied by the South African state, in defiance of the United Nations, as a kind of 'fifth province' – had spoken eloquently to South Africa's black workers of both the growing unacceptability to racial capitalism's crippling and humiliating costs – and the possibility of effective resistance.[6] Closer to home for Durbanites there were the signs of incipient strike action as manifested, over several years (April 1969, September,

---

[5] See, *inter alia*, Eddie Webster and Glenn Adler, 'Exodus Without a Map: The Labour Movement in a Liberalizing South Africa' in Bjorn Beckman and Lloyd Sachikonye (eds) *Labour Regimes and Liberalization: The Restructuring of State-Society Relations in Africa* (Harare: University of Zimbabwe Press, 2001); and Roger Southall and Eddie Webster, 'Unions and parties in South Africa: COSATU and the ANC in the wake of Polokwane' in Bjorn Beckman, Sakhela Buhlungu and Lloyd Sachikonye (eds), *Trade Unions and Party Politics: Labour Movements in Africa* (Cape Town: HSRC Press, 2010). But see also Carolyn Bassett and Marlea Clarke, 'South African Trade Unions and Globalization: Going for the "High-road", Getting Stuck on the "Low-road"', *World Organisation, Labour and Globalisation*, 2, 1 (2008); and Sakhela Buhlungu, *A Paradox of Victory: COSATU and the Democratic Transformation in South Africa* (Scottsville, S.A.: University of KwaZulu-Natal Press, 2010).

[6] The resonance of the Namibia case is well-captured in L. Douwes-Dekker, D. Hemson, J. S. Kane-Berman, J. Lever and L. Schlemmer, 'Case Studies in African Labour Action in South Africa and Namibia (South West Africa)', in Richard Sandbrook and Robin

1971, October 1972), by stevedores in the Durban (and Cape Town) docks and, Jeremy Baskin notes, there were also the 'rumblings' of Putco bus-drivers.[7]

Nonetheless, as Steven Friedman writes, just as 'the twentieth century, we are told, only began in Europe in 1914, when world war swept away its old, complacent rulers' so too

> the 1970s began for South African employers early on the morning of July 9, 1973, when 2,000 workers at the Coronation Brick and Tile Works on the outskirts of Durban gathered at a football field and demand a pay rise ... For more than a decade, African workers had been seen but rarely heard ... The job colour bar was tightened, the pass laws became ever harsher, but the workers did not resist – strikes were so rare that each was a major event ... [But] the Coronation strike broke this mould.[8]

Now industrial actions spread to other sites dotted across the Durban area, notably to the various factories of the Frame Textile Corporation, these (as Gerry Maré wrote at the time) being 'strategically placed in each of [Durban's] industrial areas' and all 'characterized by particularly low wages and bad labour relations'.[9] Soon too, Friedman notes, municipal workers were striking the Durban Corporation for a wage hike, even as 'unrest ... also spread to other Natal cities and towns and there was talk of a general African strike in Durban'! Indeed, stoppages had very soon sprung up in East London, the Johannesburg area and beyond and cumulatively these now began definitively to change the landscape of struggle.

> Between 1965 and 1971, less than 23,000 African workers had struck. In the first three months of 1973, 61,000 stopped work. By the end of the year, the figure had grown to 90,000 and employers had lost 229,000 shifts – more than seven times the number lost through African strikes in the past eight years.
>
> The strikes hastened the rebirth of African unions and jolted employers and the government into changes that would help the new [worker] organisations survive and grow. The unions would face new setbacks and the reforms were often mingled with repression. But that January morning changed the factory world in ways that still affect us today [1987].[10]

Jeremy Baskin writes to similar effect that in September, 1973, as one example, 'police opened fire on miners protesting against the rejection of a wage demand

---

[(cont)] Cohen (eds), *The Development of an African Working Class: Studies in Class Formation and Action* (London: Longman, 1975).

[7] See Jeremy Baskin, *Striking Back: A History of COSATU* (Johannesburg: Ravan Press, 1991), pp. 17–18.

[8] Steven Friedman, *Building Tomorrow Today: African Workers in Trade Unions, 1970–1984* (Cape Town: Ravan, 1987), p. 37 and *passim*.

[9] Gerry Maré's seminal paper of the time (1973) is quoted in Baruch Hirson, *Year of Fire, Year of Ash: The Soweto Revolt – Roots of a Revolution?* (London: Zed Press, 1979), p. 134, as is Maré's specific raising of the question: 'Why Durban?' His answer is situationally defined as reflecting not only the broader situation in South Africa but also the immediate 'moment' in Durban: the specific set of events at Coronation and Frame and the local 'rise in transport costs and then the rumoured train boycott'.

[10] Friedman, *Building Tomorrow Today*, p. 40.

at Anglo American's Western Deep. Twelve were killed. Sporadic strikes continued throughout the remainder of the year and into 1974. Apart from Natal, strikes occurred in East London, Johannesburg and on the mines', and he concludes pointedly that 'the rebirth of black unionism was underway'.[11] Indeed, he then itemizes in his book a complicated history of a wide range of organizational initiatives that continued to grow and to spread: the formation in Durban of an important umbrella co-ordinating organization, the Trade Union Advisory Co-ordinating Council/TUACC (forerunner of FOSATU); the emergence of various initiatives, surfacing in Cape Town and ultimately crystallizing as the General Workers Union (GWU); and, on the Witwatersrand, the stepping forward of the Urban Training Project (UTP) and other initiatives. Moreover, a number of such organizations would ultimately come together, in 1979, to form a first real federation of the re-emergent unions (20,000 workers organized in twelve unions), the Federation of South African Trade Unions (FOSATU).

It is also important to again emphasize the new perspective that characterized many of these novel worker assertions and shop-floor struggles in Durban and beyond. To begin with, the new organizations being formed out of such industrial contestations sought tactically – and so as to escape excessive negative scrutiny by the apartheid state – to avoid any overly compromising links to the ANC/SACP/SACTU exile group. As well, many within the 'new trade union movement' were suspicious of such formations-in-exile, as I heard for myself from trade union organizers in the 1970s – fearful, from the vantage point of their concern to safeguard worker interests and voice, of the ANC/SACP/SACTU's vanguardist preoccupations and also of this latter triumvirate's possible embrace of a negative, all too Soviet/Stalinist modelled, attitude towards true worker-centred empowerment from below.[12] Indeed, as Webster and Adler argue,

> The legal proscription of the nationalist movements meant that in their formative years [the] embryonic unions were able to develop leadership, organize their constituency, and define their strategies and tactics relatively independently from the ideological orientations and models of the ANC, SACP and especially their labour arm, SACTU. The space created by virtue of banning and exile meant that the new unions could develop innovative approaches to organizing that differed from the populist strategies and tactics of the nationalist-linked unions of the 1950s.[13]

It is true, of course, that the new labour activists of the seventies remained respectful of the SACTU tradition and of Congress history but many did so

---

[11] Friedman, *Building Tomorrow Today*, p. 18.

[12] Interestingly I heard this position most forcibly articulated in the late '70s at their then shared house in Durban from both then trade union activists Alec Erwin and (at that time banned) Johnny Copelyn whose own personal trajectories were ultimately to take them in quite different directions from the opinions they expressed on that earlier occasion.

[13] Webster & Adler, 'Exodus Without a Map', p. 126.

without feeling unduly beholden to their predecessors. Their actions defined themselves initially on the shop floor and, as suggested above, the sparks struck by such confrontations at the Durban port, the Coronation Brick and Tile Works, the Frame Group factories and other sites in Durban were quickly to have dramatic resonance throughout the country as a new trade union central similar to FOSATU took shape, as other labour-centred umbrella organizations (many in embryo before the Durban moment) formed and were further streamlined for effective action; and the wave of strike activity spread.[14]

In fact, it was soon clear that a nation-wide context had been created within which, even as 'labour movements throughout much of the world experienced declines in membership and influence during the 1980s and 1990s, the South African labour movement [grew] rapidly'.[15] As Webster and Adler continue:

> The membership of trade unions [expanded] ... from more than 700,000 in 1979 to nearly 3,000,000 in 1993. This involved a growth in union density from slightly more than 15 percent to 58 percent over the same period...[with] the broad trend [being] towards nation-wide industrial or sectoral unions at the core of the economy, including mining, metal, textile and clothing, retail and commercial, chemical, food and the public service.

Small wonder that Younis could see 'Durban' as the watershed that marked the revival of resistance in South Africa, suggesting that 'the strike wave that rocked the Durban area in 1972–3 would mark the beginning of the end of the decade of quiescence and, eventually, [of] the system that exacted it. The surge of strike actions that traversed numerous industries would be the biggest to hit the country since the Second World War.'[16]

Moreover, many of these unions, as the movement spread and deepened, were manifestations of what Webster has termed 'social movement unionism,' for they were fully conscious of the imperatives of the shop-floor struggles they launched while also being aware of the broader anti-apartheid resonance of their undertakings. Indeed, Joe Foster, the head of FOSATU, would make exactly this point in a widely-cited speech in the early 1980s:

> It is therefore essential that workers must strive to build their own powerful and effective organization even whilst they are part of the wider popular struggle. This organization is necessary to protect and further workers' interests and to ensure that the popular movement is not hijacked by elements who will in the end have no option but to turn against their worker supporters ... [Indeed], in relation to the particular

[14] See, *inter alia*, Institute for Industrial Education, *The Durban Strikes, 1973* (Durban: Institute for Industrial Education and Ravan, 1974); and Dennis McShane, Martin Plaut and David Ward, *Power! Black Workers, their Unions and the Struggle for Freedom in South Africa* (Boston, MA: South End Press, 1984).

[15] Webster & Adler, 'Exodus Without a Map', p. 124. See also the full range of contributions in their jointly edited volume, Glenn Adler and Eddie Webster (eds), *Trade Unions and Democratization in South Africa, 1985–1997* (London: MacMillan Press, 2000); Baskin, *Striking Back*; and Buhlungu, *A Paradox of Victory*.

[16] Younis, *Liberation and Democratization*, p. 125.

requirements of worker organization, mass parties and popular political organizations have definite limitations which have to be clearly understood by us.[17]

This was the emphasis that Bob Fine also underscored in introducing the republication of Foster's speech in the *Review of African Political Economy* at the time. There he drew a clear distinction between 'popular front' politics (where 'the working class is merely wheeled in and out like the crowd in a Shakespearean drama') and a much more assertive and effective working-class political presence, suggesting (already in 1982) that, in contrast, 'there are good reasons to believe that [the popular front] was [and continues to be?] the basic conception behind the Congress Alliance; namely that SACTU subordinated the specific interests and organization of workers first to mass protest campaigns and then to the armed struggle'.[18] Now it was precisely this latter model that many in the new unions sought to leave behind.

Not that the state was idle while all this was going on. As I have documented (writing with Stephen Gelb) elsewhere,[19] one of the state's key adjustments was exemplified in the Wiehann Report that the white government commissioned in 1979. This Report counselled the formal recognition of trade unions and the transformation of their *de facto* existence into a *de jure* one (involving the formal registration of unions, for example). Friedman signals the ambiguities of this proposed 'concession', one that was then adopted by the state, clearly:

> The unions' potential strength meant they must be controlled – their present [relative] weakness ... meant that this should be done soon. It would, the [Wiehann] report argued, be far healthier to allow the unions to register at 'an early stage' ... This would counter 'polarization,' ensure a more orderly process of bargaining' and expose African unions 'more directly to South Africa's trade union traditions and the existing institutions thus inculcating a sense of responsibility to the free market'.[20]

Indeed this real threat did at first cause tensions within the trade union movement itself, a sharp debate surfacing between various pro- and anti-registration advocates. But, as it became apparent that, by and large, the cooptative dimensions of the state's Wiehann strategy were more than outweighed by the further status and organizational thrust and momentum that the unions could now avail themselves of, this debate tended to drift away.

But this was not the only source of tension amongst the trade unions. For even if the FOSATU voice, as articulated (see above) by Joe Foster and others, was to become a particularly strong one, it was not the only trade-union voice

[17] See Joe Foster's widely-noted speech, published under the title 'The Workers' Struggle: Where Does FOSATU Stand?' in *Review of African Political Economy/ROAPE*, 9, 24, 1982, pp. 99–114.

[18] Robert Fine, 'The Workers' Struggle in South Africa', *ROAPE* 9, 24, 1982, pp. 95–99.

[19] John S. Saul and Stephen Gelb, *The Crisis in South Africa* (New York: Monthly Review Press, 1981) and in a 'Revised Edition', as expanded upon by the first of these authors (New York and London: Monthly Review Press and Zed Books, 1986); see, on the present topic, Chapter 2, Section 2 (3), 'Wiehann', pp. 125–132.

[20] Steven Friedman, as quoted in Baskin, *Striking Back*, p. 26.

to be heard during this period. Webster and Adler record a range of such diverse expressions of the time. As does Baskin[21] who emphasizes, for example, the emergence – especially in Eastern Cape cities like East London and Port Elizabeth with long histories of SACTU/ANC activity as well as in various places in the Transvaal – of what were termed to be 'community unions', those distinguished by impressive if somewhat transitory activity that 'moved rapidly, mobilizing workers across a broad front and relied on extensive organizing and mass campaigning in contrast to the intensive methods of the FOSATU bloc. They were more at home with the rally and the mass meeting than the gradual development of shop steward structures.'[22] These were the unions that helped anchor a second, powerful and much-debated, inter-union tension, one sustained both in South Africa and abroad by the SACP and the ANC – presented as voicing a sharp juxtaposition of 'national-democratic'-focused, unions (or 'populist' ones as common parlance of the time often had it), and 'shop-floor' centred unions (or 'workerist' ones, a label often attached to the more FOSATU-style trade union practices).[23]

There was much of the caricature in these various labels, even though they did also speak to something real in terms of the diverse emphases they underscored. Yet the fact is that 'workerists' and 'populists' would soon come together into a brand new union central, a union of great and continuing significance, the Congress of South African Trade Unions (COSATU). Thus, as Southall and Webster write, 'subsequently, the hostility between the two [of these] traditions [populist and workerist] declined when, in 1985, COSATU was formed as a 'strategic compromise' between the two dominant political traditions within the democratic labour movements, that is, between the national-democratic and the shop-floor traditions.'[24]

Of course, it is also important to note here another strand, one that was more embedded in the preoccupations that had characterized the Black Consciousness Movement. This was a strand which found organizational expression in 'the merging (in 1980) of several diverse unions, albeit unions generally far weaker than FOSATU's and less likely to embark on strike action ... [with] its impact on the labour scene [being] significantly less', into the Council of South Africa/CUSA. These were unions that also tended to 'reject non-racialism in favour of black leadership'. The assertions of unions that grouped within the Azanian Confederation of Trade Unions/AZACTU during this period were quite similar and indeed it was these two bodies ('12 unions from CUSA and 11 from AZACTU') that, not having participated in the union talks that led to COSATU,

---

[21] Webster & Adler, 'Exodus Without a Map', 127–128; Baskin, *Striking Back*, pp. 19–32.

[22] Baskin, *Striking Back*, p. 29.

[23] This split is well covered in Baskin, *Striking Back*, Chapter 6. 'Workerists and Populists?' The resonance was also felt as far away as Canada where SACTU and SACP actually prevailed on the Canadian Communist Party to demonize FOSATU – but also my own organization, the Toronto Committee for the Liberation of Southern Africa (TCLSAC), for our support of FOSATU, on the basis that, in the Communist Party's chosen formulation, 'direct links stink'.

[24] Southall & Webster, 'Unions and Politics in South Africa', p. 138.

were, in 1986, to form instead the National Council of Trade Unions/NACTU. Worth noting no doubt; nonetheless, the more significant contribution to the swelling of trade union growth that came from this quarter was undoubtedly CUSA's taking the lead in organizing 'black mineworkers' to launch the National Union of Mineworkers (NUM) under the leadership of Cyril Ramaphosa. NUM, located in the absolutely crucial mining industry, grew rapidly, and by 1984 could claim 110,000 members – making it, Baskin states, 'at least as large as FOSATU.' But equally noteworthy is the fact that NUM chose eventually to affiliate itself within COSATU![25]

Meanwhile, it bears emphasizing that from 1984, and right up to 1994, the trade unions generally, and COSATU in particular, were to stand out as visible and active forces of real prominence both at the work-place and in the struggles of the larger community. Thus, as Adler and Webster argue, the decisive break with 'political abstentionism' had already come in November 1984, in advance of COSATU's founding, 'when FOSATU entered into joint action with student and civic organizations to participate in the first successful worker stay-away since 1976'.[26] This kind of confrontation would only escalate. It is also true that COSATU itself (including those elements that sprang from its ex-FOSATU components) had long sensed the need for a broader political project – one that might spear-head a counter-hegemony to the historic hegemony of racial capitalism – that it could not readily imagine itself mounting alone. As it happened, and as Southall and Webster have noted, the fact of 'the invasion of the townships by the South African Defence Force in 1984 ... [did] place major pressure upon unions located within the shop-floor tradition to abandon their 'workerist' critique of 'Charterism' (or 'populism' as it was more pejoratively called), encouraging them to align with United Democratic Front, the umbrella organization of anti-apartheid civic organizations which had been formed in 1983.'[27]

But this COSATU chose not to do, opting instead to continue to safeguard the working-class/workerist thrust that defined many of its component parts, rather than to risk blunting, within a broader mass organization, its saliency as a specifically proletarian voice. It did, of course, participate actively in the mass stay-aways, boycotts and other assertive expressions of the politics that increasingly defined the broader movement. But, in terms of institutional affiliation, after 1990 it would choose ultimately to affiliate directly with the ANC and the SACP in the newly emergent 'Tripartite Alliance'. Its intention: to join the 'Alliance', Southall and Webster underscore, 'not as a subordinate partner (as had SACTU) but, formally, as an equal player with an independent power base, strategy and leadership', Of course, this was not to be the way in which the ANC increasingly chose to see things!

[25] Note, as well, the prominence of Cyril Ramaphosa, in NUM from the beginning, a figure destined to become a key point-man for the ANC during its negotiations of the early 1990s with the apartheid government, a rival of Thabo Mbeki for the presidential succession to Nelson Mandela and now the Deputy President of the country under Jacob Zuma. But thereby hangs another tale (see below)!
[26] Webster & Adler, 'Exodus Without a Map', p. 129.
[27] Southall & Webster, 'Unions and Politics in South Africa', p. 139.

Before these last stages of the run-up to a post-apartheid future, however, there were the late-1980s. It was then, when the UDF (United Democratic Front), the crucial umbrella organization of active community organizations, was temporarily banned by the government in 1988, that COSATU sprang forward to take up the political slack, anchoring the freshly minted 'Mass Democratic Movement' that now, for a period, took the UDF's place in the forefront of community struggle, helping to co-ordinate the vast internal popular movement that was now fighting back against the state's especially brutal response to the near revolution that was occurring by the mid-1980s. It is also worth noting that it was during this period, at its 1987 Congress in fact, that COSATU actually adopted a workers charter of its own, one that some saw as possibly either replacing the Freedom Charter or at least as expressing the need to 'assert working-class demands' within any broad movement to oppose apartheid. Indeed, by the time of its 1989 Congress, there had been a general acceptance of 'a national-democratic perspective combined with a transformative vision':

> The essence of 'the struggle' was to rid the country of apartheid, racial oppression and undemocratic minority rule. Freedom, however, did not simply mean handing over power to a new black, or even non-racial elite. Social and economic inequalities had to be addressed and exploitation ended. This unified perspective envisaged genuine empowerment of the mass of the people. 'Freedom means socialism' was the slogan on one NUM banner. The way to achieve this was by encouraging active workers' participation in the struggle for freedom.[28]

At the same time, COSATU itself, including its ex-FOSATU components, had long sensed the need for a broader political project – one spearheading a counter-hegemony to the historic hegemony of racial capitalism – that it could not readily imagine itself mounting alone. In this regard it also came to sense a seeming logic of its accepting, however guardedly, the broader remit that the ANC was, during the transition period, increasingly claiming for itself. Indeed, 'in one of their very first acts [after COSATU's own founding in late-1985], its new office bearers... traveled to Lusaka and endorsed the ANC's leadership of the liberation struggle'.[29] At the same time, there is also little doubt that many within the COSATU camp failed fully to appreciate the significance of the fact that, even as the ANC and COSATU first met, the ANC was already in the process of rejecting the countenancing of any counter-hegemonic perspectives whatsoever towards capitalism. Note, too, that there were some components of COSATU (for example, the remnants of the Eastern Cape unions and in, particular it would seem, the NUM) were even less wary than that as to the ANC's true goals.

It is significant, of course, that the ANC, as it moved towards power at the turn of the 1990s, did not – could not – adopt the same tactics towards COSATU that, as discussed in the following sub-section, it was to use in facilitating the 1991 dissolution of the UDF. In the event, SACTU, the presumptive liberation

---

[28] Baskin, *Striking Back*, p. 450.
[29] Webster & Adler, 'Exodus Without a Map', p. 129.

movement's trade union voice, was merely allowed, in 1990, to slip off the stage, its relative marginalization in exile from most workers' struggles on the ground now tacitly acknowledged – with COSATU's obvious ascendancy being confirmed. Yet if, as here argued, COSATU was just too strong to be, like the UDF, merely removed from the scene,[30] it was in the 1990s – in contrast to its own best intentions in its original joining of the Tripartite Alliance with the ANC and SACP (above) – slated to be permitted membership within that alliance not as a key player, nor as part of an on-going popular assertion for transformative change in South Africa's socio-economic structure, but merely as a distinctly 'junior partner' in an alliance dedicated to neo-liberalism and elite entitlement.[31] Indeed, Webster and Southall conclude that,

> the lifting of the political ban on the ANC in 1990, its return from exile, its entering into negotiations with the ruling National Party, COSATU's exclusion from the Convention for a Democratic South Africa (the forum which negotiated the making of the new Constitution), and the increasing centrality of political parties to the negotiation process meant that the ANC came to assert its hegemony over the alliance.

As they then assert,

> To be sure, during this period 1990–1994, COSATU was neither demobilized nor tamed, and it ability to mobilize mass support for the ANC's position during the negotiations was crucial. Nonetheless, with the ANC marked out as the incoming democratic government, COSATU's position within the alliance drifted into one of subordinacy.[32]

'Marked out' by whom? By capital certainly, as we shall see. For who could have been happier than capital to see COSATU subordinated to what had become, in its judgement, an increasingly 'trustworthy' ANC?

---

[30] A process discussed in the following section.

[31] As an example of COSATU's actually permitted involvement in economic decision-making – soon to prove to be more notional in its actual significance for labour assertions than real – see the account of the workings of the National Economic forum, the National Manpower Commission and the National Economic Development and Labour Council/NEDLAC to be found in Carolyn Bassett, *Negotiating South Africa's Economic Future: COSATU and Strategic Unionism*, a doctoral dissertation submitted to York University (Toronto) in June 2000.

[32] Southall & Webster, 'Unions and Politics in South Africa', p. 140. Recall, too, in Adler & Webster's observation in *Trade Unions and Democratization in South Africa*, p. 130 (written earlier albeit about the same historical moment), that 'even as COSATU was consolidating its leadership position within the democratic movement, negotiations were developing between the ANC and the apartheid state [and, we must add, capital] over what was to become a "negotiated revolution" [*sic*, this misleading phrase is quoted by Adler & Webster as deployed in Allister Sparks, *Tomorrow is Another Country: The Inside Story of South Africa's Negotiated Revolution* (Sandton, S.A.: Struik, 1994)]'. In short, Adler & Webster suggest, 'the beginnings of the transition to democracy ... initiated as well the return of the ANC's hegemonic prominence within the internal democratic movement'!

Eidelberg has made much the same argument: 'the re-emergence of the ANC, now with solid backing from the west, would decisively alter the balance of power within the tripartite alliance: the ANC would achieve hegemony and do so at the expense of both COSATU and the SACP'. This too is formulation to which we will have to return below. For the moment, however, note carefully Eidelberg's further conclusions:

> [T]he prospects for radical reform, ironically, were probably rather brighter during the 1980s, under the old regime, than they are today [2000]. In the 1980s, when the unions began negotiating with an apartheid state increasingly under siege from the international capitalist world, they had been able to exploit this conflict to their own advantage, in an often successful attempt to obtain concessions and/or support from both state and overseas capital. Likewise, in being legally recognized by the South African state, COSATU could use this advantage to help it assert hegemony over its banned ANC partner. The beginnings of union participation in massive industrial and township unrest from late 1984 helped both to consolidate their hegemony within radical opposition politics, and to justify their implicit claim to macroeconomic policy-making in any future post-apartheid stage. By the 1990s, on the other hand, this window of opportunity was contracting. The new ANC state, in obvious and sharp contrast to its apartheid predecessor, owes its coming to power to a considerable degree to the support of overseas capital [see below] and, since officially coming to power is, if anything, increasingly under capital's influence. At home, the new ANC has been steadily entrenching itself and thus is less vulnerable to internal challenges.[33]

True, Eidelberg himself (like a number of other formidably cautious commentators) did see this kind of process as virtually inevitable under South African and global capitalist conditions. Yet the attendant results have been all too clear: rather than overseeing the linking together of COSATU, the SACP and the UDF into a team which could up the ante of class struggle and push for a continuation and deepening of both an on-going liberation struggle and a more progressive and developmental future for South Africa, the ANC has merely subordinated the others to its own option of party self-aggrandizement and global neo-liberalism.

Moreover, there was (*pace* Eidelberg) nothing 'inevitable' about this decision; instead, it had been a matter of elite-driven choice, pure and simple – if also a choice fraught with consequences that are extremely unlikely to prove very positive in their implications for the overall black population of South Africa. As for COSATU, increasingly 'put in its place' by the ANC (and with many of its former leaders defecting to political and state positions), it has to date remained, as suggested earlier, a sometimes unpredictable and often quite demonstrative but generally tame 'junior partner' nonetheless – within a ruling Alliance that is as both capital and the ANC wished it to be.

Of course, it is also true that COSATU has often been slammed sharply and publicly by the ANC brass for its ascribed 'ultra-leftism'. Indeed, as we will see

---

[33] P. G. Eidelberg, 'The Tripartite Alliance on the eve of a New Millennium: COSATU, the ANC and the SACP', in Adler & Webster, *Trade Unions and Democratization in South Africa*, p. 155.

in our 'Conclusion' (Chapter 7), its future leader Zwelizinama Vavi has, in fact, been in recent years an often out-spoken critic of the overall thrust of the ANC's socio-economic policy choices. Yet, for better or worse, all of this – as Vavi himself was consistently to confirm – has occurred strictly and relatively unthreateningly from within the Alliance, with no break from that Alliance being seriously discussed. Meanwhile COSATU continues to face the real risk of becoming merely an organization of the best-paid and most organized workers (relatively-speaking, the 'labour aristocrats'), extremely hesitant, as a 'trade-union centre', to work actively either to organize the growing army of part-time and casual workers in South Africa[34] or to reach out and help mobilize the mass of the 'precariat' of 'civil society' to become partners in the building of some more promising post-apartheid brand of on-going socio-economic transformation.

The politics of the precariat: Soweto, the townships and the UDF
For the remainder of the 1970s and through the 1980s the long slow grind of building a labour movement from the shop floor up would continue, this being work of mobilization, organization and politicization of considerable long-term significance. As seen, organized labour was also to be an important participant in broader political developments right up to the present. But there were many of those who helped form the mass base of the popular movement that would overthrow apartheid who did not easily fit into the category of 'proletarian'. Hence the utility of the concept 'precariat' – but it will be necessary, with respect to the precise way in which I choose to use this concept, to add a few words of further explanation later in this section.[35]

Recall here, however, that, in the context of the 1970s, the first indications of an emergent politics of the mass of South Africans whose sociological definition lay, formally, outside the proletariat per se were to be found in the role played by black university students. True, they were themselves an ambiguous group in terms of any precise social belonging or clear future trajectory, being as they were offspring of proletariat and precariat alike. Yet, however defined, there is no gainsaying the fact that they did, in the early 1970s, launch actions on various black university campuses that signalled the turn of South African black youth more generally towards a more radical consciousness and more radical actions than heretofore. Moreover, later dramatic events in Soweto and elsewhere found their roots here.

Note that these youth tended to find the key to their comprehending and acting upon their shared plight as lying in a perspective that suggested the principal 'problem' in South Africa to be racism itself. This kind of understanding – one always potentially attractive given the grotesque pattern of socially and

---

[34] On the question of the marked expansion of 'precarious work' in South Africa on the ANC's watch and of COSATU's own failure to assert itself effectively in this sphere see Marlea Clarke, *'All the Workers': Labour Market Reform and Precarious Work in Post-Apartheid South Africa, 1994–2004*, a doctoral dissertation submitted to York University (Toronto) in April, 2006.

[35] But see also footnote 4, above.

politically empowered white racism that existed in South Africa – had already produced there a brand of anti-imperialist 'black' nationalism that had taken its most formal expression in the Pan Africanist Congress' breakaway from the more 'multi-racial' ANC in the 1950s. By the 1970s, however, such sentiments were to take on even more articulate form under the rubric of 'Black Consciousness'. This latter perspective was an important force in driving the youth rebellion of the 1970s, as were potent political figures associated with it such as Steve Biko; it was also to feed into the broader mass resistances of the 1980s, as focused, for example, through the United Democratic Front and the Mass Democratic Movement.

One key to understanding this latter development was provided by the deftly illuminating frame within which Biko located his own Black Consciousness perspective. Thus, asked in 1972[36] to reflect on the situation in the country and to identify 'what trends or factors in it ... you feel are working towards the fulfillment of the long term ends of blacks', he suggested that the regime's deep commitment to a racial hierarchy had actually acted as 'a great leveller' of class formation amongst the black population and dictated 'a sort of similarity in the community' – such that the 'constant jarring effect of the [apartheid] system' produced a 'common identification' on the part of the people. In the more liberal system envisaged by the Progressive Party of the time, 'you would get stratification creeping in, with your masses remaining where they are or getting poorer, and the cream of your leadership, which is invariably derived from the so-called educated people, beginning to enter bourgeois ranks, admitted into town, able to vote, developing new attitudes and new friends ... a completely different tone'. South Africa, too, is

> one country where it would be possible to create a capitalist black society. If the whites were intelligent. If the Nationalists were intelligent. And that capitalist black society, black middle-class, would be very effective at an important stage. Primarily because a hell of a lot of blacks have got a bit of education – I'm talking comparatively speaking to the so-called rest of Africa – and a hell of a lot of them could compete favorably with whites in the fields of industry, commerce and professions. And South Africa could succeed to put across to the world a pretty convincing integrated picture with still 70 percent of the population being underdogs.

Yet it was precisely because the whites were so 'terribly afraid of this' that South Africa represented, to Biko, 'the best economic system for revolution'. For 'the evils of it are so pointed and so clear, and therefore make teaching of alternative methods, more meaningful methods, more indigenous methods even, much easier under the present sort of setup'.

Needless to say, the Progressive Party of the 1970s was nowhere near power, and capitalists were, on the whole, still not nearly so reform-minded in the

---

36 Interview with Steve Biko, as carried out by Gail Gerhart on October 24, 1972, and available from the Aluka e-collection of anti-apartheid-related materials at www.aluka.org/action/showMetadata?doi=10.5555/AL.SFF.DOCUMENT.gerhart00 07, accessed 30 September 2013; the quotations which follow are from this interview.

1970s as Biko apparently felt the most enlightened of Progressive Party supporters already to be. In fact, as we have seen in the preceding chapter, the entire history of twentieth-century South Africa had been one much more defined by an alliance between racists and capitalists to ensure both racial and class advantage than one defined by any deep contradiction between the two camps. Flash forward, however, to the late-1980s. The reform ('intelligent') wing of the National Party (NP) – together with those of the capitalist class, both of English and Afrikaner origin, who increasingly claimed the allegiance of NP reformers – had become just what Biko imagined the Progressive Party already to be in his own time.

By then, indeed, the NP was to prove to be (at least at the top) a party capable – albeit it with great caution and much obvious reluctance – of contemplating the shedding of apartheid for a system designed, more straightforwardly, both to empower a liberal-capitalist regime and to move to facilitate black (even black majority!) participation within it. In fact, 'intelligent racists' and capitalists alike could begin to see capital's link to the politics of racial domination as having been, precisely, a 'contingent' one. Not, needless to say, that the resultant transition to a (tendentially) colour-blind capitalism would be simple or entirely straightforward; there were other dangerous alternative possibilities that had to be overcome. Nonetheless, the 'false decolonization' evoked by Biko was to be, precisely, the ultimate outcome, the new reality, to which socialist strategy for South Africa in the 21st century would have to address itself.

Biko, in evoking the 'Prog possibility' (i.e. Progressive Party), was of course following the analytical lead of Frantz Fanon. He had read and learned from[37] Fanon's analysis of 'successful' African nationalism across the northern and central portions of the continent as, in essence, fostering just such a 'false decolonization' – this to the advantage of domestic and international capital and of the newly ascendant African elites. Yet, at the same time, Biko's understanding of South Africa's quite specific possibilities led him to a different conclusion. True, he was far from naïve as regards the class dimensions of South Africa's racial capitalism; indeed, Biko had good and fruitful relations in Durban with Rick Turner and others who would spark the re-emergence of the working-class-based resistance that produced the urban strikes there (with, as seen in the preceding section, increasingly important echoes across the country) in the early 1970s.[38]

---

[37] See, on this and many other related points, Lindi Wilson, *Steve Biko* (Auckland Park, S.A.: Jacana, 2011).

[38] Eddie Webster, oral communication and also in his contributions to the (public) discussion following the presentation of his paper 'A Seamless Web or a Democratic Rupture: The Re-emergence of Trade Unions and the African National Congress (ANC) in Durban 1973 and Beyond', at the 'One Hundred Years of the ANC: Debating Liberation Histories and Democracy Today' conference', held in Johannesburg, 20–24 September 2011; see also Ian Macqueen, 'Black Consciousness in Dialogue: Steve Biko, Richard Turner and the 'Durban moment' in South Africa, 1970–1974', paper presented at the Southern African Seminar, SOAS, December 4, 2009. Rick Turner, author of 1972's very influential *The Eye of the Needle: Towards Participatory*

Nonetheless, as Biko saw it, the racial structure of the South African system was what was central, and, for him, it was the emergence of a new confidence and anti-racist consciousness – Black Consciousness – on the part of the mass of the country's oppressed black (African, Coloured and Indian) population that could most readily open the revolutionary door to a new South Africa. This, as we know, was the politics of Black self-assertion that he himself would follow in the few years of life granted him by the apartheid regime. Nor can there be any doubt as to broad resonance of such a 'Black Consciousness' emphasis – one evident in the events of Soweto (1976) and beyond – that helped fuel throughout the 1970s and 1980s, a mass movement for dramatic change in South Africa.

Partly, then, the moment was to be defined ideologically. But it was to be defined situationally as well, especially for those students who would place 'the Soweto moment', broadly defined, on the socio-political map. Here a look at the changing reality of the schools is required. For the schools and their student populations were now growing, a reluctant admission by the ruling barons of apartheid that a more skilled black population was now necessary to meet the shortfall in semi-skilled labour that was a fall-out of the apartheid boom; this because the labour requirements created by the boom and by the ever more complex system that drove it clearly demanded some expansion of the availability of educational opportunity. But while this might fit capital's needs it was a trend particularly dangerous to a white elite that was otherwise busy clearing away 'black spots' across the country and crafting a Bantustan strategy (up to and including the recognition of pseudo-'independent' African ethnic states) in order to further safeguard white power. Ironically, too, the new educational system came on stream during a period of some economic pause after the years of preceding boom. All of which was certainly trouble in the making for the apartheid regime.[39]

Moreover, the further resonance of 'the Soweto moment' was to be defined sociologically in even broader terms than that – as the entire urban and rural landscape of apartheid came to be ever more expansively interrogated and challenged in the 1980s. For however much it was emboldened by the student actions that echoed from Soweto throughout the country, the mass movement that would now surge forward in the 1980s had far wider social resonance than could simply have been derived from 'Black Consciousness' alone, or be driven simply by students. What needs countenancing here, in fact, is the full range of popular resistances that began to surface in the late-1970s and during the 1980s throughout the country's urban areas and even in the rural areas: a growing mass refusal of white-state oppression and racialized institutions and

[cont] *Democracy in South Africa* (Johannesburg: Ravan, 1980), had a profound influence on both fledgling trade unionists and their highly effective university-trained supporters in Durban in the early 1970s – before he was killed, apparently by the apartheid state, in 1978.

[39] Hirson, *Year of Fire, Year of Ash*, Chapter 5, 'Secondary Schools and the African Schools', and especially the sub-sections entitled 'Education for Black Labour' and 'New Labour Needs and School Expansion'.

of the humiliation attendant upon them. This was not unrelated to the more identifiably working-class-centred resistance of the period cited above. Yet, as noted earlier, it was not quite the same thing either, reflecting as it did a complexity in the sociology of South African resistance that must be acknowledged and further theorized.[40] In fact, a fresh conceptual distinction is actually in order here to make the point clearly, that between 'the proletariat' in the one hand and 'the precariat' on the other.

The 'precariat'? Elsewhere I have argued, in more general terms, the importance of this latter concept as regards the very many settings of the Global South where an unfinished capitalist revolution continues to pile up populations in the global cities (and also in the rural areas) whose formal employment (if any) or other guarantees of livelihood are weak and uncertain and whose life itself is therefore, generally and at best, 'precarious'.[41] In such contexts, as I have myself suggested, 'the politics of the urban dweller per se, as distinct from the politics of the urban proletariat (although there is some obvious overlap between categories of course), has a dynamic and thrust of its own'. Indeed, such assertions, focused upon effectively and designated by Jonathan Barker to be 'street-level politics',[42] are not so much a case of 'workers take to the streets' as 'street-dwellers take to the streets'! For what we see in such social circumstances, and alongside more specifically working-class action, is a 'people' who are available for socio-political upsurge (in both township and rural settings).

Indeed, their actions tend to be directed most forcefully against the state (especially at its local level) and the prevailing polity (as well as the latter's minions and programmes) rather than, directly, against the employers (and capitalism) per se. But it was, in fact, just such a 'precariat' in South Africa that (alongside an active proletariat to be sure) set itself against the racial-capitalist order throughout the 1970s and 1980s and did so in remarkable ways – its rise to special prominence in the anti-apartheid resistance being first embodied, as we have seen, by students, who were, as noted, the sons and daughters of proletariat and precariat alike. Here too the influence of Black Consciousness (BC) was front and centre – even if it was always more a mood, 'an idea whose time had come', than an organization.

Certainly, the BC mood already underlay the political volatility at the universities already in the 1960s[43] and it now found expression among a younger stratum of students, those in the schools, as well. For the BC mood would now have great resonance in sowing the seeds that would, so dramatically, become 'Soweto' – this term soon surfacing to be crucial, as both fact and as symbol, to the dawning 'South African revolution'. For Soweto, in 1976, witnessed the outbreak of a student revolt destined to spread out from its point of origin and,

---

[40] I have sought to do this in Saul, 'What Working-Class?' in Karagaac & Kaya, *Capital and Labour in Contemporary Capitalism.*

[41] Saul 'What Working Class?'

[42] See Jonathan Barker, *Street-Level Democracy* (Toronto: Between the Lines, 1999).

[43] Hirson, *Year of Fire, Year of Ash,* Chapter 3, 'The University Student Movements 1960–1969', and following chapters.

over the next decade, to galvanize a broad resistance of historic magnitude throughout South Africa. Thus, as Kane-Berman writes, 'on the morning of Wednesday, 16 June 1976, twenty thousand Soweto schoolchildren marched in protest against a decree by the South African government's Department of Bantu Education that Afrikaans had to be used as one of the languages of instruction in secondary schools'. The violence of the state's response to what initially was a peaceful march would claim 176 lives in less than a week, however, and set off a brush-fire of protest around the country.[44]

That Soweto thus became the 'epicentre' of nation-wide revolt is quite clear. For in Soweto itself, even though

> the violence that erupted in 16 June burnt itself out in a few days, calm was not really restored to the township until the beginning of 1978. During the second half of 1976, there were repeated skirmishes between students and police, some resulting in more deaths of students. The students continued to organise protests and demonstrations and their campaign against Bantu Education grew rather than diminished. Armed men in camouflage outfits became a regular sight in Soweto. Given the wide powers of the police to enter and search private homes, detain people without trial, and act drastically to prevent outdoor gatherings ..., Soweto was virtually under martial law and a state of emergency.[45]

It is equally clear the Soweto events had, in the rest of the country, a galvanizing effect: 'within two months of 16 June at least 80 communities all over the country had expressed their fury; within four months the number had risen to 160. Not only the four provinces but all the Bantustans experienced some form of upheaval, while soldiers from a military base in the north of Namibia were [also] reportedly called in to quell a disturbance in that territory'!

Kane-Berman, Baruch Hirson and other writers of the period argue all argue convincingly, then, the importance of the broad underlying contradictions alluded to above, the issue of the compulsory introduction of Afrikaans in schools then being easy to see primarily as a particular flash-point, one that merely exposed more clearly the deeper tensions embedded in the overall system. Similarly, such commentators all emphasize the crucial importance of the increasingly pervasive resonance amongst students of a 'Black Consciousness' sensibility. As Kane-Berman himself states: 'Black Consciousness ... was probably the single most important factor'. But he is surely not wrong to further suggest that one must also 'assign overwhelming weight to the shooting itself' for

> it instantly transformed a protest which might otherwise have been confined to the Afrikaans issue and to Soweto into a generalized nation-wide revolt against the total system in which black South Africans find themselves. Thereafter, inevitably, events gained a momentum of their own. The velocity of the chain reaction in other parts of the country suggests that these places were already volatile enough for news of the shooting to be in itself sufficient to trigger off explosion there.

---

[44] John Kane-Berman, *Soweto: Black Revolt, White Reaction* (Johannesburg: Ravan, 1978), p. 1.

[45] I continue here to draw heavily on Kane-Berman, *Soweto*, at pp. 2–3 and elsewhere.

A general distemper then? As the first widely known leader among the Soweto students, Tsietsi Mashanini, observed, they had 'had enough not only oppression in the schools, but of the "system of the country, the way laws are made by a white minority"'.[46] Indeed, Kane-Berman sees it as 'as much a violent protest against powerlessness, the consequence of months of frustration at the failure of the authorities to respond positively to repeated demands for the suppression of the Afrikaans decree, as it was a spontaneous explosion of anger at the shootings'. In sum, as he accurately argues, 'Black Youth was in revolt against not only specific aspects of policy, but apartheid in all its manifestations, and therefore the country's political system itself'.

No less a figure than Desmond Tutu, then Anglican dean of Johannesburg, added: '[Y]oung children learn hatred and bitterness when they sit at night and listen to their mothers and fathers talking about the indignities they suffered during the day because they are black ... what is filling black hearts more and more is naked hatred.' 'Hatred'? Black anger? Perfectly understandable, but, as Hirson (another careful and thoughtful writer on this phase of South African history) underscored, mere anger was not really sufficient, in and of itself, to produce and sustain a coherent political project. In addition, he argues, there was an important learning process – one that was at once both experiential and conceptual – facilitated by the confrontation itself, one that carried people forward to a much deeper understanding of their situation and to a more firmly anchored commitment to changing it:

> The people of Soweto had to learn with a minimum of guidance and they responded with a heroism that has made Soweto an international symbol of resistance to tyranny. Young leaders appeared month after month to voice the aspirations of the school students – and if they were now able to formulate a full programme for their people the fault was not theirs. A programme should have been formulated by older leaders – and that they had failed to do. In the event, the youth fought on as best they could – and they surpassed all expectations.
>
> Despite all the criticisms that can be levelled against the leaders of school pupils, the revolt they led in 1976–77 altered the nature of politics in South Africa. Firstly it brought to a precipitate end all attempts by the South African ruling class to establish friendly relations with the leaders of some African states, and it has made some Western powers reconsider the viability of the National Party leaders as their best allies on the sub-continent. Secondly it marked the end of undisputed white rule and demonstrated the ability of the black population to challenge the control of the ruling class.[47]

Hirson then goes on to himself document the consequent 'nation-wide response' with notable protests and instances of resistance virtually everywhere: 'In every major urban centre and in villages in the reserves the youth marched, demonstrated, closed schools, stopped transport and, on several occa-

---

[46] Kane-Berman, *Soweto*, pp. 47–48, where he quotes, as reproduced in this and the following paragraph, both Mashanini and Tutu.

[47] Hirson, *Year of Fire, Year of Ash* p. 9, from which book I continue to quote in the following paragraph (from pp. 9, 214ff, 279).

sions, brought the entire economy to a halt.' He also documents with particular thoroughness (in one of his chapters, entitled 'The Cape Province Explodes') the case of the Cape, where Black Consciousness served, as elsewhere, to draw together the goals and actions of 'Coloureds', Asians and Africans – with the savage nature of the white state's reaction to challenge now being etched quite clearly for the world to see. But what was also being exemplified here was the impressive unity of the oppressed who thus resisted racist rule. True, the 'Revolt' would, by March 1978, have temporarily 'wound down'. Yet as Hirson concludes: 'The Revolt was not over. It could not be over as long as apartheid reigned ... [even if] the phase that had opened up on June 16, 1976 was over.' For the students had demonstrated 'to South Africa and the world' that there existed in South Africa 'the will and determination to end the apartheid system'.

Hirson himself now looked primarily to the renewed centrality of 'the working class' as most ready to follow the immediate lead of the students and to keep the struggle surging forward. Nor, as we have seen in the previous subsection, was he to be disappointed in this belief throughout the 1980s. But I would further emphasize (as also argued above) that of at least equal importance was the fact that the student's lead was taken up equally by an increasingly broad range of township dwellers across urban South Africa – and by those in the rural areas as well. In particular, however, it was the actions of an urban precariat – not in any way easily reducible to being merely persons of 'proletarian belonging' – that did come to have near revolutionary effect. For the fact is that the mass of people, *qua* precariat, now chose to confront the oppressive state more directly, urgently and self-consciously, more self-consciously than many of them were moved to confront capital itself. Indeed, a battle had thus been joined that reached well beyond the shop floor.

We must be quite careful here, however, for it would be equally mistaken to assume that the responses of the 'working class' on the one hand and 'the poor' on the other were necessarily at odds. Quite the contrary, in fact, for the desired goals of the people who inhabit these two categories could fit together quite smoothly, linked as they are, potentially, by a shared interest in social and political equality and in realizing the kind of social justice of which they have been, by and large, deprived. Of course, it would take revolutionary leadership with real clarity to help people to understand ever more clearly the complementarity of the oppressions enacted respectively by capital and the state – to underscore, for example, the close and particular link that had existed between the class and racial bases of rule. Yet, truth to tell, this was the kind of leadership, as we shall argue below, that the ANC increasingly lacked both the will and the capacity to provide – a point to which we will have to return.

Meanwhile, however, the popular struggle in the townships and the rural areas surged on in the wake of Soweto. As Bundy has written of the decades we are surveying:

> Between the Durban strikes of 1973 and the Mass Democratic Movement's (MDM) defiance campaign of 1989, a long wave of popular protest surged across the South African political landscape. It eroded familiar landmarks and opened new channels,

it lapped on the beachheads of white power, and its high tide left a residue of aspirations and expectations.[48]

For now not even the state's brutal repression – and brutal it surely was – could succeed in smothering the flames so visible in so many centres throughout the country. Here in fact was a present-day expression, now dramatically magnified, of a long history of urban resistance to the closing fist of apartheid, a fight-back cast both within the ANC tradition and outside it. Thus, in 1979–80, there was, as Bundy further records, 'the shaping of a new tactical repertoire of grievance-based protests' and boycotts.[49] Moreover, this new kind of upsurge from below was to continue to trigger actions – actions to a very significant degree locally conceived and driven – that would erupt, throughout the 1980s, from an ever greater range of players and in an ever wider set of communities. True, even though such varied initiatives were linked by their sharing of apartheid as the common denominator of mass oppression, these actions were not, by and large, centrally planned or co-ordinated. Nonetheless, the intensity of this new drive towards confrontation would mark a sea-change in South Africa. For it etched the fact of a mass rejection of apartheid indelibly onto the perceptions of dominant classes (South African and globally-based alike) but also onto those of a global public more generally.

As for the details: here we find Jeremy Seekings' effective book-length history of the key national organization of the overall movement, the United Democratic Front/UDF, particularly useful.[50] For the UDF, founded in 1983, came, as Seekings records, to draw together and co-ordinate a vast range of these many manifestations of civic unrest. As he suggests, in fact, the tide had begun to flow

> strongly against the state from the end of 1983. Prospective opposition from the newly formed UDF first led the government to discard the idea of referendums among coloured and Indian voters to legitimise the process of constitutional reform. Then the elections to the new coloured and Indian houses of parliament were largely boycotted. This and other protests discredited the government's 'new deal' both within South Africa and internationally. The township revolt from the second half of 1984 forced the state onto the defensive, pushing it to use brutal repression, which served to highlight the moral poverty of even 'reformed apartheid'. The strategic framework of 'people's power' enabled the forces of revolt to be harnessed more effectively and channeled into a direct and potentially sustainable challenge to the apartheid state.

[48] Colin Bundy, 'Survival and Resistance: Township Organizations and Non-Violent Direct Action in Twentieth Century South Africa' in Glenn Adler and Jonny Steinberg (eds), *From Comrades to Citizens: The South African Civics Movement and the Transition to Democracy* (Macmillan and St. Martin's Press: London and New York, 2000), p. 26.

[49] Bundy, 'Survival and Resistance', in Adler & Steinberg, *From Comrades to Citizens*, p. 27.

[50] Jeremy Seekings, *The UDF: A History of the United Democratic Front in South Africa, 1983–1991* (Claremont, S.A,: David Phillip, 2000); see also Gregory Houston, *The National Liberation Struggle in South Africa: A case study of the United Democratic Front, 1883–1987* (Aldershot, UK: Ashcroft, 1999).

In response the government was able to stem the tide of resistance only by imposing a level of repression that was unprecedented in South Africa ... But resistance adapted and continued at a level sufficient to render the state's strategy of repression unsustainable. In mid-1988 the first talks were held towards some kind of negotiated settlement. Amidst a dramatic (if uneven) revival of popular protest during 1989, the move towards a negotiated settlement speeded up, leading to the government's decision to unban the ANC.[51]

To this last point we will have to return, but first we must also ask: just what was the state itself doing while all this was going on? A whole lot of repression is the short answer, but the state also undertook a range of moves – parallel to the new policy initiatives with respect to the proletariat that had flowed from its Wiehann Report – with respect to 'the urban question'. For here was a response to South Africa's new urban reality that sought to forestall trouble there too. Thus, the report of the state-appointed Riekert Commission[52] helped frame legislation acceding to the stabilization, even legalization, of a black urban population's 'rightful' presence in the cities – however much this was still cast in the terms of the familiar overall urban-rural split of the black population that had long underpinned racial capitalism. Not nearly enough, self-evidently. But it did signal that the premises of the most lily-white of apartheid nostrums – under which blacks could be conceived merely as 'temporary sojourners' in the city – were themselves subject to change.

More moves of a similar nature were soon afoot: the 'granting' of the status and structures of 'Black Local Authorities' (albeit virtually toothless ones) to urban Africans, for example, and as already noted previously, the attempt to oversee the incorporation of the country's Indian and Coloured communities as junior partners within a complex system of separate, racially-exclusive chambers of a new 'Tripartite' parliament for such groups. Of course, almost immediately any such 'new constitutional dispensation' proved to be merely a further provocation, adding fuel to the mounting mood of resistance manifested by all segments of the 'black' population (Africans, Indians and 'Coloureds'). Indeed, it was actually this issue – the effective rejection, marked by massive non-participation within it, of the new governmental set-up – whose formal birth, in August 1983, we have already cited: the pyramid organization of emergent groups of resistance across the country named the United Democratic Front/UDF.

Of course, the UDF was not itself the motor-force behind the myriad of local resistances that came to define a proto-revolutionary moment in South Africa in the 1980s; nor was it the sole voice of such increasingly united action. Nonetheless, it did become, to a significant degree, the presumptive *dirigeant* of South Africa's vast 'precariat' in the townships – even if, as Popo Molefe, one-time General Secretary of the UDF, put it, the UDF was forever 'trailing behind the masses'.[53] In fact, the UDF, with as many as 600 local affiliates at various

---

[51] Seekings, *The UDF*, p. 286.
[52] See, again, Saul & Gelb, *The Crisis in South Africa*, especially Ch. 2, Section II ('The Urban Question'), 1 and 2 ('Riekart' and 'The Housing Question'), pp. 117–125.
[53] Molefe, as quoted in Seekings, *The UDF*, p. 121.

points during the 1980s, became so central to resistance – perhaps the major agent in bringing South Africa, during the period 1984–86, as close to mass revolution as the country had ever been – that the state ultimately moved to attempt to smash it, banning it in 1988 and unleashing the full fury of police and military brutality on many of its leaders and functionaries.

It also bears emphasizing here that the UDF was itself a complicated entity, one that housed, it is true, many old ANC hands (including some ex-Robben Island movement loyalists), especially from areas of the country where the ANC had had particularly strong historical presence. But it also housed many other cadres of quite different political provenance. Diverse commentators have also noted the tension between the apparent petty-bourgeois ambitions of many of those who stepped forward to lead the UDF (and would become, in turn, recruits to the ANC phalanx that would step into public office with the movement's victory) and its more genuinely 'precarian' activists and 'foot-soldiers' who might well have been persuaded by a different kind of leadership to keep the struggle for a more genuine liberation alive.

For, as Seekings records in detail, a new high-point had indeed been reached with the dramatic confrontations in 1984 in the Vaal Triangle and the East Rand 'provoked by discontent over civic issues, especially increases in rents effected by unpopular township councillors, combined with student discontent around educational grievances and the state's constitutional reforms'.[54] This kind of resistance surged on: although briefly stalled after 1986 by particularly savage state repression,[55] including a banning of the UDF itself in 1988, such resistance was, by the end of the 1980s, resurgent again. Then, as emphasized above, the UDF's drive was merely refocused by COSATU and a newly minted 'Mass Democratic Movement' (the banned UDF 'under the guise of the MDM', as Seekings epitomized it), with the UDF itself 'unilaterally declar[ing] itself "unbanned" and [again] assum[ing] public activity in February, 1990'.

In summary, as Seekings suggests in a related article,[56] 'activists in African townships had sought to build a broad organizational base to extend the struggle beyond the students who had led the 1976 protests'. With regard to the ANC, he notes that only 'after some hesitation [had] the exiled ANC lent its support to the emerging civic movements'! Seekings then specifies the organization's shifts in terms of the developments in 'strategic thinking' that underlay the entire process. He finds, for example, that 'a conscious strategy of civic mobi-

---

[54] Jeremy Seekings, 'The Development of Strategic Thought in South Africa's Civic Movements, 1977–1990', in Adler & Steinberg *From Comrade to Citizens*, p. 70. See also Seekings, 'The Decline of South Africa's Civic Organizations, 1990–1996', *Critical Sociology*, 22, 3, October, 1996; Raymond Suttner, 'Legacies and Meanings of the United Democratic Front (UDF) Period for Contemporary South Africa', *Journal of Southern African Studies*, 30, 3, 2004, pp. 691–701.

[55] This widespread campaign of naked suppression was a particularly important focus of the post-apartheid Truth and Reconciliation Commission.

[56] Jeremy Seekings, 'The Development of Strategic Thought', in Adler & Steinberg, *From Comrade to Citizens*, from where the quotations in the following two paragraphs are drawn.

lization and organization emerged between 1977 and 1980', this to be followed in 1980–82 by a 'wide-spread rethinking of the structures and direction of civic organization in the light of various weaknesses and setbacks' – with the strategic assessments of those years being 'greatly promoted [in] the new alternative and "community" media, especially the student-produced *SASPU National* (South African Students Press Union publication) and *Grassroots*, and by the growing coherence of activist networks within and especially between regions'.

At this point, Seekings states, civic struggles began to be seen more clearly as 'the basis for simultaneous political struggles', with the concept of 'people's power' then being developed by strategists in 1985–86, 'to make sense of and to direct insurrectionary local activities, especially in African townships', and to 'roll back' any self-imposed limitation on the scope of civic struggle. Here, certainly, was a key to ultimate victory. Yet we must also take note of what followed from this – in 1989–90. For, again in Seekings' formulation, the 'political' and 'developmental' activities were then merely separated within extra-parliamentary strategic thinking, with civic strategies being 'reconceptualized' and turned away from the political realm. Moreover, Seekings claims, this shift towards willed depoliticization took place even as it also 'became apparent that the UDF [actually] had no choice but to disband in the aftermath of the ANC's unbanning'!

No choice? This statement is a bit glib, mere sleight of hand, one fears. In fact, Seekings himsel seems in no way to regret such a development. Indeed, he continues this line of his thinking by elsewhere writing complacently of the UDF merely 'fad[ing] away before finally disbanding formally in August, 1991'. He even adds that 'there was a certain inevitability to the organisational shift from the UDF to the ANC ... a logical, unavoidable, even unremarkable event'! Here, too, he quotes Peter Mokaba, then president of the South African Youth Congress, to similar effect, Mokaba arguing: 'Now that the ANC can operate legally, the UDF is redundant.'[57] In effect, Seekings and Mokaba were quite prepared to countenance the possibility that any future political role for the precariat would merely be consigned to the relative political passivity of participation solely through the voter's box. The voter's box, and the much more demobilized world of the newly created South African National Civic Organization/SANCO and its wards amongst the 'civics' (an alternative venue for possible practice the weaknesses of which have been crisply parsed by Elke Zuern[58]). In fact (as we now know), sadly and in the absence of any more positively empowering vision, mass action could now sometimes merely run, and all too easily, to such perverted popular purposes as evidenced in the xenophobic riots of 2008.[59]

[57] Seekings, *The UDF*, p. 260, where Makoba's 1991 statement is also cited.

[58] Elke Zuern, *The Politics of Necessity: Community Organizing and Democracy in South Africa* (Madison, WI: University of Wisconsin Press, 2011); she notes, further, that 'in 2009 the government reported that income inequality still had not been reduced despite years of economic growth', p. 12.

[59] Fortunately this was not the only possible course that politics occurring outside the tent of the ANC could take, as we will see below.

But why, we might ask, did this happen. For this way of defining the mobilized mass out of the future political equation actually signalled a very real defeat for popular struggle. True, this separation of political and developmental actions here being applauded by Seekings squared neatly with what the ANC's own agenda had become. For it was now one of facilitating a virtually 'neo-colonial' resolution of the liberation question by substituting the restrained politics of parliamentarism (of universal, if passive, 'citizenship') for the more unruly but bracingly radical politics of 'the comrades'. It is telling, therefore, that the initiatives taken by the ANC to ensure a depoliticization of civil society are much more tellingly identified by various other writers who argue along entirely different lines from those chosen by Seekings.

There is no more impressive protagonist of such an alternative assessment, perhaps, than Rusty Bernstein. For Bernstein, a highly respected ANC and SACP militant of long-standing, would write eloquently, in his waning days (2000), in an attempt to explain just why the liberation project to which he had devoted his life had become so unglued during the transition. As he saw it, 'The [ANC's] drive towards power has corrupted the political equation in various ways.' He continued:

> [When] mass popular resistance revived again inside the country led by the UDF, it led the ANC to see the UDF as an undesirable factor in the struggle for power and to undermine it as a rival focus for mass mobilization. This has undermined the ANC's adherence to the path [of] mass resistance as the way to liberation, and substituted instead a reliance on manipulation of administrative power ... It has impoverished the soil in which ideas leaning towards socialist solutions once flourished and allowed the weed of 'free market' ideology to take hold.[60]

In sum, it would seem that the dissolution of the UDF was rather less 'logical,' 'unavoidable' and 'unremarkable' than Seekings has claimed. For the ANC had actually to work quite hard to see the UDF into its grave. Indeed, it is not difficult to parse Bernstein's most sober imaginings, evoked above, as follows: the ANC, it is clear in retrospect, wanted to kill socialism and the survival of any alternative, heterodox and progressive stance to its own chosen path towards what can only be thought of as South Africa's recolonization by capital.[61] It began such a task by, quite literally, killing the UDF, killing it not for what it had done but for what, under another kind of national leadership than the ANC was prepared to offer, the UDF initiative might have become.[62]

---

[60] In a letter to the present author, which, however, I subsequently published under the title 'Rusty Bernstein: A Letter', in *Transformation* (South Africa), 64, 2007; this letter is also reproduced as an Appendix in Saul, *Liberation Lite*, pp. 104–111.

[61] See, again, Saul, *Liberation Lite*.

[62] In fact this whole process of moving the UDF to dissolve itself was a very murky one, full of apparent intrigue and even, some say, internecine violence, which many people in South Africa are still loath to discuss too openly. Yet the demise of the UDF marked a crucial moment in South Africa's recent history that has, as yet, been too seldom given the careful scrutiny it warrants.

Viewed in this light, the key fact was, as suggested earlier, precisely the ANC's very eagerness to help dissolve the UDF itself. Moreover, the truth is that this 'dissolution' of the UDF was to be as crucially significant for the direction that post-apartheid South Africa would now take as had been the implications for apartheid's fate of the UDF's rise to prominence a decade earlier! It is of course true – such was the atmosphere of all-but-achieved victory that both the ANC and capital had managed to create within the organization in the early 1990s – that the UDF's demise was actually sanctioned by the majority vote at its own final Congress in 1991. Yet the full import of the vote, and its long-run social costs – however much foreseen and embraced by ANC leaders – was perhaps lost on many UDF activists in those heady days. Costs? Van Kessel notes, for example, the very tangible 'demobilizing effect' of the UDF's demise – with the ANC doing little or nothing, in the longer run, to sustain people's waning spirit of active militancy.[63] She also quotes Alan Boesak as making a sharp distinction 'between the UDF years and the early 1990s':

> He noted a widespread nostalgia for the UDF years. 'That was a period of mass involve-ment a period when people took a clear stand. That had a moral appeal. Now it is diffi-cult to get used to compromises ... Many people in the Western Cape now say that 'the morality in politics has gone.' The 1980s, that was 'clean politics,' morally upright, no compromises, with a clear goal.'

Similarly, Mona Younis reminds us that 'as news of accommodation and concessions [during the 1990–1994 period] to the previous rulers made their way to the streets, union and community leaders and activists called for the reactivation of mass action'.[64]

The story of the contested dissolution of the UDF is thus one of the great 'lost stories' in South African historiography. For as Younis further suggests, the UDF's last conference, despite being convened to settle its fate actually witnessed a clear and strong voicing of a view quite opposed to the organization's disso-lution. This view? That, as an effective organ of 'people's power', the UDF should be retained:

> Proponents of this view envisaged the UDF's role as one of watching over the govern-ment, remaining prepared to activate mass action if the need should arrive. Many leaders and activists emphasized that the preservation of the UDF was imperative to ensure that participatory, rather than merely representative, democracy prevailed in South Africa.

---

[63] Ineke van Kessel, *'Beyond Our Wildest Dreams': The United Democratic Front and the Transformation of South Africa* (Charlotteville: The University Press of Virginia, 2000); see also Van Kessel's 'Trajectories after liberation in South Africa: mission accom-plished or vision betrayed?' in *Zuid-Afrika & Leiden* (Leiden: University of Leiden, 2011).

[64] Younis, *Liberation and Democratization*, p. 173; as Younis adds: 'For many, especially in the labour movement, 'the "national democratic" stage [a concept much favoured by the ANC] was a transitional one toward the attainment of socialism...'!

Of course, to repeat, a majority did in fact, and at the ANC's urging, vote to disband the UDF – but the loss of progressive purpose that this deed represented was a very damaging one.[65]

True, this is controversial ground, of course. Thus some observers view such a winding down of the assertive politics of resistance to oppression as virtually inevitable. But there others who would go further, even to the point of seeing the demise of the UDF as being an almost wholly benign occurrence. Such would seem to be the spirit that finds Adler and Steinberg, who entitle their own collection of essays focusing on civic action during this period *From Comrades to Citizens: The South African Civics Movement and the Transition to Democracy*.[66] 'Comrades' – those involved, in the 1980s, not only in COSATU but also, in the civics, the UDF and the MDM – to now become 'citizens'. Yet surely of the fact of becoming 'citizens' is far too comfortable a description of what would tend to befall such 'comrades' as they passed into citizenship. For, in South Africa, this was to involve the demobilization of these comrades so as to refashion them as a mass of relatively passive voters (if they now bother to vote at all); they were now to be mere consumers of the political, not active practitioners of a democratic politics in South Africa. For Adler and Steinberg seem to assume that a continuing politics of comradeship could only have connoted for a post-apartheid South Africa a univocal politics and hence a virtually totalitarian absence of genuine democracy. From such a starting-point they seem loath to contemplate the possibility that, on the terrain of struggle for a freshly minted and shared purpose of social betterment, there can in fact exist a genuine pluralism of expressed views; and that, amongst people committed to justice and equality, there can be a genuinely contested, democratic and liberated politics. Why not comrades *and* citizens, one might ask?

Other observers will continue to argue quite differently, of course, seeing in the early 1990s, the 'continued radical instincts of [various] high-quality unions, community-based organisations, women's and youth groups, Non-Governmental Organisations, think-tanks, networks of CBOs and NGOs, progressive churches, political groups and independent leftists'[67] – such assertions still manifest both because of COSATU's survival and despite the UDF's

---

[65] See also on these question Michelle Williams' valuable *The Roots of Participatory Democracy: Democratic Communists in South Africa and Kerala, India* (New York and London: Palgrave Macmillan, 2008), p. 91, in which she deftly contrasts the practices of the Communist party in Kerala (which premised its activities on 'counter-hegemonic generative politics' and 'a reliance on participatory organizing') and those of South African Communist Party (and, by extension, the ANC). In South Africa any sustained popular take-over of the process of transformation was never really on offer, the SACP/ANC merely opting for, in her terms, 'a hegemonic generative politics' and a reliance, almost exclusively, on sheer 'mass mobilizing' designed primarily to draw a crowd to popularly hail its ascendancy. There could be very little place for a pro-active UDF-like organization within such a scenario!

[66] Adler & Steinberg, 'Introduction: From Comrades to Citizens', in *From Comrades to Citizens*.

[67] Patrick Bond, *Elite Transition: From Apartheid to Neoliberalism in South Africa* (London: Pluto Press, 2000), p. 168.

demise. Yet the fact is that such voices were, at first, given little room to breathe. Here the front of gender-related struggle provides, perhaps, one particularly striking case in point of the more general problem.[68] For in the final years of apartheid distinctively feminist demands for freedom and voice had become particularly noteworthy. Not that women had been silent from the earliest days, being often quite prominent in various union and nationalist assertions and also in highly visible popular ones like the women's anti-pass demonstrations that brought thousands of women to a rally at the Union Buildings in Pretoria on August 9, 1956.

Active then but, as Cheryl Walker has underscored, there remained a very real 'ambivalence' on the part of 'the male-dominated Congress Alliance [as to] the role and scope of the women's movement within the national liberation movement'.[69] Still, women's assertions were capped by their notable involvement first within the UDF and then, at their most visible, during the phase of transition towards a post-apartheid South Africa – when strong women's voices had, as Shireen Hassim has recorded, a tangible impact on the writing of a new constitution for South Africa.[70] Nonetheless, very soon after this 'victory' it became apparent the hopes of realizing any on-going process of consolidating gender equality in the post-apartheid period was not to be easily sustained (as Hassim also demonstrates) – exactly the same trend as marked many other sites of on-going struggle, possible and proposed.

Although subsequent chapters will demonstrate that the struggle does indeed continue on many such fronts, here it is appropriate only to underscore the lessons to be learned from the UDF's demise. For the sustaining of any such revolutionary impulse as the UDF (and, more generally, a radical mass politics) seemed to have the potential to embody would have required imagination and, in practice, a shift towards confronting a new enemy, poverty, privilege and underdevelopment, in freshly innovative, imaginative and forthrightly political ways. But releasing active, assertive and sustained popular energies from below, and from an increasingly empowered citizenry, was in fact the last thing a vanguardist, ever more conservative, ANC actually was interested in – particularly as it became easier for the ANC to envisage itself soon coming to power. Just as too many UDF leaders had begun to envisage a new order – and, for themselves, new status and new jobs! – the ANC itself moved, as we have seen, to encourage the UDF, its task now ostensibly accomplished, to formally dissolve itself.

Thus, even if (as Patrick Bond admits in Chapter 4) the initial '1994–96

---

[68] On the illuminating case of the rise (notably during the period of constitutional negotiations) and fall of meaningful gender assertions see Shireen Hassim, *Identities, Interests and Constituencies: The Politics of the Women's movement in South Africa, 1980–1999*, a doctoral dissertation submitted to York University (Toronto) in June, 2002 and her subsequent book *Women's Organizations and Democracy in South Africa: Contesting Authority* (Madison, WI: University of Wisconsin Press, 2006).

[69] Cheryl Walker, *Women and Resistance in South Africa* (New York: Monthly Review, 1982 and 1991), p. 257.

[70] Hassim, *Women's Organization and Democracy.*

surge of shop-floor, student and community wildcat protests [would] subside', such outbursts of popular discontent in the very teeth of the deal between the ANC and capital did serve to provide a meaningful bridge to the awakened popular revolt that has come more recently to mark South Africa in the new century. In this connection Bond cites, as one dramatic example, the 'IMF Riots [that] continued to break out in dozens of impoverished black townships subject to high increases in service charges and power/water cutoffs.' For it is here – and in Ashwin Desai's on-going community struggles of the 'poors' and Peter Alexander's 'rebellion of the poor' – that the promise of future radical action by proletariat and precariat alike – an original promise that Rusty Bernstein had once seen to lie at the core of the UDF – continues to live.[71]

Inside from the outside:
Exile, the ANC's drive to power – and to the Right

It was, however, another force, one we have already seen to be in play, that would become most central in defining the immediate outcome, especially in the early-1990s, of the resistance in South Africa: the long-standing movement for liberation led by the ANC (together with its close ally, the South African Communist Party). Within the ANC both national-liberation assertions and those of class struggle vied for centrality. Yet insofar as a variant of Marxism provided a privileged framework of analysis in exile it was a Stalinoid one with a distinctly Soviet flavour (the Soviet Union being a major source of military support for the ANC's decision to rely on the centrality of armed struggle in its core strategy of achieving liberation). This tradition exemplified a particularly rigid brand of Marxism, one firmly wedded to a stageist theory of revolution that sought to twin class assertions with more narrowly nationalist ones, the central concept being that of a two-stage revolution, a national-democratic, national-liberation phase first and, once that was achieved, a class-defined socialist revolution next.

True, some theoretically inclined activists like Joe Slovo (veteran ANC and SACP leader, and Umkhonto weSizwe commander) did suggest that 'national liberation is impossible without social liberation and a nationalist ideology that ignores the class basis of racism is false'.[72] As he further affirmed, between the national-democratic revolution and the socialist revolution there need be 'no Chinese wall' separating the two stages.[73] But for others, wedded to the mantras

---

[71] Ashwin Desai, *We are the Poors: Community Struggles in Post-Apartheid South Africa* (New York: Monthly Review Press, 2002); Peter Alexander, 'Rebellion of the poor: South Africa's service delivery protests – a preliminary analysis', *Review of African Political Economy*, v. 37, 123, 2010).

[72] Joe Slovo, 'South Africa: No Middle Road' in Basil Davidson, Joe Slovo and Anthony Wilkinson, *Southern Africa: The New Politics of Revolution* (Harmondsworth: Penguin, 1976), p. 139.

[73] This concept has been widely used by Slovo in such core pamphlets as his *The South African Working Class and the National Democratic Revolution* (Umsebenzi Discussion

of 'colonialism of a special type' and the 'two-stage theory of revolution,' things were different. Thus future president Thabo Mbeki could assert forcefully (and presciently) in 1984: 'The ANC is not a socialist party. It has never pretended to be one, it has never said it was, and it is not trying to be. It will not become one by decree or for the purpose of pleasing its "left" critics.'[74] Nor was Mbeki alone in his abandonment of any real project of 'social liberation'. In fact, it could come as no surprise, that, ultimately and once in power, the ANC would itself and very quickly erect a particularly firm 'Chinese wall' of its own against any spread of infection from the more radical emanations of its very recent past!

That said, the ANC had had a particularly noble history of sustained struggle, if not against capitalism then certainly against apartheid itself. Nonetheless, the specific history of its interaction with the democratic protests and movements (e.g., the UDF) emerging on the ground inside the country is a complex and contradictory one that we will have to unravel below (and along the lines sketched, as seen, by Rusty Bernstein). For the ANC, despite the fact that its leadership was still largely, and until the eleventh hour, in jail or in exile, did manage to position itself skilfully to harvest the rewards of victory. Moreover, the movement even now, in the post-apartheid period, retains a striking degree of credibility because of that victory – and, judging by electoral results, a still-popularly-rooted 'right to rule'. The ANC's is a fraying credibility perhaps, but it is still a potent one.

In short, though very far from being the central player on the ground within the rising resistance movement to apartheid it was nonetheless the 'liberation movement', specifically the ANC, that came, by the early-1990s, to be the main apparent agent of the impulse for transformation in South Africa. Not that the ANC (and its close comrade organization in arms, the SACP) had been inactive during the 1970s and 1980s. Indeed, the Congress Movement was sufficiently well-organized and salient, in exile and even within the country, to capture the allegiance of a prominent number of the 'Soweto graduates' who found themselves then moving into exile. This is true, even though many more of these

---

[(cont)]Pamphlet, SACP), p. 16, and *Has Socialism Failed?* (Umsebenzi Discussion Pamphlet, SACP, 1990). As he further notes (p. 15) in the first of these two texts, 'There is ... both a *distinction* and a *continuity* between the national democratic and socialist revolutions; *they can neither be completely telescoped nor completely compartmentalised.* The vulgar Marxists are unable to understand this. They claim that our immediate emphasis on the objectives of the national democratic revolution implies that we are unnecessarily postponing or even abandoning the socialist revolution, as if the two revolutions have no connection with one another. They have a mechanical approach to the stages of our revolution, treating them simply as water-tight compartments ... It should, however, be conceded that our own formulations have sometimes been imprecise, and have invited the charge that we treat stages as compartments, as "things-in-themselves"'! (original emphasis). Yet the 'vulgar Marxists' (to employ Slovo's label) have actually been, on balance, correct, and 'abandoning the socialist revolution' is of course what has occurred on the ANC's watch in post-apartheid South Africa.

[74] Thabo Mbeki, 'The Fatton Thesis: A Rejoinder', *Canadian Journal of African Studies*, 18, 3, 1984 p. 609.

'graduates', so strongly influenced in their formation by 'Black Consciousness,' might have been expected, at least initially, to see in the 'black nationalism' of the Pan Africanist Congress/PAC a more attractive, racially-resonant, home. But the PAC itself had more or less unravelled in exile and the ANC seemed a far more convincing movement to most of the new exiles.

Unfortunately, many such exiles were destined to themselves languish in the ANC's own camps in the years ahead – the main agents of change in South Africa generally being far more internally-centred than externally so and far more premised on popular than on armed struggle. Yet the ANC would, in the end, be the most prominent 'winner' in the transition process of the 1990s – even if it would also prove itself to be, simultaneously, as much the slayer of revolutionary promise in South Africa as its facilitator, difficult as this would have been to foresee in the 60s and the 70s. For the fact is that the table for an anti-climactic outcome to liberation struggle was set well before the period of final negotiations.

A case in point: John Daniel, in discussing the transition itself has empha-sized not just the ANC's culpability in killing the UDF but also in killing the latter's fundamental spirit. For the UDF, however much he may define it as being, in essence, 'the ANC in disguise',[75] is nonetheless seen by him to have been 'a very different creature from its external progenitor': 'in orchestrating a national insurrection' it was 'not a centralized entity at all' but instead 'one that practiced a robust and raucous form of participatory democracy in which a premium was placed on grassroots consensus and accountability. It was in most respects the antithesis of the essentially conformist ANC in exile'. Indeed, it was precisely this openness that the external wing of the ANC feared most, the possi-bility that the UDF would begin 'to carry its practices into the emerging domestic structures of the ANC' – and even set in train a process of further radicalization. In sum, 'hidden largely from the view of the so-called 'magic' of the Mandela era with its policies of rainbowism and reconciliation, a subterranean struggle for the heart and soul of the ANC ensued through the early and mid-1990s,' a struggle capped by a victory for 'Lusaka' and a distinct defeat for any more progressive outcome to the South African struggle.[76]

For Daniel goes much further back than this, rooting the 'victory' in the much longer history of the ANC. Insisting that the ANC was never a mass-based party ('it embraced notions of democracy, [but] was not popularly democratic

[75] See John Daniel, 'The Mbeki Presidency: Lusaka Wins', *South African Yearbook of Inter-national Affairs, 2001/12* (Johannesburg: South African Institute of International Affairs, 2002), pp. 7–15, from which I quote liberally in the next several paragraphs. There is, of course, reason to dispute Daniel's characterization of the UDF as merely being 'the ANC's surrogate' – quite apart from the difference he admits in the texture of movement politics inside and outside the country. See, for example, the discussion of Younis' take on the dissolution of the UDF, above.

[76] 'Lusaka,' a key ANC centre of operations in exile, here becomes Daniel's code-word for the stolid, authoritarian style and substance of the ANC in exile as distinct from the more open and democratic politics internal to the mass movement in South Africa in the 1980s.

in practice ... In reality, it was a small, elite-led, top-down hierarchical party with neither a significant working class nor a rural base'). Indeed, it was this *modus operandi* that the ANC took into exile 'where, in an initially hostile Western environment, in conditions of semi-clandestinity and heavily reliant on its Soviet and East German allies, it transmogrified into a tightly-knit, highly centralized vanguard party' – its political practice that of particularly strict democratic centralism, 'with policy largely devised behind closed doors and then passed down to the lower ranks ... [and] deviation was met with expulsion and relegation'.[77]

It therefore followed, ineluctably, that when the very top leadership of such an organization took, unequivocally, the capitalist road and used its newly-won power to consolidate such a choice it was 'game over' for any who harboured, within the movement, some more radically democratic and/or socialist goals than those now enunciated by the vanguard. As McKinley writes, 'many cadres in the movement [were] angered by the apparent abandonment of long held principles and policies'. Yet, as he continues,

> The sheer pace with which the ANC leadership was traveling down the road of accommodation and negotiation instilled in its constituency the feeling there was no real alternative to a negotiated settlement which would entail compromise. This was further catalysed by the delegitimisation of socialist polices (associated with the collapsed economies of the USSR and Eastern Europe) and the accompanying confusion and demoralization experienced by movement socialists.[78]

Of course, it is precisely this that explains Rusty Bernstein's dismay when the opening offered by the UDF, with the radical possibilities that it revealed, were merely squandered by the ANC's top brass.

Daniel is also alert to the overbearing influence upon the ANC of the authoritarian ethos characteristic of the Soviet model – and also of a similar ethos within both the Front-line States bordering the region and the other liberation movements within the region itself with whom the ANC interacted.[79] For the war for southern African liberation was not a context that nurtured democracy in practice – even if its essential long-term goals were often presented in terms of democratic demands. Organizing for military confrontation against an absolutely unscrupulous and proactive enemy tended everywhere to privilege hierarchy, secrecy and even abuse of power on the part of those who would seek to lead any such resistance. But the fact is also that, as the case of the ANC's facilitating the UDF's demise hints, habits so formed would prove to be extremely difficult to shake.

Granted, such vanguardist militarism as marked the ANC did not lead readily to great success in terms of effective combat. Indeed, Janet Cherry in her book, *Umkhonto weSizwe* underscores the fact that, for the most part, 'those who left

---

[77] Daniel, 'The Mbeki Presidency', pp. 9–10.
[78] Dale McKinley, *The ANC and the Liberation Struggle: A Critical Political Biography* (London and Chicago, IL: Pluto Press, 1997), p. 109.
[79] See Saul, 'Socialism and Southern Africa' in Williams & Satgar, *Introducing New Approaches to Marxism*.

[South Africa] with a burning desire to fight for freedom of their people did not get to engage in combat at all ... the bitter reality was that the majority of those who went into exile and received military training were never deployed in South Africa'.[80] Although she does give much attention to the heroism and commitment of those who actually engaged in an uneven and sporadic programme of sabotage and like activity inside South Africa over the decades she feels forced to concede that MK's greatest achievement was the fact of its very 'presence', even if that lay chiefly over the border. In short, the ANC/MK's contribution was to be found primarily in 'raising the morale of oppressed people and delegitimising an oppressive regime'; it therefore, in her words, 'cannot be judged a failure'. Yet 'neither can MK be regarded as responsible for the overthrow of apartheid':

> The 'struggle' was conducted by millions of ordinary South Africans, without weapons or military training, who joined the trade unions, refused to carry passes, boycotted their local councilors, refused to vote in apartheid elections and, in myriad of other ways, undermined the apartheid system and made it unworkable. It was not military operations that caused apartheid to implode.[81]

Howard Barrell, another sympathetic and careful observer of MK, argues much the same position. He emphasizes that 'MK accepted the challenge of some of the most difficult conditions ever confronted by a revolutionary movement' and also states clearly MK's position 'that revolutionary armed struggle leading to a seizure of state power was both necessary and possible'. Nonetheless his book's central argument is that even 'granting the difficult conditions, the major reason for the failure of MK and the ANC to achieve this aim was their inability – despite opportunities to do so – to develop internal underground leaderships, at both regional and national levels, [and] exercising day-to-day, hands-on command and control over all aspects of political and military work. This failure, in turn, testified to lack of strategic agreement and clarity within the ANC.' As a result of his analyses, Barrell is forced to conclude that

> MK's main achievement over the three decades to 1990 was this essentially propagandistic: it helped to stimulate a combative political spirit among the ANC's support base and to further militant popular campaigning. MK cadres dared to struggle and set an example to millions. In this respect MK played a vital role in bringing South Africa to the verge of a negotiated end to white minority political domination.[82]

[80] Janet Cherry, *Umkhonto weSizwe* (Auckland Park, S. A.: Jacana, 2001), p. 142.
[81] Cherry, *Umkhonto weSizwe*, pp. 62, 66, 142. For example, Cherry adds (p. 68), 'it is ironic that while the MK was being sung about and lionized by the mass movement, which was growing into an enormously powerful force within South Africa, MK was going through [in the late 70s] what was probably its worst crisis in all the years of exile'. Even in the 1980s (p. 89), she writes, 'the bitter fact is that MK cadres continued to remain in the camps in Angola'.
[82] Howard Barrell, *MK: The ANC's Armed Struggle* (London: Penguin Books, 1990), pp. 70–1. See also Barrell, *Conscripts to their Age: African Nationql congress Operational Strategy, 1976–1986*, D.Phil thesis in Politics, Faculty of Social Studies, University of Oxford, 1993.

Martin Legassick, a third careful observer of this section's theme, would agree with Barrell's observation (and indeed expressly repeats it) that the ANC 'never ... bridg[ed] the gap between a largely externally-based MK and internal militants'. Himself an earlier advocate of a much stronger outreach by the external ANC towards the burgeoning internal worker's movement (a position for the taking of which he was actually expelled from the ANC), Legassick also saw the political mobilization and guerrilla struggle arising on the ground in the townships in 1985–86 as something that had developed 'without reference to MK and without reference even to the UDF leadership'.[83] Cherry, however, adds a further, more controversial, argument here: 'The defiance and revolt of ordinary South Africans', she writes, 'were part of a broader strategy that the liberation movement adopted and was seen as complementary to the armed struggle.' Yet the phrase 'broader strategy' seems to imply a degree of forethought, intentionality and organizational capacity that the ANC simply did not have. Moreover, was there really such a broader strategy at work or was it a case, in retrospect, of a movement being just fast enough on its feet to keep up with the mass movement?

Cherry does further insist (as does Raymond Suttner, cited below) that the ANC did have 'extensive influence on the mass movement through its underground operatives, former Robben Island prisoners and supporters'. But she also concedes that the difficulty 'remained ... of establishing consistent channels of communication with local command structures and infiltrating MK cadres'.[84] 'Broader strategy'? Again the question is left hanging as to whether the broad mass of the people, themselves already in motion, were primarily embracing a time-honoured ANC orientation and thereby assuming an increasingly popular mantle of presumed militancy ... or were they being actively recruited as members of a strongly articulated organization? The former is surely more likely. True, as the tide began to turn ever more definitively towards the possibility, even likelihood, of transition, many in leadership roles in the internal movement began to assume an ever firmer ANC identity – already beginning, perhaps, to jockey for future positions in an ANC government (rather than primarily advancing the interests of their popular base). Just where was the ANC at in actually 'leading' the people as it slowly but surely assumed such 'leadership' of the popular movement (and was, eventually, ushered into negotiations as presumptive leader of that popular movement)?[85]

* * *

We must now interrogate the particular history more closely with such questions as the latter firmly in mind. It does seems safe to say that from the Wankie

[83] Martin Legassick, *Armed Struggle and Democracy: The Case of South Africa* (Uppsala: Nordiska Afrikainstitutet, 2002), pp. 52 and 45. See also the relevant sections of his *Towards Socialist Democracy* (Scottsville, S. A.: University of KwaZulu-Natal Press, 2007).

[84] Cherry, *Umkhonto weSizwe*.

[85] Up the blind alley of neo-liberalism and recolonization, as later events would demonstrate.

campaign forward (Wankie being an ill-fated military incursion into then Rhodesia undertaken alongside Zimbabwean combatants in 1967), the ANC's practice of 'guerrilla struggle' did little, in and of itself, to shake the confidence of the regime. True, the drama of such sorties as the attacks in the early-1980s against SASOL oil refineries had a marked impact on growing popular self-confidence – as did Frelimo's defeat of the Portuguese in Mozambique in the 1970s and the Cuban/Angolan success against the South African Defence Force at Cuito Cuanavale in the 1980s. Nonetheless, the real drama of the time was being played out inside the country, on the shop-floors and in the townships themselves – in 'rising social militancy and township unrest', as Elisabeth Jean Wood emphasizes. So why then were people eager to accept the 'jailed and exiled leadership of the ANC as [their] counter elite?' she further asks. Here, in fact, is the question that must haunt all those engaged in serious interrogation of South Africa's transition. More specifically it haunts all those drawn to consider the role played by the ANC, the nature of its interface with the broader mass movement for change and the role it played in the passage to the new post-apartheid order.[86] The question: did the ANC act primarily to crystallize, to bring into sharper focus and forward the purposes of the mass movement of the 1970s and 1980s, or did it instead emerge from the shadows of exile to centre stage and then betray that movement and work to stunt its revolutionary promise?

In attempting an answer here we can first focus on Wood's own strongly argued and well-documented book-length treatment of the subject in order to underline the complexities of and difficulties in grappling adequately with such a question. For Wood covers much the same ground as does the present chapter. She notes that only 'a few isolated strikes occurred in the late 1960s [and] the mobilization of the early 1960s was suppressed and the forced quiescence endured until 1973', but that 'in (1973) ... factory workers carried out a series of strikes in the greater Durban area', launching 'a wave of strikes which broke a decades long pattern of labour calm' and signalled a significant escalation of a broader struggle. She also emphasizes the crucial significance of the wide range of community struggles that first peaked with the Soweto events and whose further elaboration in the 1980s was also crucial to popular militancy. She even underscores the fact that it was these 'massive mobilizations of the mid-1980s' and not guerrilla actions that 'constituted the ANC as an insurgent counter-elite with which negotiations would have to occur if unrest were to subside'.[87]

However, a great deal hangs on how one interprets the rather vague formu-

---

[86] Elisabeth Jean Wood, *Forging Democracy from Below: Insurgent Transitions in South Africa and El Salvador* (Cambridge and New York: Cambridge University Press, 2000), pp. 140–1; on this theme, more generally, see Younis, *Liberation and Democratization*; Williams, *The Roots of Participatory Democracy* and Kurt Schock, *Unarmed Insurrections: People's Power Movements in Nondemocracies* (Minneapolis: University of Minnesota Press, 2005).

[87] Wood, *Forging Democracy from Below*, p 112; elsewhere (p. 199) she also emphasizes that 'the ANC, by contrast [with the FMLN in El Salvador], was militarily ineffective and had much less direct contact with or control of insurgent movements in South Africa'.

lation employed: 'mass mobilizations ... constituted the ANC as an insurgent counter-elite', especially the word 'constituted'. This is so because, as we have seen, popular resistance on the ground inside the country on the one hand and the eventual ascendancy of the ANC on the other were not quite so straight-forwardly elided as Wood here implies. For there actually existed the makings of a genuinely radical insurgency in South Africa in the 1980s and early 1990s. It was only then, as we will see in the next sub-section, that capital awoke fully to the import of such a threat and began to recalculate its own historical invest-ment in apartheid structures as being the best long-term means of reaping profits and of keeping order in the country. In seeking to control any possible revolutionary fall-out of insurgency, it began to turn more and more to the ANC, not the Nationalist Party elite, as a possible partner in forestalling any outcome more dangerous to its own interests – not as an 'insurgent counter-elite' then, but as a prospective partner elite! Consider Wood's own formulation as to the way in which the various elites' now reached out for each other:

> Elites accomplished [compromise] by conceding political democracy, addressing a long-held ground of grievance; the insurgents [sic] accomplished an analogous task by agreeing to a liberalized market economy with only minor changes in the distri-bution of property rights.[88]

Consider too, Wood's (all-too-naïve) formulation as to the grounds for the ANC's response to this outreach that capital now made:

> The insurgent counter-elites abandoned their aspirations [sic] for a socialist outcome, agreed to the status quo distribution of private property rights (with few exceptions), and accepted stringent constraints on subsequent populist redistribution because, as long-excluded political actors, they valued the right to full citizenship in a democratic polity.[89]

As for why it was that the ANC was able to place itself in a position to so stunt the nature of the transition, Wood's emphasis is again instructive: 'The long-standing legitimacy of the ANC as opposition organization appears to have [become] part of the "social memory of the opposition"' – and this, taken together with the resonance of 'the personal prestige of Nelson Mandela's lead-ership ... unmatched by any other opposition figure', was the most potent factor in sealing the long-term legitimation of the ANC's claim to centrality.[90] Similarly Raymond Suttner – who otherwise argues strongly that there was a rather more active ANC underground inside South Africa during the 70s and 80s than many commentators have tended to concede – comes, nonetheless, to much the same conclusion as Wood:

> It was not inevitable or preordained that the ANC would achieve hegemony within the liberation struggle and the new democratic South Africa. Indeed, there were times in

---

[88] Wood, *Forging Democracy from Below*, p. 218.
[89] Wood, *Forging Democracy from Below*, p. 198.
[90] Wood, *Forging Democracy from Below*, p. 14–15.

the history of the organization when it was virtually dormant ... That it did survive [however] depended in the first place on the way in which the ANC had, over decades, inserted itself into the cultural consciousness of people, becoming part of their sense of being, even if at times of great repression there was no public forum of outlet for this identity.[91]

In sum, the ANC/SACP/MK tandem now served as much as very powerful myth as it did a reality – the same also being true for the quasi-mythological status that had accrued to Mandela while he was in prison during the 1980s. The result: when a capitalism-friendly ANC did finally succeed in getting the ear of capital and even of the apartheid government and was beckoned, as Fanon once said, to 'settle the problem' around 'the green baize table before any regrettable act has been performed or irreparable gesture made'[92] the stage was also well set within the resistance movement more generally for the ANC to find popular favour for its own eventual accession to formal power.

Important then, in Wood's words, was 'the movement's success in constituting the exiled leadership of the ANC as its counter-elite'.[93] But what kind of a 'success', and for whom, was the ANC's ultimate 'victory' in fact? How much of a '*counter* elite' would it really prove to be as the ANC leadership's interests came to congeal quite comfortably with those of capital. In fact, this settlement-in-the-making may be better understood as the ANC's being now both poised to cap its decades-long struggle with political victory and also to take the sting out of any such victory by means of crucial socio-economic compromises (viz., Wood above: 'only minor changes in the distribution of property rights'!). For the ANC stood ready to tame, on behalf of capital and in the furtherance of its own interests, the insurgency of the period, rather than to spearhead it and to carry it further forward. It is thus not surprising that more trenchant commentators than Wood – Daniel, McKinley and Neville Alexander[94] – have all argued

[91] Raymond Suttner, *The ANC Underground in South Africa* (Auckland Park, S.A.: Jacana, 2008), p. 148. So too does Kurt Schock tend to do (in *Unarmed Insurrections*, p. 66) in suggesting that 'more important to the anti-apartheid movement than the threat of armed insurrection was the ANC's re-established public presence after the Soweto uprising and its provision of a culture of resistance and [of] popular anti-apartheid frames'.

[92] Frantz Fanon, *The Wretched of the Earth* (Harmondsworth: Penguin, 1967), p. 48; as he then continues, 'if the masses, without waiting for the chairs to be arranged around the baize table, listen to their own voice and begin committing outrages and setting fire to buildings, the elites and the bourgeois parties will be seen running to the colonialists to exclaim "this is very serious! We do not know how it will end; we must find a solution – some sort of compromise"'.

[93] Wood, *Forging Democracy from Below*, p. 141.

[94] Neville Alexander, *An Ordinary Country: Issues in the Transition from Apartheid to Democracy in South Africa* (Pietermaritzburg: University of Natal Press, 2002). For him (p. 78), the post-apartheid state is, without qualification, a capitalist state; indeed 'to believe on the basis of some kind of populist abracadabra, as many of the ideologues of the Congress Alliance do, that [the ANC] government is purely and simply "our" government, that is, the government of the working people, or even the government of the people, is wishful thinking or irresponsible propaganda'.

that this was the actual denouement, one that both Fanon and Biko would quite readily have recognized the ultimate result of 'transition' as a kind of false decolonization. Recall Thabo Mbeki's own unequivocal 1974 statement, quoted above, to the effect that the ANC has never pretended to be socialist party. For the fact was that, by the late 1980s, Thabo Mbeki and his ANC cronies were perfectly prepared to seal a deal, unthreatening and certainly non-socialist, with capital – while adroitly outflanking Chris Hani and other potential left critics within the movement in doing so.[95]

Soon, too, Mandela himself – and despite his own provocative statements about nationalizations and other aspects of economic strategy upon his release from prison in 1990 – would retreat from such heterodox thoughts. For the ANC was actually well launched on its two-track process of negotiations – negotiations with both capital and with the apartheid state – to determine the outcome of South Africa's struggle for liberation. As for the broader movement, it had been pulled emotionally past any lingering Black Consciousness or 'workerist' sensibility and, ever more firmly, onto the ANC's symbolic terrain. What might have happened had political organization – the ANC, say – sought to build on and to draw out the revolutionary possibilities of the time is now a matter of merely disempowered speculation. The hard fact remains that ANC leadership was, quite simply, prepared to consummate a deal – one defined largely on global and local capital's own terms – in order to guarantee the consolidation of a colour-blind, formally democratic, outcome. This was a choice of strategy from which the ANC would never recover – even assuming for a moment that a fundamental transformation of South African society beyond anything defined in purely racial terms was ever a goal the ANC leadership had actually hoped to accomplish.

Finally, and before leaving this section, it is also important to note a quite different strand of the overall resistance movement: those on the left who remained staunch in their active criticism of the apartheid state but also in sharp opposition to any too unquestioning an acceptance of the ANC's unexamined 'credibility' – not least as, by the early 1990s, the ANC readied itself to move into power. This was a counter-current to the left of the ANC that had long existed in South Africa – in part as influenced by the Trotskyist tradition, in part as the reflex of a more independent, democratic and principled non-Stalinist tradition. Profoundly sceptical as to the presumed constraints of any kind of 'stageism', critics in this camp postulated, in effect, a situation of 'combined and uneven development', determined both nationally and internationally, that would make more imaginative combinations of potentially socialist and revolutionary ingredients seem possible. Put succinctly, such a formulation embraced the fact that, especially in settings at the periphery of global capitalist expansion and control, the reality of resistance may be 'overdetermined' and

---

[95] This 'Hani moment' is graphically discussed in Janet Smith and Beauregard Tromp, *Hani: A Life Too Short* (Johannesburg and Cape Town: Jonathan Ball Publishers, 2009); Mark Gevisser, in his *A Legacy of Liberation: Thabo Mbeki and the Future of the South African Dream* (New York: Palgrave Macmillan, 2009), p. 210, also draws on Hani's intervention at the NWC.

not reducible to the precise dictates of some 'correct' brand of class struggle as drawn up uncritically on the basis of a narrow reading of Marxist classics. Instead, as Michael Lowy has summarized the case, it has proven possible to envisage an 'uninterrupted transition from democratic to socialist revolution, as so-called bourgeois-democratic tasks (national independence and unity, the emancipation of the peasantry, democratic enfranchisement, and so on) [were] undertaken by workers' power in ineluctable combination with specifically socialist tasks'.[96]

Here, in fact, are glimpses of a theoretical break with the kind of class reductionism that encourages militants to be forever waiting for 'the proletariat' to speak in unequivocal and solitary tones. For example, Lowy himself (however inclined he may be to invoke 'workers' power') can also write of the importance of 'popular insurrections in which the proletariat and the urban poor [each play] the decisive role'.[97] Permit me to underscore here his suggestive distinction between the 'urban poor' and 'the proletariat'. Note, too, the importance of the democratic setting within which Lowy deems it most likely that such an 'urban poor' can prove to be available, alongside a 'working class', for progressive action.

> It is reasonable to assume ... that the intervention of the so-called 'subjective factors' – the participatory character of the revolutionary process, the democratic/pluralist outlook of the socialist vanguard, the degree of proletarian self-activity and popular self-organization, and so on – can, if not abolish, then at least limit and counter-balance the tendencies toward bureaucratization in the transition toward socialism in a poor and underdeveloped country.

For Lowy, then, the 'massive forms of popular self-organization' and 'a profound commitment to socialist democracy' on the part of the leadership could have been, could still be, the ambience of on-going liberation. This was certainly true of the days of anti-apartheid struggle itself when a vast range of South Africans – constituting an effective alliance of proletariat and precariat – came to act so effectively against apartheid. It may be so again.

The preceding formula also provides the most appropriate terms for prefiguring the kind of opposition, sited in both urban and rural South Africa, best suited to challenging the ANC and its dramatic lack of fulfilment of its promises of substantive liberation. As referred to above, Peter Alexander has written of the tangible and dramatic 'rebellion of the poor' that currently marks South Africa.[98] By what means might socio-political distemper further develop into a genuine and effectively counter-hegemonic force? Time alone will tell, but consider the fact that one recently-emergent would-be movement (the United Democratic Front) in opposition to the ANC's present hegemony speaks quite

[96] Michael Lowy, *The Politics of Combined and Uneven Development: The Theory of Permanent Revolution* (London: Verso Editions, 1981).

[97] Lowy, *The Politics of Combined and Uneven Development*, p. 202.

[98] See Alexander, 'Rebellion of the poor', and his updated survey 'SA protest rates increasingly competitive with world leader China', 23 March 2012, available from www.amandlapublishers.org.za.

specifically (in its founding document[99]) of the possibly potent combination of 'the working-class and the poor' that it envisages as crucial to South Africa's revolutionary future. 'The working-class and the poor': I will say more about this formulation and about other seeds of a ripening 'next liberation struggle'[100] in the concluding chapter to this book.

The 1970s and the 1980s: The politics of power and profit

For much of the twentieth century the phrase 'racial capitalism' accurately epitomized the nature of a social and economic system in South Africa that was intractable, even seemingly invulnerable. In this system the twin pillars of dominant social power in South Africa – the racist overrule that culminated in apartheid and the class rule inherent in capitalism's centrality to the country's economy – came to complement each other, with any possible contradictions between the two modes of ordering social hierarchy merely smoothed away with relative ease. It is this reality, as we have seen, that tempted Biko to see the fact of racial rule as trumping capital's role in setting the basic agenda of revolution in South Africa – and he offered 'Black Consciousness' as defining, under such circumstances, a way forward for an effective resistance movement. This proved to be a debatable starting-point, of course, and yet it still remained a considerable challenge to tease out the relative weight of class, race, gender and other variables within the several arenas of power that defined the South Africa of both the 'segregation' and the 'apartheid' years.

Some, already alluded to above, have insisted in seeing these two modes – that of racial domination and that of class differentiation – as being in stark contradiction throughout South Africa's history (as indeed they might appear to be in the realm of abstract model-building). Such analysts interpret (racial) prejudice as having, in fact, trumped profit in South Africa, with a colour-blind capitalism forced to concede costly and 'uneconomic' ground to the captains of racial domination. Thus, Merle Lipton, to cite merely one such analyst, highlights what she seems to feel to be the almost wholly negative racist grip upon capitalism:

> Today, as during the 1920s, Marxists are mistaken in identifying the interests of capital with the maintenance of a streamlined or 'restructured' apartheid and failing to see that capitalists – despite some reservations and ambivalence – are among the

[99] Democratic Left Front, 'Another South Africa and World is Possible!' 1st Democratic Left Conference Report, 20–23 January 2011, Johannesburg, S. A.; the phrase 'the working class and the poor of South Africa' is used a number of times, not least in the foreword (p. 2) to this important document, as is the phrase 'the anti-capitalist left'.

[100] See John S. Saul, *The Next Liberation Struggle* (Toronto, New York, Pietermaritzburg and London: Between the Lines, Monthly Review Press, University of Kwa-Zulu/Natal Press and Merlin Press, 2005).

pressures for its erosion; while white labour and the bureaucracy, despite some changes of attitude, remain its major sources of support.[101]

This is almost shockingly misleading, however. In making such a case, she highlights many of the ostensibly clarifying moments that we have also noted above: as, for example, in the period after the 1924 strike when, in her words, 'the 1924 election settled [not only the struggle against capital] over the job colour bar and civilized labour policy, but also questions of protection and subsidy for white agriculture and manufacturing'. Yet surely much more of the truth of the matter lies with the argument, cited above, of Frederick Johnstone who underscored the manner in which a crucial 'exploitation colour bar' (favouring capital) was merely complemented by a 'job colour bar' (favouring, up to point, white workers). For Johnstone has shown that any tension between the demands for entitlement based on the claims of racial and class be best conceived as representing relatively mild jockeyings for advantage within an overall structure of shared white-skin-cum-capitalist-class privilege.[102]

Other theorists have added additional dimensions to this explanation, with Harold Wolpe's emphasis on the importance of the migrant African labour system as linking two distinct modes of production, urban and rural, and serving to so cheapen the price of black labour to employers as to make a crucial contribution to capital's expanded profit margins.[103] Indeed, it was on some such bases that Stephen Gelb and I, some years ago, examined the apartheid-era contradictions of what we ourselves were content to term 'racial capitalism'.[104] Warning against 'too reductionist a position', we acknowledged that 'it would be a bold observer indeed' who suggested that racism and Afrikaner nationalism did not have some 'autonomous resonance of their own'. Yet, at the same time, we chose both to confirm our commitment to the earlier analyses of Johnstone, and Wolpe, and to attempt to further deepen them – even though we also

---

[101] Merle Lipton, *Capitalism and Apartheid: South Africa, 1910–84* (Aldershot: Gower Publishing, 1985), p. 372. The question of the extent of the state's autonomy and of the precise balance of determination that exists as between 'state' on the one hand and 'capital' on the other, and between 'race' and 'class', is an extremely complicated one, an issue not to be resolved glibly or by means of economistic or indeed any other kind of reductionism. My own position on this, which I consider to be quite sufficiently nuanced, will be apparent from the text. But other views, beyond that of Lipton, do exist: see, for example, David Yudelman, *The Emergence of Modern South Africa: State, Capital and the Incorporation of Organized Labor on the South African Gold Fields, 1902–1939* (Westport, CT: Greenwood Press, 1983).

[102] See, crucially, Fredrick Johnstone, 'White Prosperity and White Supremacy in South Africa Today', *African Affairs*, 69, 2, 1970, and also his *Class, Race and Gold: A Study of Class Relations and Racial Discrimination in South Africa* (London: Routledge and Kegan Paul, 1976).

[103] Harold Wolpe, 'Capitalism and Cheap Labour Power in South Africa: From Segregation to Apartheid', *Economy and Society* (1, 4,1972) pp. 425–456.

[104] See Saul & Gelb, *The Crisis in South Africa*; the 1986 revised edition extends my own argument in a new introduction and final chapter entitled 'The Crisis Deepens', while Gelb moved his own views forward in 'Making Sense of the Crisis', *Transformation* (5, 1987) and his *South Africa's Economic Crisis* (Cape Town: David Phillip, 1991).

emphasized the declining efficacy of the migrant labour system as the capacity of the overcrowded reserves to subsidize the African wage declined. But 'racial capitalism' was still the core logic of the system we sought to understand even in the late 1970s.

At the same time, the next two decades would reveal the link between capital logic and an institutionalized white racism as increasingly to be a much more contradictory one than had been true in previous decades. This, in turn, helped smooth the way, as we will see below, to a transition away from both apartheid and 'racial capitalism' and towards the South African present as we now know it. But there were other contradictions shaped by South Africa's history that would not prove to be quite so tractable. We must first identify these before looking at the more immediate roles of capital and the white polity in the transition that was to come in the 1990s.

Uneven and combined contradictions

For the starkest kind of 'racial capitalism,' however much it would eventually prove to be on the wane, was underpinned by some even deeper economic contradictions, these often cast more generally in terms of a pending 'crisis of under-consumption' said to dog the very footsteps of capitalism. The premise here is that there exists a tension arising from the necessary (to capitalism) existence of a wage-force 'underpaid' (in terms of its rights and its productivity) yet forced by some combination of authoritarian (racial or otherwise) and economic means, to provide their 'surplus-value' cheaply to the owners of the means of production (for both the latter's private consumption and their possible reinvestment). Closely related to this is the fact that such an 'exploited' population cannot, in consequence, offer the necessary market for any expanded production that a differently structured system might promise.

Such a perspective tends to be caricatured on much of the left as 'mere Keynesianism', a perspective that apparently is fated to offer up only reformist vistas of mild redistribution to correct any unevenness in effective demand that might exist. However, this seems to me to be a shallow criticism especially in a situation in which 'under-consumption' is locked into place, as in the case of apartheid South Africa, as a structural reality and defining feature of both the (complementary) racial and capitalist systems. Certainly, a very dramatic, even revolutionary, transformation would be required in order to establish a demand structure, both political and economic, that could push the economy – either under apartheid or even presently – towards the serving of genuinely human needs and demands. This is all the more the case when one considers, as will be done below, at least one other basic contradiction in the South African economy that demands our attention.

Here though it is also important to emphasize that the simultaneity of both racial oppression and capitalist exploitation, so central to the profitable system that 'racial capitalism' embodied in South Africa, rendered such a system distinctly vulnerable to the most sweeping kind of revolution, one that might well have challenged not only the power of institutionalized racial oppression but also that of capitalist exploitation. In fact, as we shall see, this danger was cited with increasing frequency by those charged with plotting capitalism's strategic path during the 1980s. Recall the clarity on such matters of Malcolm Fraser, the deeply conservative former Prime Minister of Australia who served as a member of the Commonwealth's 'Eminent Persons Group' (EPG) delegation to explore the situation in South Africa in 1985 and who actually wrote the mission's eloquent and tough-minded report calling for an extension of sanctions against South Africa. Why? In order to force that country to its senses before the confrontation there had escalated out of control. The EPG feared more violence and bloodshed, but Fraser, writing independently, also warned that in an escalating conflict 'moderation would be swept aside ... The government that emerged from all of this would be extremely radical, probably Marxist, and would nationalize all western business interests.'[105]

Significantly, it was at much the same time and, equally, under the growing pressure of popular resistance, that, as had Fraser, South African capitalists themselves began to recalculate the odds against the survival of a specifically 'racial' capitalism. Here, at last, the long-standing link between ruling race and ruling class could be seen as beginning, markedly, to fray – and to reveal its 'contingent' nature. Indeed (and most unfortunately), the capitalist class would, as seen, find in the ANC an extremely willing partner in deflecting any such anti-capitalist danger and in guaranteeing precisely the kind of transition to the post-apartheid present we have since witnessed.[106]

Moreover, capital did have one 'answer' with regard to this contradiction, both in South Africa and more generally, one exemplified in the shift, occurring globally, from 'demand-side' to 'supply-side' economics. In this paradigm what is necessary for economic growth is not, in the first instance, to seek to create larger markets by Keynesian or other means but, instead, to concentrate on further empowering capital to accumulate and to invest, to spread its wings, to grow. To realize this, the narrowing of the state's 'interference' in the working of the (so-called) free market became the primary preoccupation. Here is the key to the 'neo-liberalism' that has come to dominate the world in recent decades: the demand for the further freeing up of the market to capital's own prerogatives, the dramatic extension of consumer credit to sustain demand and the deepening financialization of economic activity (rather than the expansion of production per se) to keep the bubble of apparent progress in the air. But what could it mean to begin to minimize, as increasingly 'irrational', excessive state

---

[105] Malcolm Fraser, 'No More Talk. Time to Act', *The Times*, London, 30 June 1986, as quoted in John S. Saul, 'Two fronts of anti-apartheid struggle: South Africa and Canada', *Transformation*, 74, 2010, p. 140.

[106] This was also, of course, a deeply gendered process, as well as a fundamentally environmentally unfriendly one and while the transition process itself would open up, as suggested below, privileged moments for the successful assertion of a progressive feminism, this was also to be a front of relatively limited achievement and of on-going struggle. Environmental concerns were even less salient during the period of racial capitalism and of the transition from it, but were to begin to somewhat surface more strongly as a source of critical challenge to the *status quo* since 1994.

interference in the economy? This, in fact, was a broad perspective that could help further to encourage capital and its chief sympathizers in the government to think of 'apartheid' primarily as being another increasingly 'irrelevant' state intrusion into the market place. Especially when that latter policy itself was stoking the fires of civic unrest and revolutionary questioning among the subordinate population.

At the same time the further question intrudes: just what had South Africa come to look like, what has been its historical inheritance, on the supply-side of its economic equation? One way to think about this is to specify a second challenge facing capital: that which economists on the left have come to think of as capitalism's endemic 'crisis of over-accumulation and overproduction'. This is in fact a contradiction central to all capitalist systems – and one that is now ever more visible even in the northern and western citadels of global capital themselves. As Bond elaborates the theoretical point:

> In class terms ... capitalists do not and cannot systematically exploit other capitalists but they can systematically exploit workers [and] here lies the central contradiction ... With automation, the labour input becomes an ever-smaller component of the total inputs into production. And as the labour content diminishes, so too do the opportunities for exploitation, for surplus-value extraction, and for profits. Given intensifying intercapitalist competition for profits ... this situation exacerbates what becomes a self-perpetuating vicious spiral. Workers (as a whole) are increasingly unable to buy the results of their increased production [under-consumption?]. In turn this results in a still greater need for individual capitalists to cut costs. A given firm's excess profits are but temporarily achieved through productivity gains which automation typically provides since every capitalist or branch of production is compelled to adopt state-of-the-art technologies just to maintain competitiveness.[107]

In Bond's eyes this inevitably

> leads to growth in productive capacity far beyond an expansion in what consumer markets can bear ... [While] it is true that there are countervailing tendencies to this process, such as an increase in the turnover time of capital, and work speed-up, as well as expansion of the credit system ... these rarely overwhelm the dynamic for long, and there are limits to the height of the consumer debt pyramid. The inexorable consequence, a continuously worsening problem under capitalism, is termed the over-accumulation of capital.

Note too that this contradiction general to capital also has a specifically South African twist. For just as white racism had interpenetrated with capitalism exploitation in a distinctive way in defining South Africa's particular socio-political pathology, so too (under both the systems of 'segregation' and of apartheid and under the eventual rule of the ANC) did the very nature of South Africa's unique economic development in productive terms set a particular challenge to the country's further development. For South Africa remained a prisoner of the very source of its own great wealth, a prisoner of what has been seen by

---

[107] Patrick Bond, 'What is a Crisis of Overproduction' available at www.marxmail. org/faq/overproduction.htm, published July 10 1998, accessed 10 August 2013.

some observers to be the central feature of its economy, its 'minerals-energy complex'. Thus, in also defining the country's distinctive situation both under apartheid and in the post-apartheid period as being one of 'crisis', Ashman, Fine and Newman situate such a crisis as determined by this unique feature:[108]

> Global accumulation and its shifts and restructuring are necessarily mediated by the structure of particular economies and forms of class rule. We characterize the system of accumulation in South Africa as a 'Minerals-Energy Complex' (MEC) where accumulation has been and remains dominated by and dependent upon a cluster of industries, heavily promoted by the state, around mining and energy – raw and semi-processed products, gold, diamond, platinum and steel, coal, iron and aluminium.

Historically, this has meant that some of the country's 'surpluses' have been siphoned off as exportable returns to multinational firms that have been actors within the MEC. Nonetheless, many of the key firms remained, at least until quite recently, firmly embedded in the settler economy where – even if, for a significant period of the country's history, as 'English capital' sparring with 'Afrikaner political power'. For the fact is that such capital has been a major force in defining the thrust of many of the country's economic policies, not least in the disposal of the surpluses garnered from the MEC itself, and this in a particularly distinctive way.

True, the Afrikaner-controlled state did act to advance the interests of those of the bourgeoisie from its own Afrikaner community. Nonetheless, our authors assert, the interests of the MEC remained crucial in an important overall sense, and at a cost. Thus, 'both the apartheid and post-apartheid eras ... failed to diversify out of this core base in the MEC, and the strategies pursued by dominant MEC corporations, and their interconnection with and influence over state policy, have continued to be critical in determining the path of economic development'. Indeed, Bond and others who have carefully examined the costs of this tilt in policy choices regarding the use of surpluses have found them to have been bent not only towards servicing the interests of the MEC but also away from other more genuinely productive and transformative uses and from any real link to any more elevated and expansive social purposes.

This remains a charge that can be levelled against the post-apartheid regime of course although it is my co-author, Bond, who, in Chapter 4, will have the opportunity of evaluating the utility of such arguments to an understanding of the recent period – including the specific implications of the dawning epoch of an increased 'financialization' of capital, both national and global.[109] Yet

---

[108] Sam Ashman, Ben Fine and Susan Newman, 'The Crisis in South Africa: Neoliberalism, Financialization and Uneven and Combined Development', *Socialist Register* 47 (Pontypool, Wales: Merlin Press, 2011) pp. 174–295; for an earlier and more detailed statement of the position see Fine & Rustomjee, *The Political Economy of South Africa*.

[109] It is worth noting here, however, that Ashman et al. ('The Crisis in South Africa', p. 178) do argue of this later period that 'In the context of South African production, financialization has produced a particular combination of short-term capital inflows

Ashman, Fine and Newman anticipate the conclusions of the present chapter very clearly:

> The negotiations to end apartheid were in the event premised upon the achievement of political equality whilst leaving the structure and functioning of the economy intact. Yet, of course, if white capital was to be untouched how was capitalism in South Africa to be deracialized, never mind decent living standards achieved for the majority. The transitional compromise removed questions of wealth redistribution from the agenda and confined the settlement to narrowly political and constitutional issues, the establishment of bourgeois order, democratic rights and liberal democratic structures. And while white capital for a time thought that the National Party was necessary as a bulwark against the radical demands of the ANC, it quickly became clear that no such assistance was necessary, as the ANC proved itself committed to capitalism but to its neoliberal form also.
>
> This meant leaving behind the programme of nationalization enshrined in the ANC's own Freedom Charter but also other interventionist policy measures and approaches designed to address the structural legacies of apartheid. White capital, the National Party and the ANC leadership increasingly came together around the pursuit of economic growth through 'competitiveness,' faith in private sector investment, liberalization, privatization, Central Bank independence, etc. Zac de Beer's nightmare [see below], that 'the baby of free enterprise' might be 'thrown out with the bathwater of apartheid' – was not to come true.[110]

In short, the structure of over-accumulation (exaggerated as it was in its actual historical form by the continuing impact of the MEC) and the structure of under-consumption, reinforced as this was by the still largely racially defined super-inequality in South Africa, was basically left unaddressed in the transition. Much of the argument in the remainder of this chapter will seek to explain how and why this startling anti-climax to the struggle for South African liberation could have occurred.

The changing logic of capital

Not surprisingly, capitalists in South Africa had little to offer as a solution for 'over-accumulation' and other such deeply structural problems (no more than the ANC would once it came to power). After all, capital and its broader logic was very much more part of the problems with respect to this contradiction than it could ever be part of either admitting to them or solving them.[111] Nonetheless, and particularly as both popular assertions and the further threat of international economic sanctions rose ever more threateningly and effectively to the surface in the 1980s, many more capitalists could begin to contemplate the necessity to untangle at least some of the knots that tied capitalist exploitation

(cont) (accompanied by rising consumer debt largely spent on luxury items) *and* a massive long-term outflow of capital as major 'domestic' corporations have chosen offshore listing and to internationalize their operations while concentrating within South Africa on core profitable MEC sectors. The result, even before the impact of the current crisis, was a jobless form of growth and the persistence of mass poverty for the majority alongside rising living standards for a small minority, including new black elites.'

110 Ashman et al., 'The Crisis in South Africa', p. 182.

to racist oppression – notably by, slowly but surely, withdrawing their allegiance from apartheid.

As suggested above, this dawning awareness of the political dangers that the very baldest form of 'racial capitalism' created came quite unevenly to those within the capitalist class. True, some fractions of capital felt themselves to be more constrained by apartheid than others, notably, in this respect, certain sectors of manufacturing capital that could sense racial capitalism's super-exploitation of blacks to be defining a constraint on the wider domestic markets they sought. Moreover, as a more complex capitalism also emerged, the various racial discriminations within the job market – even though the apartheid system was often rather more flexible about them in practice than in theory – could also be felt as a constraint upon the capitalists' effective deployment of all labour, regardless of its pigment. Harry Oppenheimer, chairman of the Anglo American Corporation, South Africa's largest single business enterprise, and also a leading supporter, not least financially, of the still small Progressive Federal Party referred to above, put the key points clearly in the 1970s; his was a position with regard, in the first instance, to labour supplies but one with much wider implications – and also one towards which many more capitalists would gravitate throughout the following decade and a half.

> I think it presents itself to us in the Anglo American Corporation in the first place, but perhaps to business in ever widening circles, that Nationalist polices have made it impossible to make proper use of black labour. And ... that is felt to be a danger in two ways: a danger because it is necessary, in order to get economic growth, to make use of black labour because ... unless you keep the economy extremely small you can't man the skilled jobs with white people. And, on the other hand, it is felt that ... if you are going to operate business successfully you want to do so in a peaceful atmosphere and the only way to have a peaceful atmosphere is to enable black people to do better jobs and to feel a part of the economic system. And I think it is because Nationalist policy ... was felt to prevent these things happening that it was looked upon as a danger. I would think that most of the business world looked on it as a rather long-term danger. I think probably we [Anglo American] tended to think of it ... as a rather shorter term danger than many of the others did.[112]

[111] Indeed, as David Fasenfest has noted, 'it is small comfort to know that the greed of individual capitalists and their desire to externalize the costs of social and environmental reproduction may in the end be harmful to capitalism'. For this, in itself, is 'unlikely to lead to a dismantling of this system without concerted efforts coordinated at all levels'. He does see 'reason to hope', however, in the many demonstrations of 'the failure of Neoliberalism' that have served to unmask its 'true agenda of reversing the range of programs that make up the social safety net fought for by workers over many decades'. See David Fasenfest, 'Good for Capitalists, Not So Much for Capitalism', *Critical Sociology*, 37, 3, 2011, pp. 259–262.

[112] As quoted in B. Hackland, 'The Economic and Political Context of the Growth of the progressive federal party in South Africa, 1959–78' *Journal of Southern African Studies*, 7, 1, 1980, and in Saul & Gelb, *The Crisis in South Africa*, p. 86. In this volume Gelb and I set out a detailed case that anticipates the one argued here; I then extended this argument, up-dated to the mid-1980s, in several additional chapters as part of a second edition under the same title (New York and London: Monthly Review Press

Indeed, Oppenheimer – worried at the snail's pace of the reform programme of President P. W. Botha that he had earlier praised – also 'warned of possible revolution in white-minority ruled South Africa in five years unless blacks get major concessions'.[113]

The die was chiefly cast when the unrest of the 1970s, already visible enough to unsettle both capital and the apartheid state, escalated, from 1984 on, into a broad-scale eruption of black action – and also found echoes in a rising movement in support of sanctions on South Africa abroad. In such a context, the pace of the defection of capital from the apartheid project (albeit initially and most markedly its English-speaking members) continued to accelerate dramatically – a reality admirably epitomized by Dan O'Meara in his magisterial *Forty Lost Years*.[114] For soon, many far-thinking capitalists from all of capital's fractions could begin to see the future dangers, already quite visible to Oppenheimer in the 1970s, inherent in continuing to link the exploitation (indeed superexploitation) that they thrived upon any too tightly with the racial repression that marked the 'racial-capitalist' system.

In fact, with mass African resistance escalating in the 1970s and especially in the 1980s, the above-mentioned and oft-quoted remark – in the mid-1980s – of big-business insider Zac de Beer takes on its appropriate resonance: 'We all understand how years of apartheid have caused many blacks to reject the economic as well as political system ... We dare not allow the baby of free enterprise to be thrown out with the bathwater of apartheid.'[115] Of even more significance, perhaps, were the comments in 1985 of Gavin Relly, by now Oppenheimer's successor as chairman of the powerful Anglo American Corporation. For in the wake of capital's extreme crisis following international credit withdrawals,[116] Relly led a 'delegation of leading representatives of South African monopoly capital (including the Premier Group, Barclay's Bank, Sanlam and Barlow Rand) ... to Lusaka to confer with the ANC leadership,

---

(cont) and Zed Books, 1986). A number of quotations in this sub-section, notably the several quotations from the *Financial Mail*, are in fact carried over from that book.

[113] As cited in *Globe and Mail* (Toronto, February 4, 1981). On the same occasion Oppenheimer also 'told journalists that Mr. Botha and previous National Party governments, following the official policy of apartheid or racial separation, have squandered too much time in trying to reach an accommodation between South Africa's 4.5 million whites and 20 million blacks. During two years as Prime Minister, he said, Mr. Botha had raised the hopes of blacks with promises of a new deal. At the same time telling whites they must "adapt or die." But, he said, time is running out and unless "substantive changes" are made by the mid-1980s, South Africa could face violent revolution.'

[114] Dan O'Meara, *Forty Lost Years: The Apartheid State and the Politics of the National Party, 1948–1994* (Randberg, S.A. and Athens, OH: Ravan Press and Ohio University Press, 1996).

[115] As quoted in the *Financial Times*, 10 June 1986.

[116] On this topic, also crucial to capital's rethink regarding South Africa during the 1980s, see Patrick Bond, *Against Global Apartheid* (Cape Town: UCT Press, 2001), especially the section 'Geography and financial ascendance, 1970s–90s', pp. 268–270.

including Chris Hani, Thabo Mbeki, Pallo Jordan, and Mac Maharaj and led by Oliver Tambo', noting of that meeting both that 'he had the impression the ANC was not "too keen" to be seen as "marxist" and that he felt they had a good understanding 'of the need for free enterprise.'[117] Time was to demonstrate fully just how perceptive was Relly's 1985 reading of the ANC's own emerging mind-set.

As for Zac de Beer, he was soon to become a key player in progressive business councils more generally, having also assisted in the formation of the liberal Progressive Party (later a part of the Progressive Federal Party that he was briefly to lead). But much the same understanding as de Beer's was also crystallizing globally in the higher realms of the capitalist world. As, again, O'Meara reminds us, American and British capitalists were beginning to rethink the odds in South Africa and to withdraw. Recall also the dramatic warnings (cited above) by Australia's Malcolm Fraser to the South African government to come to its senses before the confrontation there escalated out of control. Fraser's intervention would in turn inspire Brian Mulroney, Canada's Prime Minister not only to put sanctions on the Canadian political agenda but also to push for them both within the Commonwealth and in the G8. Mulroney was not successful at first in the latter forum but then, slowly, Margaret Thatcher and, albeit with even greater reluctance, Ronald Reagan (he was no proponent of the Congressionally-inspired 1986 move to institute economic sanctions upon South Africa for example) began to come over to such an understanding – all the more so as the global 'threat' of the Soviet bloc itself began to wane.

To be sure, capital's tentative embrace of a rethinking about apartheid was also framed by the escalation of public pressure upon it from an emboldened anti-apartheid movement in the West – now responding dramatically to the unsettled economic horizon a turbulent South Africa had begun to present to the world.[118] But note, too, that a continuing and concerted effort to win over the ANC to a post-apartheid order extremely friendly to capitalism was clearly afoot – and beginning to promise results. Not that, in the event, much persuading of the exile group seemed to be required. After all, we have seen what Thabo Mbeki, already a key player during this period, had written, as early as 1981, about the ANC's non-socialist vocation. Now, as also seen in the previous section, 'Lusaka'[119] (along with Angola, the ANC's other main external headquarters) had shown itself quite willing to accept an opening to political power cast in terms quite unthreatening to capital – even if it meant jettisoning the more elaborate dreams of a socialist future that many in the ANC/SACP had once professed to harbour.

True, capitalists would not be very much overtly present during the negotiations period and 'transition' of the early nineties – just as they would be largely

[117] As cited in McKinley, *The ANC and the Liberation Struggle*.
[118] On this, see John S. Saul, *A Partial Victory: The North American Campaign for Southern African Liberation in Global Perspective* (New York: Monthly Review Press, forthcoming).
[119] For use of this particular short-hand to epitomize the ANC's external leadership see Daniel, 'The Mbeki Presidency'.

absent, despite their shared record of remarkable exploitation of carefully controlled African labour over many decades, from the ranks of those under the eventual scrutiny by the Truth and Reconciliation Commission. But the very private level of negotiations – a shadowy second set of parallel negotiations in fact – that capital had felt it necessary to have with the ANC was largely complete by then. Still, capital continued to evoke the promise of the wonders of the market, deploying a range of tactics to seduce 'promising' Africans into their fold: the promises of well-paid employment and position proffered by individual firms, for example, and the 'training programmes' and related 'opportunities' to 'expand their horizons' offered by the World Bank, the IMF and other major global bodies to such African players. Here, in fact, it is in point to quote the conclusion reached by Hein Marais: 'By 1994 ... the left had lost the macroeconomic battle.'[120]

The white response in the 1970s and 1980s: Reform and repression
Amongst whites there was, as seen, a liberal strand of understanding of at least some importance. This saw (from the standpoint of its world-view) the colour-blind production system of capitalism as being imprisoned within an overall racial order of political and social power that it had to accommodate to but with which it was in contradiction. A major expression of this was the aforementioned Progressive Federal Party which included, for example, so principled an advocate of such liberalism as Helen Suzman – and also the above-cited Anglo American Corporation mogul, Harry Oppenheimer, a notable funder of the party itself. This group felt that its position could be expected to slowly but surely eat away at the conscience of the white population – in the name of freedom (and, of course, capitalism). We have seen just how mistaken this liberal viewpoint was with regards to the actual workings of racial capitalism in South Africa over many decades. Nonetheless, there was a point to this position that radicals had eventually to take account of. For the exact nature of the link between racism and capitalism should have been better understood by radicals: the link was best considered as being a *contingent* one and, although long-standing, not a fixed and ineluctable one. Indeed when resistance from below in the 1980s did become potentially revolutionary in import, capital increasingly became (however late in the game) a 'liberal' anti-apartheid force – the better to co-opt the emergent nationalist insurgency into a new post-apartheid, pro-capitalist dispensation.

The National Party was much slower to come to such an understanding, with even Afrikaner capitalists themselves moving a bit more slowly towards such an understanding. Perhaps their own loyalty to the National Party arose from the fact that that Party had done so much to service their needs and aspirations over the decades. Indeed Gelb and I had already written as much in early-1980s, noting

---

[120] Hein Marais, *South Africa – Limits to Change: The Political Economy of Transition* (London: Zed Books, 1995), p. 156.

the much greater prominence of 'Afrikaans-speaking' capital, which 'now probably has as much or more in common with [its] English-speaking counterpart ... as with the blue-collar workers, teachers and civil servants who have traditionally formed the power-base of the National Party'.[121] As hinted earlier, underlying this new strength has been the establishment, since 1948, of numerous new parastatal corporations, managed by Afrikaners. The burgeoning state sector provided the groups clustered around the Nationalist project (particularly nascent Afrikaner capital) with the economic clout to direct the path of accumulation in their own interests, as distinct from the interests of foreign and local English capital. Besides ISCOR (the Iron and Steel Corporation), the Industrial Development Corporation (IDC) and Eskom (electricity), all brought forward from earlier period, there was now ARMSCOR (Armaments Corporation – weapons), SASOL (oil-from-coal) FOSKOR (phosphorus) and SAPPI (South African Pulp and Paper Industries), among others. The advantageous conditions provided for all capital by apartheid, as well as the additional benefits of favourable consideration for Afrikaners in the award of the growing number of state contracts, have linked up with the increased state activity to allow Afrikaner capital – led by financial institutions which have mobilized Afrikaners' savings (the older Cape-based Sanlam and Santam insurance companies and FVB investment company) – to move into, and build up significant stakes in, industry, mining and commerce.[122]

At the same time, it is not at all surprising that even as capital more generally was rethinking its options, so too did many wealthy Afrikaners also begin to shift their perspective as to just how important it felt the retention of apartheid to be to its interests. For this and other reasons what was occurring was, in fact, something of a sea-change within the Afrikaner polity.

Thus O'Meara and others[123] have demonstrated precisely the manner in which the fault lines of class distinction within Afrikanerdom began to eat away at the *volk* ... and at the National Party itself. For the class character of 'Afrikanerdom,' the chief electoral base of the ruling National Party, was visibly shifting, however slowly and uncertainly, and the party itself had begun to fray. In fact, one of the most interesting indices of this occurred as early as 1977, in the waning Vorster years, in a book by A. D. Wassenaar, head of Afrikanerdom's most powerful corporate body, Sanlam. Entitled *The Assault on Private Enterprise: The Freeway to Communism*, 'it lambasted the South African government for its continued paternalism and intervention in the private sector and its refusal to let the logic of the market run. Reacting at least in part to the effect of high state spending in deepening the economic crisis', Waasenaar left any further implications that adopting such a perspective might possibly have for dealing with the race question more or less unstated. But as one of the earliest statements of an apparent 'neo-liberal' position that was to become so pervasive within the definition of reality of dominant classes both Afrikaner and English, it is clear that it could readily feed into the kind of emerging deracialized socio-economic project to which capital would ultimately gravitate.

What of P. W. Botha who became Prime Minister (and eventually 'presi-

---

[121] *Financial Times*, 29 February 1980.
[122] Saul & Gelb, *The Crisis in South Africa*, p. 18–19.
[123] O'Meara's *Forty Lost Years* remains, as noted above, the *locus classicus* of analysis of the National Party's trajectory – from egg to earth as it were.

dent') after John Vorster's fall? Difficult as it may now be to remember, P. W. Botha – even granted that he was ever the bully – came to Prime-Ministerial office, in the wake of Vorster and the 'information scandal' that was Mulder-gate, as a reformer, a *verligte* (enlightened reformer) over and against the serried ranks of NP *verkramptes* (unbending deep-dyed racists). Indeed, Botha would even earn from the prestigious Johannesburg-based business journal *Financial Mail* the accolade of 1979's 'Man of the Year',[124] the magazine finding in Botha 'a driving resolve ... to move away from the narrow sectarian approach which had characterized the regimes of other Nationalist Party Prime Ministers'[125] and to move toward more straightforwardly liberal-capi-talist solutions to South Africa's pressing problems, economic and political. For, as the magazine opined editorially on various occasions near the time (1980):

> In the coming decade of crisis, what South Africa needs is skilled crisis management ... If South Africa is to enter an era of (relative) stability and prosperity, government must ensure that as many people as possible share in that prosperity and find their interests best served by an alliance with capitalism. ... Defusing the social time-bomb ... can only be achieved through negotiation – not with men with Kalashnikovs but with the authentic leaders [?] of the black people.[126]

Perhaps Botha appeared momentarily to be the man for this job. Yet, as time would reveal more clearly, Botha was seeking to 'reform' in large part in order to preserve: to preserve, in his case, the structure of racial hierarchy and not to make the much more unequivocal offer of a 'mere' class hierarchy that the capi-talists would increasingly offer as the 1980s dragged on. As Nigel Worden summarized the period to which we now turn our attention: 'The National Party government experimented with a number of reforms designed to adjust apartheid to changing economic and social circumstances, while still retaining a monopoly of political power. But the spiral of resistance and repression inten-sified.'[127] Botha would ultimately fail in his rather contradictory attempts. More-over, although his successor Eugene de Klerk was fundamentally of the same persuasion as Botha, he would feel forced to go even further in a 'reform' direc-tion than had his predecessor – while still, almost to the very end, trying to safe-guard some of the structures (such as vetoes, minority guarantees and the like) of the racist order itself!

Thus, in the 1970s and as a new wave of popular agitation begin to surface that was fired by both proletariat and precariat in the cities and in the town-ships,[128] Botha and others did know that some pre-emptive initiatives, beyond

---

[124] As discussed in Saul & Gelb, *The Crisis in South Africa*, p. 18.
[125] *Financial Mail*, 30 November 1979.
[126] *Financial Mail*, 1 February and 6 June. 1980.
[127] Nigel Worden, *The Making of Modern South Africa: Conquest, Segregation and Apartheid* (Oxford: Blackwell, 1994), p. 121.
[128] See again, on the distinction between 'proletariat' and 'precariat', Saul, 'What Working-Class?'

the Bantustan strategy and brute force, were also advisable.[129] Of course, Verwoerd's bizarre 'Bantustan' initiative did grind on in many of its particulars, now complemented by various flimsy initiatives mounted with respect to 'community councils' for urban Africans and a new 'President's Council' at the national level designed to lure into the tent the Indians and Coloured communities.[130] But the key features of the 'Total Strategy', the approach now favoured and advocated by Botha and his coterie, were several of those quite novel attempts at 'formative action' that we have earlier discussed – as framed, notably, by the Wiehann and Riekert reports. As seen, the former foresaw some stemming of growing worker radicalization as being likely to follow from the opening up to a (legalized but carefully controlled) unionization process for black workers. The latter (Riekart) anticipated some moderation of post-Soweto urban disturbances as being likely to follow from a certain firming up of access (by some blacks) to confirmed urban status and to some new (albeit limited) rights to housing.[131] The results, as the renewed (and quite dramatic) internal uprising of the mid-1980s would soon show, were to be quite different from any mere domesticating of resistance, however. For the fact is that Botha, the National Party, and the apartheid state more generally, were now trying to do several seemingly contradictory things at the same time.

The problem followed from their very interpretation of 'Total Strategy', of course – an interpretation that also rationalized the formidable centralization of power and command into Botha's own hands as Prime Minister (later President) and, under his leadership, into the hands of the 'securocrats' of the police and (especially) the military.[132] Professing themselves to be following the lead of such global gurus as Beaufre and Huntington, their 'security state' sought to 'reform' and to 'liberalize' just enough to take the steam out of the kettle of popular protest – but to make such (limited) 'reform' stick with as much force as would prove to be 'necessary'. In doing such – the acceptance of the fact of black trade unions and the legalizing of the permanency of the presence of some significant numbers of blacks in the urban areas – the National Party did, to be sure, move some distance away from the main premises of traditional 'apartheid' – far enough at any rate to accelerate the rightward drift of many amongst the lower ranks of Afrikanerdom who felt themselves to be threatened by change (these now came to strengthen the ranks of Andres Treuernicht's Conservative Party and other such dark forces of genuine reaction as Eugene

---

[129] Gelb and I in our own writing of the time (*The Crisis in South Africa*, pp. 3–4) evoked Antonio Gramsci and Stuart Hall and their concept of 'formative action' to more effectively examine steps taken by the ruling group to retain control of an 'organic crisis' of the kind we found South Africa to be confronting.

[130] For a somewhat more detailed but still admirably succinct account of these complexities see Nigel Worden's Chapter 6, 'Apartheid in Decline' in his *The Making of Modern South Africa*.

[131] On Riekert, Wiehann and related initiatives taken within the NP's new reform strategy of the late 1970s see, again, Saul & Gelb, *The Crisis in South Africa*,

[132] See Philip Frankel, *Pretoria's Praetorians: Civil Military Relations in South Africa*, Cambridge: Cambridge University Press, 1984.

Terreblanche and his Afrikaner Weerstandsbeweging (AWB) and Constand Viljoen and his Freedom Front).[133]

Nonetheless the 'reform' so envisaged could actually do very little to quell the popular (black) rejection of the fundamentally racist predilections of National Party reformers. For the black population increasingly sought not some mildly improved terms within the overall apartheid framework of power but, instead, a full-scale change, democratic and transformative, of that very framework; it was on this basis that the further push from below that fired the popular uprising of 1984–86 was launched, in fact, and this is also precisely where the other, darker, side of Total Strategy came so grimly into play. For the policing function of the 'security state' was now deemed to be absolutely essential. Finely honed as such a state apparatus had been through the preceding decades of imposing apartheid, it was fully prepared to be tough, brutal and merciless enough to attempt to force the African population to be (rather less than) 'half-free' – and to keep quiet about the rest.

This remorseless side of the story cannot be fully rehearsed here. Suffice to say that there was now locked into place a reign of terror by the state, the abuse of power that this embodied becoming much of the focus of the post-apartheid Truth and Reconciliation Commission (TRC). True, such a preoccupation would come, negatively, to deflect the TRC's attention away from the more mundane structures of corporate and political power that had long sanctioned and bolstered apartheid. Nonetheless, there were more than enough chilling accounts of the impact of this underside of Botha-ism presented to serve as a useful reminder of just what apartheid had actually meant in practice over all the years of its grim sway.[134]

Meanwhile, the neo-liberal clock was ticking for the National Party as well. Indeed, the latter-day economic strategy of the National Party-in-power was

[133] Botha's credibility, and also that of both the South African Defence Force, and of any predominantly militarized strategy for handling South Africa's contradictions more generally, were further undermined by the striking failure of the South African Defence Force to defeat the Angolans and Cubans in Angola, especially at Cuito Cuanavale. Indeed the ignominious flight from Angola in the wake of the confrontation at Cuito would soon see South African (and American) capitulation to the United Nations' writ in South-West Africa/Namibia (South Africa's 'fifth province' as it was sometimes referred to) and further shift the balance of power and influence within the South African white elite – this being one of several factors leading to de Klerk's ascendancy. See Piero Gleijeses, *Conflicting Missions: Havana, Washington and Africa, 1959–1976* (Chapel Hill, NC and London: University of North Carolina Press, 2002) and Gleijeses, *Visions of Freedom: Havana, Washington, Pretoria, and the Struggle for Southern Africa, 1976–1991* (Chapel Hill, NC and London: University of North Carolina Press, 2013).

[134] See, among other sources, the six volume official report of the TRC (Cape Town: Truth and Reconciliation Commission, 1998); in addition there as numerous nightmarish book length accounts of the most horrific nooks and crannies of the period such as Eugene de Kock's autobiographical volume, *A Long Night's Damage: Working for the Apartheid State* (Saxonwold, S.A.: Conta, 1998); Andrew Minaar et. al. (eds), *The Hidden Hand: Covert Operations in South Africa* (Pretoria: Human Sciences Research

itself, by the end of the 1980s, increasingly premised on the freshly established neo-liberal script being written by global capitalism. This was why, despite Botha's bluster, so many even within the apartheid government were particularly alert to negative signals from that quarter, and why the South African state now sought to create an ever more free-market context within which capital could operate quite freely. True, this might appear to be rather counter-intuitive in light of Botha's own otherwise *dirigiste*, and still quite racist, approach to the overall society. But it was precisely onto this kind of economic terrain that capital, and an increasing number of centrist political actors, sought, with ultimate success, to draw the ANC – itself, in any case, an increasingly willing 'victim' of this particular ploy!

In the event de Klerk himself advanced this 'strategy' dramatically, although, like Botha, he did not yield up any such 'reform' entirely straightforwardly. For he too was still trying to have it both ways. Thus (as we will see in the following chapter), even after his release of Mandela and the unbanning of the ANC, he continued, throughout most of the subsequent transition period, to deploy the state's cruel apparatus of enforcement, and to manifest a toleration (to put it charitably) of the malign activities of various so-called 'third force' elements and of Buthelezi's blood-thirsty cohort in an attempt to either defeat the ANC outright or, if not that, at least to skew the transition in the direction of more white-friendly outcomes. Not for de Klerk, until very late in the day, any mere reliance on shared trans-racial class interests to safeguard privilege beyond apartheid. Nonetheless, in the end and after a bumpy road (the grim events of Bisho and Boipatong massacres and the killing fields of KwaZulu and the Vaal townships having demonstrated the abyss that threatened to swallow the country) he came to feel he had no choice. Between chaos and the acceptance of a new ruling-class coalition transcending race he increasingly saw no realistic, more overtly racist, alternative.

(cont) Council, 1994); Terry Bell, *Unfinished Business: South African, Apartheid and Truth* (London: Verso, 2003); Jacques Pauw, *Into the Heart of Darkness: Confessions of Apartheid's Assassins* (Johannesburg: Jonathan Ball Publishers, 1997); James Saunders, *Apartheid's Friends: The Rise and Fall of South Africa's Secret Service* (London: John Murray, 2006).

3.
The Apartheid Endgame, 1990–1994

JOHN S. SAUL

On the one hand, as we have seen, capital (both local and global) was increasingly on side, its conviction growing that the ANC was the one force that could actually deliver an insurgent population to acceptance of a deal quite unthreatening in substance both to capital as well as to those whites who were securely lodged in the upper strata of society. On the other hand, however, there was the insurgent proletariat and precariat (as represented, notably, by COSATU and the UDF): yet they too were being brought, slowly but surely, to heel by the ANC – the rank and file of both proletariat and precariat now to be rendered politically, as we have suggested above, as presumptive 'citizens' rather than as assertive and active comrades in a continuing struggle for genuine liberation.

The stage was thus set for 'transition' (however contradictory it might prove to be) ... or was it? True, the ANC could look forward to the more public set of negotiations, those with the apartheid state, with some confidence – now that it had begun, by the late 1980s, to have acceptance of where it might, in the long run, really count: in the camp of that very capital with which it had, in fact, actually been negotiating for some years. But there were a number of other bridges to be crossed during the four deeply troubled years that separated Mandela's release in 1990 and the unbanning of the ANC and the SACP from the first genuinely free, all-in, election of 1994 – and there were a number of other players at the transition table to be dealt with cautiously, even somewhat nervously.

Certainly, in this then prevailing context of apparent stalemate, there was, as noted in the previous section, the substantial residue of apartheid polity, state and army, still holding the reins of governmental power, with none of these quite certain as to how much political power they could or should concede. In this crucial sphere alone the spectres of 'power-sharing', ethnic vetoes and much worse could be seen to loom. But there were other forces too, forces with even less commitment to either a deracialized capitalist or an ANC-led future than had the NP and its state. There was Gatsha Buthelezi, the Zulu leader, never quite a 'stooge' of the government but someone who was quite prepared to become its active partner in countering, in blood, the ANC. There was the White Right, too, from Eugene Terreblanche and his AWB (though this force would eventually disqualify itself with its ill-fated raid into Bophutatswana in March, 1994) through to General Viljoen. The latter's own vaunted presence was, in fact, ultimately to dwindle away into an unsuccessful bid for a special *volkstaat* to be created for exclusive Afrikaner presence within the broader boundaries of South Africa, but not before his movement, the Freedom Front, posed a shadowy threat, like that from Buthelezi, right up until a few days before the election.

We will have to return briefly to such ultra-right forces below, though we should remind ourselves that, by the late 1980s, even more salient forces had also been assembled that would feed into the change process – and facilitate the eventual erasure of apartheid. These were:

- a forceful mass movement, now partnered with a resurgent ANC but fuelled initially by black demands for liberation and by the popular actions which had given them weight (though that force was itself fragmented to some degree by alternative expressions of political purpose as manifested, principally, by the Zulu-centred manoeuvrings of Buthelezi);
- a white polity in power, intransigent and unbending at one level but vulnerable, at another, to various shifts and fissures that would be of importance as events unfolded;
- capital itself, local and international, long committed to a partnership with racial rule/apartheid in South Africa but increasingly prepared, in its most sophisticated circles, to recalculate the odds and possible range of outcomes as the situation dictated.

As we shall see, it was a deal between the ANC and capital that was in the works, and the white government would finally abandon apartheid and also accede to such a deal. The result: the ANC did ultimately win ... although capital did too.

Cutting a deal: On 'compromise' as anti-climax

How then accurately to interpret such a transition? A Fanonist framework for doing so is immediately tempting. This carries us back to an earlier section (where Steve Biko's own familiarity with Fanon's arguments was noted). After all, Fanon was the most scorching critic of the false decolonization that Biko thought South Africa might, because of its distorted, racially-structured nature, be spared. But recall Fanon's classic short-hand description of decolonization in the more northern parts of Africa where independence had arrived while he was still alive:

> The national middle class discovers its historic mission: that of intermediary. Seen through its eyes, its mission has nothing to do with transforming the nation; it consists, prosaically, of being the transmission line between the nation and a capitalism, rampant though camouflaged, which today puts on the masque of neo-colonialism [recolonization].[1]

Is this not what we can see all too clearly to have happened in South Africa as well: a power-grab by a middle class risen from among the recently oppressed population who now, riding the back of 'liberation struggle', had thrust them-

---

[1] Frantz Fanon, *The Wretched of the Earth*, p. 122. As Fanon continues, 'The national middle class will be quite content with the role of the Western bourgeoisie's business agent and it will play the part without any complexes in a most dignified manner'.

selves forward, both in the state and the private sector, to take the role of well-rewarded junior partners of global capital?

There are, of course, other possible perspectives. Some, for example, will merely offer the self-exculpatory argument that 'globalization made me do it' as sufficient explanation of the ANC's capitulation to capitalism: the Soviet bloc quickly disappearing, a much too powerful capitalist system, global and domestic, left standing. This is the kind of 'fatalism' offered up by many ANC apologists: mere resignation to 'necessity' as the rationale for the government's opting unapologetically for the capitalist road (however much such capitulation might be presented as being social-democratically-tinged). The essence of the position: Africa and Africans had no choice; whatever the outcome of taking the rightward tack, 'there is no alternative' (as Margaret Thatcher so often reiterated). Small wonder that South African President Thabo Mbeki could himself, famously and quite specifically state (and with some apparent glee): 'Just call me a Thatcherite.'[2]

One version of this position rests on the aforementioned assumption that by the late 1980s a stalemate had been reached in South Africa. As we have seen, the mass movement for democratic change, now increasingly grouped behind the African National Congress (ANC), had mounted a near-insurrection in the mid-1980s and had survived the especially brutal repression of the latter part of the decade. However, it could not expect easily to overthrow the apartheid state. As for those in command of that state, they could, up to a point, contain mass opposition but not hope to stabilize the situation sufficiently to reassure nervous investors or to calm the growing international distaste for their racist project. Linked to this there were now also marked tensions within both Afrikanerdom and within the ruling National Party itself more particularly. For a new Afrikaner business class (a principal beneficiary of NP rule over the years) had, together with its English-speaking counterpart, begun to sense that the historical marriage between the twin structures of capitalist exploitation and racial oppression, so long a profitable (if contested) one, was no longer viable economically or politically.

This would have crucial implications: in the end, the NP, now led by F. W. de Klerk who succeeded P. W. Botha to the Presidency in 1989, would see that it was becoming necessary to deal in one way or another with the ANC. Indeed, as seen, a certain rapprochement with the latter had already begun, from the mid-1980s, through a series of meetings abroad of members of the Afrikaner and business elites with ANC representatives and also through more secretive conclaves of NP leaders with the imprisoned Nelson Mandela. True, de Klerk's announcement, in February, 1990, of the unbanning of the ANC, the PAC and the SACP and the release of Mandela after 27 years in prison would come as something of a surprise and a shock to most observers. To now reconstruct the unfolding of events in the late 80s makes it seem much less so.

Beyond stalemate, then, and on to a new South Africa. Still, nothing was entirely straightforward yet with regard to the full implications of 'stalemate',

---

[2] Thabo Mbeki, then Vice-President, as cited in William Gumede, *Thabo Mbeki and the Battle for the Soul of the ANC* (Cape Town: Zebra Press, 2005), p. 89, in speaking at the June 1996 launching of the GEAR programme.

the troubled and contradictory politics that it produced also being a key reference point for the thinking of such a prominent player on this new terrain as Joe Slovo. Thus Slovo, a key South African Communist Party and Umkhonto weSizwe leader and now to be one of the major protagonists (and theorists) of the South African transition, wrote:

> We are negotiating because towards the end of the 80s we concluded that, as a result of its escalating crisis, the apartheid power bloc was no longer able to continue ruling in the old way and was genuinely seeking some break with the past. At the same time, we were clearly not dealing with a defeated enemy and an early revolutionary seizure of power by the liberation movement could not be realistically posed. This conjuncture of the balance of forces (which continues to reflect current reality) provided a classic scenario which placed the possibility of negotiations on the agenda. And we correctly initiated the whole process in which the ANC was accepted as the major negotiating adversary.

Yet the question as to how precisely the ANC could now be expected to position itself and to deal concretely with the new situation of apparent 'stalemate' was a central one – bringing into focus a whole range of questions about the transition itself.

For, after all, a quite basic prior question concerns the fact of the almost exclusive salience now granted to the ANC as the spokesman for liberation. As one noted South African historian, surveying both the ANC's overall history and, more specifically, the transition period itself, felt forced to state that 'the story of how the "exiled" ANC gained ascendancy over the internal movement, why the UDF chose to go into voluntary liquidation in 1991 and what the implications of this decision have been for the making of a non-racial democracy has yet to be fully traced and explored'.[3] Unfortunately the succeeding decade still has not produced firm, illuminating or conclusive answers to such crucial questions from either historians or relevant historical actors. It is here in fact that Rusty Bernstein's perspective, as quoted in the preceding chapter, is so instructive ... and so sobering. For, when he wrote, he was not arguing against the notion that a 'stalemate' existed. What he was registering, however, and quite critically, was the fact that the ANC, in encouraging the UDF to merely evaporate, had literally disarmed and disqualified the popular movement from playing any active and on-going role in expanding the terms of liberation in any next round of continuing struggle in which it would still, in the opinion of many, prove necessary to confront capital and/or residual 'white power'.

For this was precisely what seemed to be needed in South Africa – despite, as noted above, the oft-repeated argument on the right (and increasingly from the ANC itself) that formal democracy in a colour-blind capitalist order represented the limit of what was possible at the then-present moment of transition. In merely dismissing all possible claims to socialist aspiration, it was said that the incumbent global politico-economic order would, quite simply, not allow any more radical change to occur. This despite the fact that, as in many other countries of the

---

[3]   Saul Dubow, *The African National Congress* (Stroud: Sutton Publishing, 2000), p. 106.

Global South that had, like South Africa, been 'deeply scarred by capitalism and imperialism', little developmental promise lay in rejecting the transformation that a meaningful socialist project could deliver, and the healing that only the realization of social justice and self-conscious collective activity can promise.

I have myself spelled out elsewhere the case for such a project.[4] But so too have others, and without falling into the trap of jejune abstraction. This project would focus the production process on the centrality of meeting the actual material requirements of the people themselves (a 'socialism of expanded reproduction') and on the requirement that the people's democratic voice actually be heard in order to discipline any leadership that might assert itself, precisely to keep such a project on track. It seems clear that in a world marked ominously by the political and economic hierarchies of global capitalism, what would be required was a serious leadership of genuinely radical intent and an active and committed populace – on board for what would be a challenging and dangerous project to mount. Difficult and daunting to undertake? No doubt. Small wonder, perhaps, that the leadership of the ANC merely 'chickened out' – hesitant to become warriors in a new stage of class struggle just as, apparently, far more comfortable options, in state employment and in the private sectors, were opening up to them.

'Chickened out?' – note that this is not my phrase but that of no less an activist and observer than Ronnie Kasrils, a long-time Central Committee Member of the SACP, member of the Executive Committee of the ANC and one-time head of military intelligence for Umkhonto weSizwe, the ANC's armed wing, and MP and senior minister in the post-apartheid ANC government. Kasrils identifies, in the period 1991–96, what he labels as having been a 'Faustian moment', a moment when 'the battle for the ANC's soul got under way, and was eventually lost to corporate power; we were entrapped by the neoliberal economy – or, as some today cry, we "sold our people down the river".[5]

> [W]hat I call our Faustian moment came when we took an IMF loan on the eve of our first democratic election. That loan, with strings attached that precluded a radical economic agenda, was considered a necessary evil, as were concessions to keep negotiations on track and take delivery of the promised land for our people. Doubt had come to reign supreme: we believed, wrongly, there was no other option; that we had to be cautious, since by 1991 our once powerful ally, the Soviet Union, bankrupted by the arms race, had collapsed. Inexcusably, we had lost faith in the ability of our own revolutionary masses to overcome all obstacles. Whatever the threats to isolate a radicalising South Africa, the world could not have done without our vast reserves of minerals. To lose our nerve was not necessary or inevitable. The ANC leadership needed to remain determined, united and free of corruption – and, above all, to hold

---

4   See 'Is Socialism Still An Alternative?' – Essay 5 in Saul, *Liberation Lite*.
5   Ronnie Kasrils, 'How the ANC's Faustian pact sold out South African's poorest: In the early 1990s we in the leadership of the ANC made a serious error. Our people are still paying the price', *The Guardian*, 24 June 2013, this being an extract from the introduction to a new edition of his autobiography *Armed and Dangerous: My Undercover Struggle Against Apartheid*, first published by Heinemann Books in 1993. The extended quotations that follow are from this article as it appeared in *The Guardian*.

on to its revolutionary will. Instead, we chickened out. The ANC leadership needed to remain true to its commitment of serving the people. This would have given it the hegemony it required not only over the entrenched capitalist class but over emergent elitists, many of whom would seek wealth through black economic empowerment, corrupt practices and selling political influence.

To break apartheid rule through negotiation, rather than a bloody civil war, seemed then an option too good to be ignored. However, at that time, the balance of power was with the ANC, and conditions were favourable for more radical change at the negotiating table than we ultimately accepted. It is by no means certain that the old order, apart from isolated rightist extremists, had the will or capability to resort to the bloody repression [anticipated] by Mandela's leadership. If we had held our nerve, we could have pressed forward without making the concessions we did.

Why did they not do so? Here Kasrils is less convincing. He tends to see the ANC elite – though he does offer the above-quoted mild *mea culpa* as regards his own behaviour during this crucial period – as having been just too busy to notice that a handful of 'young ANC intellectuals schooled in western economics', and working hand-in-glove with Harry Oppenheimer, had managed to steal the game away from the masses while the ANC brass was not looking! Yet this is simply not a plausible excuse for an outcome which we have seen to be so deeply rooted in the ANC negotiating practice throughout the 1980s and concerning which Kasrils himself can only say that 'we in the leadership in the ANC made a serious error. Our people are still paying the price'! But can what he now terms to have been a 'pact with the devil' and on-going 'descent into darkness [even now] be curtailed'? He does concede that, in part, and among other things, the 'strategies and tactics of the grassroots – trade unions, civic and community organisations, women's and youth groups – signpost the way ahead with their non-violent and dignified but militant action' – and he offers the hope that more attention will be paid to those he defines as being 'most voters', these he suggests desiring 'socialist policies, not measures inclined to serve big business interests, more privatisation and neoliberal economics'.

In sum, he concludes:

All means to eradicate poverty, which was Mandela's and the ANC's sworn promise to the 'poorest of the poor', were lost in the process. Nationalization of the mines and heights of the economy as envisaged by the Freedom charter was abandoned. The ANC accepted responsibility for a vast apartheid-era debt, which should have been cancelled. A wealth tax on the super-rich to fund developmental projects was set aside, and domestic and international corporations, enriched by apartheid, were excused from any financial reparations. Extremely tight budgetary obligations were instituted that would tie the hands of any future governments; obligations to implement a free-trade policy and abolish all forms of tariff protection in keeping with neo-liberal free trade fundamentals were accepted. Big corporations were allowed to shift their main listings abroad. In Terreblanche's opinion, these ANC concessions constituted 'treacherous decisions that [will] haunt South Africa for generations to come'[6] ... [In fact] an ANC-

---

[6] Kasrils is here quoting from Sampie Terreblanche's newest book *Lost in Transformation: South Africa's Search for a New Future Since 1986* (Johannesburg: KMM Review Publishing Company, 2012) to which we return briefly in Chapter 6.

Communist party leadership eager to assume political office (myself no less than others) readily accepted this devil's pact, only to be damned in the process. It has bequeathed an economy so tied in to the neoliberal global formula and market fundamentalism that there is very little room to alleviate the plight of most of our people.

But here we slide towards reflections on the present situation in South Africa that we will have to return to in our concluding chapter (Chapter 7). For the moment, however, we must register the stark fact that in Kasrils' judgement the ANC had merely 'chickened out'. But consider too, and along somewhat similar lines, other related 'explanations' of this all-too-startling and dispiriting denouement to a liberation struggle. For example, no less an observer than Naomi Klein has offered one view as to why stalemate had led to something very close to capitulation and a largely uncritical embrace of global capital's own cherished agenda for a 'new' South Africa. For she does indeed see the ANC as having become the prisoners of capital but this had occurred, she suggests, because the ANC was merely short-sighted and naïve as regards the dangers of capitalist entanglements!

Klein does then summon up some strong witnesses to support her view: economist Vishnu Padayachee, for example, whom she paraphrases as arguing that 'none of this happened because of some grand betrayal on the part of the ANC leaders but simply because they were outmaneuvered on a series of issues that seemed less than crucial at the time – but turned out to hold South Africa's lasting liberation in the balance'. Similarly, William Gumede's view, as directly quoted by Klein, is that

> 'if people felt [the political negotiations] weren't going well there would be mass protests. But when the economic negotiators would report back, people thought it was technical.' This perception was encouraged by Mbeki, who portrayed the talks as 'administrative' and as being of no popular concern. As a result he [Gumede] told me, with great exasperation, 'We missed it! We missed the real story.'

Yet Gumede, Klein further notes, 'came to understand that it was at those "technical" meetings that the true future of his country was being decided – though few understood it at the time'. But, one is tempted to ask, had Padayachee, Gumede, and even Klein not read their Fanon?[7] For it is, in fact, impossible to think that

[7]   Vishnu Padayachee and William Gumede as quoted in Naomi Klein, *The Shock Doctrine: The Rise of* Disaster Capitalism (Toronto: Alfred A. Knopf Canada, 2007), Chapter 10: 'Democracy Born in Chains: South Africa's Constricted Freedom', pp. 233–261. It is, of course, true that the ANC was indeed wary with respect to numerous fronts – potential conflicts premised on potentially potent realities of 'difference' within South African society defined by racial, cultural, and political party/movement identifications. These have led another observer, for example, to argue that 'the balance of power and the potentially catastrophic effects of a descent into civil war dictate[d] that negotiated transition rather than revolutionary transformation is the order of the day – and that a settlement ... require significant compromises to allay the concerns of the white elite' (Steven Friedman, 'South Africa's Reluctant Transition', *Journal of Democracy*, 4, 2, 1993, p. 57). Yet the acknowledgement of such plausible reasons for caution must not be allowed to obscure the essential contribution to 'compromise' of the ANC's own

the ANC leadership, having sought assiduously to will just such an outcome, such a 'false decolonization', from at least the mid-1980s, could have 'missed it' – missed, that is, the main point as to what was happening to South Africa.

Or what of an even more recent (and even more revealing) pronouncement by Jeremy Cronin, a speech entitled 'How we misread the situation in the 1990s'? [8] Cronin, a long-time Communist Party and ANC activist (and a minister in the present Zuma government), presents an even more fatuous argument about the 'errors' of the 1990s than that of Klein though it does, nonetheless, bear a strong resemblance to hers. For naïveté is again presented as being the key, Cronin also seeing the ANC as merely having taken its eye off the ball – albeit for 19 years! His variant of this argument: 'In particular, we vastly overestimated the patriotic credentials of South African monopoly capitalism (and its soon to emerge narrow BEE [Black Economic Empowerment] hangers on)'; these advised us 'to open all doors and windows to attract inward investment flows'. The result:

> [A]lmost the exact opposite has occurred. Surplus generated inside SA, the sweat and toil of South African workers, has flown out of the open windows and open doors. Between 20% and 25% of GDP has been dis-invested out of the country since 1994. Trade liberalization in the first decade of democracy blew a cold wind though our textile and clothing sector, though our agriculture and agro-processing sector and by 2001 a million formal sector jobs had been lost.

As for the 19 years just mentioned, it is actually Cronin himself who raises this spectre, asking precisely 'Why had it taken us nearly 19 years to appreciate the need for a second, radical phase of our democratic transitions?' But he really gives no answer to his own question nor makes any attempt to explain two decades of extraordinary naïveté as to the progressive propensities of 'South African monopoly capitalism'. Instead, he now claims that the government feels a renewed responsibility to 'the organized working class' and to 'the great mass of unorganized workers, and the mass of the proletarianized unemployed, the 37% of South Africans, the urban and rural poor' (in short, 'the great mass of marginalized South Africans'), one that is moving the ANC/SACP – under the leadership of Jacob Zuma, of all people – to move away from neo-liberalism and towards both a more active and interventionist state and, indeed, a 'more radical second phase of the democratic transition'!

Kasrils? Klein? Cronin? But surely the more accurate 'explanation' for failure than any of theirs, one much more true to the facts of the 1990s, would appear to be neither mere error nor misguided naïveté; instead the key was the simple fact that an active choice *for* capitalism was being made quite consciously by those moving towards power – a decision to embrace and to celebrate capitalism, its present and its ostensibly promising future. For many, this might seem, in light of the continent's recent history a difficult project for any concerned fighter for

[(*cont*)] underlying rightist/capitalism-friendly economic calculations, as Klein's reading risks encouraging.

[8]   Jeremy Cronin, 'How we misread the situation in the 1990s', speech to the 12th National Congress of the trade union SACTWU (as issued by the SACP, 22 August 2013).

liberation to adopt? Yet in elevated circles in South Africa the choosing of such a course would soon be seen as constituting, quite simply, common sense. Mandela, for one and despite his having an apparently alternative vision immediately on his release from prison, came to accept a firmly capitalist South Africa in just such a 'commonsensical' manner.[9] Moreover, Trevor Manuel, Tito Mboweni and Thabo Mbeki (whom we have already witnessed, in the 1980s, to be playing a key role in crafting such an outcome in the ANC's meetings with South African businessmen in exile) joined right in – while many other erstwhile ANC activists themselves moved briskly into the private sector.[10]

True, as international sanctions began to bite from the mid-80s, de Klerk had (by 1989) himself begun to bend towards the overbearing 'logic' of global capitalism: transferring the state's administrative oversight from 'securocrats' to 'econocrats'; beginning the phasing out of the existing inward-oriented siege economy (state investments, border industrial zones, subsidies and low interest rates – a phasing out that would continue through the '1990s); adopting, in 1989, the IMF's macro-economic strictures; privatizing the Iron and Steel Corporation (ISCOR); installing, in 1991, a Value Added Tax recommended by the IMF; and embracing in 1993 a new, extremely market-friendly, 'Normative Economic Model'. Meanwhile, from 1990 to 1994, the ANC, at this level of policy-making at least, joined in, even as more than a dozen World Bank 'reconnaissance missions' probed every sectoral area (the ANC forcing the remnants of its erstwhile Mass Democratic Movement allies to cooperate). But Patrick Bond has further listed a whole set of crucial, global capital-friendly strategic (if also highly questionable) economic policy choices made during the first half-decade of the ANC's being in or near power.[11]

Thus, the ANC sanctioned intermediary agencies like Anglo American Corporation's Urban Foundation think-tank and the Development Bank of Southern Africa to play crucial roles in shaping a transition in hotly contested fields like housing, water, energy, land, healthcare and education. There was also the October 1993 agreement by the National Party government, ANC and foreign banks to repay the apartheid-era debt – $25 billion in foreign loans from commercial banks, which in practice prevented Mandela's first ANC government from the future undertaking of extensive social spending. But this agreement to 'to pay illegitimate apartheid era debt' was linked to taking an unnecessary IMF loan of US$850 million (December 1993) with predictable neo-liberal strings attached (including significant public sector wage and spending cuts).

[9] Recall Mandela's apparent hailing, in 1994, of the free market as a 'magic elixir' in his speech to the joint session of the Houses of Congress in Washington. For an especially smug view of the entire transition process see Michael C. O'Dowd, *The O'Dowd Thesis and the Triumph of Democratic Capitalism* (Sandton, S.A.: Free Market Foundation of South Africa, 1996).

[10] Indeed, some of these latter were also to be involved in the breakaway COPE movement that, in the wake of Mbeki's overthrow and in a [hostile but largely false] anticipation of Zuma's radicalization of the ANC project, launched itself in 2008 – and contested the 2009 election, not very successfully, as a possible national liberation-linked alternative to the right of ANC.

[11] The following several paragraphs draw on Patrick Bond, private communication, 2013.

Meanwhile, the Interim Constitution in November 1993 not only assured property rights but an 'independent Reserve Bank' as well, one banker-biased and well-insulated from democracy – thus setting the stage, in Bond's words, for the 'raising [of] interest rates to South Africa's highest real levels ever'. Then in January 1994, IMF manager Michel Camdessus apparently instructed Nelson Mandela to reappoint apartheid-era Finance Minister (Derek Keys) and Central Bank governor (Chris Stals). The *'piéce de* [non]*résistance'* of all this? By 1996, the ANC leadership would even craft for itself and the country the firmly neo-liberal GEAR ('Growth, Employment and Reconstruction') strategy – declared by Trevor Manuel, to be 'non-negotiable' – to replace 1994's mildly more left-leaning Reconstruction and Development Programme, the ANC's campaign platform.

Interestingly, Pippa Green's hagiographical biography of Trevor Manuel, one of the chief architects of the ANC's economic strategy, is entitled, boldly and altogether instructively, *Choice, Not Fate*.[12] In its pages we find the case for recolonization and for the above itemized policy package being presented as, primarily, a very smart and consciously-made developmental choice.[13] Some beneficiaries of this choice will have had quite self-interested and crass motives for making it, of course. Others may have thought – this being the perennial illusion of social democrats everywhere – that you can 'permit' capital to do the heavy lifting of accumulation and the provisioning of material requirements while 'the good guys', from on high, and through taxation and a variety of not too onerous 'controls', bend such a capitalist system to meet a range of humane social preferences and less tangibly material 'needs'.

Lost to this latter version of the project, however, is the way in which class imperatives and the uneven distribution of power almost inevitably rot out shared social purpose under capitalism, even as capitalism is also fostering a broad culture of consumerism and 'possessive individualism' that is unlikely to readily sustain any alternative, more high-minded, popular politics. Operating here is a kind of Gresham's law that affects every case of a politics that is merely mildly progressive: under this 'law' one witnesses, invariably, the gradual debasing of the coinage of progressive socio-political purpose and the fostering of a merely parasitic state and a self-seeking governing class. This is, at best, what I would myself judge to have become of South Africa's presumed transi-

[12] Pippa Green, *Choice, Not Fate: The Life and Times of Trevor Manuel* (Johannesburg: Penguin Books, 2008); this book, which focuses primarily on Manuel's crucial role post-apartheid in helping further to shape such a truncated transition once in power is also a startling example of hagiography (both as regards Manuel and also the ANC at its most conservative). But its title is also an arresting short-hand advertisement for the way in which the ANC would apparently like to present itself to right-thinking readers!

[13] We might be forgiven for thinking that this 'choice' has not proven to be quite so 'smart' from the point of view of the vast mass of the South African population, however. Meanwhile, for another clear statement of the 'official' position – as articulated by Alan Hirsch, Chief Director of Economic Policy in the Presidency – see Hirsch's book *Season of Hope: Economic Reform under Mandela and Mbeki* (Pietermaritzburg: UKZN Press, 2005), to which we will also have occasion to return in the following chapter.

tion – and even this kind of pretence as to the retention of some higher aspiration and some higher purpose was fast to fade away in ruling circles.

Floating a deal: Mandela and Mbeki, de Klerk and capital

To become more concrete, we can first remind ourselves that serious negotiations did actually begin in the second half of the 1980s with the ANC increasingly invited inside the tent of compromise and deal-making. Such negotiations were based, quite precisely, on the above-cited apparent 'fact' of stalemate – that both the government and the ANC thought increasingly to be the appropriate way to interpret things. As argued above, the state was certainly in a major bind: capable, up to a point and by means of an ever escalating reliance on sheer force, to hold the line but no longer able to reassure its capitalist backers at home and abroad that such a 'solution' could really hope to service their long-term requirements. Moreover, for de Klerk to now opt, in however guarded a manner, in favour of the ANC also implied a further exacerbation of tensions within Afrikanerdom – between those closer to endorsing the new crystallizing logic of capital in general and those with a more vested interest, material and ideological, in racist rule per se.

Still, we have seen that a certain rapprochement between the principal parties to transition – state, capital and the ANC – was in train, this having been capped by de Klerk's startling February 1990, pronouncement of an apparent truce. This in turn meant for de Klerk and company that in any forthcoming negotiations process real concessions would have to be made. But it is important to emphasize that they also envisaged a continued playing of the Buthelezi card, some further discrediting of the ANC, and the sustained prioritization of a racially defined constitutional agenda as a possible winning gambit. In fact, until quite late in the day, the de Klerk group imagined their having some chance of crafting success in terms of arriving at an outcome that would be at least semi-familiar to old racist hands like themselves.

Meanwhile, although the ANC, for its part, was now increasingly able to place itself at the head of the mass movement for democratic change, it could not dream of overthrowing the apartheid state by its long preferred, if now abandoned, means: guerrilla struggle.[14] At the same time, as we have seen, it had no apparent interest in any much broader radical purpose – one that could have been defined in terms of such goals as sustained popular empowerment and socio-economic equality, for example – and therefore had no particular taste for the kind of on-going popular struggle that might have been necessary to realize such an outcome. Most important was the fact that it could now readily envision – and would proceed to seek to mount – an effective negotiation strategy designed merely to deliver on what, *faute de mieux*, had become its own

---

[14] Note, however, the one last gasp of armed liberation activity that was 'Operation Vula'; on this episode see Padraig O'Malley, *Shades of Difference: Mac Maharaj and the Struggle for South Africa* (London and Johannesburg: Penguin, 2007).

version of a radical agenda: one-person, one-vote in a united South Africa.

The shifting terrain for this shuffle to a new South Africa – increasingly, in the political realm, a *pas à deux* between the NP and the ANC – began with the meetings throughout the 1980s between Mandela on the one hand and, on the other, representatives of the National Intelligence Service throughout the 1980s and then with even more elevated political players. Of course, as also noted above, this same shadow-play of negotiations about negotiations was complemented by the important meetings outside South Africa itself between the ANC's exile group and various players from white South Africa as drawn from the ranks of capital and the academy. Then, however, and even with the ban on the ANC lifted, the process merely to limp along for two years, the Groote Schuur Minute (4 May 1990), the Pretoria Minute (6 August 1991) and the National Peace Accord of September 1991 only serving to signal little more than 'on-going discussions' and 'the best of intentions' all round. This all too tentative process ultimately culminated, from late 1991, in the several meetings of the 'Convention for a Democratic South Africa' (CODESA and CODESA II), with the latter process itself breaking down in June 1992 amidst considerable national disarray.

At this point, however, the Slovo-sponsored 'sunset clauses' initiative served to signal the possibility of even greater inter-racial compromise, foreseeing a coalition government of five years between the major players, and also various other tactical concessions designed in part to defuse specific white fears and concerns. This served to keep the immediate process of negotiations on course as the agreement between the ANC and capital now found greater traction amongst the formal (NP) holders of white power, with both major parties eventually accepting an important jointly-agreed 'Record of Understanding' of September 1992. Then, throughout much of 1993, it fell to a 'Multiparty Negotiating Forum' to put the finishing touches on a deal that ultimately permitted a 'Transitional Executive Council' to help supervise the interim period and to organize the historic 1994 election – with an agreement also being reached on a set of constitutional guidelines that would serve to structure a final constitution-making process after the elections themselves.

It does bear emphasizing that these four years of 'transition'[15] were, of course, turbulent ones. For de Klerk's own attempts to retain the initiative and as much as possible of white minority privilege continued. His NP still held the reins of state power throughout the period and, in fact, he moved only slowly towards acceptance of any more genuinely democratic outcome. In addition, as underscored above, the state's military and police apparatuses continued to harass opponents, while also backing the brutal undertakings of Chief Buthelezi of KwaZulu and his Inkatha Freedom Party (IFP) which, as we have suggested, moved to manipulate Zulu nationalism in order to advance Buthelezi's own interests and to render difficult the consolidation of the ANC as a national political force. Not surprisingly, therefore, levels of violence rose precipitously, particularly in Natal and on the East Rand. Indeed, the death toll was extremely high throughout the transition, in part owing to Inkatha's ruthlessness and the

---

[15] See, Saul 'Race, Class, Gender and Voice' in *Liberation Lite*.

apparent activity of some state-sponsored 'Third Force'. Thus one close observer, Janet Cherry, has written: 'The figure of deaths due to political violence in South Africa between 1960 and 1994 is commonly given as between 20,000 and 30,000' but that from 'February 1990 to April 1994 ... 14,000 to 15,000 deaths occurred.' In short, she concludes, 'the fact remains that more people died in the four-year transition period ... than in the preceding three decades'![16]

As all this was going on, de Klerk himself did have a clear victory, amongst whites, for his reform strategy in his winning a whites-only referendum in March, 1992, and this certainly further consolidated the NP's central place in the negotiations. Nonetheless, as emphasized above, there remained, situated further to the right, Afrikaners who now threatened civil war, forged bizarre alliances with corrupt Bantustan leaders, and even argued, as seen, for the creation of a separatist white *Volkstaat*. Thus both the Conservative Party and the more overtly fascist movement, the AWB – each fuelled by unalloyed racism and by the hatreds and fears of lower-class whites who, more than their middle-class white counterparts, had good reason to dread any forced equality (and competition for jobs) with blacks – remained committed to rolling back the clock to the days of unqualified apartheid. They were, in fact, the potential protagonists of a fresh civil war.

Here, perhaps, the greatest danger from the White Right was represented by General Constand Viljoen.[17] For he, not Ferdy Hartzenberg (of the CP) or Eugene Terreblanche (of the AWB), had lines into a security establishment not otherwise inclined towards putschist activity and he also had a much better chance of linking up with divisive forces in the African community (with Buthelezi, for example, and with the 'independent Bantustan' governments of the Ciskei and Bophuthatswana). Yet, as a realist, Viljoen had also begun to conclude that the Afrikaners' last best hope lay in separatism, not apartheid overlordship. The foiling of white intervention to shore up Lucas Mangope's regime in Bophuthatswana narrowed Viljoen's options, however, and when the ANC skilfully allowed some space in the negotiations for the separatist notion of a *Volkstaat* to remain a possibility the general chose, late in the day but fatefully, to commit himself to the electoral process. Despite a spate of bombings on the eve of the elections, the White Right was thus largely corralled into the fold of peaceful transition.

[16] Janet Cherry, *Umkhonto weSizwe*, pp 135–36. Another estimate suggests that 'over the period of the negotiations from February 1990 to April 1994, as South Africa was supposedly normalizing, 14,807 people were killed, according to the South African Institute of Race Relations. This is in stark comparison to the previous five years, when the Institute reported 5,387 deaths from political violence' (Brandon Hamber, 'Dr Jekyll and Mr Hyde: Violence and Transition in South Africa', in E. Bornman et al., (eds) *Violence in South Africa*, Pretoria: Human Sciences and Research Council, 1998, pp. 349–370).

[17] See Jonathan Hyslop, 'Why was the White Right not able to stop South Africa's democratic transition?' in Peter Alexander, Ruth Hutchison and Deryck Schreuder (eds), *Africa Today: A Multi-disciplinary Snapshot of the Continent in 1995* (Canberra: The Humanities Research Centre, 1995); this point is summarized in John S. Saul, *Millennial Africa: Capitalism, Socialism and Democracy* (Trenton, NJ: Africa World Press, 2001), p. 187.

As for Buthelezi's own last-minute entry into the election in 1994, it was surely produced, at least in part, by Viljoen's decision to abandon his own resistance. Nonetheless, Buthelezi did continue to pose a challenge to the electoral process and some deft handling by the ANC would be necessary before all was done. For the IFP had developed a significant base amongst many (although by no means all) Zulu-speakers in the rural areas and squatter settlements of the KwaZulu Bantustan and in workers' hostels especially on the East Rand. It also brought to the table a particularly bloody record of harassment of the ANC, such harassment often carried out hand-in-glove with the apartheid state. Moreover, de Klerk almost certainly was knowledgeable as to the various on-going attempts by the South African military and police both to strengthen the hand of Buthelezi and the IFP and to actively undermine in other ways the ANC's attempt to emerge as a fully hegemonic force in a new South Africa. Yet, paradoxically enough, Buthelezi was in the end also to prove to be a beneficiary of the very process – that of constitution-making – that he had himself chosen to boycott.

For it was primarily white politicians, increasingly denied any more direct guarantees of minority privilege, who successfully held out for a federal division of powers as one possible means of hamstringing an ANC government that, they feared (mistakenly, as it happened), might with victory seek to use the central government actively for progressive purposes. Another line of defence to secure established socio-economic inequalities was the successful attempt to bind the ANC to a constitutionally-prescribed protection not so much to individual human rights but, particularly, to a strong guarantee of the right to property. In addition, the above-mentioned 'sunset clauses' safeguarded for a period the positions of whites in public employment – while, as indicated, an agreement on a 'Government of National Unity' meant positions for National Party and IFP politicians (including both de Klerk and Buthelezi) in the cabinet formed by the ANC after its electoral victory! In addition, an amnesty offered some protection to those who had committed various gross abuses of power in defence of apartheid (albeit it was to be an amnesty sufficiently qualified so as to prepare the ground for the subsequent establishment of the Truth and Reconciliation Commission).

True, the de Klerk team itself had remained reluctant, until quite late in the day, to commit itself unequivocally to the notion of the possible establishment of, in the end, an ANC government: they still harboured hopes of further safeguarding various attributes of the existing racial order within any new constitutional/political dispensation that might eventually emerge from negotiations. Nonetheless, the NP was now cornered, trapped between rising pressures from capital (including its Afrikaner wing) to settle the situation on the one hand, and the escalating and dangerous reality of bloodshed and social chaos that fed off a festering lack of resolution on the negotiations front on the other. How much choice, at the last, did de Klerk have? In the event, he felt forced to accede to history and to embrace the role of statesman – even as he still hoped against hope that the pending election itself might yet deny the ANC its victory. But in acceding to a deal that would ultimately clear the way for such an ANC victory he had apparently done enough to win – however bizarrely – a share (with Mandela) of a joint Nobel Peace Prize!

For its part, the ANC continued to consolidate itself at the head of the forces pressing for change despite the fact that negotiations between the two chief protagonists – the ANC and the Nats – had remained, at first, so intermittent and slow to ensure progress. As seen, the initial Convention for a Democratic South Africa (CODESA I and II), created as a negotiations' forum in late 1991, broke down on several occasions. But mid-1992 witnessed a massacre at Boipatong and the shooting of demonstrators at Bisho in the Ciskei, as well as a massive trade-union-led general strike in support of meaningful change. Both parties central to the process now sensed the need to guide a volatile situation towards compromise, their respective elites having developed a mutual vested interest in a smooth transition under their own joint control: the 'Record of Understanding' they signed in September, 1992, was then, as we have seen, to produce much more serious negotiations at Kempton Park in 1993. Their intentions further focused by the massive outcry that followed the assassination of popular SACP leader Chris Hani by white extremists,[18] the negotiators finally did set in train the process that led to the historic 1994 election.[19]

The loss of Hani, who had opted during the transition (and, apparently, for the foreseeable future) to play his most active role within the SACP rather than the ANC, should be especially noted here. After all, Hani was still saying, shortly before his assassination, that

the ANC will have to fight a new enemy. That enemy would be another struggle to make freedom and democracy worthwhile to ordinary South Africans. Our biggest enemy would be what we do in the field of socio-economic restructuring: the creation of jobs, building of houses, schools, medical facilities, overhauling our education, eliminating illiteracy, building a society which cares, and fighting corruption and those moving into the gravy train of using power, government positions to enrich individuals. We must build a different culture in this country, different from Africa, different from the Nationalist Party. And that culture should be one of service to people.

Some of us, especially we in the [Communist] Party, have been discussing how we should cut down the salaries of Ministers, of parliamentarians and all the subsidies, so that if you are in parliament in Cape Town or Pretoria, you actually rent a flat like everybody. We are thinking in terms of a number of guidelines so that those people who go into parliament or go into the government should be those who are prepared to serve the people, not because it is a way of enriching people. And I think the ANC therefore must now position itself to tackle the problems of grassroots people. And that is why the ANC must allow the formation of many democratic formations in this country, organs of civil society, like the civics, independent trade unions, students' organisations, teachers organisations, organisations of housewives, women, gays and everybody else, so that it is kept reminded of the need of the people on the ground.[20]

[18] On Hani see Smith & Tromp, *Hani: A Life Too Short.*
[19] For my own first hand observations of this election see John S. Saul 'Now for the Hard Part', *Southern Africa Report*, 9, 5 & 10, 1 (July, 1994), and other first-hand materials in John S. Saul, *Revolutionary Traveller: Freeze-Frames from a Life* (Winnipeg: Arbeiter Ring, 2009).
[20] Chris Hani, from an interview by Luli Callinicos, March 31, 1993 (in a transcript from her files kindly made available to me by Callinicos.

How Hani would have played his hand in future is, of course, now a matter of mere speculation. But, as articulated above, his was not the kind of project that, either at the time or in the near future, was much favoured or advocated by a number of significant others amongst those returning from exile. Indeed, as we have seen, effective 'elite-pacting' of the kind the ANC now pursued was closely linked to continuing efforts by many of the ANC leadership's to facilitate the demobilization of those very popular energies (cf. the fate of the UDF, above) that had been so crucial to the weakening of the apartheid state in the first place.

To be sure, everything was not quite so straightforward within ANC circles as this may suggest. For example, a senior ANC cadre (Pallo Jordan) would at this time speak nervously of the danger that the ANC was merely 'committing suicide by concessions'.[21] Others within the ANC, Jeremy Cronin for example, worried as to the precise meaning and extent of the 'principled compromises' (in Joe Slovo's phrase) made by the ANC during the negotiations process[22] while Raymond Suttner expressed his fears as to the degree of 'demoralization' the ANC's approach to negotiations was increasingly producing:

> JS [Joe Slovo] is absolutely right to underline the massive victory we have scored at the negotiations. He fails, however, to mention that the past three years have also seen the transformation of our organizations, particularly the ANC. This transformation could have a serious, long-term impact. In particular, the negotiations have had a dissolving effect on mass organization, a tendency for our constituency to become spectators. If we conduct the coming election campaign in a narrow electoralist manner, the dissolution could be deepened. Whatever the victory, we should not underrate the strong sense of demoralization in our organizations.[23]

Moreover there was some firm expressions of demands from below that had some real impact upon the negotiations themselves: for example, COSATU effectively manifested its unease at late-apartheid government policy initiatives (and at its own absence from the formal negotiations process) with a dramatic two-day general strike against a proposed new Value Added Tax (as earlier noted). Negotiators were further reminded of the mass presence beyond the conference halls when, at a crucial moment, the above-mentioned series of rolling mass demonstrations (climaxing in the Boipatong massacre and the shooting by Ciskei soldiers into a large group of protesters marching on Bisho) helped to reactivate stalled talks.[24]

---

21   Pallo Jordan, 'Strategic Debate on the ANC' (mimeo, 1992; an abbreviated version of this paper appears as 'Committing Suicide by Concession', *Weekly Mail* (12–19 November 1992).
22   Jeremy Cronin, Nothing to Gain from All-or-Nothing Tactics', *Weekly Mail* (13–19 November 1992).
23   Suttner's comments appear as a part of the account of the SACP's 'Central Committee Discussion of Joe Slovo's Presentation', *The African Communist*, 135, Fourth Quarter, 1993, p. 14.
24   On this event, see Pallo Jordan's illuminating 'Bisho Martyrs Commemoration Lecture', presented on September 6, 2012 and sent to me by the author. Note, too, that Jeremy Cronin spoke forcefully at the time (see footnote 6 above) against the possible danger of such actions as Bisho and Boipatong merely manifesting a

All of which was too little and too late in any event – especially since on the second socio-economic front, there was actually even more to worry about, though even less was said. For as we have consistently emphasized above there had, beyond constitutional negotiations and electoral politics, been a virtual second set of negotiations going on. Much more informal, these had seen the ANC during the transition continuing to reassure various international capitalist actors (the bourgeoisies of both South African and international provenance, Western governments, and the World Bank and the IMF) as to the modesty of its claims – which had sometimes seemed to be rather more radical in exile – to challenge the existing economic status quo. The road to a successful political-cum-constitutional transition was, as noted, eased, both locally and internationally, by this increasing domestication of the ANC to the requirements of global capitalism. We have seen that some have, perhaps too charitably, suggested that the ANC had little room for manoeuvre in this arena. Yet the fact remains that, by 1994, the movement/party had bound itself to an economic strategy with very doubtful promise of changing for the better the material conditions of the mass of South Africans in the post-apartheid period.

For, in the long run, at least as dangerous to realizing the betterment of the prospects of the bulk of South Africa's impoverished people as the machinations of either Buthelezi or de Klerk were those of the wielders of corporate power who would now to live to tell the tale of this dual transition with increasingly self-satisfied smiles on their faces. In fact, in the end, the relative ease of the political transition was principally guaranteed by the ANC's withdrawal from any form of genuine class struggle in the socio-economic realm and the abandonment of any economic strategy that might have been expected directly to service significantly the immediate material requirements of the vast mass of desperately impoverished South Africans. This was to produce a society where the income gap between rich and poor has been, and remains, among the widest in the world: a society in which some could suggest in the mid-1990s that the poorest 60 percent of households share of total expenditure was as little as 14 percent and the share of the richest 20 percent was then some 69 percent, and where, across the decade of the nineties, a certain narrowing of the income gap between black and white (as a growing number of blacks have edged into elite circles) has been paralleled by an ever greater discrepancy in class terms.[25]

Granted, the 'negotiations' in the sphere of economic/class relationships

---

(cont) tendency for such 'mass action' to be viewed primarily as a 'tap' to be turned on and off at will by the ANC rather than as an earnest of on-going popular empowerment.

25 See, for useful source on such matters, Haroon Bhorat et al., *Income and non-income inequality in post-apartheid South Africa: What are the Drivers and Possible Policy Interventions?* (Capetown: Development Policy Research Unit, 2009); Sampie Terreblanche, *A History of Inequality in South Africa, 1652–2002* (Scottsville: University of Natal Press, 2002). See also Jeremy Seekings and Nicoli Nattrass, *Class, Race and Inequality in South Africa* (New Haven and London: Yale University Press, 2005); Michael McDonald, *Why Race Matters in South Africa* (Cambridge and London: Harvard University Press, 2006).

were much less public than the formal meetings of the Convention for a Democratic South Africa (CODESA) and the Kempton Park negotiations. But they were, perhaps, even more important. As one close observer wrote in 1994:

> Since 1990, when the democratization process began, some foreign governments, notably the US and some of its allies – Britain, Germany, Italy and Japan – successfully induced the ANC to move away from its socialist economic policies, including that of nationalization. Instead, they succeeded in persuading the movement to embrace Western-style free market principles which the ANC increasingly, albeit reluctantly [*sic*, see below], adopted. It is interesting to note, for example, that Mandela's evolving position on fiscal responsibility was a direct response to pressures from foreign investors and governments.[26]

But this brand of compromise was merely part of a decade-long process of accommodation, one hailed in retrospect by no less a source than South Africa's corporate think-tank par excellence, the Centre for Development and Enterprise (CDE): 'The evolution of the ANC's policy position was ... influenced by foreign perceptions and pressures (from foreign investors, potential investors, the World Bank, IMF and others). Other important policy influences were the 'Growth for All' document of the South African Foundation (representing the country's 50 largest corporations) published in February 1996. The result: 'Throughout the 1990s the ANC's economic policies have shown a clear shift towards greater acceptance of the market ... (one sealed) finally in the Growth, Employment and Redistribution (GEAR) proposals of June, 1996.'[27]

Indeed, as Asghar Adelzadeh wrote nearer the time, what was happening both before and after 1994 (culminating with GEAR in 1996) was 'a lame succumbing to the policy dictates and ideological pressures of the international financial institutions', the 'adoption of the essential tenets and policy recommendations of the neo-liberal framework advocated by the IMF in its structural adjustment programmes', an outcome, Adelzadeh argues, that was

> all the more remarkable in view of the limited, even negative impact of such programmes, especially in southern Africa, the lack of leverage that the international financial institutions such as the IMF and World Bank had over South African policymakers, the lack of any dramatic shifts in the economic and political environment to warrant such major shifts in policy orientation, and the lack of a transparent and fully argued justification for the adoption of an entirely different policy framework.[28]

---

[26] Chris Landsberg, 'Directing from the Stalls: The International Community and the South African Negotiation Forum', in Steven Friedman and Doreen Atkinson (eds), *The Small Miracle: South Africa's Negotiated Settlement*, South African Review 7 (Braamfontein: Ravan, 1994), pp. 290–91.

[27] Ann Bernstein, *Policy-Making in a New Democracy: South Africa's Challenges for the 21st Century*, Centre for Development and Enterprise Research 10 (August 1999), a report funded by South African Breweries, p. 83.

[28] Asghar Adelzadeh, 'From the RDP to GEAR: The Gradual Embracing of Neo-Liberalism in Economic policy', *Transformation*, 31, 1996.

But if 1996 was the crucial year for putting the finishing touches on the ANC's capitulation to neo-liberal orthodoxy, it seems plausible to argue that the die had already been cast during the transition period itself. To repeat something that in a previous section we quoted Hein Marais as having observed: 'By 1994 ... the left had lost the macroeconomic battle.'[29]

Sealing the deal: The troubled transition (1990–94) and the 'Freedom Compromise'

The day was soon to come, in fact, when *The Economist* could crow of the post-transition reality that

> For all the fears that resentful ANC socialists would confiscate wealth, the new breed shares the same capitalist aspirations as the old. Though black incomes are barely a sixth of white ones, a black elite is rising on the back of governmental jobs and the promotion of black business. It is moving into the leafy suburbs, such as Kelvin and Sandton, and adopting the outward symbols of prestige – the BMW, swimming pool, golf handicaps and black maid – that so mesmerize status-conscious whites.

Indeed, as early as 1992 Mandela himself would, revealingly, warn a journalist interlocutor that 'we are sitting on a time bomb ... The enemy is now you and me, people who have a car and have a house. It's order, anything that relates to order [that has become the target], and it's a very grave situation.'

But this was a reality that would post-date the transition and we will have to return to it in subsequent chapters. For now, in 1994, it remained only for the April election to formally 'seal the deal' and usher the ANC into power – the latter thereby achieving its long-term goal of a democratic political system. Make no mistake: this marked an historic accomplishment of staggering proportions that the world quickly and vocally acknowledged as such – as did a large majority of South African voters. This despite Inkatha's only eleventh-hour conversion to participation in the 1994 polls, the fraud, violence and considerable chaos that marked the electoral process in Natal, and the existence of virtual 'no-go' areas for various of the parties during the election period (especially in Inkatha-dominated rural Natal). In the end, no accurate count of the vote proved to be remotely possible in Natal: the result, 'accurate' or not, was quite simply diplomatically brokered and in the IFP's favour, this being a choice of tactic made by the national-level ANC in order to draw Buthelezi further into the tent of compromise. The upshot was that the IFP would form the government in the province of KwaZulu-Natal, one of nine such provincial units established within the new federal system affirmed in the constitutional guidelines that inter-party negotiations preceding the elections had produced. Beyond the inclusion of Buthelezi (along with de Klerk!) in the new ANC-dominated national cabinet there was the additional fact that

---

[29] Marais, *South Africa – Limits to Change*, p. 156.

in spite of being named in the TRC report as carrying responsibility for 'gross violation of human rights' Buthelezi has escaped with scarcely a blemish and with
apparent absolution from the ANC itself ... his position as an elder states-person
acknowledged through the number of times that he has served as Acting State President in the frequent absence of both Mandela and [then Deputy President] Mbeki.[30]

A small price to pay for peace, perhaps. Meanwhile even as Buthelezi was being
awarded a negotiated victory in KwaZulu-Natal, the National Party, with
considerable Coloured support, took the Western Cape. More broadly, however,
the ANC won 7 of 9 provinces and an overwhelming national majority of 62.6
per cent of the twenty million South Africans who voted. Although short of the
two-thirds majority that would have enabled it unilaterally to rewrite the
Constitution (had it been so inclined), the ANC now dominated the government
and its leader Nelson Mandela became the first President of a democratic South
Africa on May 10, 1994. A nation-wide, all-in election had thus witnessed the
transfer of power from a racial oligarchy to a new, pan-racial majority. Small
wonder that the negotiations which served to realize such democratic possibilities and to hold in check many dangerous contradictions have been a magnet
for the attention of students of the 'political science' of transition. Here was a
case, if ever there was one, of the 'setting up [of] government in diversity as a
way of defusing conflict'. Accordingly, the temptation has been irresistible for
political practitioners and political observers alike to merely place the ebb and
flow of political in-fighting, of intra-elite trade-offs and of constitutional
compromise to the centre of their analyses.

Thus a book by Allister Sparks has usefully documented the manner – as we
have ourselves seen here – in which the relevant negotiations had actually
begun well before the release of Nelson Mandela from prison in 1990. Sparks
traces their continuation right up to the 1994 election[31] – although, interestingly enough, he also notes with the transition the growing centrality of 'a new
class stratification gradually beginning to overlay South Africa's old racial
strata, never completely eliminating the old divisions but blurring them and
adding a different dimension'. Equally impressive have been the two important
volumes on the South African transition prepared by Steven Friedman and his
colleagues: *The long journey: South Africa's quest for a negotiated settlement* and
also their *The small miracle: South Africa's negotiated settlement*.[32] In these books,

---

[30]   Gerhard Maré, 'Makin' Nice with Buthelezi', *Southern Africa Report*, 14, 3, 1999, p.
      10. As Maré (esteemed author of many books and articles on Buthelezi, Inkatha and
      KwaZulu over the years) also observes of Buthelezi's cronies, people 'closely associated
      with horrendous acts of violence', they have 'simply defied or ignored the storm and
      survived – often as members of various provincial parliaments or the central parlia-
      ment, such as warlords David Ntombela and Mandla Shabalala, and the notorious
      prince Gideon Zulu'.

[31]   Sparks, *Tomorrow is Another Country*.

[32]   Steven Friedman (ed.), *The Long Journey: South Africa's Quest for a Negotiated Settle-
      ment* (Johannesburg: Ravan, 1993) and Friedman & Atkinson, *The Small Miracle*; see
      also Hassen Ebrahim, *The Soul of a Nation: Constitution-making in South Africa* (Oxford:
      Oxford University Press. 1998); and *Review of Constitutional Studies*, special issue, the

and others, one finds painstaking analyses of the intense interactions that took place, over the four-year period 1990–94, amongst political elites regarding transitional political and bureaucratic arrangements, long-term constitutional dispensations and the proposed workings of the electoral system that finally came into play in 1994.

True, there is some discussion in such works of the moments at which political actors outside the formal negotiating framework broke into the process: as discussed above, the mass action campaign, spearheaded by the trade unions in August 1992, and the more chaotic events at Bisho and Boipatong that same month are cited in this regard. On the left, there was concern that such mass action had come to be treated, as we have seen Cronin to warn, as a mere 'tap', to be turned on and off at the ANC leadership's whim as short-term calculation of advantage at the bargaining table might dictate: 'We must not confine or inhibit mass struggle ... Instead we need to encourage, facilitate and indeed build the kind of fighting grass-roots organizations that can lead and sustain a thousand and one local struggles against the numerous injustices our people suffer', Cronin continued.[33] But most academic analysts seemed to accept both as inevitable and as benign the fact that, on balance, the negotiations' process tended to sideline many of the bearers of popular resistance who had done so much to place negotiations on the table in the first place. 'Elite coalescence has been the hallmark of South Africa's transition', writes Timothy Sisk approvingly, adding that 'elite-concluded accords do not work unless elites are able to demobilize their own constituencies'! The election itself was hailed, in effect, as locking the results of such 'coalescence' – and such judicious 'demobilization' – into place.[34]

And yet, and yet. For these elections had also been, as Suttner feared, fully revelatory of what little has become of popular mobilization in South Africa – as has been the virtual collapse of the ANC as a mass political organization (although not as an electoral machine) since 1994. True, the 1994 election had the distinction of being a 'freedom election': under the prevailing circumstances one could not have asked for much more than that, such a massive African vote for the ANC marking the coming into the political kingdom of a population that had been denied any such voice for centuries. By 1999, however, it was difficult to miss the significance of the fact that South African elections had become mere popularity contests, the ANC still floating to a considerable degree on its legitimacy amongst Africans as a successful liberation movement rather than on any record of delivery on popular expectations during its first term in office. Meanwhile, in 1994, the vote in KwaZulu-Natal continued to fall along quasi-ethnic lines (producing, once again, a narrow victory for the IFP) and the vote in Western Cape along racial ones (producing a National Party/Democratic Party government – with the two parties since

(cont) introductory article to which (by Richard Bauman and David Schneiderman) is entitled 'The South African Constitution in Transition', 3, 1, 1996.

33 Jeremy Cronin, 'The Boat, the Tap and the Leipzig Way', *African Communist* (130, 1992) pp. 41–54.

34 Timothy D. Sisk, *Democratization in South Africa: The Elusive Social Contract* (Princeton: Princeton University Press, 1995), p. 123.

merged into a new 'Democratic Alliance'). Nationally, the Democratic Party became the official opposition (albeit with only 11 per cent of the vote compared to the ANC's near two-thirds share of the poll): it did so, significantly, on the basis of a campaign pitched to whites, 'Coloureds' and Indians in terms of issues of crime, corruption and the dangers of abuse of power inherent in a one-party dominant (read, also, African-dominant) political system, issues that were given, tacitly, a racial, even racist, spin.

But there was something else as well. For this tendency to a hollowing out of the elections and moving them away from moments of genuine ideological substance may also have reflected the fact that there was not so very much more to campaign about – other than the black population's understandable claim to, at long last, political power (a claim which the ANC represented in the electoral arena as did no other party). As for the Democratic Party, it did hew to a particularly business-friendly, neo-liberal line as regards socio-economic policy during the election but by at least as early as 1999 and probably much earlier this did not much distinguish the party from the ANC itself in policy terms. For on many potentially important strategic issues the space for democratic disagreement and contestation had by then been papered over by a crippling consensus amongst the main political contenders regarding the presumed imperatives of economic orthodoxy.

Small wonder that some observers have found it difficult to avoid a relatively narrow and unenthusiastic reading of what, substantively, was actually being accomplished in South Africa in democratic terms. Thus, David Howarth distinguishes the 'democratic transition' South Africa has achieved from the 'democratic transformation' that had not really been attempted – using the term 'democratic transition' to refer 'to the process by which negotiating elites manage to oversee the installation of formal liberal-democratic procedures, whereas [democratic transformation] designates the longer-term process of restructuring the underlying social relations of a given society'. Since, in South Africa, these 'underlying social relations' encompass a measure of socio-economic inequality that is virtually unparalleled elsewhere in the world (only Brazil and Guatemala are ever mentioned as being in the same league on the Gini scale), it is not difficult to see what Howarth is driving at.[35]

Nonetheless, the fact remained that a page had been turned. Time alone would tell what was written on the next one.

---

[35] David Howarth, 'Paradigms Gained? A Critique of Theories and Explanations of Democratic Transitions in South Africa', in D. Howarth and A. Norval (eds), *South Africa in Transition: New Theoretical Perspectives* (New York : St Martin's Press, 1998), p. 203 (as also cited in Saul's 'Post-War and Post-Apartheid: The Costs and Benefits of Peacebuilding South African Style', in Taisier M. Ali and Robert O. Matthews, *Durable Peace: Challenges for Peacebuilding in Africa*, Toronto: University of Toronto Press, 2004).

Part II
The Present as History[1]:
Post-Apartheid and Post-1994

---

[1] Cf. Paul Sweezy, *The Present as History* (New York: Monthly Review Press, 1953).

Part II
The Present as History:
Post-Apartheid and Post-1994

4.
Contradictions Subside then Deepen:
Accumulation and Class Conflict, 1994–2000

PATRICK BOND

South Africa won its democracy in 1994. But in far too many respects, it has been a 'choiceless democracy' in socio-economic policy terms and more broadly a 'low-intensity democracy', to borrow terms coined respectively by Thandika Mkandawire for Africa, and by Barry Gills and Joel Rocamora for many ex-dictatorships.[2] The self-imposition of economic and development policies – typically at the behest of financial markets and the Washington/Geneva multilateral institutions – required an extraordinary insulation from genuine national determinations: in short, an 'elite transition'.[3] This insulation of policy from democracy was facilitated by invoking the mantra of seeking 'international competitiveness', and initially peaked with Nelson Mandela's 1996 *Growth, Employment and Redistribution* policy. As Chapter 5 shows, Pretoria's obeisance to multinational corporations, revealed in this core policy, helped to mould the platinum belt in a manner that inexorably led to the Marikana Massacre. In the South African case of low-intensity democracy, it must be stressed, the decision to reduce any real room for strategic manoeuvre was made as much by the local principals as it was by the Bretton Woods Institutions, other financiers and investors.

As these next chapters document, South Africa's democratization was profoundly compromised by an intra-elite economic deal that, for most people, *worsened* poverty, unemployment, inequality and ecological degradation, while also exacerbating many racial, gender and geographical differences. In this chapter we consider the critical choices and outcomes from 1994–2000. These confirmed the late-apartheid turn to neo-liberal macro-economic management

---

[2]   Thandika Mkandawire, 'Crisis Management and the Making of "Choiceless Democracies" in Africa', in R. Joseph (ed.) *The State, Conflict and Democracy in Africa* (Boulder, CO: Lynne Rienner, 1999); Barry Gills et al. (eds), *Low Intensity Democracy* (London: Pluto, 1993). This condition led a series of formerly anti-authoritarian critics of old dictatorships – whether from right-wing or left-wing backgrounds – to transform into 1980s–90s neo-liberal rulers whose policies generally made poor people, women and the environment suffer: Alfonsin (Argentina), Aquino (Philippines), Arafat (Palestine), Aristide (Haiti), Bhutto (Pakistan), Chiluba (Zambia), Dae Jung (South Korea), Havel (Czech Republic), Mandela (South Africa), Manley (Jamaica), Megawati (Indonesia), Mugabe (Zimbabwe), Museveni (Uganda), Nujoma (Namibia), Obasanjo (Nigeria), Ortega (Nicaragua), Perez (Venezuela), Rawlings (Ghana), Walesa (Poland) and Yeltsin (Russia).

[3]   Patrick Bond, *Elite Transition: From Apartheid to Neoliberalism in South Africa* (London: Pluto Press, 2000 and 2014, New Edition).

and micro-economic deregulation. The policy choices amplified South Africa's vulnerability to world neo-liberal hegemony until – and beyond – the 1998 East Asian crisis. In the next chapter we move to the twenty-first century, because it is sometimes presumed in Pretoria to have ushered in a 'new', 'post-neo-liberal' era, with policies and growth patterns associated with a so-called 'developmental state' and deeper welfare support, although I argue that the evidence of any such shift is ultimately unconvincing.

Indeed, each of the country's first four democratic governments – led by Mandela (1994–99), Thabo Mbeki (1999–2008), Kgalema Motlanthe (2008–9) and Jacob Zuma (2009–present) – failed to redistribute the country's wealth and establish conditions for thoroughgoing participatory democracy, thus leaving the door open for widespread social protest, populist demagoguery and apathy. But in the first two decades of free political activity, after the February 1990 unbanning of black parties, the government's lamentable record of delivery failed to generate the long-awaited rise of a political party to the left of Mandela's African National Congress (ANC). To understand why, requires combining analysis of the changing structure of capital – especially its worsening unevenness and financialization – with the study of divisions within the subordinate classes. This will in turn set the stage for considering a variety of public policies adopted after apartheid, many of which reflected more continuity than change.

Ending the apartheid regime was one of the greatest human achievements of the past century. However, according to those engaged in the process, the transition agreement between the racists and the ANC was full of unfortunate compromises. Whites kept the best land, the mines, manufacturing plants and financial institutions. They exported vast quantities of capital, and benefited most from the economic policies adopted during the 1990s. For there had been only two basic paths that the ANC could have followed. One was to mobilize the people and all their enthusiasm, energy, and hard work, use a larger share of the economic surplus (through state-directed investments and higher taxes), and stop the flow of capital abroad, including the repayment of $25 billion in illegitimate apartheid-era debt. *The other, which was ultimately the one chosen, was to trudge down the neo-liberal capitalist road, with merely a small reform here or there to permit superficial claims to a 'National Democratic Revolution'.* Because the latter path was chosen, we start this chapter by considering the economic barriers to deepened democracy – before proceeding to examine the economic outcomes themselves, followed by a discussion of social policy patterns, the commercialized state, environmental concerns and the reactions of civil society.

Economic barriers

The neo-liberal path was prefigured in the transitional years. As already discussed by John Saul in Chapter 3, the ruling bloc's political strategy included weakening the incoming ANC government through repression and provocation of internecine township violence. Perhaps most devious, though, were the divide-

and-conquer blandishments offered to black leaders by way of elite-pacting. The initial softening up process entailed Mandela's controversial talks-about-talks with National Intelligence Agency director Neil Barnard in prison and the Afrikaner intellectuals' and English-speaking business leaders' approaches to exiled ANC leaders during the late 1980s. The unbanning of the ANC allowed many of the pacting processes to come above ground into a certain kind of rose-coloured sunlight. For example, methodologies included 'scenario planning' gimmicks to generate a coerced harmony, promoted first by Shell Oil and then Anglo American, Nedbank, Sanlam and other corporations during the critical 1990–94 period, willingly embraced by the ascendant ANC neo-liberals.[4]

Another crucial force in the battle for hearts and minds at that time was the World Bank. Along with International Monetary Fund (IMF)'s periodic visits and an $850 million loan in late 1993, the Bank's 1990–93 Reconnaissance Missions allowed the neo-liberal agencies' to shape policy framings for a post-apartheid market-friendly government. These were far more persuasive for the ANC leadership than the more populist ambitions of the 1994 Reconstruction and Development Programme (RDP), the main document of election promises. The Bretton Woods Institution's influence was ironic, since the Bank and IMF had such a regrettable history in southern Africa:[5]

- the Bank's US$100 million in loans to Eskom from 1951–67 provided only white people with electric power, but all South Africans paid the bill;
- the Bank refused point-blank to heed a United Nations General Assembly instruction in 1966 not to lend to apartheid South Africa;
- the IMF provided apartheid-supporting loans of more than $2 billion between the Soweto uprising in 1976 and 1983, when the US Congress finally prohibited Bretton Woods Institution lending to Pretoria;
- the Bank lent tens of millions of dollars for Lesotho dams which were widely acknowledged to help apartheid South Africa 'sanctions-bust' financial boycotts in 1986, via a London trust;
- the Bank and IMF were prolific in financing the region's worst dictators and then in imposing the 'Washington Consensus' through unworkable Structural Adjustment Policies;
- the IMF advised Pretoria in 1991 to impose the regressive Value Added Tax, in opposition to which 3.5 million people went on a two-day stay-away.

Subsequently, lending and policy advice to Mandela's team from the Bretton Woods twins included:

- Bank promotion of 'market-oriented' land reform in 1993–94, which established such onerous conditions (similar to the failed policy in neighbouring Zimbabwe) that instead of 30 per cent land redistribution as mandated in the RDP, less than 1 per cent of good land was redistributed;

[4] Bond, *Elite Transition*, Chapter 2.
[5] The points below are elaborated in Bond, *Elite Transition*, Chapter 4.

- the Bank's endorsement of bank-centred housing policy in August 1994, with recommendations for smaller housing subsidies;
- Bank design of South African infrastructure policy in November 1994, which provided the rural and urban poor with only pit latrines, no electricity connections, inadequate roads, and communal taps instead of house or yard taps;
- the Bank's promotion of water cut-offs for those unable to afford payments, opposition to a free 'lifeline' water supply, and recommendations against irrigation subsidies for black South Africans in October 1995, within a government water-pricing policy in which the Bank claimed (in its 1999 Country Assistance Review) it played an 'instrumental' role;
- the Bank's conservative role in the Lund Commission in 1996, which recommended a 44 per cent cut in the monthly grant to impoverished, dependent children from R135 per month to R75;
- the Bank's support to the Growth, Employment and Redistribution policy in June 1996, through contributing two staff economists and providing its economic model to help frame 'Growth, Employment and Reconstruction' (GEAR) and offer unworkable policy targets;
- the Bank and IMF's consistent message to South African workers that their wages are too high, and that unemployment can only be cured through 'labour flexibility';
- the Bank's role in Johannesburg's Egoli 2002 plan, aimed at commercialising city functions, including research support and encouragement of municipal privatization;
- the Bank's repeated commitments to invest, through its subsidiary the International Finance Corporation, in privatized infrastructure, housing securities for high-income families, for-profit 'managed healthcare' schemes, and the now-bankrupt, US-owned Domino's Pizza franchise.

Even without going through the process of lending to transitional South Africa – until the IMF's huge 1993 credit – the Bretton Woods Institutions exercised enormous clout. The Bank carefully recruited select ANC officials to work with them in Washington during the early 1990s, and also gave substantial consultancies to ideologically-compatible local allies in South Africa. But notwithstanding all the political manoeuvres associated with the rise and fall of personalities, blocs and ideas during the 1990–94 period, perhaps the most important fusion of the old and new occurred on the economic terrain five months prior to the April 27, 1994 democratic election, when the 'Transitional Executive Committee' (TEC) took control of the South African government, combining a few leading ANC cadre with the ruling National Party, which was in its last year of 45 in power.

Thus, even as racist laws were tumbling in Parliament and as the dignity of the majority black population was soaring, the TEC accepted, on December 1, 1993, an $850 million loan from the IMF, signed first by subsequent Finance Minister Pravin Gordhan. It was ostensibly for drought relief, although the searing drought had ended 18 months earlier. The loan's secret conditions –

leaked to *Business Day* in March 1994 – included the usual items from the classical structural adjustment menu: lower import tariffs, cuts in state spending, and large cuts in public sector wages. In addition, Michel Camdessus, then IMF managing director, put informal but intense pressure on incoming President Mandela to reappoint the two main stalwarts of apartheid-era neo-liberalism, the Finance Minister and Central Bank governor, both from the National Party.[6]

So it was in May 1994, just after the ANC won an overwhelming victory, Mandela announced a 'Government of National Unity' (GNU) that included F. W. de Klerk's National Party and the Zulu-nationalist Inkatha Freedom Party. This was justified to an adoring society desperate for reconciliation, because highly creative vote tallying gave the National Party (NP) just over 20 per cent and Inkatha 10 per cent of electoral support and denied the ANC the two-thirds which Mandela himself had stated would be an adverse outcome, insofar as it would dent investor confidence to know the *Constitution* might be alterable.[7] The subsequent roles of de Klerk (an honorary-type deputy president) and Inkatha's Mangosuthu Buthelezi (Home Affairs Minister) were relatively unsubstantial, and the NP dropped out of the government in 1996 without much notice, soon to merely dissolve as a party and be folded into the ANC by de Klerk's successor Marthinus van Schalkwyk. The latter was rewarded with the Environmental Affairs and Tourism Ministry, playing his part with the same loyalty as he served apartheid, to the general disgust of his former and subsequent constituencies. De Klerk faded away into maintaining a Foundation, whose spokesperson David Steward was occasionally voluble on civil and political rights problems, entirely lacking the humility that should have accompanied de Klerk's amnesty for his numerous crimes against humanity.

De Klerk could comfortably retire because by mid-1996 with a neo-liberal economic policy in place, the elite transition was cemented and only provincial power shifts – from Inkatha to ANC in 2004 in KwaZulu-Natal, and from ANC to the Democratic Alliance in 2009 in the Western Cape – disturbed the political power-balance arrangements established in 1994. The ANC continued to receive between 60 and 67 per cent of the national votes, and Mandela continued to be venerated after he departed the Presidency for having guided the 'miracle' of a political solution to the surface-level problems of apartheid.

However, seen from below, the replacement of racial by what we might term 'class apartheid' was decisive under Mandela's rule. Those behind-the-scenes economic policy agreements forged during the early 1990s meant the Afrikaner regime's own internal power-bloc transition from apartheid 'securocrats' (e.g., Defence Minister Magnus Malan and Police Minister Adriaan Vlok) to transitional-apartheid 'econocrats' (such as Finance Ministers Barend du Plessis and Derek Keys and especially Reserve Bank Governor Chris Stals who lasted in power until 1999) was matched by a similar process of deradicalization in the ANC. There, party managers led by Mbeki – Mandela's first Deputy President

---

[6] Patrick Bond, *Against Global Apartheid* (London: Zed Books, 2003).
[7] Alan Fine, 'SA Electorate Repeats 1994's "Perfect Fluke"', *Business Day*, 9 June 1999.

and *de facto* prime minister from 1994–99 – renamed its Department of Economic *Planning* as the Department of Economic *Policy*. Trevor Manuel was appointed to lead it in 1990, replacing a man (Max Sisulu) with more Keynesian leanings. Along with Tito Mboweni and Maria Ramos (his future wife, who became head of Absa Bank), Manuel ensured that a small group of neo-liberal managers were gradually brought into the Treasury and SA Reserve Bank. The Congress of SA Trade Unions (COSATU) and SA Communist Party (SACP) offered similar pragmatists who could be trusted to impose neo-liberal policies, including future Trade Minister Alec Erwin, Reconstruction and Development Programme Minister Jay Naidoo, Housing Minister Joe Slovo, Transport Minister Mac Maharaj, and Minister-at-large Essop Pahad.

In sum, this neo-liberal group now overseeing the ANC-COSATU-SACP Alliance became eminently 'trustworthy' in the eyes of Afrikaners and English-speaking businesses, as well as the 'international community', also known as imperialists.[8]

Two decades on, top ANC official Ngoako Ramatlhodi offered a vivid description of the mandate given the incoming government: 'In a sense we are managing a white-man economy on behalf of white men who ran the economy under apartheid, but they have changed in form, not in politics'.[9] As a result, former ANC leader Ronnie Kasrils confessed in 2013, 'the battle for the soul of the ANC got underway and was lost to corporate power and influence ... To lose nerve, go belly-up, was neither necessary nor inevitable... My belief is that we could have pressed forward without making the concessions we did.'[10] In other words, answering the question 'Were we pushed or did we jump?' Kasrils favours the latter – but the former (external pressure) was also a formidable force.

Aside from the 1990–94 deal-making and ideological panel-beating, various other international economic constraints emerged. A few weeks after liberation in May 1994, when Pretoria joined the General Agreement on Tariffs and Trade on disadvantageous terms as a 'transitional' not 'developing' country (as a result of pressure from Bill Clinton's White House), the economy's de-industrialization was guaranteed. In January 1995, privatization began in earnest, with Mbeki facilitating the sale of a few minor parastatals, and much bigger targets loomed, including Eskom and Transnet. There was ever more rapid financial liberalization, beginning with Financial Rand exchange controls abolition in March 1995, in the immediate wake of Mexican capital flight that destroyed the peso's value. Without these capital controls, the Reserve Bank lost its main protection against a currency run. When capital flight began in earnest due to an inaccurate rumour about Mandela's health 11 months later, the only strategy left was to raise interest rates to a record high, resulting in a long period of double-digit prime interest rates, the highest in the country's modern history.

The most important post-apartheid economic decision was taken in June

[8] Bond, *Elite Transition*, Chapter 1.
[9] Moloko Moloto, 'Even the fish will vote for ANC, says official', *The Mercury*, 1 July 2013.
[10] Ronnie Kasrils, *Armed and Dangerous*, Fourth Edition (Johannesburg: Jacana, 2013).

1996, when the top echelon of ANC policymakers imposed what Finance Minister Manuel termed a 'non-negotiable' macro-economic strategy without bothering to properly consult its Alliance partners in the union movement and SACP, much less its own constituents. Introduced in the wake of the February 1996 currency crash, mainly in order to promote investor confidence, GEAR allowed the government to psychologically distance itself from the somewhat more Keynesian RDP, a 150-page document which in 1994 had served as the ANC's campaign platform, and which the ANC's civil society allies continued to support. An audit of the RDP (conducted for ANC leadership) showed that only the document's more neo-liberal features were implemented by the dominant bloc in government during the late 1990s, and promises to meet basic needs were, in the main, abandoned.[11]

The constraints would tighten in the years after GEAR codified liberalization as the official ideology. Successive Reserve Bank governors loosened exchange controls even further (nearly 40 times in the next 15 years), and Finance Minister Manuel let the capital flood out when in 1999 he gave permission for the relisting of financial headquarters for most of the largest companies listed on the London Stock Exchange. The firms that took the gap and permanently moved their historic apartheid loot offshore include Anglo American, De Beers diamonds, Investec Bank, Old Mutual insurance, Didata ICT, SAB Miller breweries (all to London), and Mondi paper (to New York).[12] Earlier, giants like Gencor (later BHP Billiton) and Liberty Life had run away – the former with the dubious help of Keys, who came from Gencor to the Finance Ministry and then left in 1994 (to Mandela's disappointment) so as to again lead the firm which he had notoriously aided by approving exchange control relaxation. Of the largest Johannesburg Stock Exchange firms, only a few old Afrikaner corporates kept their primary listing in South Africa, perhaps in part because of their lack of global marketability.

It is here that the core concession made by the ANC during the transition deal was apparent, namely in meeting the desire by white businesses to escape the economic stagnation and declining profits born of a classical 'over-accumulation crisis' – in which too much capital piles up in a given territory without sustainable ways to increase consumer purchases of goods, employment of idle labour, new investment of fixed capital, or value production. There was simply no further route to growth within stagnant, conflict-ridden apartheid South Africa, leading corporates to promote both geographic escapism and what came to be known as 'financialization'.

A symptom of the over-accumulation crisis was declining corporate profits, which actually resembled quite a roller coaster: a downward slide from 1960s

---

[11] Bond, *Elite Transition*, Chapter 3; Patrick Bond and Meshack Khosa (eds), *An RDP Policy Audit* (Pretoria: Human Sciences Research Council Press, 2000).

[12] Earlier, Keys had allowed Billiton (formerly Gencor) to escape to Melbourne in a merger with BHP, and Liberty Life insurance went to London. Keys had formerly been Gencor's executive chairperson, and in 1986 became Minister of Economic Co-ordination, Trade and Industry, switching to finance in 1992. After leaving Mandela's government in September 1994, he became chief executive of Billiton.

levels which were amongst the world's highest, to extremely low rates by the 1980s.[13] (The falling profits trajectory closely followed those of the world's largest firms, in the United States.) But by the late 1990s, mainly through disinvesting from South Africa, deregulating business internally, moving funds from production to commerce and financial speculation, and in the process shifting profit/wage ratios from negative to positive, the major Johannesburg and Cape Town conglomerates reversed the downward slide. By 2001 they were achieving profits that were the ninth highest in the industrialized world.[14]

Looking back, it is apparent that the four most critical processes in shifting resources to capital after apartheid ended were 1) the demise of the sanctions-induced *laager* – and its associated inward-oriented economic policies – so that business elites could escape the saturated South African market, 2) a quickening financialization process which rewarded holders of assets, 3) the deregulation of a variety of SA industries, and 4) the channelling of the 1970s–80s rise of black militancy in workplaces and communities into corporatist union arrangements and patronage politics. Reflecting the success of the latter strategy, there was a steady shift of the national surplus from labour to capital after 1994, amounting to an 8 per cent redistribution from workers to big business in the post-apartheid era. The major decline in labour's share – a full 5 per cent fall – occurred during the mini-crisis from 1998–2001.[15] These dynamics confirmed the larger problem of choiceless democracy in which the deal to end apartheid on neo-liberal terms prevailed: *black nationalists won state power, while white people and corporations would remove their capital from the country, but also remain welcome for domicile and the enjoyment of yet more privileges through economic liberalization.*

Economic outcomes

In the controversial words of one observer: 'I am sure that Cecil John Rhodes would have given his approval to this effort to make the South African economy of the early 21st century appropriate and fit for its time.' That was Nelson Mandela in mid-2003, when launching the Mandela-Rhodes Foundation in Cape Town.[16] 'Fit for its time' meant the Minerals-Energy Complex and financial institutions at the South African economy's commanding heights were

---

[13] Nicoli Nattrass, 'Post-war Profitability in South Africa: A Critique of Regulation Analysis in South Africa', *Transformation*, 9, 3, 1989.

[14] Laura Citron and Richard Walton, 'International Comparisons of Company Profitability', *UK National Statistics Publication Hub*, Oct. 2002, available from www.ons.gov.uk/ons/rel/elmr/economic-trends—discontinued-/no—587—september-2002/international-comparisons-of-company-profitability.pdf, accessed on 2 October 2013.

[15] COSATU, 'Strategic Policy Framework, Ten-Year Plan', Johannesburg, 2004, p. 96, available from www.nehawu.org.za/images/Congress_June2004_Book5_SPF.pdf, accessed on 2 October 2013.

[16] Reported in *The Sowetan*, 26 August 2003.

given priority in all policy decisions, as had been the case over the prior century and a third, along the lines Rhodes had established.[17] As a result:[18]

- the most profitable, fast-growing sectors of the SA economy, as everywhere in the world during the roaring 1990s, were finance, insurance and real estate, as well as communications and commerce, due to speculative and trade-related activity associated with neo-liberalism;
- but the context was stagnation, for overall GDP/capita declined in the late 1990s, and even in 2000 – a growth year after a mini-recession in the wake of the Asian crisis – there was a negative per person rate of national wealth accumulation recorded by the World Bank if we subtract non-renewable resource extraction from GDP so as to more accurately reflect economic activity and net changes in wealth;[19]
- labour-intensive sectors such as textiles, footwear and gold mining shrunk by 1–5 per cent per year (gold hit its low point of $250/ounce in 1998 after peaking in 1981 at $850/ounce), and overall, manufacturing as a percentage of GDP also declined;
- private gross fixed capital formation was a meagre 15–17 per cent during the late 1990s, only picking up to slightly higher levels after 2004 (public sector fixed investment surged, but largely for the construction of white elephant projects);
- the sustained over-accumulation problem in highly-monopolised sectors continued, as manufacturing capacity utilization continued to fall from levels around 85 per cent in the early 1970s to 82 per cent in 1994 to below 80 per cent by the early 2000s;
- instead of funding new plant and equipment in this stagnant environment, corporate profits were redirected into speculative real estate and the Johannesburg Stock Exchange, which by the late 1990s had created the conditions that generated a 50 per cent increase in share prices during the first half of the 2000s, while the property boom which began in 1999 had by 2008 sent house prices up by a world record 389 per cent (in comparison to just 100 per cent in the US market prior to the burst bubble and 200 per cent in second-place Ireland over the 1997–2008 period).[20]

The South African transition is often said to have been characterized by 'macro-economic stability', but this ignores the easiest measure of such stability: exchange rate fluctuations. The currency crashes witnessed over a period of a

---

17 This history is reported upon in Saul's prior chapters, as well as in Bond, *Against Global Apartheid.*

18 Unless otherwise specified, the data below are drawn from two sources: South African Reserve Bank *Quarterly Bulletins* – e.g., www.resbank.co.za/Publications/Quarterly-Bulletins/Pages/QuarterlyBulletins-Home.aspx, accessed 10 October 2013; the annual IMF Article IV Consultations, e.g. www.imf.org/external/pubs/ft/scr/2012/cr12247.pdf, accessed 2 October 2013.

19 World Bank, *Where is the Wealth of Nations?* (Washington DC, 2006), p. 66.

20 *The Economist*, 20 March 2009.

few weeks in February–March 1996 and again in June–July 1998 exceeded 30 per cent, and both led the SA Reserve Bank to impose vicious interest rate increases which in turn sapped growth and rewarded the speculators. Another four such crashes of more than 15 per cent within a few weeks occurred in the dozen years after 2000, as discussed in the next chapter. Moreover, in terms of the quantities of paper wealth destroyed in the process, the main post-apartheid moments of macro-economic *instability* were as dramatic as any other South African economic dislocations during the previous two centuries, including even the 1929–32 Depression and the September 1985 financial panic that split big business from the apartheid regime and paved the way for ANC rule. Domestic investment remained sickly (with less than 2 per cent increase a year during the late 1990s GEAR era when it was meant to increase by 7 per cent), and were it not for the partial privatization of the telephone company (disastrous by all accounts), foreign investment would not have even registered during Mandela's Presidency. Domestic private sector investment was net negative (below replacement costs of wear and tear) for several years, as capital effectively went on strike, moving mobile resources offshore as rapidly as possible.

Recall the mandate for 'Growth, Employment and Redistribution'. Yet of all GEAR's targets over the period 1996–2000, the only ones successfully reached were those most crucial to big business: reduced inflation (down from 9 per cent to 5.5 per cent instead of GEAR's projected 7–8 per cent), the current account (temporarily in surplus prior to the 2000s capital outflow, not in deficit as projected), and the fiscal deficit (below 2 per cent of GDP, instead of the projected 3 per cent). What about the main targets?

The 'G' for growth was actually negative in per capita terms using GDP as a measure (no matter how biased that number is in a 'resource-cursed' society like South Africa, in which the uncompensated depletion of non-renewable minerals is actually an official statistical *positive*). The driving forces behind South African GDP were *de*creasingly based in real 'productive' activity, and increasingly in financial/speculative functions that are potentially unsustainable and even parasitical. The contribution of manufacturing to GDP fell from 21.2 per cent in 1994 to 18.8 per cent in 2002, although the crashing Rand helped push the mining sector up from 7.0 per cent to 8.1 per cent over the same period, while the agriculture, forestry and fishing sectors ranged between 3.2 per cent (2000) and 4.0 per cent (1997). Most tellingly, the category of 'financial intermediation' (including insurance and real estate) rose from 16 per cent of GDP in 1994 to 20 per cent eight years later.

The 'E' for employment was the most damaging initial result of South Africa's embrace of the neo-liberal economic approach, for instead of the employment growth of 3–4 per cent per year promised by GEAR proponents, annual job losses of 1–4 per cent characterized the late 1990s. South Africa's official measure of unemployment rose from 16 per cent in 1995 to 30 per cent in 2002. Adding frustrated job-seekers to that figure brought the proportion of unemployed people to 43 per cent. Meanwhile, labour productivity increased steadily and the number of days lost to strike action fell, the latter in part because of ANC demobilization of unions and hostility to national strikes undertaken for political purposes. These still did happen regularly (e.g. repeated national actions against privatization), but were now more like somewhat formulaic 'set-pieces' in character, entailing no fundamental disruption of power relations.

Finally, the 'R' – redistribution – benefited corporations most because a succession of Finance Ministers – Keys, Liebenberg and Manuel – lowered primary company taxes dramatically, from 48 per cent in 1994 to 30 per cent in 1999. They also maintained the fiscal deficit below 3 per cent of GDP by restricting social spending, notwithstanding the avalanche of unemployment. As a result, according to even the government's own statistics, average black African household income *fell 19 per cent from 1995–2000* (to $3,714 per year), while average *white household income rose 15 per cent* (to $22,600 per year). Not only relative but absolute poverty intensified, as the proportion of households earning less than $90 of real income increased from 20 per cent of the population in 1995 to 28 per cent in 2000. Across the racial divide, the poorest half of all South Africans earned just 9.7 per cent of national income in 2000, down from 11.4 per cent in 1995. The richest 20 per cent earned 65 per cent of all income. The income of the top 1 per cent went from under 10 per cent of the total in 1990 to 15 per cent in 2002. (That figure peaked at 18 per cent in 2007, the same level as in 1949.) The most common measure, the Gini coefficient, soared from below 0.6 in 1994 to 0.72 by 2006 (0.8 if welfare income is excluded).[21] A major United Nations Development Report in 2003 acknowledged that although from 1995 to 2002, the ratio of South Africans living in poverty (defined as $2/day) fell from 51.1 per cent to 48.5 per cent, the absolute number of people living in poverty rose from 20.2 to 21.9 million thanks to population growth. Moreover, extreme poverty (under $1 per day) increased in both absolute and relative terms, from 9.4 per cent to 10.5 per cent.[22] Matters did not subsequently improve, for University of Cape Town economist Haroon Bhorat reported in July 2013, 'Using the national poverty line of $43 per month (in current prices), 47 percent of South Africans remain poor. In 1994, this figure was 45.6 percent.'[23] One may debate the merits of the highly dubious '$/day' measures, but the oft-stated claim by government officials that poverty was reduced during ANC rule appears to be falsified by the state's own rudimentary statistics.

In sum, the acronym GEAR might have more accurately been revised to DUPE – Decline, Unemployment and Polarization Economics. A great many South Africans were duped by Mandela's persuasiveness into thinking that the economy Cecil Rhodes would have found fit for its time would somehow also fit the aspirations of the majority. The big question was whether a variety of social protests witnessed after apartheid by civil society – including many groups asso-

---

[21] Hilary Joffe, 'Growth has helped richest and poorest', *Business Day*, 5 March 2008.
[22] United Nations Development Program, *Human Development Report South Africa* (Pretoria, UNDP, South Africa, 2003).
[23] Haroon Bhorat, 'Economic Inequality Is a Major Obstacle'. *New York Times*, 28 July 2013, available from www.nytimes.com/roomfordebate/2013/07/28/the-future-of-south-africa/economic-inequality-is-a-major-obstacle-to-growth-in-south-africa, accessed 2 October 2013.

ciated with the Mass Democratic Movement – would shift social policy away from its moorings in apartheid white privilege and instead towards a transformative approach empowering of poor people, women, youth, the elderly, the disabled and the ill. Or would social policy instead represent what we might rename 'tokenistic welfarism' and half-baked political patronage?

Social policy in philosophy and practice

In a crude, cynical political sense – i.e., the sentiment needed to interpret elite relations to the masses – the biggest challenge for the new ANC government was how to use state patronage to demobilize South Africa's once-formidable mass movements. On two occasions, in 1992 after the Bisho massacre and in 1993 after the Hani assassination, Mandela had already taken upon himself the duty of corking the anger building below. As he warned at the opening of Parliament in 1995: 'The government literally does not have the money to meet the demands that are being advanced.' As for social policy: 'We must rid ourselves of the culture of entitlement which leads to the expectation that the government must promptly deliver whatever it is that we demand.'[24] Minimalist approaches to social democracy characterized his public policies, since so many of the concrete strategies were suffused with neo-liberal market-oriented characteristics.

The first programme along these lines was Operation Masakhane, 'Let's Build Together', a campaign that Pretoria used to link improved state services – although the initial allocation was only a relatively petty R700 million – to resident payment of rent/service bills. Notwithstanding advertisements by Archbishop Desmond Tutu and former radical trade unionist Moses Mayekiso, its failure coincided with rapid increases in water and electricity prices that were required by the 85 per cent cut in central-to-local state operating subsidy funding transfers. These cuts left many municipalities effectively bankrupt, just at the stage they were taking on responsibility for vast numbers of new residents. Previously, the apartheid-era 'Black Local Authorities' had mainly been funded by Regional Services Councils, and the 1995–96 municipal elections were meant to legitimize the increasingly decentralized municipalities that combined white and black residential areas for the first time.

But even that combination was suspect, because white, Indian and 'Coloured' councillors were overrepresented due to ward-based voting. Thanks to the compromised Interim Constitution of November 1993, 50 per cent of the municipal council seats were allocated to that odd combination, while 50 per cent went to African townships, serving to break the unity of combined 'black' politics. Moreover, the Interim Constitution gave the former grouping inordinate power over planning and budgeting, with a veto possible by mobilizing just a third of a council's seats. Together, these provisions reinforced residual white

[24] Patrick Bond and Greg Ruiters, 'The Development Bottleneck', *Southern Africa Report*, April–May, 1996.

power and made rapid change impossible. Such compromises within the Interim Constitution meant that prospects for genuinely democratic local government, with more engaged social participation, were much reduced. When, in 2000, the municipal demarcation exercise reduced the numbers of local authorities from 843 to 284 – which had the effect of increasing the geographical requirements for service delivery in Bantustans and other poor areas to untenable distances – this also further cut back on the possibility of meaningful local democracy.[25]

By 2002, the result of these shifts of responsibility – 'unfunded mandates' – was that service charges on water and electricity consumed 30 per cent of the income of those households earning less than $70 per month. As unemployment rose during the late 1990s, an upsurge of disconnections resulted, with an estimated 10 million people losing service from 1994–2001. Of these, 60 per cent were not reconnected within six weeks, indicating that poverty was primarily to blame and not the so-called 'culture of non-payment' that those now in power alleged to be a negative legacy from the days of effective anti-apartheid activism.

The worst disconnection rate was for fixed telephone lines, where, of 13 million people connected for the first time, 10 million were cut by 2000, as prices per call soared. This was due to the partial privatization of Telkom that resulted in the demise of internal cross-subsidies, for the new Texan and Malaysian investors attempted to maximize profits, at the expense of poor-customer retention, during the late 1990s. Reflecting the cost-recovery approach to service delivery and hence the inability of the state to properly roll out *and maintain* these functions, the category of GDP components known as 'electricity, gas and water' fell steadily from 3.5 per cent to 2.4 per cent of that GDP's total from 1994 to 2002.[26]

One reason for lack of capital investment was lack of *return* on investment, as the state became increasingly commercialized – thus slowing the rate of electrification in rural areas and even to outlying schools, for example. As noted later, attempts to privatize Eskom's electricity supply were resisted by trade unions. But most importantly, efforts to introduce new Independent Power Producers to the generation mix were foiled by how expensive it was to set up a new power plant, in relation to the residually low cost of production via Eskom's dirty 1970s/80s-era coal-fired plants. Eskom needed to generate higher surpluses to finance a new generation of power plants, and while its bureaucrats ignored the long-term inexpensive renewable options, which had short-term higher capital costs, the state was pumping billions of Rands of subsidies into nuclear research and development, as well as absurd discounts to BHP

---

25 Patrick Bond, *Cities of Gold, Townships of Coal* (Trenton, NJ: Africa World Press, 2000).
26 Patrick Bond, *Unsustainable South Africa* (London: Merlin Press, 2002). For more on the debate regarding water disconnection statistics, see Patrick Bond, *Talk Left, Walk Right* (Pietermaritzburg: University of KwaZulu-Natal Press, 2006), Chapter 8; Ronnie Kasrils, 'Report on Water Cut-offs a Case of Sour Grapes among US Populists', *Sunday Independent*, 8 June 2003; David McDonald, 'Attack the Problem Not the Data', *Sunday Independent*, 15 June 2003.

Billiton and Anglo American Corporation so as to mop up the large 1990s surpluses. Hence in the chaos, there was insufficient new capacity built by the time of the mid-2000s commodity boom, leading to the 2006 Cape Town power outage that cost the ANC its municipal ruling status, and the 2008 national load-shedding that frightened the entire society.

Ordinary people felt the implications of the chaotic decision making. The 1998 national electricity policy called for Eskom to apply 'cost-reflective' pricing policies, which meant much higher charges to poor people, especially those who during the 1980s and early 1990s had fought successfully for a nominal township service charge (often as little as $3 per month). In contrast, recognizing how vital it was to provide cheap electricity and water, the RDP had endorsed the progressive principle of cross-subsidization, which imposed a block tariff that was meant to rise for higher-volume consumers. This redistributive approach would have consciously distorted the relationship of cost to price and hence sent economically 'inefficient' pricing signals to consumers. Such signals would have meant that *poor people should consume more essential services* (for the sake of gender equity, health and economic side benefits), while rich people should save the environment by cutting back on hedonistic consumption, as well as cross-subsidizing everyone else.

The neo-liberal critics of progressive block tariffs correctly insisted that such distortions of the market logic introduce a disincentive to supply low-volume users; their assumption is that the whole point of public utility supply is now to make profits or at least to break even in narrow cost-recovery terms. In advocating against the proposal for a free lifeline and a rising block tariff, a leading World Bank expert advised the first democratic Water Minister, Kader Asmal, that privatization contracts 'would be much harder to establish' if poor consumers had the expectation of getting something for nothing. If consumers weren't paying, the advisor argued, South African authorities required a 'credible threat of cutting service'.[27]

That approach trumped a genuinely redistributive strategy. Not even the next Water Minister, Ronnie Kasrils, could fulfil his promise to revert to the RDP and finally implement a free basic water policy. Indeed Kasrils' high-profile promise led the authors of the Bank's *Sourcebook on Community Driven Development in the Africa Region* to quickly lay out a typical neo-liberal policy for pricing water: 'Work is still needed with political leaders in some national governments to move away from the concept of free water for all.'[28] In 1999, the Bank claimed that the water advisor's 1995 recommendation was 'instrumental in facilitating a radical revision in South Africa's approach to bulk water management'[29] – and also to Asmal's revision away from the micro-economic mandate for Free Basic Water (FBW). When the FBW mandate was finally honoured by Kasrils,

[27] John Roome, 'Water Pricing and Management: World Bank Presentation to the SA Water Conservation Conference', unpublished paper, South Africa, 2 October 1995.

[28] World Bank, *Sourcebook on Community Driven Development in the Africa Region: Community Action Programs* Annex 2 Africa Region (Washington DC: World Bank, 2000).

[29] World Bank, *Country Assistance Strategy: South Africa*, Annex C (Washington DC: World Bank, 1999), p. 5.

as we see in the next chapter, the commercialization instinct was already thoroughly accepted by municipal government suppliers. As a result, FBW ended up either being sabotaged, or delivered in a tokenistic way. To illustrate, in Durban – the main site of FBW pilot-exploration starting in 1997 – the overall cost of water ended up doubling for poor households. This had the direct impact of causing a decline in consumption by a third in the subsequent six years.[30]

Matters were even worse in rural South Africa. After a 1994 White Paper was adopted by Minister Asmal which prohibited subsidies on operating and maintenance costs, his officials began a major capital investment roll-out of community water supply projects featuring communal standpipes at an average distance of 200 metres (c. 650 feet) from residences. Despite the array of problems associated with collecting payment for water from communal standpipes, the principle of full payment for the operating, maintenance and replacement costs was insisted upon. Once projects were built, especially by Mvula Trust and other non-governmental suppliers, communities were meant to receive no further support. Inexorably, extremely serious problems arose in the community water supply projects. Where monitoring and evaluation did take place there were varying estimates about project sustainability, but most were desultory. Even the pro-government Mvula Trust acknowledged that roughly half of the projects it established failed because of inability to maintain the system. The main reasons for unsustainability of a water system invariably included genuine affordability constraints. There was also an unwillingness to pay for communal standpipes as they were often not viewed as a significant improvement on existing sources of water. Other important reasons for failure include poor quality of construction, areas within communities without service and intermittent supply.[31]

Reflecting the rise in capital expenditures and subsequent decline in maintenance across the terrain of social policy, government's 'general services' role in GDP rose from 16.2 per cent in 1994 to 17.3 per cent in 1998, but fell back to 15.8 per cent by 2002.[32] On the one hand, state fiscal support for the social wage increased a little, and recipients of existing apartheid programmes were broadened to include all South Africans. But this expansion was not necessarily a commitment to either social democracy or the 'developmental state' (although that was talked of through the 2000s), given how little the fiscal commitment represented in absolute and relative terms. Instead, as Susan Booysen remarked, the social grants formed a crucial part of the ruling party's 'political regeneration', for the 'ANC-in-government is the dispenser, the patron that ensures social grants and other benefits. This is recognised as the "ANC doing good".'[33]

[30] Patrick Bond, 'Water, Health and the Commodification Debate', *Review of Radical Political Economics*, 2010, 42, 3, September 2010.
[31] David Hemson, 'Rural Poor Play a Role in Water Projects', *Business Day*, 1 July 2003.
[32] Cited in United Nations Development Programme, *South Africa Human Development Report 2003*, Appendix 12 (New York: UNDP, 2003).
[33] Susan Booysen, 'The ANC and the Regeneration of Political Power, 1994–2011', Paper presented at the conference, One Hundred Years of the ANC: Debating Liberation Histories and Democracy Today, Johannesburg, 20–24 September 2011, p.15.

There were some who claimed that these budgetary shifts were profound, including Stellenbosch University professor Servaas van der Berg. He argued that between 1993 and 1997, social spending increased for the poorest 60 per cent of households, especially the poorest 20 per cent and especially the rural poor, and that state subsidies decreased for the 40 per cent who were better off; taken together and by counting in non-pecuniary support from the state, Pretoria could then claim a one-third improvement in the Gini coefficient. Hence the overall impact of state spending, he posited, would lead to a dramatic decline in actual inequality. Unfortunately, van der Berg (a regular consultant to the neo-liberal Treasury Department) made no effort to calculate or even estimate state subsidies to capital, i.e. corporate welfare. Such subsidies remained enormous because most of the economic infrastructure created through taxation – roads and other transport, industrial districts, the world's cheapest electricity, R&D subsidies – overwhelmingly benefits capital and its shareholders, as do many tax loopholes.

Moreover, at the same time, the size and orientation of social grants were not particularly satisfactory, for according to University of KwaZulu-Natal researchers Nina Hunter, Julian May and Vishnu Padayachee:

> The grants do not provide comprehensive coverage for those in need. Unless they are able to access the disability grant, adults are largely excluded from this framework of assistance. It is only possible for the Unemployment Insurance Fund to be received by the unemployed for a maximum of six months and then only by those who were registered with the Fund, for the most part the formally employed.

There were other problems: means-testing was utilized with the inevitable stigmatization that comes with a state demanding proof of poor people's income; cost-recovery strategies were still being imposed, by stealth, on recipients of state services; the state's potentially vast job-creating capacity was never utilized aside from a few short-term public works activities; and land and housing were not delivered at appropriate rates.[34]

In addition, according to Hunter, May and Padayachee, Pretoria's spending on public education was definitely not

> pro-poor, since the share going to the poor and the ultra-poor was substantially smaller than their share of the population. In South Africa, education should be free, but in practice schools require school fees and other costs (such as uniforms, school books and stationery, transport to school) [that] are making it increasingly more difficult for the poorest to access basic education.

In a 2001 state survey, it was revealed that 35 per cent of learners dropped out by Grade 5 (worse than neighbouring Namibia, Lesotho and Swaziland) and 48 per cent left by Grade 12. The state schools were in terrible shape, with 27 per cent lacking running water, 43 per cent without electricity, and

---

[34] Nina Hunter, Julian May and Vishnu Padayachee, *Lessons for PRSP from Poverty Reduction Strategies in South Africa* (Durban: University of KwaZulu-Natal School of Development Studies, 2003).

80 per cent without libraries and computers.[35]

On the brighter side, gender relations recorded some improvements in those early years, especially with the inclusion of reproductive rights in health policy, albeit with extremely uneven access. But one measure of women's poverty in the 1994–2002 period – a $1/day income or below – showed a rise from 10.1 per cent to 11.1 per cent.[36] Women were also victims of other forms of post-apartheid economic restructuring, with unemployment broadly defined at 46 per cent (compared to 35 per cent for men), and a massive late-1990s decline in relative pay, from 78 per cent of male wages in 1995 to just 66 per cent in 1999.[37] Women certainly made major gains in political terms, especially as the new elite consolidated with extensive anti-sexism rhetoric. To illustrate, under white rule before 1994, the share of women in Parliament was 2.7 per cent, and by 2009 it was 42 per cent, fourth highest in the world. By 2009 there were 30 women cabinet ministers and deputy ministers (fourteenth in the world), and a majority of the nine provinces were run by women premiers.[38] The World Economic Forum's 'Global Gender Gap Index' offered comprehensive data for 2011, when South Africa was ranked fourteenth overall of 135 countries.

But there were shockingly low ranking levels when gender intersected class (not to mention race): 67th in wage equality, 69th in primary school enrolment, 72nd in labour force participation, 83rd in literacy and 107th in life expectancy.[39] The class/gender correlations are extreme in areas such as pay for formal work, measured by Statistics South Africa in 2011, as 44.4 per cent of women earned below R2000/month, compared to just 30.5 per cent of men. The average African woman earned R23/hour compared to R91.5/hour for white males. As for time spent on unpaid housework, care of others and collection of water and fuel, a typical day for an African women included 4.43 hours, compared to 1.4 for a white male and 3.3 for a white female.[40] After researching 1997–2006 data, economists Rulof Burger and Rachel Jafta concluded that 'race and gender both played an important role in determining labour market outcomes – although the former is much more important than the latter – and that there is very little evidence to suggest that these effects are disappearing over time'.[41]

One reason was that contemporary South Africa retained apartheid's patri-

[35] Salim Vally and C.A. Spreen, 'Education Rights, Education Policy and Inequality in South Africa', *International Journal of Educational Development*, 26, 4, 2006.

[36] Cited in UNDP, *South Africa Human Development Report 2003*, Appendix 12.

[37] Statistics South Africa, 'The South African Labour Market', Pretoria, 2002 p.147.

[38] Phumla Williams, 'Celebrating our women's liberation', *The South African Government blog*, 30 July 2013.

[39] Ricardo Hausmann, Laura D. Tyson and Saadia Zahidi, 'The Global Gender Gap Report 2011' (Geneva, World Economic Forum, 2012).

[40] Statistics South Africa, 'Gender Statistics 2011', available from http://beta2.statssa.gov.za, accessed on 2 October 2013.

[41] Rulof Burger and Rachel Jafta, 'Affirmative Action in South Africa: An Empirical Assessment of the Impact on Labour Market Outcomes', Working Paper 76 (University of Oxford Centre for Research on Inequality, Human Security, and Ethnicity, March 2010).

archal modes of surplus extraction, thanks to both residual sex discrimination and the migrant (rural-urban) labour system – that is subsidized by women stuck in the former Bantustan homelands. Such women were, quite simply, not paid for their role in social reproduction, something that in a normal labour market would be handled by state schooling, health insurance and pensions. The migrant labour system's deepening after apartheid formally ended was reflected in a survey of rural households in which 24 per cent recorded a reliance on at least one migrant worker in 1993, a figure which increased to 34 per cent in 2004.[42] This structured super-exploitation was exacerbated by an apparent increase in domestic sexual violence associated with rising male unemployment and the feminization of poverty. Women also remained the main caregivers in the home, there again bearing the highest burden associated with degraded health.

With the public healthcare services in decline due to underfunding and the increasing penetration of private providers, infectious diseases such as tuberculosis, cholera, malaria, and AIDS became rife, all far more prevalent than during apartheid. Life expectancy fell from 65 at the time of liberation to 52 a decade later.[43] Diarrhoea killed 43,000 children a year, as a result mainly of inadequate potable water provision. Most South Africans with HIV had, until the mid-2000s, little prospect of receiving antiretroviral medicines to extend their lives. On the other hand, the 1997 *White Paper for the Transformation of the Health System* did at least set out the following national objectives:

(a) unify the fragmented health services at all levels into a comprehensive and integrated National Health System (NHS);
(b) reduce disparities and inequities in health service delivery and increase access to improved and integrated services, based on primary health care principles;
(c) give priority to maternal, child and women's health; and
(d) mobilise all partners, including the private sector, NGOs and communities in support of an integrated NHS.

Four programmes received strategic focus: free health care, the clinic building and upgrading programme, HIV/AIDS, and the Primary School Nutrition Programme.[44]

There was, in fact, some progress to report because most importantly, perhaps, the national Department of Health committed, in 1994, to the prin-

---

[42] Lisa Steyn, 'Measuring the waves of migration', *Mail & Guardian*, 11 January 2013. A subsequent fall in this rate to 18 per cent in 2008 is apparently so far from statistical validity that it is considered to be a quirk.

[43] Statistics SA, 'State of the World Population 2004', Pretoria, 17 September 2004, available at www.statssa.gov.za/news_archive/17sep2004_1.asp. Accessed on 2 October 2013; CNN, 'Life expectancy in Africa cut short by AIDS', 18 March 1999.

[44] Patrick Bond, Yogan Pillay and David Sanders, 'The Rise of Neo-Liberalism in South Africa: Developments in Economic, Social and Health Policy', *International Journal of Health Services*, 27, 1, 1997, pp. 25–40.

ciple, that primary health care (PHC) would be free for pregnant women and children under age six. In 1996 it expanded the commitment to ensure that all South Africans would not pay for 'all personal consultation services, and all non-personal services provided by the publicly funded PHC system', according to government's *Towards a National Health System* statement. As a result, there was a major budget shift from curative care to PHC, with the latter projected to increase by 8.3 per cent in average real terms annually. Closures of hospital facilities in several cities were anticipated to save money and allow for redeployment of personnel (although the closures also affected access, since many consumers used these latter in lieu of clinics).

But other areas of implementation – the District Health System especially for rural areas; clinic building; free primary health care, maternal and child health, and reproductive rights; child nutrition; staffing – relied not only on provincial departments taking the vast bulk of resource, planning and implementation responsibilities.[45] For at a micro level, the rapid establishment of a District Health System was also required. Personnel constraints were also severe. On the one hand, transformation of Department of Health senior management was relatively rapid, with a reduction in the number of white male managers from 99 per cent in 1994 to 50 per cent in 1997. But on the other hand, of even greater concern was the difficulty in staffing new clinics (particularly those in isolated areas). There were, for example, serious shortfalls in medical personnel willing to work in rural South Africa and this required immediately two major programmatic initiatives: the deployment of foreign personnel (especially several hundred Cuban general practitioners) in rural clinics; and the imposition of a two-year Community Service requirement on students graduating from publicly-subsidized medical schools.

Yet if the personnel issue remained a barrier to implementation, regrettably the Department of Health was ambivalent about mobilizing civil society in areas where Community Health Workers could have supported service delivery. The RDP had suggested that 'Communities must be encouraged to participate actively in the planning, managing, delivery, monitoring and evaluation of the health services in their areas'. But Community Workers were excluded in the policy document *Restructuring the National Health System for Universal Primary Health Care*, thus denying the system a potential source of both enthusiastic people and of community eyes and ears on diverse health problems.

The most severe blight on South Africa's post-apartheid record of health leadership was, without question, its HIV/AIDS policy. This could be blamed upon both the personal leadership flaws of presidents Mandela and Mbeki and their health ministers, and also upon features of the socio-political structure of accumulation. With millions of people dying early because of AIDS, and with approximately five million HIV-positive South Africans by 2000, the battle against the disease was one of the most crucial tests of the post-apartheid government.

Pretoria's problem began, arguably, with Mandela's reticence even before

---

[45] Bond et al., 'The Rise of Neo-Liberalism in South Africa'.

1994. In an interview, he explained his hesitation to raise AIDS as a social crisis: 'I was very careful because in our culture you don't talk about sex no matter what you do.' He remarked on advice he received in Bloemfontein by a school principle after asking her: 'Do you mind if I also add and talk about AIDS?' As Mandela recounted, 'She said, "Please don't, otherwise you'll lose the election." I was prepared to win the election and I didn't talk about AIDS.'[46] But Mandela was, at the same time, also prone to accepting quack AIDS 'remedies' like the industrial solvent Virodene, a toxic substance proposed for human ingestion by local researchers, and apparently financed with Mbeki's assistance as an ANC money-making strategy.[47] After this gimmick inevitably failed, Pretoria's subsequent refusal to provide medicinal treatment for HIV-positive patients led to periodic charges of 'genocide' by several authoritative figures: the heads of the Medical Research Council (Malegapuru William Makgoba), SA Medical Association (Kgosi Letlape) and Pan Africanist Congress health desk (Costa Gazi), as well as leading public intellectual Sipho Seepe. Beyond the oft-cited peculiarities of the President himself, there were three deeper reasons why local and global power relationships meant that the battle against AIDS was mainly lost in the first years of liberation.

One reason was the pressure exerted by international and domestic financial markets to keep Pretoria's state budget deficit to 3 per cent of GDP, as mandated in GEAR. The financiers typically oppose increased state spending on healthcare and other social services in a context of massive unemployment (i.e. unprecedented numbers of people who are surplus to the requirements of the capitalist economy). Reflecting this pressure, consider the telling remark of the late Parks Mankahlana, Mbeki's main spokesperson, who in March 2000 justified to *Science* magazine why the government refused to provide relatively inexpensive anti-retrovirals (ARVs) like nevirapine to pregnant, HIV-positive women: 'That mother is going to die and that HIV-negative child will be an orphan. That child must be brought up. Who is going to bring the child up? It's the state, the state. That's resources, you see.'[48]

A second reason was the residual power of pharmaceutical manufacturers to defend their rights to 'intellectual property', i.e., monopoly patents on life-saving medicines. Nor did this pressure end in April 2001 when the Pharmaceutical Manufacturers Association withdrew their notorious lawsuit against the South

---

[46] Interview by Padraig O'Malley, Available at www.nelsonmandela.org/omalley/cis/omalley/OMalleyWeb/03lv00017/04lv00344/05lv01388/06lv01397.htm, accessed on 2 October 2013.
[47] Fiona Ford, 'Mbeki link to toxic cure', *The Star*, 15 September 2007, available at www.iol.co.za/news/south-africa/mbeki-link-to-toxic-cure-1.370777#. UHOjiFE6zdU, accessed 2 October 2013.
[48] *Mail & Guardian*, 21 July 2000. A few months later, Mankahlana reportedly died of AIDS, and in between had also failed two paternity tests. See Jaspreet Kindra, 'Aids drugs killed Parks, say ANC', *Mail & Guardian*, 22 March 2002; SAPA, 'Mankahlana misses maintenance-court hearing', 5 September 2000. Available from http://mg.co.za/article/2002-03-22-aids-drugs-killed-parks-says-anc; and http://www.thepost.co.za/mankahlana-misses-maintenance-court-hearing-1.45811#.Uh6HND84pq0, both accessed 2 October 2013.

African Medicines Act of 1997, which permits parallel import or local production, via 'compulsory licenses', of generic substitutes for brand-name antiretroviral medicines.

A third reason for the elongated HIV/AIDS holocaust in South Africa was the vast size of the reserve army of labour. This feature of the socio-political structure of accumulation allowed companies to readily replace sick HIV-positive workers with desperate unemployed people, instead of providing them with treatment. In 2000, for example, Anglo American Corporation had 160,000 employees. With more than a fifth HIV-positive, the firm began planning 'to make special payments to miners suffering from HIV/AIDS, on condition they take voluntary retirement'. Aside from bribing workers to go home and die, there was a provisional hypothesis that 'treatment of employees with antiretrovirals can be cheaper than the costs incurred by leaving them untreated'. However, in October 2001, a detailed cost-benefit analysis showed the opposite. As a result, 'the company's 14,000 senior staff would receive antiretroviral treatment as part of their medical insurance, but the provision of drug treatment for lower-income employees was too expensive'.[49] This remark summed up so much of post-apartheid South Africa's approach to poor and working-class people: human expendability in the face of corporate profitability. Yet as we will celebrate in the next chapter, these three reasons associated with financial, pharmaceutical and employer profitability were all ultimately overcome by a different reasoning. The victorious view, to prolong life even at the expense of corporate well-being, reflected a shift in the balance of forces in favour of HIV-positive activists in the Treatment Action Campaign, as a result of their tireless work.

Commercialization of the state

It is important to add that the government's regular claim of 'insufficient state capacity' to solve economic, social and environmental problems was matched by a willingness to turn resources over to the private sector. If outsourcing, corporatization, and privatization could have worked anywhere in Africa, they should have done so in South Africa – with its large, wealthy markets, relatively competent firms and advanced infrastructure. However, contrary evidence emerges from the four major cases of commodification of state services: telecommunications, transport, electricity, and water.

In the lucrative telecommunications sector, 30 per cent of the state-owned Telkom was sold to a Houston-Kuala Lumpur alliance in 1996. The cost of local calls skyrocketed, leading the vast majority of new lines to be disconnected. Meanwhile, twenty thousand workers were fired. Attempts to cap fixed-line monopoly pricing by the regulator were rejected by the Texan-Malaysian joint venture via both a court challenge and a serious threat to sell their Telkom shares in 2002. As a result, Telkom's 2003 Initial Public Offering on the New

---

[49] *Wall Street Journal,* 16 April 2002.

York Stock Exchange raised only $500 million, and so, in the process, an estimated $5 billion of Pretoria's own funding of Telkom's late 1990s capital expansion evaporated. A pact on pricing and services between the two main private cellular operators and persistent allegations of corruption combined to stymie the introduction of new cellular and fixed-line operators.

In the field of transportation there was a variety of dilemmas in the first years of democracy associated with partial privatizations. Commercialized toll roads were unaffordable for the poor. Air transport privatization led to the collapse of the first regional state-owned airline. South African Airways was disastrously mismanaged, with huge currency-trading losses that continued well into the 2000s, and an inexplicable $20 million pay-out to a short-lived US manager. The Airports Company privatization led to security lapses and labour conflict. Constant strife with the ANC-aligned trade union threw ports privatization into question. The increasingly corporatized rail service shut down many feeder routes that, although 'unprofitable', were crucial to rural economies.

As for the electricity sector, Pretoria announced in 2004 that 30 per cent of the Eskom parastatal (the world's fourth largest electricity producer) would be sold. That position shifted after a COSATU protest, and soon state policy was to allow 30 per cent of generating capacity to come from new Independent Power Producers. Meanwhile, still anticipating deeper institutional privatization, a corporatizing Eskom fired 30 thousand electricity workers during the 1990s. While a tiny pittance was invested in renewable energy, the state expanded spending on nuclear energy research. This occurred first through pebble-bed reactor technology in partnership with US and British firms and then, after that investment (in the range of $2 billion) was written off, ordinary nuclear reactors were authorized that were estimated to cost $60 billion or more. At the same time, tariffs for residential customers rose much higher as cross-subsidies came under attack during the late 1990s, and the process would intensify dramatically a decade later. As a result of increasingly unaffordable tariffs, Eskom slowed the extension of the rural electricity grid while millions of people who fell into arrears on inflated bills were disconnected – leading to massive (often successful) resistance such as illegal reconnections. With tuberculosis and other respiratory illnesses reaching epidemic levels, those who did not reconnect their electricity illegally were forced back to paraffin or coal fires for cooking, with all the hazards that entailed.

The drive to privatize was not only manifest at national level. Virtually all local governments turned to a 100 per cent cost-recovery policy during the late 1990s, at the urging of central government and the World Bank, largely to prepare for a wave of water and solid waste commercialization. Attempts to recover costs from poor communities inflicted hardships on the most vulnerable members of society, especially women and those with HIV-positive family members susceptible to water-borne diseases and opportunistic AIDS infections. Although water and sanitation privatization applied to only 5 per cent of all municipalities, the South African pilot projects run by world's biggest water companies (Biwater, Suez, and Saur) resulted in a number of problems related to overpricing and underservice: contracts were renegotiated to raise rates because of insufficient profits; services were not extended to most poor people; many low-income residents were disconnected; pre-paid water meters were widely installed; and sanitation was often substandard. It was simply not in the interests of Paris or London water corporations to provide water services to people who could not afford to pay at least the operations and maintenance costs plus a profit mark-up. Cost-recovery policy applied in northern KwaZulu-Natal led to the continent's worst-ever cholera outbreak, catalysed by mass disconnections of rural residents in August 2000, for want of a $10 per household connection fee, which forced more than a thousand people to halt consumption of what had earlier been free, clean water.

For the 10 per cent or so wealthiest whites and a scattering of rich blacks who, throughout, enjoyed insulation from crime and segregation from the vast majority, lifestyles remain at the highest level in the world, however. This was evident to any visitor to the slightly-integrated suburbs of South African cities. The residential 'arms race' – private security systems, sophisticated alarms, high walls and razor wire, gated communities, road closures and booms – left working-class households more vulnerable to robberies, house-breaks, car theft and other petty crime (with increases of more than one third in these categories from 1994–2001[50] and only slight declines since), as well as epidemic levels of rape and other violent crimes. In sharp contrast, escalating corporate crime (including illicit capital flight) was generally not well policed, or suffered from an apparently organized penetration of the South African Police Service's highest ranks, especially during the reign of Jackie Selebi as police commissioner.

Racial apartheid was always explicitly manifested in residential segregation, and, after liberation in 1994, Pretoria adopted World Bank advice that included an avoidance of public housing (virtually no new municipal or even cooperatively-owned units have been constructed), smaller housing subsidies than were necessary, and much greater reliance upon banks and commercial developers instead of state and community-driven development. The privatization of housing was, indeed, one of the most extreme ironies of post-apartheid South Africa, not least because the man taking advice from the World Bank, Joe Slovo, was chair of the SA Communist Party. (Slovo died of cancer soon thereafter and his main ANC bureaucrat, who was responsible for designing the policy, soon became a leading World Bank functionary.) With privatization came more intense class segregation. By 2003, the Provincial Housing Minister responsible for greater Johannesburg admitted to a mainstream newspaper that South Africa's resulting residential class apartheid had become an embarrassment: 'If we are to integrate communities both economically and racially, then there is a real need to depart from the present concept of housing delivery that is determined by stands, completed houses and budget spent.' His spokesperson added: 'The view has always been that when we build low-cost houses, they

[50] Ted Leggett, 'Is South Africa's Crime Wave a Statistical Illusion?' *SA Crime Quarterly* 1, July 2002, available at www.issafrica.org/uploads/CQ1Leggett.pdf, accessed 2 October 2013.

should be built away from existing areas because it impacts on the price of property.' However, the head of one of Johannesburg's largest property sales corporations, Lew Geffen Estates, insisted: 'Low-cost houses should be developed in outlying areas where the property is cheaper and more quality houses could be built.'[51]

Unfortunately it was the likes of Geffen, the commercial bankers and allied construction companies who drove housing implementation, so it was reasonable to anticipate no change in Johannesburg's landscape – featuring not 'quality houses' but what many black residents term 'kennels'. Several hundred thousand post-apartheid state-subsidized starter houses were often half as large as the 40 square meter 'matchboxes' built during apartheid, and located even further away from jobs and community amenities. In addition to on-going disconnections of water and electricity, the new slums suffer lower-quality state services ranging from rare rubbish collection to dirt roads and inadequate storm-water drainage.[52]

Early signs of ecological decay and 'resource curse'

The story is the same when we consider the environment, for South African ecology degenerated in many crucial respects – e.g., water and soil resources mismanagement, greenhouse gas contributions to global warming, fisheries, industrial toxics, genetic modification, the early manifestations of Acid Mine Drainage – in the years immediately after apartheid. Official research conceded this point by 2006 when the *Environmental Outlook* report acknowledged 'a general decline in the state of the environment'.[53]

For example, in spite of water scarcity and water table pollution in the country's main megalopolis, Gauteng, the first two mega-dams within the Lesotho Highlands Water Project were built during the late 1990s, with destructive environmental consequences downriver, and the extremely high costs of water transfer deterring consumption by poor people in Gauteng townships. One result was the world's highest-profile legal case of third-world-development corruption. Another result was the upsurge of social protest in which South Africa's main 'water war' – between Soweto residents and their municipal supplier outsourced to a Paris water company, Suez (whose construction subsidiary was one of the firms prosecuted for corruption in Lesotho) in the early 2000s – can be traced to the higher prices and a commercialized system to which the protesters objected. The wealthiest urban (mainly white) families continued to enjoy swimming pools and English gardens, which meant that in some of the most hedonistic suburbs water consumption was 30 times greater each day than in low-income townships (some of whose resi-

[51] *Saturday Star*, 7 June 2003.
[52] Bond, *Cities of Gold, Townships of Coal*.
[53] South African Government Information, 'The State of our environment should remain under a watchful eye', Pretoria, 29 June 2007, vailable at www.info.gov.za/speeches/2007/07062911151001.htm, accessed 2 October 2013.

dents continue doing gardening and domestic work for whites). Rural (black) women still stand in line for hours at communal taps in the parched former Bantustan areas. The location of natural surface and groundwater remained skewed towards white farmers due to apartheid land dispossession and, with fewer than 2 per cent of arable plots redistributed by 2000 (as against a 1994–99 RDP target of 30 per cent), Pretoria's neo-liberal land policy had conclusively failed.

Other examples of residual apartheid ecology could be cited, including numerous unresolved conflicts over natural land reserves (while displacement of indigenous people continues), deleterious impacts of industrialization on biodiversity, insufficient protection of endangered species, and state policies favouring genetic modification for commercial agriculture. Marine regulatory systems have become overstressed and hotly contested by European and East Asian fishing trawlers, as well as by local medium-scale commercial fishing firms fending off new waves of small-scale black rivals. Expansion of gum and pine timber plantations, largely for pulp exports to East Asia, remained extremely damaging, not only because of grassland and organic forest destruction – leading to soil adulteration and far worse flood damage downriver, such as Mozambique suffered in 2000–2001 – but also due to the spread of alien invasive plants into water catchments across the country. There was a constructive, high-profile state programme, 'Working for Water', that slowed but it did not reverse the growth of alien invasives.[54]

Thanks to accommodating state policies, South African commercial agriculture remained extremely reliant upon fertilizers and pesticides, with Genetically Modified Organisms increasing across the food chain and virtually no attention given to potential organic farming markets. The government's failure to prevent toxic dumping and incineration led to a nascent but portentous group of mass tort (class action) lawsuits. The victims included asbestos and silicosis sufferers who worked in or lived close to the country's mines. Other legal avenues and social activism were pursued by residents who suffered persistent pollution in extremely toxic pockets like South Durban and, just south of Johannesburg, the industrial sites of Sasolburg and Steel Valley. In these efforts, the environmental justice movement almost invariably fought both corporations and Pretoria, which from 1994 downplayed ecological crimes (a Green Scorpions anti-pollution team did finally emerge but with subdued powers that barely pricked). Indeed by 2012, South Africa was recognized as the fifth worst environmental performer out of 132 countries surveyed by Yale and Columbia University ecologists.[55] Moreover, the South African economy's contribution to climate change was amongst the world's highest – twenty times higher than even that of the US – when carbon intensity is measured (that is, carbon dioxide equivalents emitted each year per person per unit of GDP).

One immediate problem that was obvious to even the World Bank by 2000,

54 Bond, *Unsustainable South Africa*.
55 Columbia University and Yale University, *Environmental Performance Index 2012*, New York.

was the way South Africa's reliance upon non-renewable resource extraction gave the country a *net negative per capita income*, once adjustment to standard GDP is made. The typical calculation does not take into account pollution or depletion of minerals, and once such corrections are made, the South African Gross National Income (GNI) per person in the year 2000 of $2837 would be reduced to -$2 per person in total wealth (including 'natural capital'). This decline appears largely due to non-renewable resource depletion, which amounted to 1 per cent of GNI in 2000. Using quite conservative ways of estimating the 'natural capital' in South Africa in 2000 (with rural land valued at nearly $1900 per person, minerals at around $1100 and timber at $300) South Africa relied a great deal more on intangible capital ($49,000) and the urban built environment ($7300).

Neither of these grew sufficiently to offset the shrinking natural capital, wear and tear on manufacturing and costs of pollution. A 2011 edition of *Changing Wealth of Nations* calculates a 25 per cent drop in South Africa's natural capital mainly due to land degradation. By 2008, according to the 'adjusted net savings' measure, the average South African was losing $245 per person per year.[56] Although methodologies are subject to debate, the overall message is fairly straightforward, namely that even relatively industrialized South Africa is dependent upon natural resources, and this makes the proper calculation of income and genuine 'wealth' an increasingly vital task. The conclusion: the more platinum, gold, coal and other metals are being dug from the soil, the poorer South Africa becomes.

Early indicators of social unrest

The question raised by the failure of Mandela's government to solve all these foundational problems is whether matters could have been different if activists and leadership had agreed on a strategy of transformation based on popular empowerment, as well as renewed international solidarity to change global power relations. To some extent, many of the policy papers drafted during the second half of the 1990s contained rhetoric promoting popular participation, but these were consistently undermined by the harsh realities of power relations experienced in every sector.[57]

To some extent, too, the rise of international solidarity was another critical factor; so very important in apartheid's fall it had great potential to assist in addressing South Africa's external economic constraints. For example, poet-activist Dennis Brutus and Archbishop Njongonkulu Ndungane founded Jubilee South Africa in 1998, and argued that the $25 billion in debt that the Mandela government allegedly owed Western banks should be repudiated. They made the case for default on grounds of 'Odious Debt'. Yet on that point, and on many

---

[56] World Bank, *Where is the Wealth of Nations*, Washington DC: World Bank, 2006; World Bank, *The Changing Wealth of Nations*, Washington DC: Workd Bank, 2011.
[57] Bond, *Elite Transition*.

others, post-apartheid foreign policy did not return the favour of anti-apartheid solidarity.

There were other examples of Pretoria's anti-solidaristic foreign relations, in which democrats and social justice activists suffered because of elite links between the ANC and tyrants: the Indonesian and East Timorese people suffering under the corrupt dictator Suharto, Nigerian democracy activists who in 1995 were denied a visa to meet in Johannesburg, the Burmese people (thanks to the Myanmar junta's unusually friendly diplomatic relations with Pretoria), and victims of murderous central African regimes which were SA arms recipients. For example, the National Conventional Arms Control Committee reported that, in the period from 1996 to 1998, undemocratic regimes like those of Colombia, Algeria and Peru purchased more than R300 million Rand worth of arms from South Africa.[58] Pretoria's support for tyrants in Swaziland and Zimbabwe offered the most extreme cases, especially after Mbeki took power in 1999, and Zimbabwean democrats continued to challenge tyrants there.

In general, Mandela's government, instead of combating adverse global, regional or local power balances, chose to legitimize the *status quo.* The occasional exception – Mandela's outrage at the execution of Nigerian environmental activist Ken Saro-Wiwa – proved the rule; the unanimous backlash against Mandela in that case by other African elites merely further convinced Pretoria not to side with democratic movements. Only Palestine solidarity was durable, but this not until after Pretoria's pro-Zionist (black) ambassador was replaced in the early 2000s. Because the post-apartheid era's internal social unrest festered, one result was to prove to be amongst the world's worst cases of xenophobia, as noted in the next chapter.

While the ANC was soon co-opted into an extremely Bantustan elite-like role in helping to manage global apartheid, as shown in the next chapter, the internal South African struggle against injustice also started from day one. By 1995, for example, Mandela was moved to pronounce: 'Let it be clear to all that the battle against the forces of anarchy and chaos has been joined', here referring to the growing rumble of mass actions, wildcat strikes, land and building invasions and other disruptions.[59] In short, while often dismissed as Mandela's honeymoon period, the 1994–99 phase of post-apartheid capitalist consolidation actually included anti-neo-liberal protest by trade unions, community-based organizations, women's and youth groups, Non-Governmental Organizations, think-tanks, networks of CBOs and NGOs, progressive churches, political groups and independent leftists. To illustrate, while the initial 1994 upsurge of confident liberatory shop-floor, student and community wildcat protests gradually subsided, nonetheless sustained critiques of macro-economic and micro-economic policies were periodically recorded against such worthy targets as the Finance Ministry, the Reserve Bank and Minister of Trade and Industry, for:

[58] Peter Batchelor, 'South Africa: An Irresponsible Arms Trader?' *Global Dialogue*, 4, 2, 1999, p. 17.
[59] Bond & Ruiters, 'The Development Bottleneck'.

- imposing sometimes draconian fiscal conservatism;
- leaving Value Added Tax intact on basic goods;
- amplifying tax cuts favouring big firms and rich people;
- repaying apartheid-era foreign debt;
- restructuring the state pension funds to benefit old-guard civil servants;
- letting the country's largest corporates shift their financial headquarters to London;
- liberalizing foreign exchange and turning a blind eye to capital flight;
- granting permission to demutualise the two big insurance companies;
- failing to more aggressively regulate financial institutions;
- not putting discernable pressure on the Reserve Bank to bring down interest rates;
- advancing legislation that would have transferred massive pension fund surpluses (subsequent to the stock-market bubble) from joint-worker/employer control straight to employers;
- making deep cuts in protective tariffs leading to massive job loss;
- giving out billions of dollars' worth of 'supply-side' subsidies for Spatial Development Initiatives, considered 'corporate welfare';
- cutting decentralization grants which led to the devastation of ex-Bantustan production sites;
- generating merely tokenistic attempts at small business promotion;
- lifting the Usury Act exemption (i.e., deregulating the 32 per cent interest rate ceiling on loans);
- failing to impose a meaningful anti-monopoly and corporate regulatory regime.

These were merely a few of the late 1990s economic policy grievances that attracted critique from radical civil society activists, along with campaigns in a variety of other sectoral development fields: land reform, water, energy, housing, welfare, education, local government, environment, defence, policing, foreign affairs, labour, broadcasting, health, transport, public works, public services, justice, public enterprises and sports.[60] Some of these concerned mid-1990s governance debates during the chaotic transition, especially given the truncated nature of municipal democracy described above.[61] The state soon turned to its continuing of its task of systematic demobilization of community groups that had played such an important role in destabilizing apartheid.[62] Recall, for example, the example of the destruction of the United Democratic Front, or the ANC's late 1990s funding of the SA National Civic Organisation (SANCO) in order to sustain a much denuded community institution which invariably backed the Mbeki faction.

[60] Bond, *Elite Transition*, pp. 217–223.
[61] See, e.g. David Everatt et al., 'Civil Society and Local Governance in the Johannesburg Mega-city', Community Agency for Society Enquiry, Johannesburg, for the United Nations Research Institute for Social Development, Geneva, 1997.
[62] Shamim Meer, 'The Demobilisation of Civil Society: Struggling with New Questions', *Development Update*, 3, 1, 1999.

For it was in the urban sphere where real struggles now unfolded (although as we see in the next chapter, in 2001 a 'Landless Peoples Movement' did also briefly arise). In this sphere, capital had begun to earn the status of the ANC's ally of deracialization. Here the most important voice of business was the Johannesburg-based Urban Foundation, later renamed the Centre for Development and Enterprise, which attempted to win civics to their position. One of its leading strategists, Jeff McCarthy, had argued that winning civics over to a 'market-oriented' urban policy would 'hasten the prospect of alliances on broader political questions of "vision"'.[63] In other words, a consensus on urban issues would, McCarthy was suggesting, form the basis for a new post-apartheid political order. The choice of whether or not to join up with this political-economic project was thus perhaps the most important choice that civics faced in the short and medium term. Until 1994, the civics had been resolutely anti-capitalist, but after demobilization began in earnest in 1994, the leadership of SANCO, the supposed pyramid organization of such civics, favoured a corporatist relationship with the ruling party. As a result, genuinely critical civics began to revive in the late 1990s in a much more oppositional guise, and were soon more commonly referred to as the 'new social movements'.

These new movements started off in Durban when ANC stalwart Fatima Meer – Mandela's first authorized biographer – came to the mainly Indian suburb of Chatsworth to gather votes for the ruling party ahead of the 2000 election. Along with local charismatic intellectual Ashwin Desai, she very quickly realized that ANC elites were the main opponents of poor and working-class Chatsworth residents, and switched political sides in 1999. A few months later, in Soweto, Trevor Ngwane did the same, moving from regional leader of the ANC and Johannesburg City Councillor, to the main face of left opposition. After being fired from the ANC because he opposed water commercialization, he organized the Soweto Electricity Crisis Committee and then the Anti-Privatisation Forum in 2000. In Cape Town, the Anti-Eviction Campaign appeared soon afterwards.

Critical civil society of this sort had been meant to be nurtured, according to official documents such as the 1994 RDP: 'Social Movements and Community-Based Organisations are a major asset in the effort to democratise and develop our society. Attention must be given to enhancing the capacity of such formations to adapt to partially changed roles. Attention must also be given to extending social-movement and CBO structures into areas and sectors where they are weak or non-existent.'[64] But this, quite simply, did not happen. For example, an enormous funding boost meant for civics and other CBOs in late 1994 was diverted by Roelf Meyer and Valli Moosa of the Ministry of Constitu-

---

[63] See Mark Swilling, 'Deracialised Urbanisation: A Critique of the New Urban Strategies and Some Policy Alternatives from a Democratic Perspective', *Urban Forum*, 1, 2, 1990; Bond, *Cities of Gold, Townships of Coal*, Chapter 10.

[64] African National Congress, *Reconstruction and Development Programme* (Johannesburg: Umanyano, 1994), Chapter 5. For more on how this would ideally have been implemented, see South African National Civic Organization, *Making People-Driven Development Work* (Johannesburg: SANCO, 1994).

tional Development into advertising (by Saatchi & Saatchi) the state's unsuccessful Masakhane campaign, aimed at getting poor people to start paying for state services they had boycotted payment for during apartheid. Perhaps the most charitable interpretation of the state-society relationship desired by the ANC can be found in an important discussion paper circulated widely within the party. Author Joel Netshitenzhe insisted that, due to 'counter-action by those opposed to change', civil society should instead serve the ruling party's agenda:

> Mass involvement is therefore both a spear of rapid advance and a shield against resistance. Such involvement should be planned to serve the strategic purpose, proceeding from the premise that revolutionaries deployed in various areas of activity at least try to pull in the same direction. When 'pressure from below' is exerted, it should aim at complementing the work of those who are exerting 'pressure' against the old order 'from above.'[65]

However, by the late 1990s, Pretoria's neo-liberal policies ('from above') were causing severe problems in urban South Africa. Because of a simultaneous political break from the African National Congress, the most substantial community groups that formed the Concerned Citizens Forum of Durban in 1999 and Johannesburg's Anti-Privatisation Forum in 2000 became largely disconnected from the more mainline SANCO civics, even if many of their leaders (like Meer, Desai and Ngwane) had themselves been forged in the earlier round of urban struggles.

The composition of South Africa's urban working class was, likewise, changing. The new social subjectivities that were emerging merit study in and of themselves, often becoming sites of 'autonomist' politics.[66] According to a proponent of this analysis, Franco Barchiesi, the new social movements that resulted from neo-liberal policy pain are based on 'community self-management, construction of grassroots discourse, direct action in ways that are so rich, plural and diversified as to be totally at odds with the hierarchical organisational practices of the traditional Left'.[67] That traditional Left was split between tiny (and by 2000 mostly defunct) Trotskyist parties or an SA Communist Party which, though numbering members in the tens of thousands, apparently had no interest in supporting the growing insurgencies from below. Nor was there any credible political party alternative on the left of the ANC Alliance, given how hard it was to win the necessary 50,000 votes to gain a seat in Parliament, as the Azanian People's Organization and Pan Africanist Congress learned as they slipped into oblivion. As a result, local leaders insisted that the new social-movement left had reconstituted itself through novel and appropriate forms of community activism, with the traditional goals of socialism via state power remaining intact. This was the interpretation forcefully reiterated by both the Soweto Electricity Crisis Committee and Anti-

---

[65] African National Congress, 'The State, Property Relations and Social Transformation', discussion document, *Umrabulo*, 5, 3, 1998, p. 12.

[66] Ashwin Desai, *We are the Poors* (New York: Monthly Review, 2002).

[67] Franco Barchiesi, 'After the March on the Left', *Khanya Journal*, December 2002.

Privatisation Forum during its peak years in the early 2000s, for example.[68]

In sum, as the first Mandela moment of post-apartheid South Africa passed, something bigger had begun to jell around 1999 as two kinds of social movement emerged to offer radical challenges to the status quo: the Treatment Action Campaign with their stunningly successful single-issue concerns about AIDS medicines, and the new urban social movements that had even broader potential. The fate of these two models for continuing South Africa's liberation momentum is something that will be taken up in the following chapters.

[68] Trevor Ngwane, 'Sparks in the Township', Interview, *New Left Review*, 22, July–August 2003.

5.

Consolidating the Contradictions:
From Mandela to Marikana, 2000–2012

PATRICK BOND

The evolution of the South African state and society in the early twenty-first century confirmed the more pessimistic predictions: neo-liberalism would fail, thus leading to systemic corruption (sometimes termed neo-patrimonialism), followed by open ruptures thanks to extreme inequality, unemployment and low pay in varied communities and workplaces. The Marikana massacre on August 16, 2012, reflected these trends, as the next chapter reports. However, the story would have been yet more grim if, during the dozen years after 2000, Pretoria had not adopted what we can characterize as 'tokenistic welfarism' in several social policy innovations. Most important was a victory won by civil society activists against President Thabo Mbeki that led to free access to AIDS medicines and then to a dramatic rise in life expectancy. Some social policies, such as Free Basic Services for lifeline water and electricity, were of global importance, yet at the same time suffered severe limitations because of their tokenistic character. All of these developments reflected the overarching problem of neo-liberalism in public policy, operating within a structurally dysfunctional economy that excluded around 40 per cent of the working-age population from employment, overlaid with new gender and race biases, not to mention extreme disregard for the environment.

Ultimately, as we will see, the extreme political turmoil within the ruling party – with three presidents serving in the course of nine months in 2008–09 following the prior year's 'palace coup' against Mbeki at the Polokwane conference of the African National Congress – did not lead to changes in core state processes. The most explicit shifts were Zuma's blind eye to corruption, the addition of a more clumsy securocratic element, a blatant roll-back of constitutional values so as to preserve rulers' power, and the swatting away of challenges from radical youth leader Julius Malema and Zuma's deputy Kgalema Motlanthe at the 2012 Mangaung party Congress.

In this context, the 2000s witnessed a revival of political-economic sloganeering: all manner of newly-adopted phrases were clumsily deployed to characterize state strategy. Of course, these semantic tricks did not seem to work very well in practice. Meant to overcome 'two economies' by spreading the wealth of the first downwards, the much-advertised 'developmental state' failed to materialize. Major government construction projects, soon to be recharacterized as White Elephants, consumed vast public investment funds, such as the ten soccer stadiums built or refurbished for the 2010 World Cup which briefly distracted the society's attention. The 'War on Poverty' was rapidly lost, while subsequent claims to a 'New Growth Path' and 'National Development Plan' were just as misleading. Although $100 billion in new state infrastructure subsidies were promised in 2012, they would be too little, too late – and far too generous to corporations engaged in extraction and processing of minerals, and hostile to ordinary people's basic needs – to address the society's extreme political-economic tensions and ecological damage.

As a result, deep-seated contradictions that had subsided in the mid-1990s deepened throughout the economy and society. The tensions finally boiled up into public view in 2012. As noted below, the idea of Constitutionalist solutions to socio-economic crisis was attractive, but the judicial system was too class-biased in favour of property rights to contain the social anger – not to mention its victimization by presidential meddling and rank favouritism. As a consequence of the failure of internal systemic routes for resolving grievances, South Africa's world-leading rate of community protest during the 2000s was joined – immediately following the Marikana massacre – by wildcat strikes in 2012 affecting a fifth of the country's half-million mineworkers as well as other critical sectors.

Protesters were deterred neither by repression nor by the country's down-graded credit ratings from global financiers. But the lack of a coherent opposition – either in Parliament from liberals, or in the streets, factories and mines from the left – was, as the next chapter documents, notable, notwithstanding such favourable conditions. The failure to generate a progressive post-nationalist politics soon provided an opportunity for an elite reconsolidation by the alliance of pro-business nationalists, communists and more conservative labour activists at the ANC's 2012 Mangaung Conference. The broader neo-liberal project therefore continued and the overall configuration for capital accumulation was still the 'Minerals-Energy Complex' suffused with financialization, better understood by the time of Marikana as a perpetual 'resource curse'.

Economic miracle myths

According to conventional wisdom, Mandela's rejection of a populist turn to nationalization or even slightly more generous fiscal and monetary policies during the late 1990s allowed South Africa to enter the 2000s with much greater 'fiscal space'. There was renewed confidence in state macro-economic management borne of an economic recovery after a low point in 2001. That in turn both allowed an expansion of the welfare state, and reflected growing investor confidence – thanks to the combination of Trevor Manuel at the Treasury and Tito Mboweni at the Reserve Bank through mid-2009, Alec Erwin at Trade and Industry until 2004 and then at Public Enterprises until 2008, and with Mbeki directing the overall ensemble. After a crash, the Rand strengthened from a late-2001 trough in which US$1 bought R13.85, to a mid-2004 peak of R6 to the US$. By then, just after another landslide ANC victory in the national elections (with nearly 70 per cent of the vote) it was easy for the ruling party's defenders to declare that neo-liberal policies 'worked' and now permitted more generous social programmes.

The self-confidence was reflected in the way the government's main policy strategist, Joel Netshitenzhe, wrote about ANC accomplishments: '10 million people [were] connected to water which cannot by any stretch of the imagination be compared with the *few households occasionally cut off* (emphasis added).[1] A few months later, in the *Mail & Guardian*, the government's chief water official conceded that in 2003, '275,000 of all households attributed interruptions to cut-offs for non-payment', which affected in excess of 1.5 million people that year alone.[2]

These are the kinds of positions that must be interrogated in coming pages, before turning to their political implications. So to start, consider in more detail the most eloquent analyst on behalf of the South African economic 'miracle' narrative, Alan Hirsch.

[A]t the centre is a social democratic approach to social reform – it is the state's job to underwrite the improvement in the quality of life of the poor and to reduce inequalities, but with a firmly entrenched fear of the risks of personal dependency on the state and of the emergence of entitlement attitudes ...

The ANC's approach is sometimes summarized as elements of a northern European approach to social development combined with elements of Asian approaches to economic growth, within conservative macroeconomic parameters. This remains the intellectual paradigm within which the ANC operates ...

[B]ecause the ANC was confident of electoral success for at least 10 to 15 years, reaping the liberation political dividend, it did not feel forced to introduce risky, populist economic or fiscal policies to retain electoral support. Long-term growth prospects are brighter today in South Africa than at any other time in its recent history. The macroeconomy is in good shape and is well managed; new state and civic institutions are growing in authority and competence; developmental strategies have been tested and modified, and are now making headway. The country is stable and the government has elicited new levels of trust and confidence ...

Government and businesses in South Africa have learned to manipulate the levers of growth, and redistributive policies are reinforcing the positive growth trajectory. Where the ceiling is no one really knows.[3]

There was little question that 'conservative' parameters were adopted, of course, and in the form of a core set of policies that are applauded, more generally, by Washington when applied in South Africa and similar countries:

* government budget discipline, increased user fees for public services and privatization or commercialization of state enterprises;
* the lifting of price controls, subsidies and any other distortions of market forces;
* liberalization of currency controls;
* higher interest rates and deregulation of the local financial industry;

[1]   *Sunday Times*, 5 April 2004.
[2]   Mike Muller, 'Turning on the Taps', *Mail & Guardian*, 25 June 2004.
[3]   Alan Hirsch, *Season of Hope* (Ottawa: International Development Research Centre; Pietermaritzburg: University of KwaZulu-Natal Press, 2005).

- steady removal of import barriers (trade tariffs and quotas);
- an emphasis on promotion of exports, above all other economic priorities.

In South Africa as elsewhere, the effects of these neo-liberal policies were consistent. Budget cuts depressed most economies' effective demand, leading to declining growth rates compared to the prior Keynesian or statist era. Often the alleged 'crowding out' of productive investment by government spending that justified the policies was not, in fact, the reason for low investment levels. As a result, budget cuts were not compensated for by private sector growth. Privatization processes typically did not distinguish which state enterprises may have been strategic in nature; were too often accompanied by corruption; and often suffered from foreign takeover of domestic industry with scant regard for maintaining local employment or production levels (the buyers' incentive was sometimes simply gaining access to markets or stripping assets).

Moreover, the World Bank and IMF economists who most forcefully promoted privatization and commercialization were unconcerned about supply of 'public goods' which would be widely accepted as more broadly socially beneficial. For example, the positive effects of water supply on public health, environmental protection, local economic activity and gender equality were never calculated, thus never used to justify higher subsidies. As a result, disputes over the price of water graduated into full-fledged social protests during the early 2000s when the state more actively disconnected those who could not afford services. State services were increasingly reduced to mere commodities, requiring of their recipients full cost recovery even though a small, tokenistic subsidy might be provided for initial consumption: 6000 litres (1585 US gallons) per household of water and 50 kilowatt hours of electricity each month (the norm suggested in 2001). As for consumption after that small amount, the water and electricity tariffs chosen universally across South African municipalities meant the price rise for the second block of consumption was prohibitive. The result was higher non-payment rates, higher disconnection levels and lower consumption levels by poor people.[4]

As another reflection of extreme uneven development in South Africa during the 2000s, cities hosted the world's most speculative residential real estate bubble, with an inflation-adjusted price rise of 389 per cent from 1997 to 2008, more than double the second biggest bubble, Ireland's at 193 per cent, according to *The Economist*. (Spain, France and Britain were also above 150 per cent while at the centre of the sub-prime home mortgage crisis, the rise in the US national index was only 66 per cent over the same period.)[5] But inequality

---

4   In the case of Durban, where Free Basic Water was initiated, the doubling of overall water prices from 1997 to 2004 – during the AIDS pandemic, a cholera epidemic and long-lasting diarrhoea – led to a cut in low-income households' consumption by an average of one third. See Bond, 'Water, Health and the Commodification Debate'; Patrick Bond, 'Durban's Water Wars, Sewage Spills, Fish Kills and Blue Flag Beaches', in Patrick Bond (ed.), *Durban's Climate Gamble: Trading Carbon, Betting the Earth* (Pretoria, University of South Africa Press, 2011).

5   *The Economist*, 20 March 2009.

is perhaps most extreme in residential capital flows. Although there were many more houses built for lower-income people annually with state subsidies in the post-apartheid period compared to the last decade of apartheid, World Bank advice in 1994 meant that these were typically half as large, and constructed with flimsier materials than during apartheid; located even further from jobs and community amenities; characterized by disconnections of water and electricity; and with lower-grade state services including rare rubbish collection, inhumane sanitation, dirt roads and inadequate storm-water drainage. True, the policy improved slightly during the early 2000s but the charge that these were worse products than the apartheid regime's 'matchbox' houses for black people continued to hold. Suggestions in the *Reconstruction and Development Programme* that there be somewhat more socialized housing and a very different building system were completely ignored by policy makers.[6]

How were the property and financial bubbles sustained? First, there were crucial residual exchange controls that limited institutional investors to 15 per cent offshore investments during most of the post-apartheid era, and which still – although steadily relaxed (30 times since 1994) – restrict offshore wealth transfers by local elites. Second, a false sense of confidence in macro-economic management prevailed, with property rights sacrosanct in the Constitution and in public policy. The oft-repeated notion is that under Manuel, 'macro-economic stability' was achieved. Yet no emerging market had as many currency crashes (defined as 15 per cent in nominal terms within a month) over that period: South Africa's were in early 1996, mid-1998, late 2001, late 2006, late 2008 and late 2011. By early 2009, *The Economist* ranked South Africa as the most 'risky' of seventeen emerging markets, in large part because corporations caused an enormous balance of payments deficit. The outflows of profits and dividends – which during the 1990s stayed within South Africa – were, after 2000, mainly to the corporates' overseas financial headquarters.[7] BHP Billiton had moved Gencor's old operations to Melbourne, while Anglo American and so many other large firms relocated their financial base to the London Stock Exchange. Amongst the largest South African firms, only the Sanlam insurance conglomerate remained primarily listed in Johannesburg during the early 1990s.

To cover the outflows, a vast new borrowing spree began, with foreign debt rising from $25 billion in 1994 to $80 billion by late 2010 – much associated with World Cup-related construction – and then to more than $140 billion by 2012 as the outflow of profits, dividends and interest accelerated (in 2012 alone, amounting to $12 billion). Moreover, dramatically rising consumer credit was responsible for a buyers' boom – albeit not of local products but mainly those from East Asia (imports were consumed at a rate greater than South African exports after apartheid, even during the 2002–8 commodity price bubble when South Africa rapidly increased its base metals and raw platinum production).

[6]   Bond, *Cities of Gold, Townships of Coal*, Chapters 6–10.
[7]   *The Economist*, 26 February 2009.

If there was a factor most responsible for the 5 per cent GDP growth recorded during most of the 2000s it was, by all accounts, consumer debt; households' debt to disposable income ratios soared from 50 per cent to 80 per cent from 2005–08. As a result, overall bank lending rose from 100 per cent to 135 per cent of GDP. But this overexposure began to become an albatross, with non-performing loans rising from 2007 by 80 per cent on credit cards and 100 per cent on home mortgages compared to the year before, and full credit defaults as a percentage of bank net interest income rising from 30 per cent at the outset of 2008 to 55 per cent by year's end.[8] The big shift after the real estate market peaked in 2007 was the rise of unsecured credit, including 'pay-day lenders' which enforced repayment through garnishee orders that left workers impoverished at the end of each month. By 2012, more than 20 per cent of the $12 billion in quarterly credit extensions were of this nature, causing growing consternation amongst financial regulators.[9] These may appear to be dry numbers, but at the same time the world microfinance industry was crashing, with its guru Muhammad Yunus fired as head of Grameen Bank in 2011 and 250,000 suicides recorded in India by over-indebted small farmers from 2005–11. The pain of excess debt was the source of enormous personal and social conflict, including at Marikana, as we observe in the next chapter.

At the same time, global credit was also dangerously overextended. The world financial meltdown and subsequent crash in trade and production in 2008–09 left South Africa especially exposed, with more than one million jobs lost as a result from early 2009. The decline in corporate tax revenue drove the budget deficit to a near-record 7.6 per cent of GDP for 2009, yet South Africa was not pursuing a classical Keynesian strategy. To get through the crisis, the state was simply carrying through massive construction projects contracted earlier. Anticipated increases in state spending based upon ruling-party promises – especially for job creation – were deferred by the new Finance Minister, Pravin Gordhan, in his maiden budget speech in October 2009. The post-apartheid share of social spending in the total budget only rose from around 50 per cent during the mid-1990s to 57 per cent at the peak of crisis, as a result of social grant transfer payments.[10] Given how little had been spent on blacks during apartheid, this increase hardly represented a major step in building a welfare state.

In short, South Africa's high corporate profits and steady GDP growth during

---

[8]   All data are from the International Monetary Fund 'Article IV Consultations' available at www.imf.org and from the South African Reserve Bank (SARB) *Quarterly Bulletins*, available at www.resbank.co.za/Publications/QuarterlyBulletins/Pages/QuarterlyBulletins-Home.aspx, both accessed 3 October 2013.
[9]   See quarterly issues of the National Credit Regulatory, 'Consumer Credit Market Report,' Johannesburg, available at www.ncr.org.za, accessed 3 October 2013.
[10] SARB, *Quarterly Bulletins*. This increase is mainly explained by the rise in the number of recipients of sub-poverty social grants, which – as noted earlier – were inadequate for anything beyond survivalism. See Nina Hunter, Julian May and Vishnu Padayachee, *Lessons for PRSP from Poverty Reduction Strategies in South Africa'*, Durban, University of KwaZuluNatal School of Development Studies, 2003.

the 2000s did not reflect sustainable accumulation, investment and economic development. The problems were ominous: currency volatility; rapid depletion of non-renewable resources with very little reinvested; wealth derived more from financial markets than from production of real products (in part because of extremely high real interest rates that persisted until 2009); and the continued rise in the Gini coefficient measuring inequality during the 2000s. Zuma might have preferred denial – 'Notions that the gap between the rich and poor in South Africa is widening is a farce', he claimed in late 2012[11] – but all the data available prior to the 2011 Census showed rising inequality.[12]

While the increase in welfare state expenditures continued as a result of rising life expectancy (from a 2004 low of 52 to 60 by 2012), itself a function of social activism with respect to AIDS-medicines access, distribution of the society's surplus continued to malfunction within the labour markets. As Dick Forslund of the Alternative Information and Development Centre explained: 'In 1994, the wage share to GDP was 55.9%. In 2010 it had fallen to 50.6% ... [which] corresponds to R150bn not paid out this year to ordinary employees, and which therefore cannot boost demand, to the benefit of small businesses and industry.'[13]

Moreover, the problem of 'capital strike' – large-scale firms' failure to invest – continued, as national gross fixed capital formation hovered around just 15–17 per cent annually until 2006, hardly enough to cover wear and tear on equipment. After 2006, it was only investment by the state and parastatal agencies that raised the rate, yet these major purchases – such as new South African Airways airplanes, new coal-fired power plants, the 2010 World Cup stadiums, new airports and refurbishments, rail and road transport systems in greater Johannesburg, and a new oil pipeline from Durban – without exception proved extremely expensive, coming in way over budget – not least because of illegal construction company price collision – and with far fewer customers than plan-

---

[11] Babalo Ndenze, 'Inequality gap in SA is a "farce" and media spin, says Zuma', *The Star*, 2 November 2012.

[12] Perhaps the most rigorous review of official data available is Murray Leibbrandt, Ingrid Woolard, Arden Finn and Jonathan Argent, 'Trends In South African Income Distribution and Poverty Since the Fall of Apartheid', OECD Social, Employment And Migration Working Papers No. 101, Cape Town: Southern Africa Labour and Development Research Unit, School of Economics, University of Cape Town, 2010. At the time of writing, the 2011 Census was being debunked for errors, with implications for Gini coefficient data still unclear. Prior to this book's publication, the most recent data came from a 1993–2008 study by a state bureaucrat, Justin Visagie. As *Business Day* reported, 'The upper class also dramatically increased its share of the national income, from 17 to 32 percent, showing a rising concentration of wealth at the top. The middle and lower classes actually lost ground in terms of their combined income share, which decreased from 83 to 68 percent.' Carol Paton, 'SA's upper class "more African – and ever wealthier"', *Business Day*, 29 July 2013.

[13] Dick Forslund, 'Wages, profits and labour productivity in South Africa', *Amandla!* 23 May 2012, available at www.amandla.org.za/special-features/the-wage-and-productivity-debate/1142-wages-profits-and-labour-productivity-in-south-africa-a-reply, accessed 3 October 2013.

ners anticipated. The result was a series of 'white elephants', hardly the basis for building a 'developmental state'.

In the 'second economy', the state wages war on the poor

'We need to disabuse people of the notion that we will have a mighty powerful developmental state capable of planning and creating all manner of employment', said Manuel in October 2008, just as the International Monetary Fund's managing director Dominic Strauss-Kahn told the rest of the world to embark upon quick-fix state deficit spending.[14] This echoed Manuel's 2001 statement to a Sunday newspaper: 'I want someone to tell me how the government is going to create jobs. It's a terrible admission, but governments around the world are impotent when it comes to creating jobs.'[15]

The idea of a 'developmental state' did, at least, provide fixed investment opportunities whereas earlier, private sector investment was at the level of merely maintaining plant and equipment. As the artificial construction-sector boom moved from residential real estate to state projects around 2006, South Africa found itself with many more uneconomic mega-projects:

- the Coega complex in Nelson Mandela Metropole (the old Port Elizabeth and Uitenhage), where massive amounts of electricity and water could one day be consumed in a new smelter (Alcan and subsequently Rio Tinto made initial commitments although in 2008 these were cancelled as electricity shortages became crippling);[16]
- the Lesotho Highlands Water Project dams (Africa's highest), which, since 1998, diverted Lesotho's water out of the Senqu River feeding the Free State water table into the insatiable Gauteng industrial complex, especially for coal-fired power-plant cooling and for Johannesburg swimming-pool fill-ups and the watering of golf courses (a third mega-dam was due for 2013 construction, with more planned through the 2020s);[17]
- the unnecessarily expensive new and refurbished soccer stadiums for the 2010 World Soccer Cup, which soared by a third over budgeted expenditure due to the excessive imports;[18]

---

[14] Cited in Richard Lapper and Tom Burgis, 'South Africans Urged to Beware Left Turn', *Financial Times*, 27 October 2008.

[15] *Sunday Independent*, 9 January 2000.

[16] Patrick Bond, 'Coega, Energy, Corporate Welfare and Climate Crisis', in G. Ruiters (ed.), *Development Challenges in the Eastern Cape* (Pietermaritzburg: University of KwaZulu-Natal Press, 2011), pp. 164–72.

[17] Patrick Bond, 'A Political Economy of Dam Building and Household Water Supply in Lesotho and South Africa', in D. McDonald (ed.), *Environmental Justice in South Africa* (Columbus, OH: Ohio University Press; Cape Town: University of Cape Town Press, 2002), pp. 223–269.

[18] Patrick Bond and Eddie Cottle, 'Economic Promises and Pitfalls of South Africa's World Cup', in E. Cottle (ed.), *South Africa's World Cup: A Legacy for Whom?* (Pietermaritzburg: University of KwaZulu-Natal Press, 2011).

- the corruption-ridden $5 billion Arms Deal was one of the most important markers of the ANC's fall from grace and morality, for companies like Thales from Paris allegedly bribed Jacob Zuma's aide Schabir Shaik, ThyssenKrupp bribed Tony Yengeni and BAE Systems bribed Stella Sigcau, while other highly influential politicians and officials accused of malfeasance include Thabo Mbeki, Trevor Manuel, Joe Modise, Chippy Shaik, Fana Hlongwane and Mac Maharaj;[19]
- nuclear energy – initially Pebble-Bed Nuclear Reactors but after R14 billions of wasted expenditures these were scrapped in 2011 – potentially costing hundreds of billions of rands, alongside hundreds of billions more rands spent on coal-fired power plants (notwithstanding South Africa's already vast existing contributions to climate change through energy-related carbon dioxide emissions);
- the R30 billion Gautrain fast rail network that links Johannesburg, Pretoria and the OR Tambo Airport, subsidized at R350 million per year (because ridership was about one third of what was planned)[20] and affordable only to elite travellers – as were the upgrades of highly-subsidized South African Airways (SAA) and the undertaking of airport refurbishments (including construction of a new one in Durban which was so expensive that SAA cancelled its flights between Durban and Cape Town to save money).[21]

The justification for many such projects was that they will stimulate foreign direct investment,[22] tourism, and other multipliers that bring returns beyond the original capital investment. That these benefits do not necessarily follow was evident in the rhetoric concerning 'two economies'. To make his case, Mbeki divided the South African economy into first world and third world components in a 2003 speech. The former

[19] Terry Crawford-Browne, *Eye on the Money* (Cape Town: Umuzi, 2007). Thanks to Crawford-Browne's hard work, the investigation of the Deal continued in the form of a highly controversial Commission that Zuma picked Judge Willie Seriti to run. The Commission was thrown into crisis in mid-2013 when one of its three members and a senior staffer resigned because of Seriti's alleged 'second agenda'. Core documents showing widespread corruption in government and amongst Zuma associates are available at www.armsdeal-vpo.co.za and http://amabhungane.co.za/article/2011-06-24-the-arms-deal-cache, both accessed 3 October 2013.

[20] Louise Flanagan, 'Taxpayers to Subsidise Gautrain', *The Star*, 21 June 2011.

[21] Sake24 'SAA Stops Durban, Cape Town Flights', 6 October 2010, available at www.sake24.com, accessed 3 October 2013.

[22] To illustrate, on the one hand Hirsch insisted that 'long-term and direct foreign investment entered South Africa in significant volumes'. On the other, Hirsch also provided data that proved the very *opposite*, that until 2001, only the year 1997 witnessed more than a paltry $1.4 billion foreign investment inflow (the year of state phone company Telkom's partial and ultimately unsuccessful privatization), as compared to an average $4 billion a year for *financial* inflows and outflows. As for the $8 billion that flowed in during 2001, Hirsch concedes in an explanatory note: 'The high figures in the direct investment columns for 2001 result from a transaction between Anglo American and De Beers, which resulted in Anglo American moving its domicile to London' (from 1999). In other words, it is only by considering Anglo American as 'foreign' capital that foreign investment rose. Aside from expansion of temporary auto components

is the modern industrial, mining, agricultural, financial, and services sector of our economy that, everyday, become ever more integrated in the global economy. Many of the major interventions made by our government over the years have sought to address this 'first world economy', to ensure that it develops in the right direction, at the right pace. It is clear that this sector of our economy has responded and continues to respond very well to all these interventions. This is very important because it is this sector of our economy that produces the wealth we need to address the many challenges we face as a country ... The successes we have scored with regard to the 'first world economy' also give us the possibility to attend to the problems posed by the 'third world economy', which exists side by side with the modern 'first world economy' ... Of central and strategic importance is the fact that they are *structurally disconnected* from our country's 'first world economy'.[23] (emphasis added)

This approach – reminiscent of old-fashioned 1950s-era modernization theory – become the prevailing discourse in government by 2005. The opposite thesis is that *uneven development* typically generates the 'development of underdevelopment' in certain sites, because the more capital accumulation there is in an economy the more impoverished become those parts of it that are structured to be exploited. Gill Hart adds another angle to the debate as to how Mbeki's shift should be understood:

The operative question, then is not whether the First/Second Economy is an accurate portrayal of reality, but rather how it is being constructed and deployed to do political – or, perhaps more accurately, depoliticising – work. What is significant about this discourse is the way it defines a segment of society that is superfluous to the 'modern' economy, and in need of paternal guidance ... they are deserving of a modicum of social security, but on tightly disciplined and conditional terms.[24]

To illustrate, the migrant labour system did not end with apartheid, and accordingly, many of the same old processes by which urban capital were subsidized by the old racial system continued into the new. What is termed 'the reproduction of labour power' was, after 1994, accompanied by a slightly expanded social wage (a pension and child grant system now reaching into rural areas), which in turn provided an even greater social subsidy to employers. Indeed, employers took an ever-greater share of the national surplus during the 2000s, leaving a substantially lower portion to workers. One of the explanations for this was that urban 'reserve armies of labour' – i.e., poor, unemployed people – were useful insofar as they created competition for unskilled and semi-skilled jobs, and hence cheapened labour. Immigrant workers contributed to the rise in the reserve 'army', with the reproduction of cheap labour reaching much further

(cont) and the subsequent purchases of existing enterprises Absa by Barclays and Vodacom by Vodafone, the amount of foreign direct investment in South Africa was paltry, in turn reflecting the excess idle capacity in most South African manufacturing industries due to local oligopolization, product uncompetitiveness and earlier periods of overinvestment. There were no other major greenfield investments after 2000.

23 Thabo Mbeki, 'Steps to End the Two Nations Divide', *ANC Today*, 3, 33, 2003.

24 Gillian Hart, 'Beyond Neoliberalism? Post-Apartheid Developments in Historical and Comparative Perspective,' in V. Padayachee (ed.), *The Development Decade? Social and Economic Change in South Africa 1994–2004* (Pretoria, HSRC Press, 2005).

into the region after 1994, as millions of new Zimbabweans, Congolese, Mozambicans, Malawians and others were added, often with greater skill and determination levels and, given their desperate conditions at home, a willingness to work for much lower pay. Xenophobia was a logical, tragic outcome.

As a result of these processes, poverty increased, in contrast to the bragging by then Finance Minister Trevor Manuel, who in October 2007 claimed in Parliament that South Africans in poverty 'dropped steadily from 52.1% in 1999 to 47% in 2004 and to 43.2% by March this year.'[25] In reality, a 2010 report of the Organisation for Economic Cooperation and Development prepared by University of Cape Town (UCT) experts declared that since 1994, 'poverty incidence barely changed in rural areas, while it increased in urban areas'.[26] Another UCT report disclosed that the per centage of people below $43 per month income had risen from 45.6 per cent in 1994 to 47 per cent in 2012.[27] This meant that the supposed 'ladder' between the alleged first and second economy had broken.

Even though Mbeki and his colleagues made extravagant claims (e.g., that 1.6 million net new 'jobs' were created between 1995 and 2002[28]) such claims required some pretty ingenious accounting, as journalist Terry Bell exposed:

> Homemakers who help sustain themselves and their families out of backyard vegetable plots or who keep a few chickens are part of the new employed class. In fact, that vast army of the barely hidden jobless who stand forlornly on street corners for hire or who sell coat hangers, rubbish bags or handful of sweets at traffic lights or railway stations in the hope of making a few rand all add to this two million jobs figure. According to the latest statistics, in September 2001, 367,000 workers earned nothing for their labour, while a further 718,000 were paid between R1 and R200 a month.[29]

This sector of the society could not advance during the 2000s, leading in 2008 to a 'War on Poverty' (WoP), announced in Mbeki's final State of the Nation speech. However, within two years, the WoP was lost, and moved to the responsibility of Minister of Rural Development and Land Reform, Gugile Nkwinti, who allowed it to fizzle out almost entirely.[30] In a speech to Parliament in 2010, he confessed the losses he was suffering on rural terrain:

[25] Shaun Benton, 'SA Winning the War on Poverty', *South Africa info*, 31 October 2007, available at www.southafrica.info/about/social/minibudget-311007.htm, accessed 3 October 2013.

[26] Leibbrandt et al., 'Trends in South African Income Distribution and Poverty', p. 36.

[27] Haroon Bhorat, 'Economic Inequality Is a Major Obstacle', *New York Times*, 28 July 2013, available from www.nytimes.com/roomfordebate/2013/07/28/the-future-of-south-africa/economic-inequality-is-a-major-obstacle-to-growth-in-south-africa, accessed 2 October 2013.

[28] SA Government Communications and Information System, *Towards a Ten Year Review* (Pretoria, 2003), p. 36.

[29] Terry Bell, 'How "Non Jobs" come to the Aid of Government Election Propaganda', *Sunday Independent*, 15 February 2004.

[30] Gugile Nkwinti, 'Speech by the Minister of Rural Development and Land Reform, Mr G. Nkwinti (MP), Debate on the Budget Vote of the Department of Rural Development and Land Reform', National Assembly, Parliament, March 24 2010.

Nkwinti suggested that the government's land reform programmes had not been sustainable and confirmed that the target of transferring 30 percent of agricultural land to black farmers by 2014 would not be reached. He revealed that at least nine out of ten emerging farmers given land under the government's land reform policy had failed to make a commercial success of their farmland. A total of 5.9 million hectares had been redistributed since the end of apartheid but 90 percent of that land was not productive.[31]

The reason this part of the WoP was failing, according to Nkwinti, was the beneficiaries' own failure to 'continue producing effectively and optimally on the land'. Yet, according to one report, the government itself had 'failed to pay R3.4bn in post-settlement grants to beneficiaries of land reform with potentially damning consequences'.[32] Nkwinti's spending choices became even more controversial in 2013, when he used his out-of-court willing-seller, willing-buyer power to overrule his own land-claims commissioner and compensate the (white) owners of Mala Mala Game Reserve $100 million on behalf of 15,000 members of the Mhlanganisweni Community in a restitution case. Over the two prior years, a total of $250 million went to settle 800 claims, so this was a remarkably generous deal, according to Rhodes University historian Nomalanga Mkhize:

> When it comes to the resolution of the land question, it is pretty clear that the ANC was outwitted and outplayed at the pre-1994 negotiating table. Perhaps they should have negotiated a comprehensive land settlement package before agreeing on our post-1994 constitutional dispensation. After all, land dispossession was always the fundamental basis of South Africa's 300 years of conflict.[33]

Not even a much-lauded National Development Plan published during 2012 could put the pieces back together again. Headed by former Finance Minister Trevor Manuel, the National Planning Commission (NPC) included talented technical, political, civil society and business thinkers. But its 2011 diagnostic analysis of South Africa's durable problems neglected any consideration of the economic mismanagement described above, and hence no structural changes in macro-economic policy were envisaged. The NPC's main revelation was striking: 'State agencies tasked with fighting corruption are of the view that

---

[31] SAPA 'Land Beneficiaries owed R34 billion', Pretoria, 25 July 2010, available at www.timeslive.co.za/business/article534467.ece/Land-reform-beneficiaries-owed-R3.4bn, accessed 10 October 2013.

[32] iAfrica News, 'Why Land Reform is Failing', 6 July 2010, available at http://business.iafrica.com/features/860926.html, accessed 6 October 2013.

[33] Naledi Nomalanga Mkhize, 'Why the Mala Mala Case Should Compel us to a Second CODESA ... and Fast', *The Con*, 11 August 2013. The only hope was a revival of the Landless People's Movement or some configuration that would gather aggrieved rural South Africans. In mid-2013, the Land, Race and Nation conference provided strong indications of the potential for rural activism, uniting groups like Tshintsha Amakhaya, the Food Sovereignty Campaign, Makukhanye, Mawubuye Land Rights Forum, Coastal Links, Siyazakha, Ilizwi Lamafama, Urban Food and Farming, iThemba Farmers, Mopani Farmers' Union, and the Rural People's Movement.

corruption is at a very high level. Weak accountability and damaged societal ethics make corruption at lower levels in government almost pervasive. Corruption in infrastructure procurement has led to rising prices and poorer quality.'[34] But this was by then an easy critique. The NPC diplomatically deferred analysing the deeper corruption of the economy, the wasting of productive capacity in favour of what is now regularly termed 'financialization'. Capital is incorrectly said to be 'scarce' when in reality there was the opposite problem: excess liquidity in ultra-speculative markets. Moreover, in 2011 the NPC failed even to take notice of the on-going loss of jobs (more than a million since late 2008), instead making the extraordinary claim that 'Unemployment levels are decreasing since 2002'.

The NPC's inability to diagnose economic problems was matched by its disjointed approach to broader socio-environmental decay. On the one hand, the NPC listed atop its infrastructure priority plan two objectives: 'The upgrading of informal settlements' and 'Public transport infrastructure and systems.' But on the other hand it proclaimed that 'users must pay the bulk of the costs' (albeit with 'due protection for poor households'). This contradiction could not be reconciled, however, not when the vast bulk of state investments in commuter rail were in luxury Johannesburg-Pretoria train lines that only a tiny fraction of the public could afford to use and which required more than R1 million per day subsidy, and when an 'e-tolling' system for Gauteng highways was so onerous for ordinary people that the Congress of SA Trade Unions and its allies threatened a national strike to have the toll system revoked.

Similarly, in supplying electricity (the source of so many service-delivery protests), Eskom's huge price increases – already 127 per cent between 2008 and 2011 with many more years of double-inflation annual percentage rises on the horizon – applied to poor households but not to BHP Billiton and Anglo American Corporation. The latter two firms were recipients of special pricing agreements made with apartheid's officials two decades earlier (two such officials, Finance Minister Derek Keys and Eskom Treasurer Mick Davis, promptly joined BHP Billiton after apartheid). Depending upon the source of information, the agreements apparently run through to 2030, supplying power to smelters – transforming imported bauxite into aluminium that is priced too high for local consumption – at R0.12 per kilowatt hour, around a tenth of what poor households pay via self-disconnecting pre-payment meters.[35] The NPC report was silent on such contradictions.

Ironically, the NPC diagnostic argued, 'South Africa needs to move away from the unsustainable use of natural resources' and optimistically asserted: 'South Africa can manage the transition to a low-carbon economy at a pace consistent with government's public pledges, without harming jobs and competitiveness.' Yet the Plan's next two infrastructure priorities would amplify that

[34] National Planning Commission, 'Diagnostic Report', Pretoria, July 2011.
[35] Patrick Bond and Khadija Sharife, 'Above and Beyond South Africa's Minerals-Energy Complex', in D. Pillay et al. (eds), *New South African Review 2*, Johannesburg: University of Witwatersrand Press, 2012, pp. 279–299.

very unsustainability and carbon intensity. 'The development of the Durban-Gauteng freight corridor, including the development of a new dug-out port on the site of the old Durban airport' was part of a $25 billion 'back of ports' strategy to expand the shipping, freight, and petrochemical industry, in spite of near universal South Durban community opposition. Second, the Plan called for 'The construction of a new coal line to unlock coal deposits in the Waterberg, extension of existing coal lines in the central basin' – this in spite of the vast damage (not acknowledged) caused by the coal industry to local and global ecologies.

What the NPC report demonstrated, in short, was that South Africa's control by the 'Minerals-Energy Complex' meant that no change to *status quo* climate-destroying policies was on the cards.[36] Just prior to Durban's hosting of the United Nations COP17 climate summit, Pretoria's November 2011 *Climate White Paper* also failed to grapple with fossil fuel addiction. For as the NPC also argued as its top priority for economic growth South Africa must 'raise exports, focusing on those areas where South Africa has the endowments and comparative advantage, such as mining', even though this *status quo* strategy was so destructive to economy, society, polity and ecology as to represent a profound resource curse. Interestingly, *Business Day* editor Peter Bruce put the point in a fashion quite similar to the position of the government, urging on Gordhan's $100 billion infrastructure spending in early 2012 with the mantra: 'Mine more and faster and ship what we mine cheaper and faster.'[37]

It was obvious that in both the first and second economies, South Africa's 'developmental state' continued to wage war on the poor. There was a nonstop push to deregulate business, make labour markets flexible, and privatize or corporatize state-owned enterprises and this was accompanied by an urging of quite similar and quite specific mandates on various social sectors as well: the elimination of subsidies, promotion of cost recovery and user fees, disconnection of basic state services from those who do not pay, means-testing for social programmes, and reliance upon market signals as the basis for local development strategies. As Stephen Gill has argued, enforcement is crucial, through both a 'disciplinary neo-liberalism' entailing constant surveillance, and a 'new constitutionalism' that locked these policies in over time.[38] Ironically, it was in this context that, in fighting neo-liberalism within social policy, many poor people were persuaded to turn to what would ultimately prove to be a frustrating strategy – demanding constitutionally-guaranteed rights beyond 'first generation' ones (those in the spheres of civil and political freedoms) as their response to state failure.

[36] Patrick Bond, *Politics of Climate Justice*, Pietermaritzburg: University of KwaZulu-Natal Press, 2012.

[37] Peter Bruce, 'Thick End of the Wedge', *Business Day*, 13 February 2012, available at www.bdlive.co.za/opinion/columnists/2012/08/20/the-thick-end-of-the-wedge-the-editors-notebook, accessed on 3 October 2013.

[38] Stephen Gill, 'Globalisation, Market Civilisation, and Disciplinary Neoliberalism', *Millennium*, 24, 3, 1995.

Constitutional rights and wrongs

Defence of the South African Constitution's celebrated socio-economic rights clauses became a cottage industry during the 2000s, especially for liberals and social democrats seeking legalistic answers to the deepening social crisis. In response, neo-liberal critics bemoaned a new 'culture of entitlement' in which the government was expected to solve all social ills,[39] and former Black Consciousness Movement revolutionary leader Mamphela Ramphele (a Managing Director at the World Bank during the early 2000s and later a wealthy venture capitalist) argued forcefully against the rights-based strategy: 'The whole approach of the post-apartheid government was to deliver free housing, free this, free the other. This has created expectations on the part of citizens, a passive expectation that government will solve problems.'[40] Moreover, as we shall see, the courts were only occasional allies of poor South Africans, for they usually worked explicitly within the framework of budgetary limitations and existing public policy, rarely pushing the boundaries on genuine socio-economic progress.

The judges' wariness of supporting social movements requesting even basic civil and political rights was on display on Human Rights Day, 21 March 2004. Just before the grand opening of the Constitutional Court's new building in central Johannesburg, at the site of the old Fort Prison where Nelson Mandela had been incarcerated, community activists in the Anti-Privatisation Forum (APF) called a march to demand their rights to water. They were specifically protesting against the installation of pre-paid water meters in Soweto by the French company Suez, which was running the city's outsourced water company. City officials banned the peaceful protest on grounds of potential traffic disturbances – on a Sunday. The police arrested 52 activists and bystanders, some simply because they were wearing red shirts, and blocked travel of APF buses into Johannesburg. Neither the judges nor Mbeki – who attended the opening ceremony – uttered a word in the protesters' defence, revealing the true extent of their underlying regard for civil and political rights.

The country's highest court had by then heard three major cases on socio-economic rights. The first, in 1997, led to the death of a man, 41-year-old Thiagraj Subramoney, who was denied renal kidney dialysis treatment because the judges deemed it too expensive. Inspired by the Constitution, Subramoney and his lawyers had insisted that 'No one may be refused emergency medical treatment' and that 'Everyone has the right to life.' Chief Justice Arthur Chaskalson replied, 'The obligations imposed on the state by sections 26 and 27 in regard to access to housing, health care, food, water and social security are dependent upon the resources available for such purposes, and that the corresponding

[39] See, e.g., Lungile Madywabe, 'A Compelling need for African Innovation' (Johannesburg: The Helen Suzman Foundation), 2005, p.1.
[40] Cited in Pippa Green, '100 days, 11 issues', *Mail & Guardian*, 17 August 2009.

rights themselves are limited by reason of the lack of resources.' The day after the ruling, Subramoney's plug was pulled and he died.[41]

The next high-profile Constitutional Court case on socio-economic rights was over emergency municipal services, in a lawsuit brought by plaintiff Irene Grootboom in her Cape Town ghetto of Wallacedene. Although she won, the outcome was not positive, for the Court decided simply that the 1994 *Housing White Paper* that was Housing Minister Joe Slovo's last major initiative before he died of cancer in 1994 was unconstitutional for not considering the needs of poor people. That document had as its main priority the 'normalization of the market' for housing in townships. By 2000, when the Grootboom case went to the Constitutional Court, the Slovo policy had left national, provincial and municipal housing authorities without a mandate and plan to supply emergency housing and associated services.

The Court's decision was, however, merely 'negative', for it slapped down existing policy for failing to meet constitutional standards. But the Court did not have the courage and self-mandate to prescribe the policies and practices that *would* be considered of minimal acceptability. As a result, Grootboom and her community remained as destitute as ever, and by 2008, it was tragic yet also logical to read the headline, 'Grootboom dies homeless and penniless', according to Pearlie Joubert in the *Mail & Guardian*:

> Judge Richard Goldstone, a Constitutional Court judge at the time of the hearing, described the Grootboom judgement as unique, saying it will be remembered as 'the first building block in creating a jurisprudence of socio-economic rights.' Grootboom's victory gave legal muscle to the poorest of the poor and has been studied around the world. Her legal representative at the time, Ismail Jamie, said the Grootboom decision was 'undoubtedly one of the two or three most important judgements the Constitutional Court has made since its inception.' This week Jamie said that Grootboom's death 'and the fact that she died homeless shows how the legal system and civil society failed her. I am sorry that we didn't do enough following-up after judgement was given in her favour. We should've done more. I feel a deep regret today,' he said.[42]

The third high-profile case was more encouraging. In 2001 the Treatment Action Campaign insisted that the drug nevirapine be offered to HIV-positive women who were pregnant in order to prevent transmission of the virus to their children. Recall (from Chapter 4) that, a year earlier, Mbeki spokesperson Parks Mankahlana had explained the state's reluctance in an interview with *Science* magazine in cost-benefit terms, essentially arguing that refusing to supply nevirapine was logical in terms of saving state resources.[43] The callous nature of his cost-benefit analysis was confirmed by state AIDS policies, often termed by critics as being basically 'denialist'. The result, according to Harvard School of

---

[41] Constitutional Court of South Africa, 'Soobramoney Decision', 1997, available at www.escr-net.org/usr_doc/Soobramoney_Decision.pdf, accessed 3 October, 2013.

[42] Pearlie Joubert, 'Grootboom dies Homeless and Penniless', *Mail & Guardian*, 8 August 2008.

[43] *Mail & Guardian*, 21 July 2000.

Public Health researchers: 'More than 330,000 people died prematurely from HIV/AIDS between 2000 and 2005 due to the Mbeki government's obstruction of life-saving treatment, and at least 35,000 babies were born with HIV infections that could have been prevented.'[44] The word for this scale of death, genocide, was used to describe Mbeki's policies by the then president of the Medical Research Council Malegapuru Makgoba, by leader of the SA Medical Association Kgosi Letlape, by Pan Africanist Congress health desk secretary Costa Gazi, by leading public intellectual Sipho Seepe, by Young Communist League of SA leader Buti Manamela and by others.

In its mid-2002 judgement, the Constitutional Court criticized the state: 'The policy of confining nevirapine to research and training sites fails to address the needs of mothers and their newborn children who do not have access to these sites. It fails to distinguish between the evaluation of programmes for reducing mother-to-child transmission and the need to provide access to health care services required by those who do not have access to the sites.' One of the lawyers on the successful case, Geoff Budlender, observed that this victory 'was simply the conclusion of a battle that TAC had already won outside the courts, but with the skilful use of the courts as part of a broader struggle.'[45] As argued below, the lessons learned from the TAC struggle are vital to further political development in South Africa, with or without constitutional components.

However, the limits of rights talk became evident in the fourth of the highest-profile socio-economic rights cases, over the right to water. Activists in the Phiri neighbourhood of Soweto insisted upon a social entitlement to an acceptable supply of clean water, amounting to at least 50 litres per person per day and delivered via a metering system based on credit and not pre-payment meters. In October 2009, the Constitutional Court overturned a seminal finding in lower courts that human rights activists had hoped would substantially expand water access to poor people: *Mazibuko et al. vs Johannesburg Water.* In the first ruling, Johannesburg High Court Judge Moroa Tsoka had found that pre-payment meters were 'unconstitutional and unlawful', and ordered the city to provide each applicant and other residents with a 'free basic water supply of 50 litres per person per day and the option of a metered supply installed at the cost of the City of Johannesburg'.[46] Tsoka accused city officials of racism for imposing credit control via pre-payment 'in the historically poor black areas and not the historically rich white areas'. He noted that meter installation apparently occurred 'in terms of colour or geographical area'.[47] It

[44] Amy Roeder, 'The Cost of South Africa's Misguided AIDS Policies,' *Harvard Public Health*, Spring 2009, available at www.hsph.harvard.edu/news/magazine/spr09aids, accessed 3 October 2013.

[45] Geoff Budlender, 'A Paper Dog with Real Teeth', *Mail & Guardian*, 12 July 2002.

[46] *Mazibuko & Others v the City of Johannesburg & Others.* Unreported case no 06/13865 in the Johannesburg High Court, 2008.

[47] Patrick Bond and Jackie Dugard, 'The Case of Johannesburg Water: What Really Happened at the Pre-paid "Parish Pump"'. *Law, Democracy and Development*, 12, 1, pp. 1–28, 2008.

was the first South African case to adjudicate the constitutional right of access to sufficient water.[48]

Johannesburg's appeal was also joined by the national water ministry, and was based on the decision by Johannesburg officials, just a few weeks prior to Judge Tsoka's decision, to retract the ANC promise of universal free basic water service. In the 2000 municipal election campaign, the ANC's statement had been clear: 'The ANC-led local government will provide all residents with a free basic amount of water, electricity and other municipal services so as to help the poor. Those who use more than the basic amounts, will pay for the extra they use.' Initially, Johannesburg Water officials reinterpreted the 'right to water' mandate regressively by adopting a relatively steep-rising tariff curve. In this fee structure, all households received 6000 litres (1585 US gallons) per month for free, but were then faced with a much higher second block (i.e., the curve was convex-up), in contrast to a concave-up curve starting with a larger life-line block, which would have better served the interests of lower-income residents. The dramatic increase in their per-unit charges in the second block meant that for many poor people there was no meaningful difference to their average monthly bills even after the first free 6000 litres. Moreover, the marginal tariff for industrial/commercial users of water, while higher than residential, actually declined after large-volume consumption was reached.[49]

What is the impact of these kinds of water price increases on consumption? The 'price elasticity' – the negative impact of a price increase on consumption – for Durban was measured during the doubling of the real (after-inflation) water price from 1997–2004. For rich people, the price hike resulted in less than a 10 per cent reduction in use. In contrast, the impact of higher prices was mainly felt by low-income people (the bottom one third of Durban's bill-paying residents, in one study) who recorded a very high 0.55 price elasticity, compared to just 0.10 for the highest-income third of the population.[50] Johannesburg and other cities' data are not available but there is no reason to suspect the figures would be much different, and international evidence also bears out the excessive impact of high prices on poor people's consumption.[51] Hence, ironically, as the 'right to water' was fulfilled through Free Basic Water, the result of price changes at higher blocks in Durban and Johannesburg was further water depri-

[48] Republic of South Africa. Constitution of the Republic of South Africa, Act 108 of 1996, Cape Town.
[49] See, e.g. Bond, *Unsustainable South Africa*, and *Talk Left, Walk Right*. In early 2008, changes to Johannesburg Water pricing policy meant that although there was a higher Free Basic Water allotment, of 10,000 litres (2600 US gallons) per month, the promise of free basic water would be kept only for the small proportion of the population declared 'indigent', instead of on a universal basis to all. Facing the lawsuit, and following the departure of the French water company which set the original prices, there was scope for a slightly more redistributive and conservationist pricing system, and the 2008/09 water price increases included very slightly above-inflation rises for higher blocks of consumption.
[50] Reg Bailey and Chris Buckley, 'Modelling Domestic Water Tariffs', presentation to the University of KwaZulu-Natal Centre for Civil Society, Durban, 7 November 2005.
[51] Veronica Strang, *The Meaning of Water*. Oxford: Berg, 2004.

vation for the poor alongside increasing consumption in the wealthier suburbs – with this is in turn creating demand for more bulk water supply projects (including another Lesotho Highlands Water Project dam) which will then have to be paid for by all groups, and which will have major environmental impacts.

Resistance strategies and tactics developed over time. Activists attempted to evolve what was already a popular township survival tactic on diverse fronts – illicitly reconnecting power once it was disconnected by state officials due to non-payment for example (in 2001, 13 per cent of Gauteng's connections were illegal) – to a more general strategy. Thus socialist, but bottom-up, ideological statements of self-empowerment were regularly made by the APF and member organizations such as the Soweto Electricity Crisis Committee. Indeed, within a few months of Johannesburg Water's official commercialization in 2000, the APF had united nearly two dozen community groups across Gauteng, sponsoring periodic mass marches of workers and residents. The APF was also the core activist group in the Coalition Against Water Privatisation, which supported the Phiri complainants in a court process that lasted from 2003 through 2009.

The Constitutional Court's October 2009 ruling, however, vindicated Johannesburg Water, affirming that the original amount of 25 litres (6.6 US gallons) per person per day plus pre-payment meters were 'reasonable and lawful' because self-disconnections were only a 'discontinuation', not a denial of water services: 'The water supply does not cease to exist when a pre-paid meter temporarily stops the supply of water. It is suspended until either the customer purchases further credit or the new month commences with a new monthly basic water supply whereupon the water supply recommences. It is better understood as a temporary suspension in supply, not a discontinuation.' The Coalition Against Water Privatization was disgusted with the Court's logic, however: 'We have the highest court in the land saying that those poor people with pre-paid water meters must not think that their water supply has discontinued when their taps run dry ... Such "logic", and even worse that it is wrapped up in legal dressing and has such crucial practical consequences, is nothing less than mind boggling and an insult both to the poor and to the constitutional imperatives of justice and equality.'[52]

The case was useful nonetheless in revealing the broader limits to the merely constitutional framing of socio-economic rights, one such limitation being the concomitant 'domestication' of the politics of need, as Tshepo Madlingozi put the point. By taking militants off the street and putting them into courts where their arguments had to be panel-beat – removing any progressive and quasi-socialist intent, for example – the vain hope was to acquire judges' approval.[53] Another critical legal scholar, Marius Pieterse, complained that 'the transformative potential of rights is significantly thwarted by the fact that they are typi-

[52] Coalition against Water Privatization, Press Statement: 'One Step Forward, Two Steps Back'. Johannesburg, 25 March 2009.
[53] Tshepo Madlingozi, 'Good Victim, Bad Victim: Apartheid's Beneficiaries, Victims and the Struggle for Social Justice', in W. le Roux and K. van Marle (eds), *Law, Memory and the Legacy of Apartheid*, Pretoria: University of Pretoria Press, 2007.

cally formulated, interpreted, and enforced by institutions that are embedded in the political, social, and economic status quo'.[54] Added Daniel Brand: 'The law, including adjudication, works in a variety of ways to destroy the societal structures necessary for politics, to close down space for political contestation.' Brand specifically accuses courts of depoliticizing poverty by casting cases 'as private or familial issues rather than public or political'.[55]

Commoning medicines during the AIDS pandemic

One solution, both proposed and acted upon, has been the moving of rights talk to that of 'commoning', articulating more clearly and politically the collective claim for public goods. For this, in turn, can represent a more consistent form of sustained resistance to neo-liberalism, one potentially ranging from mass protest to micro-level mutual aid. The AIDS victory in the Constitutional Court could not have been achieved without the broader political sensibility won in 1999–2002 by activists who converted AIDS from a personal health stigma into a social cause that required a commoning of medicines that had earlier been privately consumed, at great cost, by only those with class and race privileges.

Because so many lives were lost in the early 2000s, and because the struggle to save subsequent lives of millions of HIV-positive South Africans was ultimately victorious, it is worth understanding in detail how a small, beleaguered group of activists with compromised immune systems had such an extraordinary impact on public policy while also challenging the whole notion of commodified healthcare. The South African government's 1997 Medicines Act had actually made provision for compulsory licensing of patented drugs, and this in turn helped to catalyse the formation in 1998 of a Treatment Action Campaign (TAC) that lobbied for AIDS drugs. In the late 1990s, such anti-retroviral medicines (ARVs) were prohibitively expensive for nearly all the five million people who would need them once their blood counts ('CD4') fell below 250.

That campaign was immediately confronted by the US State Department's 'full court press' against the Medicines Act (the formal description provided to the US Congress), in large part to protect intellectual property rights generally, and specifically to prevent the emergence of a parallel inexpensive supply of AIDS medicines that would undermine lucrative Western markets. The campaign included US Vice President Al Gore's direct intervention with SA government leaders in 1998–99, to revoke the law. (Significantly, in July 1999, Gore launched his 2000 presidential election bid, a campaign generously funded by big pharmaceutical corporations). As an explicit counterweight,

---

54 Marius Pieterse, 'Eating Socioeconomic Rights: The Usefulness of Rights Talk in Alleviating Social Hardship Revisited', *Human Rights Quarterly*, 29, 2007, pp. 796–822.
55 Danny Brand, 'The Politics of Need Interpretation and the Adjudication of Socio-Economic Rights Claims in South Africa', in A. J. van der Walt (ed.), *Theories of Social and Economic Justice*, Stellenbosch: Stellenbosch University Press, 2005.

TAC's allies in the AIDS Coalition to Unleash Power (ACTUP) began to protest at Gore's campaign events in the United States. The protests ultimately threatened to cost Gore far more in adverse publicity than he was raising in Big Pharma contributions, so he changed sides and withdrew his opposition to the Medicines Act – as did Bill Clinton a few weeks later at the World Trade Organization's Seattle Summit.

Big Pharma did not give up, of course. The main South African affiliates of the companies that held patents filed a 1999 lawsuit against the constitutionality of the Medicines Act, counterproductively entitled 'Pharmaceutical Manufacturers Association of SA v. Nelson Mandela' (a case which even *Wall Street Journal* editorialists found offensive). It went to court in early 2001, but by April there were also additional TAC solidarity protests world-wide against pharmaceutical corporations in several cities by *Medicins sans Frontiers*, Oxfam and other TAC solidarity groups. Such public pressure compelled the Association to withdraw the suit and by late 2001, the Doha Agenda of the World Trade Organization adopted explicit language permitting violation of Trade-Related Intellectual Property Rights for medical emergencies.

It is also true that Big Pharma's reluctance to surrender property rights so as to meet needs in the large but far-from-lucrative African market coincided with the rise of philanthropic and aid initiatives to provide branded medicines. The Bill and Melinda Gates Foundation's parallel health services in countries like Botswana undermined state health services; it was no coincidence that Gates himself stood more to lose than anyone on the planet in the event intellectual property was threatened. Given such prevailing power relationships, the South African government did not invoke any compulsory licensing of medicines even after the 2001 lawsuit was withdrawn. Local generics manufacturers Aspen and Adcock Ingram did, however, lower costs substantially through voluntary licensing of the major AIDS drugs. It is in this sense that not only decommodification, but also deglobalization of capital was considered vital to expanding access to the ARVs. Similar local licensing arrangements were soon arranged for firms in Kampala, Harare and other places.

This struggle was one of the most inspiring in the context of Mbeki's neoliberal-nationalist years. Elsewhere in South Africa, independent left movements struggled to turn basic needs into human rights, making far-reaching demands (and even occasionally winning important partial victories): the provision of improved health services (which led to endorsement of a National Health Insurance in 2010), an increase in free electricity from the tokenistic 50 kilowatt hours per household per month, especially given the vast Eskom price increases starting in 2008, thoroughgoing land reform; a prohibition on evictions and the disconnection of services, free education, lifeline (free) access to cellphone calls and text messages, and even a 'Basic Income Grant', as advocated by churches and trade unions. The idea in most such campaigns was that services should be provided to all as a human right by a genuinely democratic state, and to the degree that it was feasible, financed through cross-subsidization by imposition of much higher prices for luxury consumption.

Because the 'commodification of everything' was still under way across

Africa however, *decommodification* could actually form the basis of a unifying agenda for a broad social reform movement, if linked to the demand to 'rescale' many political-economic responsibilities that were handled by embryonic world-state institutions. The decommodification principle was already an enormous threat to the West's imperial interests, as in, for example, the denial of private corporate monopolies based on 'intellectual property'; resistance to bio-piracy and the exclusion of genetically modified seeds from African agricultural systems; the renationalization of industries and utilities (particularly when privatization strategies systematically failed, as happened across Africa); the recapture of indigenous people's territory via land grabs; and the empowerment of African labour forces against multinational and local corporate exploitation.

To make further progress along these lines, delinking from the most destructive circuits of global capital would also be necessary, combining local decommodification strategies with traditional social movements' calls to close the World Bank, IMF and World Trade Organization (WTO), and with rejection of the United Nations' neo-liberal functions and lubrication of US imperialism. Beyond that, the challenge for Africa's and South Africa's progressive forces, as ever, was to establish the difference between 'reformist reforms' and reforms that advanced a 'non-reformist' agenda (in the terminology of Andre Gorz – but also termed 'structural reforms' by John Saul). The latter attempts were to win gains that did not strengthen the internal logic of the system, but that instead empowered the system's opponents. Hence, unlike reformist reforms, non-reformist reforms would not have a co-optive character. Neither would they lessen the momentum of reformers (as did many successful reformist reforms). Rather, they would heighten the level of meaningful confrontation by opening up new terrains of struggle. The non-reformist reform strategy would include generous social policies stressing decommodification, exchange controls, and more inward-oriented industrial strategies allowing democratic control of finance and ultimately of production itself. These sorts of reforms would strengthen democratic movements, directly empower producers (especially women) and, over time, open the door to the contestation of capitalism itself.

However, not only did imperialism stand in the way of such change, so too did Pretoria's own diverse sub-imperial concerns. For, notwithstanding their occasionally leftist rhetoric, Mbeki, Motlanthe and Zuma situated their country as the continent's leading bourgeois-aspirant state, i.e., as the modern international equivalent of an old-fashioned South African Bantustan, where the co-opted elite prospered under conditions both of global apartheid and of indefensible local (and widening) class divisions.

Looking outward

Another confusing feature of South African society in the twenty-first century is foreign policy, especially in view of the ruling party's traditions of hot rhetoric about global realities. Just prior to the 'Coalition of the Willing' invasion of Iraq in 2003, for example, Nelson Mandela declared that George W. Bush, 'who cannot think properly, is now wanting to plunge the world into a holocaust. If there is a country which has committed unspeakable atrocities, it is the United States of America.'[56] Yet within weeks, three Iraq-bound US warships had docked and refuelled in Durban, and South Africa's state-owned weapons manufacturer, Denel, had sold $160 million worth of artillery propellants and 326 handheld laser range-finders to the British army and 125 laser-guidance sights to the US Marines. Bush visited the South African capital Pretoria in July 2003, and left the impression, according to Johannesburg's *Business Day* newspaper, 'of a growing, if not intimate trust between himself and Mbeki. The amount of public touching, hugging and backpatting they went through was well beyond the call of even friendly diplomatic duty.'[57] By May 2004, Mandela had telephoned Bush in a cowed and conciliatory mood, for, as he put it, 'The United States is the most powerful state in the world and it is not good to remain in tension with the most powerful state.'[58]

In spite of the confusing signals from South Africa's leaders – occasionally talking left while mainly walking right – there can be no doubt that from the late 1990s the international political power centres showed increasing trust in Mandela, Mbeki, Manuel and Trade Minister Alec Erwin, giving them insider access to many elite forums. At the time, global-establishment institutions were coming under strong attack at sites like the Seattle and Cancun World Trade Organization summits, the annual meetings of the World Bank and International Monetary Fund, G8 meetings, a Gothenburg summit of the European Union, and the Davos World Economic Forum. Given the global elites' need for legitimacy, Pretoria's lead politicians were now to be allowed to preside over the UN Security Council, the board of governors of the International Monetary Fund and the World Bank, the United Nations Conference on Trade and Development, the Commonwealth, the World Commission on Dams, and many other important international and continental bodies. Simultaneously assuming third world leadership, Pretoria also headed the Non-Aligned Movement, the Organisation of African Unity, and the Southern African Development Community.[59]

In addition, during a frenetic two-year period beginning in September 2001, Mbeki and his colleagues hosted, led, or played instrumental roles at the following dozen major international conferences or events: the World Conference against Racism (Durban, September 2001); the launch of the 'New Partnership for Africa's Development/NEPAD' (in Abuja, Nigeria, October 2001); the WTO ministerial summit in Doha, Qatar (November 2001); the UN Financing for Development conference in Monterrey, Mexico (March 2002); the G8 summit in Kananaskis, Canada (June 2002); the launch of the African Union (Durban, July 2002); the World Summit on Sustainable Development

---

[56] *Independent* Online, 30 January 2003.
[57] *Business Day*, 11 July 2003.
[58] *Mail & Guardian*, 24 May 2004.
[59] Bond, *Against Global Apartheid.*

(WSSD) (Johannesburg, August–September 2002); the World Economic Forum in Davos, Switzerland (January 2003); the G8 summit in Evian, France (June 2003); George W. Bush's first trip to Africa (July 2003); the WTO ministerial summit in Cancun, Mexico (September 2003); and the IMF/World Bank annual meeting (Dubai, September 2003).

In the event, Mbeki's administration failed to capitalise on these opportunities, however:

- at the UN racism conference, Mbeki colluded with the European Union to reject the demand of NGOs and African leaders for slavery/colonialism/apartheid reparations;
- NEPAD provided merely a home-grown version of the Washington Consensus;
- at Doha, Trade Minister Alec Erwin split the African delegation so as to prevent a repeat of the denial of consensus that had foiled the Seattle WTO summit in December 1999;
- Manuel was summit co-leader in Monterrey, where he legitimized on-going IMF/World Bank strategies, including its lack of progress on debt relief;
- from G8 meetings, Mbeki departed with only rhetorical commitments, invariably to be violated in practice;
- the African Union supported both NEPAD and the Zimbabwean regime of President Robert Mugabe, suggesting that good governance would not be considered a component of Africa's new partnerships;
- at the Johannesburg WSSD, Mbeki undermined UN democratic procedure, facilitated the privatization of nature, and did nothing to address the plight of the world's poor majority;
- in Davos, global elites ignored Africa;
- for hosting a leg of Bush's Africa trip, Mbeki became the US 'point man' on Zimbabwe, and avoided any argument as regards Iraq's recolonization;
- in Cancun, the collapse of WTO trade negotiations – again (like Seattle) catalysed by an African walkout – left Erwin 'disappointed';
- at Dubai, with Manuel leading the IMF/World Bank Development Committee, there was no Bretton Woods democratization, new debt relief or post–Washington Consensus policy reform.[60]

After 2003, the pace slowed, with the focus shifting to three major hosting responsibilities: the 2010 World Cup, 2011 United Nations Climate Summit and 2013 Brazil-Russia-India-China-South Africa summit. In the meantime, problems in establishing NEPAD as an all-encompassing assertion of South Africa's strength and values on the continent deserve more consideration for, by all accounts, this too petered out in disappointment. The origins of NEPAD and the African Peer Review Mechanism are revealing. Mbeki had embarked upon a late 1990s 'African Renaissance' branding exercise, which he endowed with poignant poetics but not much else. The lack of content was somewhat reme-

[60] See Bond, *Talk Left, Walk Right*.

died during 2000 in a PowerPoint skeleton unveiled in Mbeki's meetings with Clinton in May, at the Okinawa G8 meeting in July, at the UN Millennium Summit in September, and at a subsequent EU gathering in Portugal. The skeleton was fleshed out in November 2000 with the assistance of several economists and was immediately ratified during a special South African visit by World Bank President James Wolfensohn. By this stage, Mbeki had managed to sign on as partners two additional rulers from the crucial north and west of the continent: Abdeleziz Bouteflika of Algeria and Olusegun Obasanjo of Nigeria (both leaders of countries that suffered frequent mass protests and various civil, military, religious and ethnic disturbances). Later, he added Senegal's Abdoulaye Wade, who in 2012 was to be ousted from power by mass popular protest.

Addressing an international gathering in Davos, January 2001, Mbeki made clear whose interests NEPAD would serve: 'It is significant that in a sense the first formal briefing on the progress in developing this programme is taking place at the World Economic Forum meeting. The success of its implementation would require the buy-in from members of this exciting and vibrant forum!'[61] Of course, international capital would benefit: from large infrastructure construction opportunities, privatized state services, on-going structural adjustment (which lowers the social wage and workers' real wages), intensified rule of international property law, and various of NEPAD's sectoral plans, all to be co-ordinated from a South African office at the Development Bank of Southern Africa, a World Bank-style institution staffed with neo-liberals and prone to economic and geopolitical gatekeeping. Once Mbeki's plan was merged with an infrastructure-project initiative offered by Wade, it won endorsement at the last meeting of the Organisation of African Unity, in June 2001. (In 2002, this became the African Union, and NEPAD would long serve as its official development plan.)[62]

The actual NEPAD document was publicly launched in Abuja, Nigeria, by African heads of state on 23 October 2001. In February 2002, global elites celebrated NEPAD at venues ranging from the World Economic Forum meeting in New York to the summit of self-described 'progressive' national leaders (but including Britain's Tony Blair) who gathered in Stockholm to forge a global 'Third Way'. Elite eyes were turning to the 'scar on the world's conscience' (as Blair described Africa), hoping NEPAD would serve as a large enough band-aid, since G8 leaders at their June 2002 summit in Canada had already rejected Mbeki's plea for an annual $64 billion in new aid, loans and investments for Africa.

For perhaps the main reason for international doubts about Mbeki's commitment to neo-liberalism and the rule of law was his repeated defence of the continent's main violator of liberal norms, Mugabe. This loyalty was in spite of NEPAD promises: 'Africa undertakes to respect the global standards of democracy, the core components of which include political pluralism, allowing for ... fair, open and democratic elections periodically organised to enable people to

---

[61] *Business Day*, 5 February 2001.
[62] Patrick Bond (ed.), *Fanon's Warning* (Trenton: Africa World Press, 2005).

choose their leaders freely.' Yet Mbeki would term Zimbabwe's demonstrably unfree and unfair March 2002 presidential election as 'legitimate', and repeatedly opposed punishment of the Mugabe regime by the Commonwealth and the UN Human Rights Commission. In February 2003, South African Foreign Minister Nkosazana Dlamini-Zuma even stated: 'We will never criticise Zimbabwe.' It is not surprising then that NEPAD secretariat's Dave Malcomson, responsible for international liaison and co-ordination, once admitted to a reporter that 'Wherever we go, Zimbabwe is thrown at us as the reason why NEPAD's a joke.'[63] At the June 2003 G8 meeting in Evian, France, world elites were well aware of NEPAD's lack of street credibility. They thus provided only paltry concessions to Mbeki, what the *Financial Times* termed 'year-old pledges to provide an extra $6 billion a year in aid to Africa' – a fraction of the amount spent on the Iraq War just weeks earlier.

Why did South Africa's rulers consistently support Mugabe? In mid-2001, Mbeki told the British television show *Hard Talk* that he had tried persuading Mugabe to reform, but that the Zimbabwean ruler 'didn't listen to me'. By November, Mbeki publicly attributed Zimbabwe's problems to 'twenty years of economic policies' (with no details – e.g., was Mugabe's failed 1990s IMF-blessed Economic Structural Adjustment Program included?). Mugabe was often blamed for 'socialist' policies, yet his social spending spree was, in reality, a brief two-year period of rising education and health expenditures until 1984, followed by systematic cutbacks and deprivation under IMF and World Bank guidance. It is more likely that Pretoria backed Harare because of a common trajectory, for as Zimbabwe began to implode during the late 1990s, and as Mugabe appeared to have squandered both political popularity and the legitimacy to govern, the ANC leadership must have looked north and observed the following as if in a mirror:

- a liberation movement which won resounding electoral victories against a terribly weak opposition, but under circumstances of worsening abstentionism by, and depoliticization of, the masses;
- concomitantly, that movement's undeniable failure to deliver a better life for most of the country's low-income people, while material inequality soared;
- rising popular alienation from, and cynicism about, nationalist politicians, as the gulf between rulers and the ruled widened inexorably and as numerous cases of corruption and mal-governance were brought to public attention;
- growing economic misery as neo-liberal policies were tried and failed;
- the sudden rise of an opposition movement based in the trade unions, quickly backed by most of civil society, the liberal petit-bourgeoisie and the independent media – potentially leading to the election of a new, post-nationalist government.[64]

[63] *Financial Times*, 'G8 Vows to "Fully Commit" to Developing African Nations', 2 June 2003.
[64] Patrick Bond and Masimba Manyanya, *Zimbabwe's Plunge*, London: Merlin Press, 2003.

There were also material economic reasons for letting Zimbabwe's economy suffer, insofar as South African business was the primary beneficiary of de-industrialization just across the Limpopo River. As for other cases within what became known as South Africa's 'sub-imperialist' drive up continent, Johannesburg businesses were assertive especially in banking, breweries, construction, mining, services and tourism. The largest South African corporations benefited from NEPAD's lubrication of capital flows out of African countries – though the money did not stop in Johannesburg. For a financial flight was taking place, mainly to London, where the Anglo American Corporation, De Beers, Old Mutual insurance, South African Breweries, Liberty Life insurance and other huge South African firms had relisted. Moreover, the regional acquisitions by South African corporations were in any case mainly takeovers, not 'greenfield projects' involving new fixed investments. Thus, on the one hand, in spite of a high-profile mid-2002 endorsement of NEPAD by 187 business leaders and firms, led by Anglo American, BHP Billiton and the Absa banking group, there had been no investments made in twenty key infrastructure projects to be reported two years later, though there were plenty of vocal corporate complaints that NEPAD's peer review mechanism had insufficient teeth to discipline errant politicians. According to the chief reporter of (pro-NEPAD) *Business Day* in mid-2004: 'The private sector's reluctance to get involved threatens to derail NEPAD's ambitions.'[65]

On the other hand, the prospect that Johannesburg-based corporations were becoming 'new imperialists' was of 'great concern', according to Pretoria's then Public Enterprises Minister, Jeff Radebe, speaking in early 2004: 'There are strong perceptions that many South African companies working elsewhere in Africa come across as arrogant, disrespectful, aloof and careless in their attitude towards local business communities, work-seekers and even governments.'[66] But Radebe could also have been describing his Cabinet colleague Mbeki. The *Sunday Times* reported from the July 2003 African Union meeting in Maputo that Mbeki was viewed by other African leaders as 'too powerful, and they privately accuse him of wanting to impose his will on others. In the corridors they call him the George Bush of Africa, leading the most powerful nation in the neighbourhood and using his financial and military muscle to further his own agenda.'[67]

That agenda continued after Mbeki, becoming evident in March 2013 when tragically, 15 corpses of SA National Defence Force (SANDF) soldiers were recovered in Bangui after apparently trying to guard Johannesburg businesses – some linked to ANC's Chancellor House and other ANC leaders – in the Central African Republic's capital against the Chad-backed Seleka rebel movement. A few weeks later, another 1350 SANDF soldiers were deployed in the resource-rich eastern Democratic Republic of the Congo as part of a peace-keeping force

[65] Rob Rose, 'Companies "Shirking" their Nepad Obligations', *Business Day*, 24 May 2004.

[66] SAPA, 'SA's "Imperialist" Image in Africa', 30 March 2004.

[67] Ranjeni Munusamy, 'The George Dubya of Africa', *Sunday Times*, 13 July 2003.

(not far from where Zuma's nephew Khulubuse had bought into a major oil exploration project).

South African critics of Mbeki were joined by African intellectuals who demanded better from their leaders as well, and many such critics seemed to understand clearly Pretoria's continental ambitions. To illustrate, at a joint conference in April 2002 in Accra, Ghana, the Council for Development and Social Science Research in Africa (CODESRIA) and Third World Network Africa identified the 'most fundamental flaws of NEPAD' as follows:

- the neo-liberal economic policy framework at the heart of the plan ... which repeats the structural adjustment policy packages of the preceding two decades and overlooks the disastrous effects of those policies;
- the fact that, in spite of its proclaimed recognition of the central role of the African people to the plan, the African people have not played any part in the conception, design and formulation of the NEPAD;
- notwithstanding its stated concerns for social and gender equity, it adopts the social and economic measures that have contributed to the marginalization of women;
- that in spite of claims of African origins, its main targets are foreign donors, particularly in the G8;
- its vision of democracy is defined by the needs of creating a functional market.[68]

Nor did not take long for the pessimists' predictions to come true, as even on its own terms NEPAD was fundamentally flawed. As Senegalese President Wade stated in October 2004: 'I am disappointed. I have great difficulties explaining what we have achieved when people at home and elsewhere ask me ... We're spending a lot of money and, above all, losing time with repetition and conferences that end and you're not quite sure what they've achieved.'[69] In June 2007, at the World Economic Forum meeting in Cape Town, Wade acknowledged that NEPAD 'had done nothing to help the lives of the continent's poor'.[70] Later that year, Wade was even more frank: 'The redirection of the project has become inevitable, because nobody has yet understood anything from NEPAD and nobody implemented NEPAD.'[71] As Mbeki himself confessed a few weeks after his ouster from power, in December 2008, 'I am afraid that we have not made the progress we had hoped for. Indeed, and regrettably, I believe that we have lost some of the momentum which attended the launch and detailed elaboration of the NEPAD programmes.'[72]

[68] Council for Development and Social Science Research in Africa, Dakar and Third World Network-Africa, 'Declaration on Africa's Development Challenges', Resolution adopted at the Joint Conference on Africa's Development Challenges in the Millennium, Accra, 23–26 April 2002, p. 4.

[69] BBC, 'Africa's big plan "disappointing"', London, 22 October 2004.

[70] L. Ensor, 'South Africa: Get Down to Brass Tacks – Mbeki', *Business Day*, 18 June 2007.

[71] *Daily Observer*, 'Wade: Nepad has failed', 4 October 2007.

[72] SAPA, 'Nepad losing momentum: Mbeki', 12 December 2008.

Mbeki's African Peer Review Mechanism (APRM) itself was conceived so that African regimes – including South Africa's (to great internal consternation) – would essentially review themselves with kid gloves and, when civil society's own critique emerged, this was merely repressed.[73] According to Bronwen Manby from AfriMAP (a pro APRM NGO):

> Although each country that has undergone the APRM process is supposed to report back to the APR Forum on its progress, there is no serious monitoring exercise of how effectively this is done. Nor any sanctions for failure to act. Nor, apparently, is there any real system to ensure that the commitments the government makes address the most important problems highlighted in the APRM review ... The implementation of the APRM programme of action is also left entirely to the executive, with no formalised role for parliamentarians or civil society to hold the government's feet to the fire should it fail to perform ... Even the continental APRM secretariat failed to engage in any serious way with national institutions ... Without this sort of integration into other national planning systems, debates and oversight mechanisms, the APRM process seems doomed to become little more than a cosmetic exercise without effect in the real world of policy and decision making.[74]

In sum, the imposition of NEPAD's neo-liberal logic soon amplified uneven development in Africa, including South Africa. Added to the invasion by Chinese firms specializing in neo-colonial infrastructure and extractive industries, as well as cheap (but de-industrializing) manufactured goods, and to the West's preparations for military interventions from the oil-filled Gulf of Guinea in the west to the Horn of Africa in the east, it was apparent that Africa was now to be squeezed even harder. Patents, marketing restrictions and inadequate state-financed research made life-saving medicines unreasonably scarce; genetically modified food threatened peasant farming; and trade was also increasingly exploitative because of the 'Singapore issues' advanced in their own interests by the G8 countries as regards investment, competition, trade facilitation and government procurement. Indeed, the new conditionalities merely amplified the grievances of developing nations as regards the negative impact upon them of the G8's vast agricultural subsidies, unfair industrial tariffs, incessant privatization of services, and intellectual property monopolies. Together, these prompted African–Caribbean–Pacific withdrawal from the ministerial summit of the World Trade Organization (WTO) in Cancun in September 2003, leading to its collapse, with no subsequent improvements in the following years.

Throughout this period, there was a larger Washington geopolitical agenda for Africa, which Bush's first Secretary of State, Colin Powell, described in a document, *Rising US Stakes in Africa*: political stabilization of Sudan (whose oil was craved by Washington); support for Africa's decrepit capital markets, which could allegedly 'jump start' the Millennium Challenge Accounts (a new aid

---

[73] Patrick Bond, 'Removing Neocolonialism's APRM Mask: A Critique of the African Peer Review Mechanism', *Review of African Political Economy*, 36: 122, 2009, pp. 595–603.

[74] Bronwyn Manby, 'African Peer Review Mechanism: Lessons from Kenya', *Pambazuka News*, 362, 15 April 2008.

regime); more attention to energy, especially the 'massive future earnings by Nigeria and Angola, among other key West African oil producers'; promotion of wildlife conservation; increased 'counter-terrorism' efforts, which included 'a Muslim outreach initiative'; expanded peace operations, transferred to tens of thousands of African troops thanks to new G8 funding; and more attention to AIDS. On all but Sudan, South African cooperation was crucial to the US imperial agenda. In late 2006, for example, when Bush wanted to invade Somalia to rid the country of its nascent Islamic Courts government, he called in Mbeki to assist with legitimating the idea, though it was ultimately carried out by Meles Zenawi's Ethiopian army three weeks later.[75] When in 2011, Obama wanted to invade Libya to rid the country of Muammar Gaddafi, South Africa voted affirmatively in the UN Security Council, even though Zuma had tried to intervene to save him via an African Union peace-keeping plan.[76]

On occasions such as the 2009 and 2012 recapitalizations of the International Monetary Fund, especially to generate larger bailout financing options for Europe, South Africa's finance ministers could be relied upon. Manuel consistently promoted the kind of debt relief that resulted in low-income African countries actually paying a much *higher* percentage of export income on debt relief – because, while the un-repayable capital was written down, the on-going repayment obligations actually increased.[77] As for South Africa's financial role in Africa, mid-2002 witnessed Manuel promising the Commonwealth Business Council he would 'fast-track financial market integration through the establishment of an internationally competitive legislative and regulatory framework' for the continent.[78]

---

[75] White House Press Office, 'Press Release: Remarks by President Bush and President Mbeki of South Africa in Photo Opportunity,' Washington, 8 December 2006. Specifically, Mbeki referred to: 'the difficult situation in Somalia' – ('Yes, sir,' Bush intervened) and Mbeki continued, 'and the President, together, we are very keen that, indeed, something must move there. This was a failed state. It's necessary to support the transitional government, to restoring a government and to reunify the country, and so on. It's an important thing because the problem, one of the big problems is that as it is, it provides a base for terrorists, find safe haven there and then can spread out to the rest of the continent. It's something that is of shared concern.' Within three weeks, at Washington's behest, Ethiopia invaded Somalia. (See *Sudan Tribune*, 10 December 2010, reporting on WikiLeaks cables, http://www.sudantribune.com/spip.php?article37189, accessed 3 October 2013).

[76] An opponent of Mbeki in contesting continental politics, Gaddafi's own links to Zuma were potentially important prior to the 2011 uprising; the 'Browse Mole' report by veteran journalist Ivor Powell – who was then working for the Scorpions special police unit dedicated to corruption – named Zuma as a beneficiary of largesse from both Libya and Angola, an allegation the *Mail & Guardian* considered 'credible'. See Sam Sole, 'Browsed and Beaten', *Mail & Guardian*, 1 May 2009 and Ivor Powell, 'Smoke and Mirrors', *Mail & Guardian*, 1 May 2009.

[77] Lynley Donnelly, 'Throwing Good Money at EU Troubles', *Mail & Guardian*, 22 June 2012.

[78] Trevor Manuel, 'Mobilizing International Investment Flows: The New Global Outlook', speech to the Commonwealth Business Council, Johannesburg, 24 September 2002.

But without any Africa-wide progress to report two years later, Manuel's director-general Lesetja Kganyago announced a new 'Financial Centre for Africa' project to amplify the financialization tendencies already evident in Johannesburg's exclusive new Sandton central business district: 'Over the five years to 2002, the financial sector grew at a real rate of 7.7% per year, more than twice as fast as the economy as a whole.'[79] Responsible for a full quarter of post-apartheid South African GDP growth, the sector required further room to expand. According to Kganyago:

> What is needed is a financial hub especially focused on the needs and circumstances of the region, much in the same way that Singapore and Hong Kong cater for the capital needs of the Asian continent ... International financial centres tend to have a foundation in common. Elements include political stability, free markets, and what is best described as the rule of commercial law.

Pretoria's specific aims included 'opening South Africa's markets to African and global issuers; global lowest trading costs and trading risk; global leadership in investor protection; and a global hub for financial business process outsourcing'. Concluded Kganyago: 'Africa's economies cannot wait the slow maturing of national financial markets to provide the necessary channel for large-scale foreign capital flows for development. Only a regional financial centre will be in a position to provide these services in the foreseeable future.'

In the same spirit, Reserve Bank deputy governor Daniel Mminele acknowledged in November 2012 that Pretoria stood alongside Washington in *opposing global regulation* such as the 'Robin Hood tax' on financial transactions that was supported by more enlightened countries, including those from Europe being roiled by global financiers. Moreover, Mminele conceded, 'South Africa is aligned with advanced economies on the issue of climate finance' and against those of the South, especially when it came to the matter of paying 'ecological debt' to increasingly desperate countries already losing 400,000 people per year to climate-caused deaths. South Africa, in other words, stood out in the world as an extremist advocate of neo-liberal global financial governance.[80] Yet ironically, by 2012 Mbeki was reinventing himself as a leading critic of illicit capital flight from Africa.[81]

A telling incident in mid-2002 illustrated the responsibility that the South African government had taken on to police such world financial mechanisms. A Cabinet meeting in Pretoria concluded with this statement: 'The meeting noted the provision by South Africa of a bridge loan to the Democratic Republic

---

[79] Lesetja Kganyago, 'South Africa as a Financial Centre for Africa', speech to the Reuters Economist of the Year Award Ceremony, Johannesburg, 11 August 2004.

[80] Daniel Mminele, 'South Africa and the G20 – Challenges and Opportunities', presentation to the SA Institute of International Affairs and the University of Pretoria, Pretoria, 31 October 2012.

[81] Thabo Mbeki, 'Tackling Illicit Capital Flows for Economic Transformation', Thabo Mbeki Foundation, Johannesburg, 2012, available at www.thabombekifoundation.org.za/Pages/Tackling-Illicit-Capital-Flows-for-Economic-Transformation.aspx, accessed 3 October 2013.

of the Congo of Special Drawing Rights (SDR) 75 million. This will help clear the DRC's overdue obligations with the IMF and allow that country to draw resources under the IMF Poverty Reduction and Growth Facility.'[82] In ensuring the rollover of the debt, Pretoria thus sanitized the earlier generation of IMF loans made to Mobutu Sese Seko, riven with corruption and capital flight to European banks.

Continuities with an earlier sub-imperial project were obvious, for the people of the DRC were previously victims of South Africa's apartheid-era allegiance with Mobutu, an arrangement that especially suited the ecology-destroying mineral extraction corporations headquartered in Johannesburg. The people's struggle against oppression had initially spawned another ruler in 1996, Laurent Kabila, who unfortunately refused democracy and later fell to an assassin's bullet. Thanks to his son Joseph's connections in Union Buildings and Finance Ministry, however, the old 'odious' Mobutu loans were honoured and serviced with Pretoria's new credits. They should have been repudiated. In addition, IMF staff would be allowed back into Kinshasa with their own new loans, and with neo-liberal conditionalities again applied to the old victims of Mobutu's fierce rule. A similar process was offered to regimes such as Mugabe's Zimbabwe and King Mswati's Swaziland for the purpose of repaying the IMF first and foremost, although Pretoria's conditionalities were just as tough as the IMF's so these did not materialize. For these reasons, and others, the 2000s was a period that could be considered South Africa's 'sub-imperialist' era.[83]

The big question raised by Zuma's Presidency was whether the momentum from Mbeki's years would continue, given the former's preoccupations with domestic matters. Only in 2012 was the answer decisively affirmative: Nkosazana Dlamini-Zuma's election as African Union Commission chairperson was engineered, and Pretoria secured entry into the Brazil-Russia-India-China bloc (previously BRIC, now BRICS). The next question was whether these interventions would generate a return, because BRICS' attempts to adjust global governance in the large emerging economies' interests were revealed as hapless when three BRICS governments lined up publicly in support of three different candidates for World Bank President in 2012: South Africa favoured a neo-liberal Nigerian finance minister, Brazil promoted a progressive Keynesian economist from Colombia and Russia backed Washington's inevitably-victorious choice of US citizen Jim Yong Kim. Also in 2012, BRICS committed to support the IMF's recapitalization with $75 billion, of which South Africa gave $2 billion[84] – in spite of

[82] South Africa Government Communications and Information System, 'Statement on Cabinet Meeting', Pretoria, 26 June 2002.

[83] For more on the role that South Africa has come to play vis-à-vis its neighbours in southern Africa, see D. Miller, O. Oloyede, R. Saunders (eds), 'South Africa in Africa – African perceptions, African realities', special issue of the *African Sociological Review*, 12, 1, 2008.

[84] Explaining the SA contribution – initially he said it would be only one tenth as large – Gordhan told *Moneyweb* that it was on condition that the IMF became more 'nasty' (*sic*) to desperate European borrowers, as if the Greek, Spanish, Portuguese and Irish

simultaneously arguing the need for a 'BRICS Development Bank' because the Bretton Woods Institutions were unresponsive. Meanwhile, the 'Bank of the South' project advocated for many years by the Venezuelan leader Hugo Chavez did not get South Africa's support. In sum, the critique of Mbeki – that in the cases of NEPAD and so many other global-governance strategies he was only polishing the chains of global apartheid, not breaking them – applied equally to Zuma.

Conclusion

Liberated South Africa, approaching its two-decade birthday, was very different than what was claimed for it at its 1994 birth – and as was still advertised at the time that Mandela stepped down from the Presidency in 1999. As argued in the last chapter, many of the structural problems that left the edifice shaky after 2000 were due to compromises his government had overseen in the early years, and that were then amplified during Mbeki's nine-year reign. As a result of this combination, an ever more extreme fusion of nationalist rhetoric and neo-liberal practice made South Africa amongst the most difficult countries to read, politically, by late 2012. At that point, the society was beset by such severe contradictions – such as the Marikana massacre – that matters nearly came to a head during the main political conventions. Only the centripetal forces that were threatening to break the ruling party, the trade union movement and the Alliance could restore the power brokers at the centre, especially Zuma, SACP leader Blade Nzimande, and COSATU general secretary Zwelinzima Vavi. All were reelected handily in 2012. Had the nervous constituencies not returned these men to power, however, a fracturing of the Alliance and its components might well have begun in earnest that year.

The contradictions would become worse, as one of the most prescient observers of South African politics, William Gumede, forecast just after the 2007 ANC leadership putsch of Mbeki at the Polokwane Congress: 'For all the doubts that hang over Zuma's character, many argue that he offers a crit-ical conduit for the poor's grievances. These people are going to be disap-

---

(cont) poor and working people were not suffering enough. The result of this BRICS intervention was that China gained dramatically more IMF voting power, while Africa actually lost a substantial fraction of its share. Gordhan then admitted at the September 2012 Tokyo meeting of the IMF and Bank that it was likely 'the vast majority of emerging and developing countries will lose quota shares – an outcome that will perpetuate the democratic deficit'. Given 'the crisis of legitimacy, credibility and effectiveness of the IMF', it 'is simply untenable' that Africa only has two seats for its 45 member countries. Yet Gordhan's role in promoting the BRICS' expanded capital commitment to the IMF was the proximate cause of perpetuating the crisis of legitimacy. (*Moneyweb*, 'Special report podcast: Pravin Gordhan – Minister of Finance', 29 September 2011, available at www.moneyweb.co.za/moneyweb-special-report/special-report-podcast-pravin-gordhan—minister-of,.; also Pravin Gordhan, 'IMFC Statement by Pravin J. Gordhan, Minister of Finance, South Africa', Wash-ington, IMF, 13 October 2012, available at www.imf.org/external/am/2012/imfc/statement/eng/zaf.pdf, both accessed 3 October 2013.

pointed.'[85] Indeed the personal quickly became all too political, as Zuma turned to controversial private accumulation strategies that included $35 million spent on his homestead and nearby roads, while his own family accumulated fortunes in the process. Asked in 2010 about the lucrative and extremely dubious deal that global steelmaker ArcelorMittal (formerly SA's state-owned ISCOR) cut with a consortium including his son, Duduzane, as well as questions regarding his nephew Khulubuse's role in hotly-contested oil prospecting claims in the Democratic Republic of the Congo, Zuma replied, 'Nobody has said, "Here is corruption." I think for people to think that if you are a Zuma you can't do business is a very funny thing, I tell you.'[86] Not everyone was amused, and one dissident Communist leader, David Masondo, offered a frank rebuttal, speaking of 'ZEE – Zuma Economic Empowerment'. For Masondo, 'ZEE is not only an assault on the Young Communist League and South African Communist Party resolutions – which called for the nationalization of monopoly industries – it amounts to a burial of the Freedom Charter. Only a few can be misled to believe that there is no link between Zuma's rise to the Presidency and his family's rise to riches.'[87]

But this was not only about a family of fat-cats, in which the first B, 'Broad' (as in Broad-Based Black Economic Empowerment, itself promised as the antidote to Mbeki's elite-oriented Black Economic Empowerment), was apparently replaced in popular parlance with a new B: Belt-size (given the vast girth of several Zuma beneficiaries). More substantially – and in addition to the general rise of a wide array of corrupt practices – three main ruling-party power blocs were apparently at war within the party:

- a group bent on personal accumulation projects who were willing to associate (mostly privately) with former ANC Youth League leader Julius Malema (expelled for indiscipline in 2011), although this group was somewhat on the wane as Malema suffered repeated political defeats;
- those of the centre-left intent on gaining more influence on policy decisions (albeit with virtually nothing to show for their efforts to date), some of whom backed Kgalema Motlanthe in his quixotic campaign to unseat Zuma at the 2012 ANC Congress (as did a few in the first camp);
- the President's KwaZulu-Natal regional allies, initially under stress because of corruption probes that seemed to have emanated from Zuma's office, but later absolved in legally-unsatisfactory ways, as was Zuma's own 2009 prosecution on multiple graft charges.

As to the outcomes of such internal struggles, only time would tell. As the next chapter argues, the ANC, more broadly, faced a sobering period in the wake of the horrors of the Marikana massacre. The Mangaung conference made the

[85] William Gumede, 'Zuma's Victory may Trigger the Break-up of the ANC', *The Guardian*, 19 December 2007.
[86] Ray Hartley, 'An Interview with Jacob Zuma', *The Times*, 9 September 2010.
[87] David Masondo, 'BEE has Evolved into a Family Affair', *CityPress*, 5 September 2010.

ANC increasingly appear as the very post-liberation political party that Frantz Fanon had warned of a half-century earlier in *The Wretched of the Earth*:

> Powerless economically, unable to bring about the existence of coherent social rela-
> tions, and standing on the principle of its domination as a class, the bourgeoisie
> chooses the solution that seems to it the easiest, that of the single party. It does not yet
> have the quiet conscience and the cairn that economic power and the control of the
> state machine alone can give. It does not create a state that reassures the ordinary
> citizen, but rather one that rouses his anxiety. The state, which by its strength and
> discretion ought to inspire confidence and disarm and lull everybody to sleep, on the
> contrary seeks to impose itself in spectacular fashion. It makes a display, it jostles
> people and bullies them, thus intimating to the citizen that he is in continual danger.
> The single party is the modem form of the dictatorship of the bourgeoisie, unmasked,
> unpainted, unscrupulous and cynical.[88]

[88] Frantz Fanon, *The Wretched of the Earth* (New York: Grove Press, 1963).

Part III
Conclusions:
The Future as History[1]

---

[1] Cf. Richard Heilbroner, *The Future as History* (New York: Grove Press, 1961). See also C.L.R. James, *The Future in the Present* (Westport, Conn.: Lawrence Hill and Company, 1977).

6.

Uneven and Combined Resistance:
Marikana and The Trail to 'Tunisia Day' 2020

PATRICK BOND

The prior two chapters showed how the wholehearted embrace of neo-liberalism by the African National Congress from the early 1990s left the economy especially fragile, reliant upon asset bubbles and subject to capital flight at the first sign of trouble. Although from 1993–2008 there was technical GDP growth each year, it was terribly stilted. Although South Africa technically began recovering from formal recession in late 2009, this did not reverse the economic rot: i.e., the rise of mass unemployment, further property market turmoil, manufacturing stagnation, a severe credit squeeze and a return to dangerous current account deficits (as the big extractive and financial corporations shipped out funds to London, and as trade slipped into deficit, too). As inequality increased and reports became more frequent of corporate managers 'earning' millions of dollars in salary and perks, South Africa became a microcosm of growing global concerns about the '1 per cent' versus the '99 per cent'.

One of the most visible representatives of the latter was Congress of SA Trade Unions (COSATU) general secretary Zwelinzima Vavi. He regularly articulated the limits of worker patience during his long career in trade-union leadership, although in the second half of 2012 this role was constrained by shifting power balances and in mid-2013 he became embroiled in a major controversy concerning his sexual behaviour with a subordinate, leaving the momentum within the left of the labour movement to be forged by the National Union of Metalworkers of South Africa (NUMSA). The turmoil in organized labour was either a tragic distraction for those with deeper liberation ambitions – or a harbinger of a split in COSATU that would distinguish the 'sweetheart' unions from the class-struggle wing of the labour movement. After a long period of below-inflation wage settlements and sub-contracted ultra-cheap labour that left workers far poorer in relative terms in the years after 2000, desperation created a new sense of militancy under Zuma's reign.

All this culminated in the explosion at Marikana and the follow-up wildcat strike wave in 2012–13, but even by 2010, unions were demanding – and often won – substantially-above-inflation wage concessions in several crucial sectors. Rising militancy was most intense in the public sector but included an upsurge of strikes in public and private transport just prior to South Africa's hosting of the World Cup, when the SA Transport and Allied Workers Union tightened its chokehold on ports and rail for three weeks before winning a large increase. NUMSA members also won large wage increases at the time, but also became increasingly vocal about macro-economic policy, regularly engaging the SA

Reserve Bank governor in debate about interest rates and capital controls.

There were broader links made to poor people's and middle-class concerns as well. For example, COSATU's mini-revolt in 2010 included threats of a national strike to halt electricity price increases far above the inflation rate and in 2012–13 to halt new tolls on Gauteng highways. COSATU was also angered that Finance Minister Pravin Gordhan's first full budget in February 2010 not only ignored a promised National Health Insurance plan and the need to phase out labour brokers (which were responsible for mass hiring/firing of casualized workers) but even tried introducing a 'dual labour market' by subsidizing young workers at a cheaper entry-level wage, an approach Gordhan continued pushing into 2013 even after worker protests soared.

In the meantime, thousands of minor service-delivery protests occurred each year, unstoppable yet apparently unlinkable, given the lack of organizations – such as a Workers Party, as had been built in Brazil a quarter century earlier – that might have provided ideological and strategic coherence. COSATU had done something similar during the late 1980s and early 1990s with the 'civics', through deploying their leaders into the main urban social movements. But COSATU's contemporary outreach to civil society was much less ambitious, drawing ire from the ANC when the Treatment Action Campaign and centre-left NGOs were invited to a 2010 conference. COSATU apparently lacked the courage needed to seek out more militant grassroots and leftist social-movement 'small-a' alliances, as John Saul had earlier suggested would be necessary.[2] However, in 2013 a metalworkers union break from COSATU heralded a Workers Party.

The lack of community rootedness proved a huge barrier to the next stage of mobilization and control of extremely disgruntled labour, by mid-2012. There were similar limits elsewhere in civil society, but contradictions continued to rise. Within the faith community, the SA Council of Churches (SACC) leadership was obsequious under Mbeki. But from 2009, Zuma made alliances with evangelical and traditional African faith leaders, alienating SACC figures such as Bishop Jo Seoka, who at Marikana played an important role in legitimizing the grievances of the striking workers. By late 2012, the SACC's main bishops offered a powerful public critique of Zuma, which was dismissed contemptuously by the ANC.

There were many other surface-level manifestations of spreading cracks in the Alliance between COSATU, the SA Communist Party (SACP) and the neo-liberal wing of the ANC. These cracks Zuma patiently attempted to paper over with strong support from hard-line communists, but they grew ever deeper and wider within months of his 2009 election. Indeed, COSATU had vastly underestimated the extent of social despair and popular anger, and by mid-2012, starting in the mining belt and moving to transport and then the Western Cape farms, periodic explosions of wildcat strike activity by tens of thousands of workers at a time put unprecedented socio-economic stress on post-apartheid South Africa. To understand why – and where it may go in the years following

---

[2] John S. Saul, *The Next Liberation Struggle* (Toronto: Between The Lines, 2005).

the ruling party's 100th anniversary – means first considering the events of August 16 2012 in more detail.

A moment at Marikana

When a ruling party in any African country sinks to the depths of allowing its police force to serve white-dominated multinational capital by killing dozens of black workers so as to end a brief strike, it represents an inflection point. Beyond just the obvious human rights and labour-relations travesties, the incident offered the potential for a deep political rethink, unveiling extreme depths of ruling-class desperation represented by the fusion of Cyril Ramaphosa's black capitalism, Lonmin's collaboration (through Ramaphosa) with the Mining and Police Ministers, the brutality of state prosecutors who charged the victims with the crime, the alleged 'sweetheart unionism' of the increasingly unpopular National Union of Mineworkers (NUM), and the fragility of a COSATU split between Zuma/Ramaphosa loyalists and those with worker interests at heart. Positions quickly hardened and those culpable became defensive. Only a few in the society – including several former ANC apparatchiks who began openly questioning tactics of the dominant political class (as documented by Saul in Chapter 7) – openly confronted the chilling lessons about the moral degeneration of a liberation movement that the world had supported for decades.

The site of the immediate conflict was the platinum belt. South Africa's share of world platinum reserves is more than 80 per cent. The belt stretches in a distinct arc around the west side of the Johannesburg-Pretoria megalopolis of ten million people, and up towards the Zimbabwe border. The area also has vast gold and coal deposits, and the nine main mining firms operating mainly in this region recorded $4.5 billion in 2011 profits from their South African operations. In this context, there are six basic factual considerations about what happened at Marikana, in the platinum belt northwest of Johannesburg, beginning around 4pm on 16 August:

- The provincial police department, backed by national special commando reinforcements, ordered several thousand striking platinum mineworkers – rock-drill operators – off a hill where they had gathered as usual over the prior four days, surrounding the workers with barbed wire and firing teargas;
- the hill was more than a kilometre (about three-quarters of a mile) away from Lonmin property, the mineworkers were not blocking mining operations or any other facility, and although they were on an 'unprotected' wildcat strike, they had a constitutional right to gather;
- as they left the hill, 34 workers were killed and 78 others suffered bullet-wound injuries, all at the hands of police weapons, leaving some crippled for life, with sixteen shot dead while moving through a small gap in the fencing, and the other eighteen murdered in a field and on a smaller hill nearby, as they fled;
- no police were hurt in the operation – although it appears that a sole miner with a pistol fired as he entered the gap – and some of the police attempted a

clumsy cover-up by placing crude weapons next to the dead bodies of several men after their deaths;

- 270 mineworkers were arrested that day, followed by a weekend during which state prosecutors charged the men with the 'murder' of their colleagues (under an obscure apartheid-era 'common purpose' doctrine of collective responsibility), followed by an embarrassed climb down by the national prosecutor after the society registered utter disgust;
- there was no apparent effort by police to discipline errant troops in subsequent months, even when massacre-scene photographs showed that weapons were planted on dead mineworker bodies (a year later there was still no publicized discipline for whoever tampered with the scene), and indeed the police moved into Marikana shack settlements again and again to intimidate activists in the wake of the massacre, including fatally shooting – with rubber bullets one Saturday morning – a popular local councilwoman (from the ruling party), Paulina Masuhlo, who sided with the protesting mineworkers and communities.

The details about how the massacre unfolded were not initially obvious, for mainstream media embedded behind police lines (unaware at the time of the 'killing *kopje*') and official police statements together generated a 'fog of war', as former Intelligence Minister Ronnie Kasrils remarked.[3] The effect was to stigmatize the mineworkers. It was only a few days later that observers – the September Imbizo Commission, University of Johannesburg researcher Peter Alexander and his research team, and *Daily Maverick* reporter Greg Marinovich – uncovered the other shootings.[4] Most journalists relied on official sources, especially the police and National Prosecuting Authority, even when they were discredited by their own persistent falsehoods.

Such media bias allowed the impression to emerge in conventional wisdom that police were 'under violent attack' by irrational, drugged and potentially murderous men from rural areas in the Eastern Cape's Pondoland, as well as from Lesotho and Mozambique, who used '*muti*' (traditional medicine) to ward off bullets. Plenty of press reports and even the SACP's official statement refer to the workers' pre-capitalist spiritual sensibilities – 'a *sangoma* [traditional healer] is today still able to convince sections of the working class that bullets turn into water if you have used "*intelezi*" [traditional medicine]'[5] – to try to

[3] Ronnie Kasrils, 'The slayings grow more sinister', *Amandla!* September 2012.
[4] Peter Alexander, Thapelo Lekgowa et al., *Marikana: A View from the Mountain and a Case to Answer*, Johannesburg: Jakana, 2012. The various reporters at *Daily Maverick* led the SA press corps; available at www.dailymaverick.co.za, accessed 4 October 2013. There was an allegation from the Black-Consciousness-oriented September National Imbizo people's movement that the white researchers did not sufficiently credit their findings, as in: http://septembernationalimbizo.org/bloody-marikana-what-the-media-didnt-tell-you and http://septembernationalimbizo.org/theft-of-sni-material-used-to-maintain-anti-black-agenda, both accessed 4 October 2013.
[5] Blade Nzimande, 'Our condolences and sympathies to the Marikana and Pomeroy victims'. Johannesburg, SA Communist Party, 24 August 2012, available at www.sacp.org.za, accessed 4 October 2013.

explain why they might have charged towards the police, through the five-metre (16-feet) gap in the barbed wire, with their primitive spears and wooden sticks. *Business Day's* editor opined that the strikers 'were convinced by a sangoma a few days earlier that if they let him smear some black powder into cuts on their foreheads they would become invincible. This is not necessarily a demanding audience.'[6]

Although the facts will always remain clouded, subsequent film footage gathered from police cameras a year after the event confirms that the first few dozen mineworkers were leaving the enclosed area in a non-hostile way, and they initially moved directly into the line of fire of heavily armed police, whose weapons were cocked for firing well in advance. The police claim six handguns were recovered from dead, wounded and arrested mineworkers, but this was thrown into question by evidence of systematic post-massacre tampering at the scene of the crime – the weapons placed next to bodies at some point after the massacre – because, by mistake, they surrendered photographs taken both before and after the deed to the Farlam Commission that Zuma mandated to investigate the massacre.

Another layer of complexity related to prior murders of six workers, two security guards and two policemen close by, starting when a march on 11 August by striking workers against the NUM – accused of selling out the workers – was met with gunfire, allegedly from NUM officials. Tension in the area mounted quickly, and when the security guards and police were killed during the confrontations, apparently by some of the Marikana mineworkers, this generated a sensibility of vindication. Gruesome footage of the murdered cops circulated amongst the provincial police who were on duty on August 16. Later, the assassination of NUM shop stewards increased in pace, as well. But it must be recalled that this was not brand new conflict, for strike-related violence over the prior year at Lonmin and the other major platinum mining operations left scores of other workers dead, just six months earlier, when 17,000 mineworkers were temporarily fired nearby at the world's second-largest platinum firm, Impala Platinum Holding (Implats), before gaining wage concessions.

South Africa learned a great deal about labour's desperation in subsequent days, because explaining the intensity of the Lonmin workers' militancy required understanding their conditions of production and reproduction. The typical rock-drill operator's take-home pay was said to be in the range of $511 per month, with an additional $204 per month as a 'living out allowance' to spare Lonmin and other employers the cost of maintaining migrant-labour hostels. Most workers were from the Eastern Cape's Pondoland, Lesotho and Mozambique; many therefore maintained two households, having families to support in both urban and rural settings. At the same time, structural changes in the mines were blurring the distinction between shop steward and foreman, hence drawing NUM local leaders into a cozy corporatist arrangement with the mining houses. But controlling the workers would be another matter, and NUM

---

[6]   Bruce, 'Thick End of the Wedge'.

found itself challenged by a new union that had come from its own dissident ranks, the Association of Mining and Construction Union (Amcu).

Indeed, tens of thousands of workers who subsequently went on wildcat strikes in the North West, Limpopo, Free State, Mpumalanga, Northern Cape and Gauteng Provinces did not do so out of the blue. They began leaving NUM in droves from late 2011 because of its worsening reputation as a sweetheart union, mostly moving to Amcu. This sudden structural shift in power within the working class seemed to panic the ANC, whose local deputy leader, Buti Makhongela, told a loyal group of NUM workers in mid-2013, 'We cannot be intimidated. We have defeated apartheid. This [Amcu] is a small cockroach that needs a mild spray to solve it.'[7]

Amcu's members had participated in various forms of labour and community-based protests over the prior few years, as the 350 per cent price increase for the metal during the 2002–08 boom left the main companies – AngloPlats (Anglo American Platinum), Implats and Lonmin – extremely prosperous, without evidence of trickle-down to the semi-proletarianized workforce. So it was that 3000 Lonmin rock-drill operators demanded a raise to $1420/month as a basic gross 'package' amount; they struck for over a month (three weeks beyond the massacre) and ultimately received what was reported as a 22 per cent wage package increase, which in turn catalysed prairie-fire wildcat strikes across the immediate mining region and then other parts of the country in September–November.[8] Similar militancy was soon evident in trucking, the auto sector, municipal labour and other sectors.

But as with a vast proportion of ordinary South Africans (see Chapter 5) this was a time of extreme household indebtedness. It soon became clear that the Marikana workers were victims not only of exploitation at the point of production, but also of super-exploitative debt relations. Remarked Milford Bateman, a leading financial economist critical of such exploitation: 'We have perhaps just witnessed one of the most appalling microcredit-related disasters of all in South Africa.'[9] Financial desperation was compounded by legal abuse, carried out by the same race/gender/class power bloc – white male Afrikaners – who had, in their earlier years and in the same geographical settings, been apartheid beneficiaries. Microfinance short-term loans that carry exceptionally high interest rates were offered to mineworkers by institutions ranging from established banks – one (Ubank) even co-owned by NUM and another (Capitec)

---

[7] Sapa, 'ANC backs NUM, urges recruitment', 21 July 2013, available at http://news24. com/fin24/Companies/Mining/ANC-backs-NUM-urges-recruitment-20130721, accessed 4 October 2013.

[8] There are some very serious doubts about whether the 22 per cent that was advertised was genuine, because the rock drill operators had already won a 10 per cent increase, and then there were other anomalies. The demand originally made, for R12,500/month – effectively $15,000per year for one of the world's most demanding, dangerous jobs – was revived as a result. But the point of the '22 per cent' victory was that it resonated across the South African industrial landscape. See Kwanele Sosibo, 'After Marikana: The Missing 22% and the Return of R12500', *The Con*, 23 August 2013.

replete with powerful ANC patrons – down to fly-by-night '*mashonisa*' loan sharks. Another (African Bank) had such high levels of unsecured loans that investors started a mid-2013 run that crashed 40 per cent of its share value within a few days of trading. The extremely high interest rates charged by these desperate lenders, especially once arrears began to mount, were one of the central pressures requiring workers to demand higher wages.

As a political-economic phenomenon, this was actually not unusual, for the move to liberalized economic relations in 1994 shifted the power system from one of direct coercion in the spheres of labour control (especially migrancy from Bantustans under apartheid-allied dictators) and socio-political power, to indirect coercion by finance and law. The formalized migrancy system and evolution of labour relations on these mines did not improve the socio-economic conditions of workers, given the rising debt burden. By 2012, this left 'anywhere between 10–15 per cent of SA's workforce with a garnishee order issued' to compel repayment, according to Malcolm Rees of *MoneyWeb*.[10] As discussed in the prior chapter, wages as a share of the social surplus had fallen by more than 5 per cent from 1994 to 2010.[11] In addition, much greater inequality in wage income was also a factor, contributing to a rapid rise in the Gini coefficient over the same period. One reaction by the working class was to turn to rising consumer debt, in order to cover rising household consumption expenditures. Having risen rapidly to $4.96 billion in 2007, the outstanding unsecured credit load registered with the national credit regulator escalated to $13.75 billion by 2012.[12] This was a huge load, for according to Rees, '*Moneyweb* reports indicate that at least 40 percent of the monthly income of SA workers is being directed to the repayment of debt.'[13]

An additional experiential reason for the heightened conflict was recorded by Democratic Left Front leader Mazibuka Jara: 'The strike at the Lonmin mine in Marikana has deep systemic roots in the conditions of workers in that mine. For several years now that mine has increasingly used labour from labour brokers. So they would hire a company to bring workers on a part-time basis to work the mines, particularly underground.'[14]

[9] For documentation, see Lisa Steyn, 'Marikana Miners in Debt Sinkhole', *Mail & Guardian*, 7 September 2012; Ron Derby, 'Could Debt Costs be Behind Miners' Pay Demands?' *Business Day*, 14 September 2012; Malcolm Rees, 'Financially Illiterate Miners Debt Shocker', *Moneyweb*, 1 October 2012; Milford Bateman, 'Microcredit and Marikana: How they are Linked', *The Star*, September 18 2012.

[10] Rees, 'Financially Illiterate Miners Debt Shocker'.

[11] Dick Forslund, 'Wages, profits and labour productivity in South Africa', *Amandla!* 24 January 2012, available at www.amandla.org.za/special-features/the-wage-and-productivity-debate/1142-wages-profits-and-labour-productivity-in-south-africa-a-reply, accessed on 4 October 2013.

[12] Steyn, 'Marikana Miners in Debt Sinkhole'.

[13] Rees, 'Financially Illiterate Miners Debt Shocker'.

[14] Mazibuko Jara, 'The Marikana Massacre and the New Wave of Workers' Struggle', *New Politics*, 14, 3, Summer 2013, available from http://newpol.org/content/south-africa-marikana-massacre-and-new-wave-workers%E2%80%99-struggle-0, accessed 4 October 2013.

Still, none of this labour-capital conflict – implicating mining houses and financiers – would have flared into such an explosive situation at Marikana, many believe, were it not for the relationships between state, ruling party and trade-union elites that developed over the prior two decades with the major mining houses. These cozy relations, evident when even former mineworker leaders like Ramaphosa and James Motlatsi relegitimized companies with very low morals, apparently incensed ordinary workers. That is one reason their staying power was raised to such high levels.

Corporate-state-labour sweethearts

Lonmin was long ruled by Tiny Rowland, a man so venal that his London and Rhodesia Company was named 'the unacceptable face of capitalism' by British Prime Minister Edward Heath in 1973 after just one episode of his bribery and bullying was unveiled. Rowland died in 1998, after losing control of the company five years earlier due to his ties to Libyan dictator Muammar Gaddafi. Lonmin then rebranded and its 'Integrity, Honesty & Trust' slogan adorns billboards at Marikana – and by 2010 the firm's 'Sustainable Development Report' was ranked 'excellent' by Ernst and Young. Lonmin was even featured on the World Bank's website as the leading example of International Finance Corporation (IFC) 'strategic community investment', worthy of a 2007 Bank commitment of $150 million in equity investment and credit. Exactly two weeks after the massacre, the new Bank president Jim Yong Kim came to Pretoria and Johannesburg for a visit. Tellingly, he neglected to check on his Lonmin investment in nearby Marikana, and instead gave a high-profile endorsement to an IFC deal with a small junk-mail printing/posting firm that is prospering from state tenders.[15]

Lonmin must also have been confident that with the World Bank backing its community investment strategy, it could mainly ignore the nearby Nkaneng shack-settlement's degradation. The lack of clean running water, sanitation, storm-water drainage, electricity, schools, clinics and any other amenities make Nkaneng as inhospitable a residential site to reproduce labour power as any other in South Africa, yet Lonmin's approach to the community's troubles was tokenistic. Instead of building decent company housing for migrant workers, for example, it relied on the inadequate living out allowance, much of which was just added to wages targeted for remittance to the home region. This arrangement left Nkaneng uninhabitable from the standpoint of decency – but a place of desperation that was never upgraded, not even a year after the massacre. Mineworkers had continued migrancy relations but what had changed with the economic restructuring and job bloodbath was that the

---

[15] Patrick Bond, 'Jim Yong Kim's trip to South Africa was just a PR exercise for the World Bank', *The Guardian Poverty Matters* blog, 12 September 2012, available at www.guardian.co.uk/global-development/poverty-matters/2012/sep/12/jim-yong-kim-world-bank-south-africa, accessed 4 October 2013.

number of dependants per mineworker rose dramatically, from eight to fifteen, according to labour expert Gavin Hartford.[16]

Lonmin's successful public relations onslaught prior to 2012 probably gave its executives confidence that long-standing abuse of low-paid migrant labour could continue. After all, NUM was itself so co-opted that shop stewards were reportedly paid three times more than ordinary workers. According to Jara,

> NUM had increasingly become removed from the conditions, the grievances, and the demands of the lowest rank of the workers, the most exploited – particularly those who drill the rocks. Because those who drill the rocks must be physically strong, since they work the hardest and work the longest, and they were not getting increased wage rates at all. The NUM had increasingly been led by a layer of quite streetwise, English speaking, white-collar workers. Most of them had been working above the ground, as mining clerks or other officers in the system. So this combination of factors meant that there was no outlet, there was no forum, to hear and address the grievances of underground workers.[17]

NUM general secretary Frans Baleni earned $160,000 per year at that stage, and gained notoriety when he had advised Lonmin to fire 9000 of the same Marikana mineworkers at its Karee mine in late 2011 because they went on a wildcat strike. As Baleni's former deputy, Archie Palane, put it, 'It's absolutely shocking – completely unheard of – that a union advises an employer to fire workers. No matter what your differences or what they did, this should simply not happen. It gives the impression that you just don't care. How can you ever expect those workers to trust you to represent them in any negotiations?' Of the 9000, 7000 were rehired but they quit NUM and joined the rival Amcu. One result, at nearby Implats, was that of the 28 000 workers, 70 per cent had been NUM members in late 2011, but by September 2012 the ratio was down to 13 per cent.[18] Indeed NUM went from being the country's largest single union in 2012 to approximately fourth largest in 2013, having lost at least 40,000 workers.

On the ecological front, the entire platinum belt contributes to the toxicity and overall pollution that means South Africa's 'Environmental Performance Index' slipped to fifth worst of 133 countries surveyed by Columbia and Yale University researchers in early 2012.[19] The Minerals-Energy Complex's prolific contribution to pollution is mainly to blame, including its coal mining that generates coal-fired power used in electricity-intensive mining and smelting operations. In this context, Lonmin might have considered its on-going destruction of the platinum belt's water, air, agricultural and other eco-systems to be of little importance – within a setting in which pollution was ubiquitous.

---

[16] Gavin Hartford, 'The mining industry strike wave', Manuscript, September 2012, and presentation to the *Amandla! Colloquium*, Magaliesburg, 18 November 2012.

[17] Jara, 'The Marikana Massacre and the New Wave of Workers' Struggle'.

[18] Jan de Lange, 'Archie Palane points finger at NUM failings'' *Miningmx*, 10 September 2012, available at www.miningmx.com/page/news/markets/1388854-Archie-Palane-points-finger-at-NUM-failings, accessed 4 October 2013.

[19] Yale University Environmental Performance Index, available at http://epi.yale.edu, accessed 4 October 2013.

Moreover, the North West provincial and Rustenburg municipal governments were apparently rife with corruption. Emblematic was the 2009 assassination of a well-known ANC whistle-blower, Moss Phakoe, found by a judge to have been arranged by the ANC's Rustenburg mayor, Matthew Wolmarans. Again, in this context, Lonmin and the other big mining houses in the platinum belt might have considered South Africa just one more third-world site worthy of the designation 'resource-cursed' – a phrase usually applied to sites where dictatorial and familial patronage relations allow multinational capital in the extractive industries to, literally, get away with murder. Around two dozen anti-corruption whistle-blowers like Phakoe were killed in the first few years of Zuma's rule.[20]

And, of course, family enterprise suited the Zumas, who had a reported 220 businesses. It was not surprising to learn, for example, that along with the infamous Gupta brothers Ajay, Atul and Rajesh – generous sponsors of Zuma's patronage system, although at huge cost in the form of the humiliating scandal over a private airplane landing at the Pretoria presidential air field in mid-2013[21] – Zuma's son Duduzane was co-owner of JIC Mining Services (JIC), the platinum belt region's largest firm specializing in short-term labour outsourcing (sometimes called 'labour broking', though JIC denies this, and NUM has a recognition agreement with the firm).[22] Soon after the airplane incident, Duduzane teamed up with the Guptas to launch a 24-hour television news channel.

Nor was it a secret that the President's nephew Khulubuse Zuma played a destructive role in nearby gold-mining territory as Aurora co-owner, along with

---

[20] For updates on this facet of the crisis, see www.corruptionwatch.org.za, accessed 4 October 2013.

[21] According to Kalim Rajab, 'In May 2010 during a State visit to India, when President Zuma played the global statesman ahead of the upcoming World Cup, a banquet was given for the great and the good of the sub-continental diplomatic and trade world. From the South African side, the President was accompanied by the usual mix of industrialists, BEE beneficiaries, trade delegates and motley acolytes. In a public forum, the president made it clear his love for samosas, the strong bond the two countries shared … and, not so subtly, that for the multitude of heavyweight Indian titans in the room who were thinking of investing in South Africa, the suitable way of channelling it would be through the Gupta family. I'm not sure if there are any historical precedents for such a blatant (and downright dodgy) show of support by an administration towards politically connected businessmen, but at first it didn't seem to have the required effect. Several top Indian industrialists left in disgust. At the time, it was perhaps not surprising. After all, few of them would have heard of the Gupta family or thought of them as major players. Before arriving in South Africa, they had been a middleweight family in the power stakes on the sub-continent. Those in the know used to scoff at them for having embellished their credentials through a clever sleight of hand, by naming their companies outside India 'Sahara' – thereby trading off the powerful (and unconnected) brand name of the famous billionaire Subrata Roy's Sahara Group'. Kalim Rajab, 'Message to Cabinet: It is NOT just a wedding', *Daily Maverick*, 6 May 2013.

[22] Glynnis Underhill, 'Duduzane Zuma to be Gupta news channel's BEE partner', *Mail & Guardian*, 9 August 2013.

Nelson Mandela's grandson Zondwa and Zuma's lawyer. Indeed, that particular mining house had perhaps the single most extreme record of ecological destructiveness and labour conflict in the post-apartheid era, reflecting how white-owned mining houses gave used-up mines with vast Acid Mine Drainage liabilities to new black owners who were ill equipped to deal with the inevitable crises. The result, for Zuma and co-directors, was likely criminal prosecution in future on grounds of 'acting recklessly'.[23]

This in turn was all part of the much-proclaimed deracialization of apartheid capitalism. As *Business Day* editor Peter Bruce wrote in 2003, 'The government is utterly seduced by big business, and cannot see beyond its immediate interests.'[24] As noted in Chapter 4, ten years later, the same 'system' was confirmed by the ANC's head of elections, Ngoako Ramatlhodi, a sophisticated lawyer who was formerly premier of Limpopo Province: 'In a sense we are managing a white-man economy on behalf of white men who ran the economy under apartheid, but they have changed in form, not in politics.'[25]

The interests converged when it came to facilitating capital accumulation – 'we must strive to create and strengthen a black capitalist class', said Thabo Mbeki, upon taking over from Mandela in 1999 – specifically within the ANC's leading political power blocs.[26] This entailed channelling social surpluses in at least a tokenistic manner, so as to underwrite the power of patronage required to ensure the ANC could gain voting majorities into the indefinite future. Here, a critical linkage factor to keep the ruling party financially prosperous was the ANC's investment arm, Chancellor House, which was to become involved in all manner of controversial projects as a tender partner, such as the Medupi coal-fired power plant and minerals trade in the Central African Republic.[27]

[23] Xolela Mangcu, 'Far Cry from Biko's Political Approach', *The Sowetan*, 25 September 2012, available at www.sowetanlive.co.za/columnists/2012/09/25/far-cry-from-biko-s-political-approach; Loyiso Sidimba, 'Khulubuse, Others Face Criminal Charges – Liquidators', *City Press*, 27 March 2013, available at www.citypress.co.za/politics/khulubuse-others-face-criminal-charges-liquidators (both accessed 4 October 2013); INet Bridge, AFP, 'Zuma, Mandela Family Assets Seized in Mining Bankruptcy', 16 April 2012.

[24] Peter Bruce, 'SA Needs a Market Economy', *Business Day*, 4 June 2003, available at http://allafrica.com/stories/200306040569.html, accessed 4 October 2013.

[25] Moloko Moloto, 'Even the Fish will Vote for the ANC', *The Mercury*, 1 July 2013.

[26] Thabo Mbeki, 'Speech of the President of South Africa, Thabo Mbeki, at the Annual National Conference of the Black Management Forum', Johannesburg, 20 November 1999, available at www.thepresidency.gov.za/pebble.asp?relid=2596&t, accessed 4 October 2013.

[27] For the ill-fated Medupi job, Chancellor House bought a quarter share of the local subsidiary of Hitachi, which, in a suspicious deal, won a tender for the supply of $5 billion worth of boilers to the vast coal-fired power plant. The World Bank made its largest-ever project loan to support that deal. With then Eskom chair Valli Moosa also a member of the ANC Finance Committee at the time, the SA Public Protector labelled his conflict of interest 'improper'. But reflecting the balance of political power and financial facilitation by Robert Zoellick's World Bank, the deal went through and two subsequent years of delays could be blamed, perhaps not surprisingly, on faulty boilers. (The day that Jim Kim arrived in Johannesburg, on 4 September 2012, several

One man who had lubricated the process of corrupting the ANC was the afore-mentioned Rowland, formerly a member of Hitler Youth in Hamburg, and then mainly schooled in England. After a World War II internment due to his German background, he was a porter in London's Euston station but by migrating to what was then Southern Rhodesia, he made his wealth in tobacco and rose rapidly within that colony's racist business environment. After taking control of Lonrho, from the early 1960s he became a leading confidante to a succession of African dictators as well as liberation strugglers, including Zimbabwe's. It was from these sorts of leaders and their countries' natural resources, railroads and newspa-pers that he extracted a vast fortune for his tightly controlled firm. Rowland's accomplishments included platinum trading to help bust apartheid-era sanc-tions against South Africa. He also assisted Jonas Savimbi and ensured the Angolan rebel got CIA assistance. For these pro-apartheid acts, he perhaps made amends by flying Oliver Tambo around in a jet and buying the ANC leader a mansion in one of Johannesburg's most fashionable white suburbs, Sandhurst. In 1996, Mandela honoured Rowland with the Order of Good Hope award, South Africa's most prestigious honour; he died in 1998.

Mandela, too, was showered with a small financial fortune by friendly tycoons after release from 27 years of prison in 1990, sufficient to soon amass a $10 million asset base, as revealed in his ugly divorce proceedings with Winnie Madikizela-Mandela.[28] It is not known whether and how the gifts influenced Mandela, and whether he used his world-historic prestige on behalf of bene-factors. But as one illustration, the donation of $25 million from the Indonesian dictator Suharto to the ANC's 1994 election campaign may explain Mandela's award of another Order of Good Hope medal to that tyrant in 1997, a few weeks before popular protests forced him to flee Jakarta.[29] For reasons that were never clear, Mandela also bestowed upon Zuma a R1 million gift in 2005 shortly after the latter was fired as Mbeki's Deputy President. Later, the image of Mandela's selflessness, humanity and humility was repeatedly soiled by the in-fighting and indeed unseemly greed exhibited by at least one of his lawyers (Ismail Ayob) and several of his family members, especially grandson Mandla, who filed one

---

[(cont)] hundred Medupi construction workers embarked on a strike that included burning some of the facilities, resulting in the evacuation of 17,000 workers, a problem that did not attract his attention while in the country or in his blog upon returning.) As for the Central African Republic, Chancellor House was implicated in deal-making (with CAR 'fixer' Didier Pereira) for a diamond monopoly that in turn provided crucial background to why the SA National Defence Force 'protected assets' in Bangui in March 2013, at the cost of losing 13 soldiers in a coup. (Amabhungane reporters, 'Is this what our soldiers died for?', *Mail & Guardian*, 28 March 2013, avail-able at http://mg.co.za/article/2013-03-28-00-central-african-republic-is-this-what-our-soldiers-died-for, accessed 4 October 2013.)

[28] *Jet*, 'Nelson and Winnie Mandela Divorce', 8 April 1996.

[29] In a similar episode, the same medal – renamed Order of the Companions of O. R. Tambo – was granted to the late Guyanan President Linden Forbes Burnham, perhaps best known for his role in the assassination of Walter Rodney, but who donated substantial sums of solidarity funds paid for by the Guyanan people during the 1980s. The award was 'deferred' after an international outcry in May 2013.

lawsuit after another against each other. By December 5, 2013, when Mandela died after several months of incapacitation, Mandla lost the battle over grave site location.

According to *Daily Maverick*'s Ranjeni Munusamy,

> Mandla claimed that his family targeted him because he refused to join the court action undertaken by his aunts Makaziwe and Zenani to gain control of Nelson Mandela's artworks and riches ... After stating at the media briefing that he did not want to air the family's dirty laundry in public, he proceeded to do just that ... 'At the moment it seems like anyone can come and say I am a Mandela and demand to be part of decision-making process of the family. Individuals have abandoned their own families and heritage and decided to jump on the Mandela wagon,' Mandla said. It has been rather curious that all of Mandela's children, grandchildren and great children bear the surname, but nobody has dared to question it before. The name is clearly a hot ticket to stardom and is being passed down the line even when there is no entitlement to it ... When Graca Machel married Nelson Mandela on his 80th birthday, she opted to keep her first husband, former Mozambican president Samora Machel's name. Therefore she is the only person in Madiba's immediate family not bearing his name, and yet is the only one trying to protect it and uphold his legacy. Irony doesn't get more pointed than that.[30]

Venality by a revered generation of struggle leaders and their offspring may seem sufficiently disheartening to provoke South Africans to political depression and apathy. One antidote, explored below, was to take inspiration from the spirit of popular resistance evident even immediately after the massacre. But a complementary recourse would be to learn lessons drawn for politics after Marikana: precisely by learning from prior massacres.

Marikana massacre: historical metaphors and political lessons

The South African state's prior mineworker massacre was in 1922 when Johannesburg's white gold miners rebelled against the increasing use of competing black labour, to the sound of the Communist Party of South Africa's notorious slogan, 'Workers of the World Unite for a White South Africa!' They were resoundingly defeated and then co-opted, a fate that Marikana workers and 100,000 others who went wildcat – in the weeks following that massacre – avoided, at least in the short run. Those workers began moving by the tens of thousands from COSATU affiliates to upstart – albeit economistic, wages-oriented and openly apolitical – trade unions like the Amcu, predictably labelled by Alliance leaders – the ANC's Gwede Mantashe, SACP's Blade Nzimande and even COSATU's Vavi) – as the new 'counter-revolutionaries'.[31]

---

[30] Ranjeni Munusamy, 'Mandla Mandela and the Chamber of Secrets', *Daily Maverick*, 5 July 2013.

[31] Getrude Makhafola, 'Mantashe: Marikana Breeds Counter-revolution', *Business Report*, 26 August 2012, www.iol.co.za/business/business-news/mantashemarikana-breeds-counter-revolution-1.1369789; SABC, 'Nzimande Condemns Exploitation of Mine Workers', 28 October 2012, available at www.sabc.co.za/news/a/

The periods after more recent political massacres may have more to teach us. After 21 March 1960 at Sharpeville, an hour's drive south of Johannesburg, where 69 were shot dead for burning the apartheid regime's racist passbooks, there was an immediate downswing in mass-resistance politics, followed by a hapless turn to armed struggle and the shift of resources and personnel to ineffectual exile-based liberation movements. It was not until 1973 that mass-based organizing resumed, starting in the Durban dockyards with resurgent trade unionism.

The next big apartheid massacre was in June 1976 when in Soweto as many as 1000 school children were murdered by the police and army for resisting the teaching of Afrikaans and taking to the streets. In the 1980s and early 1990s, there were periodic massacres by men who apparently fused ethnic interests of migrant workers (mainly from KwaZulu) to the Inkatha Freedom Party and the regime's 'Third Force' provocateurs. But that era's most comparable event to Marikana was the Bisho Massacre in which 28 were shot dead by a Bantustan army at the conclusion of a march in the Eastern Cape's Ciskei homeland.

What are the most powerful lessons? In 1960, the effect of the killings was first desperation and then more than a decade of quiescence. In 1976, the Soweto uprising put South Africa on the world solidarity map and, along with liberation movement victories in Mozambique, Angola and then Zimbabwe, kick-started other communities, workers, women and youth into the action-packed 1980s. In 1992, the revulsion from what happened at Bisho, followed by anger at Chris Hani's assassination in April 1993, were the catalysts required to finally set the April 1994 date for the first one-person one-vote election.

For Marikana, is there a historical analogy to pursue? In other words, if post-Marikana struggle was explicitly against what might be termed 'class apartheid', then was the disparate resistance signified by the desperate platinum workers similar to the crack-down of the early 1960s – and hence would there be much more state repression before a coherent opposition emerged? Or would the contagion of protest from this and thousands of other micro-protests across the country start to coagulate, as in the 1976–94 period, into a network similar to the United Democratic Front – implying an inevitable split in the ANC-COSATU-SACP Alliance, led by genuine communists and progressive post-nationalist workers – and then the formation of Worker's Party to challenge ANC electoral dominance?

Or might something happen quite suddenly to rearrange power relations, as in 1992, and as happened in Egypt in the wake of courageous independent labour organizing against state-corporate-trade-union arrangements in the years prior to the massive January 2011 Tahrir Square mobilizations? If a slower scenario plays out, a 'Tunisia Day' could come to South Africa in 2020, according to high-profile commentator Moeletsi Mbeki, younger brother of the

(cont) 7fbbfb804d3dc362af9affe570eb4ca2/Nzimande-condemns-exploitation-of-mine-workers—20121028; SAPA, 'Cosatu to Reclaim Rustenburg from "Forces of Counter Revolution"', 20 October 2012, available from www.timeslive.co.za/local/2012/10/20/cosatu-to-reclaim-rustenburg-from-forces-of-counter-revolution, all accessed 4 October 2013.

former president.[32] But if we look back at the generally successful strike wave of 2012 as a time for revitalized confidence at a time that capital insisted the state put its foot down on the workers (as aided by sweetheart unions and co-ordinated by Ramaphosa) that confluence of events would be an augury for matters coming to a head much sooner. Zuma's remarks in October 2012 about the need for strikers to 'get back to work' had an ominous sound.[33] The very next day, the Marikana workers went on another wildcat strike because the police moved in to the platinum mine once again, arresting a few central leaders. Zuma's subsequent appeal to big business and parastatal executives to adopt a salary freeze in search of greater legitimacy fell on deaf ears, with no visible compliance. The President clearly lacked authority, and no wonder, what with extreme divisions tearing apart the ANC's big tent just prior to the Mangaung Congress in December 2012.

COSATU, Malema, Ramaphosa, and a fractured ruling party

The stage was set, immediately after Marikana, for renewed debates over whether the Tripartite Alliance was a progressive or now regressive political arrangement, especially between the centre-left unionists and communists who are close to official power and thus defensive of the political *status quo*, on the one hand; and on the other, critical, independent progressives convinced that South African politics could become more acutely polarized. Overlaying the crisis and these debates was the internal ANC split between pro- and anti-Zuma forces, which spilled over into COSATU prior to its September 2012 Congress prior to, at the Mangaung electoral conference of the ruling party, Zuma squashing his opponent (then deputy President) Kgalema Motlanthe with three quarters of the vote. This political battle was just one of the indications of a paralysed labour leadership. NUM threatened to open a leadership challenge to Vavi at a conference shortly after Marikana.[34] In August 2013, Vavi was exposed for having an office affair and was suspended from COSATU. With NUM's decline in the platinum and goldfields, the new leading union was the metalworkers, and their late 2013 campaign to resurrect Vavi's position through a COSATU mass congress was unsuccessful. At the time of writing, a new union movement of the left appeared inevitable.

Such political manoeuvring left COSATU mostly silenced about Marikana, as NUM's weight and the parallel subversion of other union leaders made it too difficult for the federation to visibly back the upstart platinum, gold and other

---

[32] Moeletsi Mbeki, 'South Africa: Only a Matter of Time before the Bomb Explodes', Leader, 21 February 2011, available at www.leader.co.za/article.aspx?s=23&f=1&a=2571, accessed 4 October 2013.

[33] Piet Rampedi and Shaun Smillie, 'Get back to work', *The Star*, 18 Oct 2012, available at www.iol.co.za/the-star/get-back-to-work-1.1405430, accessed 4 Oct 2013.

[34] Ranjeni Munusamy, 'Move to Dislodge Vavi may Fire Back at Zuma', *Daily Maverick*, 13 August 2012, available at http://dailymaverick.co.za/article/2012-08-13-move-to-dislodge-vavi-may-fire-back-at-zuma, accessed 4 October 2013.

mineworkers. In any case, what these wildcat strikers were doing might, more conservative unionists believed, even throw the institutions of centralized bargaining into chaos. The demand for higher wages was both extreme, and thus opposed by NUM, and ultimately successful in the case of Marikana's courageous workers. The reported 22 per cent raise that the workers won – at a time inflation was around 6 per cent – after a month of striking inspired the country's labour force to look at their own pay packets askance.

But by failing to issue immediate statements about Marikana, much less mobilize workers for solidarity against the joint onslaught of multinational capital and the state, COSATU was simply unable in late 2012 to intervene when so many cried out for a shift from the proverbial 'War of Position' to a 'War of Movement'. COSATU's longing gaze to Zuma for a genuine relationship reminded many of its support for him during the darkest 2005–07 days of corruption and rape charges. Yet it was now, in the Marikana moment, even more apparent that COSATU's conservatism was the principal barrier to social progress. Its weakness was tangible at two levels.

First, in sharp contrast to COSATU's posture, into the void stepped Julius Malema, the ANC's former youth leader. Malema had been partially discredited by his alleged implication in corrupt 'tenderpreneurship' (insider deals for state contracts) in the neighbouring province of Limpopo. Yet he managed to gather 15,000 angry people at Marikana two days after the massacre, and voiced powerful critiques of Zuma, Lonmin and their associated black capitalist allies, such as Lonmin part-owner Ramaphosa. He did the same on the one-year anniversary of the massacre, when the main COSATU union, NUM, refused to participate in the memorial. Malema stole the show.

Meanwhile, the second way in which COSATU's weakness was manifested was in the subsequent rise of Ramaphosa to renewed power within the ANC. Any such rebirth of Ramaphosa had seemed virtually inconceivable immediately after the Farlam Commission began. There, a startling series of revelations emerged about Ramaphosa's 'smoking-gun' emails sent to other Lonmin executives and government ministers exactly 24 hours before the massacre.[35] To further contextualize this, recall that Ramaphosa's company Shanduka was the majority shareholder of the Lonmin black empowerment subsidiary, which gave him 9 per cent ownership in Lonmin and a seat on the board. Shanduka was in 2012 being paid $360,000 a year by Lonmin for providing 'empowerment' consulting, not to mention Ramaphosa's board salary and dividend returns on Lonmin share ownership.

This was not a bad arrangement for the mining house, as Ramaphosa's emails on August 15 reflected the power relations that Lonmin gained in its association with the former mineworker leader. Revealing these, the lawyer for the 270 arrested mineworkers, Dali Mpofu, explained:

[35] David Smith, 'Ramaphosa has blood on his hands, say miners', *The Guardian*, 25 October 2012. For more on his battered credibility, see Sam Mkokeli, 'Ramaphosa e-mail is a gift to his detractors', *Business Day*, 25 October 2012, available at www.bdlive.co.za/national/politics/2012/10/25/news-analysis-ramaphosa-e-mail-is-a-gift-to-his-detractors, accessed 4 October 2013.

It's a long line of emails under, in the same vein, effectively encouraging so-called concomitant action to deal with these criminals, whose only crime was that they were seeking a wage increase ... At the heart of this was the toxic collusion between the SA Police Services and Lonmin at a direct level. At a much broader level it can be called a collusion between the State and capital and that this phenomenon is at the centre of what has occurred here ...

This collusion between State and capital has happened in many instances in this country. In 1920 African miners went on strike and the government of Jan Smuts dealt with them with violence, and harshly, and one of the results of that was that they reduced the gap between what white mineworkers were getting and what black mineworkers were getting, was reduced and the pact that had been signed in 1918 of introducing the colour bar in the mines was abandoned. That abandonment precip-itated a massive strike by the white mineworkers in 1922 and that strike was dealt with by the Smuts government by bringing in the air force – the air force and about 200 people were killed. This is one of the most important happenings in the history of this country, and in 1946 under the leadership of the African Mineworkers Union, the African workers, 70 000 African workers also went on a massive strike and the government sent 16 000 policemen and arrested, like they did to our, the people we represent, some of the miners under an act called the War Measures Act.

So this has happened, this collusion between capital and the State has happened in systematic patterns in the history of, sordid history of the mining industry in this country. Part of that history included the collaboration of so-called tribal chiefs who were corrupt and were used by those oppressive governments to turn the self- suffi-cient black African farmers into slave labour workers. Today we have a situation where those chiefs have been replaced by so-called BEE partners of these mines and carrying on that torch of collusion.[36]

The BEE billionaire Ramaphosa's collaboration with white elites was also reflected in his attempt a few months earlier to purchase a prize buffalo at a game auction for \$2.3 million,[37] an event underscored by Malema as indica-tive of the gulf between the new South Africa's 1 per cent and the workers. One of the most eloquent critics of the arrangement was 'Cyrilina Ramaphoser', also known as Masello Motana, here explaining her video dance tune 'Makerena on Marikana':

I am crushed by the ANC's latest enigmas. Electing Cyril Ramaphosa as their deputy after Marikana. I cannot get over it. I went into a deep depression once I realized that he had every intention of not only attending the conference, but in getting elected into the executive and even the highest position possible. All this barely a hundred days after those bodies had been buried. It's like someone raping your cousin, then coming to your party, and having the biggest slice of cake and the best booze. I went into a deeper depression than the one I went through after the massacre itself. As for the media! Cheering on as it usually does with capital lubricants like Ramaphosa. I

[36] Farlam Commission, 'Transcription of the Commission of Inquiry: Marikana – Days 1 to 7, 1 to 31 October 2012', pp. 218–220, available at www.seri-sa.org/images/stories/marikana_consolidatedtranscript_days1-7.pdf, accessed 4 October 2013.

[37] Having withdrawn from bidding at the final moment, he remarked, 'I spent my budget on other animals. And, like any businessman, you must know when to stop', *City Press*, 'Buffalo Soldier Cyril Loses out', 14 April 2012, available at www.citypress.co.za/news/buffalo-soldier-cyril-loses-out-20120414, accessed 4 October 2013.

could not in all good conscience see how I could live in such a country. So it was either Cyrilina or exile.[38]

Chester Missing, the comic ventriloquist character, was led to remark, 'The problem is politicians and the poor live in different worlds. We're paying for air-conditioning at Nkandla but can't find cash for the Marikana victims' lawyers: 67 minutes of hypocrisy for Madiba. It's so surreal the lawyer is called Dali.'[39] Not surprisingly in this context of exploding cynicism about the ANC, Malema was quickly rewarded with overwhelming support from Marikana miners on two occasions – including a memorial ceremony he arranged, at which he kicked out several of Zuma's cabinet ministers who had come to pay respects. But, on his third visit, police denied him his constitutional rights to address another huge crowd. Even while contesting fraud charges in his home base (where facilitating provincial tenders had made him rich) Malema thus became, briefly, an unstoppable force across the mining belt in North West and Limpopo Provinces, and even Zimbabwe, calling for radical redistribution. At one point three weeks after the massacre, the SA National Defence Force was declared on 'high alert' simply because Malema addressed a group of disgruntled soldiers.[40]

Yet money still talked in South Africa. By December 2012, Malema's own apparent power had ebbed, as he was expelled from the ruling party, and Ramaphosa had won the ruling party's deputy presidency against Malema's two main allies – with more than three quarters of the vote. COSATU was also very clearly in retreat with Vavi nervously appealing to Ramaphosa not to act like a capitalist. Malema himself was completely out of the national political equation, humiliating himself with a co-authored letter to the ANC leadership just before the Mangaung conference began, begging that he be allowed back into the organization: 'We remain loyal supporters and members of the ANC, willing to be corrected and guided under its principles.'[41]

This request was simply rebuffed by Zuma's team, leaving Malema to found a new political formation in mid-2013, the Economic Freedom Fighters (EFF). Although some polls put his youth support at over 20 per cent, without a strong institutional base it was likely this new ruse by the formidable rhetori-cian would fail, given on-going politically-motivated tax and corruption inves-tigations by Zuma loyalists into Malema's prior bling-riddled, tender-

---

[38] Zachary Rosen, 'Popstars Politics in the New South Africa: A Conversation with Masello Motana', *Africa is a Country*, 28 March 2013, available at http://africasacountry.com/2013/03/29/popstars-politicians-and-personhood-a-conversation-with-masello-motana, and for the video, see www.youtube.com/watch?v=UWT2SGK95uM, both accessed 4 October 2013.

[39] Chester Missing, 'SA Politics so Surreal, We Have Lawyers Named Dali', *City Press*, 29 July 2013.

[40] Andrea van Wyk, 'Take a Chill Pill and Sit Down, Malema tells Defence Minister', *Eyewitness News*, 12 September 2012, available at http://ewn.co.za/2012/09/12/Take-a-chill-pill-Malema-tells-defence-minister, accessed 4 October 2013.

[41] *City Press*, 'Please take me back, I'll be good – Malema', 17 December 2012, available at www.citypress.co.za/news/buffalo-soldier-cyril-loses-out-20120414, accessed 4 October 2103.

preneurship lifestyle.[42] Malema's rebuttal: 'You can't wage a war against capital and not expect a reaction. Revolution is painful. EFF is not calling for blood on the floor. It is calling for a constructive redistribution of resources of this country in a radical way.... Show me a country that practised market-related economy which has prospered in Africa, or created an equal society, free of poverty, where the wealth is shared among people.' Zuma's team is, he argued, 'a kleptocracy, a government of thieves ... We want them out of power. They have failed our people.'[43]

Big business expressed relief at Malema's expulsion from the ANC, and openly celebrated Ramaphosa's defeat of anti-Zuma candidates Tokyo Sexwale and Matthews Phosa at Mangaung. Sexwale was evicted from the Housing Ministry within six months. With Ramaphosa as the new deputy President, ANC Secretary-General Mantashe could brag: 'He will open up avenues for the ANC to interact with business, and maybe reduce the suspicion on the part of business about an ANC that is supposedly hostile to business – although it is not.'[44] There remained some question as to whether Ramaphosa would himself simply be swallowed up by the Zuma team's own corrupt practices. Indeed, this was precisely the equation posed by *Business Day's* Bruce: 'He [Ramaphosa] will provide Zuma with the sort of credibility cover only the likes of Trevor Manuel still have to offer ... Of course, as much as Ramaphosa can save Zuma, so can Zuma defile Ramaphosa if he is unable to wean himself off what appears to be a staple diet of financial dependency on friends of one kind or another, or business 'associates' who see in the President an easy mark.'[45] Time alone would tell.

For the moment, however, the vociferous endorsements of Ramaphosa by big business meant the ANC's economic talk-left-so-as-to-walk-right strategy was even more clearly signalled, especially when it came to the National Development Plan, which Ramaphosa co-chaired the creation of, and which was endorsed by business, the Democratic Alliance and the ANC's neo-liberal wing. In the words of commentator Adam Habib: 'The ANC says it's committed to the notion of economic transformation. If that is true, how do you elect a billionaire as your deputy President? He has an admirable political record, but his track record on economic transformation is abysmal.'[46] The potential for Ramaphosa to act in the interests of South Africa's untransformed business-in-general coin-

[42] For the impressive Founding Manifesto of the Economic Freedom Fighters, see www.politicsweb.co.za/politicsweb/view/politicsweb/en/page71619?oid=393903&sn=Detail&pid=71616, accessed 4 October 2013.

[43] Pascal Fletcher, 'Former-ANC "bad boy" plans election bid against the odds', Reuters, Johannesburg, 24 July 2013.

[44] Sam Mkokeli and Carol Paton, 'Ramaphosa SA's Prime Minister,' *Business Day*, 20 December 2012, available at www.bdlive.co.za/national/politics/2012/12/20/ramaphosa-sas-prime-minister--mantashe, accessed 5 October 2013.

[45] Bruce, 'Thick End of the Wedge'.

[46] Robyn Dixon, 'South African President Jacob Zuma Retains ANC Leadership', *Los Angeles Times*, 18 December 2012, available at www.latimes.com/news/nation-world/world/la-fg-south-africa-zuma-20121219,0,340440.story, accessed 5 October 2013.

cided perfectly with his own personal portfolio's tentacles, spread right across the South African economy, as Mandy de Waal pointed out:

> As executive chair of Shanduka, the investment company he founded in 2001, Ramaphosa has interests in resources, energy, financial services, food and beverages, and property. Shanduka has investments in some of the most influential and powerful businesses in South Africa (and in some cases globally). These include Macsteel, Scaw Metals SA, Lonmin (through Incwala Resources), Kangra Coal, McDonald's SA, Mondi Plc, Lace Diamonds, Pan African Resources Plc, Coca- Cola, Seacom, MTN, Bidvest, Standard Bank, Alexander Forbes, Investment Solutions, and Liberty Group. Besides the executive role he has at Shanduka, he is the joint Non-Executive Chairman of Mondi Group, and the non-executive chair of MTN, and a number of other companies Shanduka has interests in like Standard Bank and Bidvest. He is also on the board of SABMiller.[47]

Rebuilding from micropolitics

With Zuma reelected ANC President at Mangaung and with Ramaphosa as his Deputy and presumed replacement in 2019 after Zuma's second term would end, the ruling party's political turmoil appeared to stabilize. This was not necessarily a durable stability, however, because as *Daily Maverick* reporter Ranjeni Munusamy put it in mid-2013

> Businessman Cyril Ramaphosa would return from the political wilderness and help the Zuma slate at the ANC's Mangaung conference to a landslide victory. In exchange Ramaphosa would get what he always wanted: a no-contest ticket to the presidency. The first part worked like a charm. Unfortunately for Ramaphosa, though, he has no guarantee that he will be the next Number One. And there's not very much he can do if the current Number One and his supporters change their minds about the deal ...
>
> All Ramaphosa had to do was be number two on the Zuma slate in Mangaung, and his path to the presidency in 2019 would be cleared. In the meantime he would scale down his business interests and become deputy president of the state in 2014, thus making for a smooth transition for him to take power in five years. In terms of this deal, the Zuma camp would back him for ANC president in 2017 and make sure it was a walkover ...
>
> The problem is that Ramaphosa accepted the deal without any guarantees – and realistically, how could there be any? The deal was based on trust that Zuma and his campaigners would honour the agreement. Predictably, this now looks shaky.[48]

A different micropolitical struggle – between the state and civil society – was even more tumultuous and unpredictable than internal ANC manoeuvres. An early 2013 call for a national strike from the most militant of mineworkers reflected on-going frustrations. But the forces for genuine change had not, by

---

[47] Mandy de Waal, 'Cyril Ramaphosa: ANC Deputy, Captain of Industry', *Daily Maverick*, 20 December 2012, available at http://dailymaverick.co.za/article/2012-12-20-cyril-ramaphosa-anc-deputy-captain-of-industry, accessed 5 October 2013.

[48] Ranjeni Munusamy, 'Concomitance can mean Dancing with the Devil, Mr Ramaphosa', *Daily Maverick*, 22 July 2013.

the end of 2012, been properly gathered from below. Prospects for labour and community activists unifying at the base needed more attention, for to exist in Marikana and similar mining towns was to face incessant police repression bordering on unqualified brutality.

For example, the brief emergence of a women's mutual-aid movement amongst mineworker wives and girlfriends, as well as other women from the impoverished Marikana community, was one reflection of a new bottom-up politics. At least one martyr emerged from their ranks: Paulina Masuhlo, an unusually *sympatico* ANC municipal councillor in Marikana who sided with the workers, was shot in the abdomen and leg with rubber bullets during a police and army invasion of Nkaneng on September 15. She died of the wounds on September 19. Yet for the subsequent week and a half, police and malevolently bureaucratic municipal officials refused the women's attempts to memorialize Masuhlo with a long protest march from Nkaneng to the Marikana police station. Persistence and legal support prevailed, so 800 demanded justice in a women's-only trek from Nkaneng to Marikana police station on September 29, dignified and without casualties.

But the political opportunities that might fuse worker, community and women's interests in improving conditions for the reproduction of labour power – perhaps one day too joined by environmentalists – were fragile and easy to lose. Male migrant workers typically maintained two households and hence channelled resources back to the Eastern Cape, Lesotho, Mozambique and other home bases. This process of mixing short-term residents with long-term Tswana-speaking inhabitants was fraught with potential xenophobia and ethnicism, not to mention gendered power relations. Migrancy has also facilitated syndicates of illicit drugs, transactional sex (even forced sexual labour), traditional patriarchy, dysfunctional spiritual suspicions (e.g., the use of traditional medicine, *muti*, against bullets, which allegedly wears off quickly in the presence of women), widespread labour broking and other super-exploitative relations.

As a result, as discussed earlier, it was extremely expensive to swim within this sea of poverty, with desperation microfinance leading to even more extreme exploitation. It remained to be seen whether this fusion of mining and financial exploitation would generate strategic responses. For example, new versions of a debt moratorium or organized debtor's cartel – such as the 'bond boycott' strategies that were so common in the early 1990s, in which borrowers banded together to gain strength for collective defaults – would be a logical progression for a micropolitics of resistance in Marikana and so many other similar situations. The 'repo man' tended to resort to threats and practices of violence, of course, so this is not a decision to be taken lightly; in Mexico in early 1995, it took a jump in interest rates from 14 to 120 per cent to catalyse the 'El Barzon' – the yoke – movement which gathered a million members to renegotiate debts on the basis of the financial reality, 'Can't pay, won't pay!'

The South African precedent was the earliest recorded bond boycott, in Port Elizabeth's Uitenhage township in 1988 in which a Volkswagen autoworkers strike led to Standard Bank attempting to repossess workers' newly-built houses, because of loans which they were having trouble servicing as a result of the strike. Labour and community activists successfully turned the tables on that alliance of a multinational auto corporation and domestic financial capital by engaging in a collective refusal to repay. The strategy and tactic changed power relations sufficiently so that instead of Volkswagen compelling Standard to pressure workers to go back to the assembly line, the workers and communities compelled Standard to request Volkswagen to settle the strike. With many dozens of such local bond boycotts and a semi-successful national bond boycott campaign by the SA National Civic Organisation (SANCO) in 1992,[49] there was some sense by the mid-1990s that, from below, society could and should unify against financial power.

In mid-1996, a 'Campaign against the Bank Rate Increase' began, fusing 'Cosatu and its affiliate unions, the ANC, ANC Youth League, SACP, Sanco, SA Students' Congress (Sasco), Congress of SA Students, Muslim Youth Movement, Young Christian Students and the Call of Islam', as *Shopsteward* reported:

> The campaign's immediate demand was for the reversal of the one percent increase. But there was agreement that, even if the big four drop their one percent hike [of May 1996], interest rates are still too high, particularly when compared to other countries. This has a detrimental effect on economic growth, housing, job creation and the budget deficit, to mention but a few. Many coalition organisations want to take the campaign a step further to review monetary and interest rate policies and there are moves afoot to look at measures, including legislation, to regulate banks' behaviour ...
>
> The coalition is the first of its kind since the 1994 general elections, involving a broad alliance of organisations, unseen since the days of the anti-VAT campaign in 1991. The campaign has also pleased alliance activists concerned that the ANC has neglected grassroots campaigns in favour of exclusively parliamentary politics. There is a view that parliamentary avenues should complement campaigns at a mass level and that the ANC should continue to act in concert with civil society organisations in transforming the country.[50]

That brief 1996 campaign did launch several mass actions, but suddenly, in mid-June, momentum was reversed when the ANC acted against civil society by unilaterally imposing the *Growth, Employment and Redistribution* home-grown structural adjustment policy. Nonetheless, in spite of its truncated nature, the bank campaign was, in concept, one of the ways the 'small-a alliance' vision

[49] As a result of the resistance, township housing foreclosures which could not be consummated due to refusal of the defaulting borrowers (supported by the community) to vacate their houses, and the leading financier's US$700 million black housing bond exposure in September 1992 was the reason that its holding company (Nedcor) lost 20 per cent of its Johannesburg Stock Exchange share value (in excess of US$150 million lost) in a single week. Locally, if a bank did bring in a sheriff to foreclose and evict defaulters, it was not uncommon for a street committee of activists to burn the house down before the new owners completed the purchase and moved in. Such power, in turn, allowed both the national and local civic associations to negotiate concessions from the banks. The practice is reviewed in Mzwanele Mayekiso, *Township Politics* (New York: Monthly Review Press, 1996); and Bond, *Cities of Gold, Townships of Coal.*

[50] *Shopsteward*, 'Banks buckle under public pressure', 5, 3, 1996, available at www.cosatu.org.za/show.php?ID=2080#INTERVIEW, accessed 5 October 2013.

found an early manifestation. Later the SACP too attempted several banking reforms but without substantial benefits, as the balance of forces grew continually more adverse under Mbeki's rule. But this was not unusual during the early 2000s; the country with one of the world's fastest growth rates, India, also suffered a quarter of a million suicides by small farmers, invariably because of over-indebtedness. Bankers really did rule the world, as was evident when the bailout funding of 2008–09 went entirely to creditors and not to the debtors. However, in unlikely places (even the United States), impressive attempts to generate social pressure against banks suddenly emerged in 2008–09, with Occupy Wall Street only the most visible.

South Africa missed out on the first phase of the complaining against the '1 per cent', one reason being that the traditions of South African progressive politics always paralleled classical socialist reasoning. As a result capitalist malevolence – Marikana being only one example – invariably called forth the simple demand that the means of production be nationalized. In late 2012, Zuma, Shabangu and their pro-business allies succeeded rather easily in ridding the ANC of such chatter, not least because Malema's own troubles rose to crisis proportions, thus temporarily neutralizing his more populist voice. Indeed, the expulsion of the ANC Youth League faux-radicals left virtually no major figures aside from the general secretary of the National Union of Metalworkers of South Africa, Irvin Jim, to demand nationalization of strategic resources.

Nationalizing Lonmin and other platinum corporations would have been a smart move, of course, for South Africa controls more than 80 per cent of world platinum reserves, and the price spike occasioned by the Lonmin, Implats and Angloplats strikes – 30 per cent over six weeks – suggested great potential for a platinum cartel similar to the Organization of Petroleum Exporting Countries's oil cartel. The main buyer of platinum in 2012 was the European auto industry, but while the EU economic crisis continued, demand was intrinsically soft. This meant major platinum mines could make plausible threats that if workers did not return, they would simply close shafts. The same week that Lonmin conceded the big wage increase to several thousand Marikana rock-drill operators, it found it could cancel short-term contracts of another 1200 workers.

Revolution, revulsion and rearguard defence

Because of this convoluted political conjuncture, the most hopeful outcome of Marikana was to be an 'economistic' one, namely the wage increase won by the striking workers. This in itself was no mean feat, as Peter Alexander argues:

> In other settings, events of this kind have led to the defeat of a movement, or at least its abeyance. But that is not what happened here. On the contrary, the strike got stronger. Workers faced trauma, the tribulations of burying their dead in far-away places, threatened sackings, lack of money for food, and attacks from unions and politicians. But, by 7 September the company was reporting that attendance at work was down to two per cent, and after that it gave up providing statistics. There was an

undeclared state of emergency and a community leader was killed, but still the workers fought on, until, on 18 September, they agreed to a settlement that secured them victory. Had the strike collapsed, people across the country fighting poverty and injustice would have been cowed. The opposite happened and, from the perspective of the state and the bosses, the killings were an appalling miscalculation, an enormous setback. Somehow, despite 34 colleagues being killed and with many more injured or detained, workers found the strength to pull themselves together and determine that the strike would continue. This was one of the most remarkable acts of courage in labour history, anywhere and at any time.[51]

But if the acts of courage were, Alexander reminds us, forged from frustration and anger, they also lacked a sufficiently strong and clear political agenda. And some such agenda was been necessary to mobilize the tens of millions of disgruntled South Africans into a force capable of breaking sweetheart relations between state, ruling party, labour aristocrats, parasitical capital and the London/Melbourne mining houses. For some, Marikana was potentially the breakthrough event that independent progressives long sought, one that could reveal more graphically the intrinsic anti-social tendencies associated with the ANC-Alliance's elite transition from revolutionaries to willing partners of some of the world's most wicked corporations. Such a narrative was indeed the one promoted by the otherwise extremely fractured South African left.

For example, some factions associated with the relatively broad-based (though labour-less) Democratic Left Front and the Marikana Support Campaign, did sponsor regular political meetings from Johannesburg and Cape Town and also solidaristic activities in the platinum belt. Nonetheless, because the first such meeting at the University of Johannesburg a week after the Marikana massacre provisionally included a leading NUM representative on the programme (he was shouted down and chased from the hall),[52] another left faction led by Johannes-

---

[51] Peter Alexander, 'Analysis and conclusion', in Alexander et al., *Marikana*, p. 195.
[52] The most evocative description of that meeting is probably by Athi Mongezeleli Joja, 'White tears cheapening black suffering' (available at http://septembernationalimbizo.org/white-tears-cheapening-black-suffering, accessed 5 October 2013). To illustrate the divisions that quickly emerged, although an impressive revival of the Black Consciousness (BC) tradition had risen since the early 2000s through the *New Frank Talk* series, the sole public intervention on Marikana by the September National Imbizo was to visit two days after the massacre to begin the reconstruction of events, but without subsequent commentary or activism. A month after the massacre, BC adherents along with an unusually subdued left-autonomist network conjoined in an intellectual conference at Johannesburg's Wits University, in an event known as the 'Tribe of Moles', led by an emerging black intelligentsia suspicious of classical socialist formulations and friendly to insurgent opportunities. But surprisingly, in a whole day of debating race, representation and radical politics, the word Marikana was not mentioned once from the stage or floor. When asked during a break about the evolving situation, including Marikana women's organizing, the country's most prominent BC proponent, Andile Mngxitama, called the cross-racial/class/geographical gender organizing underway (including middle-class women from NGOs) a distraction, for after all the corpses were 'black bodies' – and hence he gave impetus to the frequent claim that contemporary South African BC argumentation soon degenerates into race essentialism.

burg's Khanya College broke away to found the 'We are all Marikana' campaign.[53] Resolutely opposed to any legitimation of COSATU's Alliance unionism, this network also gathered ordinary workers for educational events (although momentum appeared to slow within a month of the massacre).

In contrast, one other small revolutionary party in Marikana engaged in much higher-profile recruiting and consciousness-raising: the Democratic Socialist Movement (associated with the Committee for a Workers' International). However, its limitations were also obvious, for in December 2012, as its representative conceded: 'The modest founding of the Workers and Socialist Party with just 20 delegates present has made concrete the idea of an alternative based on a socialist programme committed to nationalisation of the commanding heights of the economy of which the mining industry remains a key component.'[54]

For the fact remains that even though it may often have seemed that a 'pre-revolutionary' situation existed in a South Africa that had one of the highest protest rates in the world, the lack of connection between those with grievances remained the most crippling problem. This 'disconnect' continued amongst traditional critics of ANC neo-liberalism in late 2012. One critical example was the lack of any real attempt to co-ordinate international solidarity. This was a huge void in Marikana-related political work, an opportunity lost by South Africans despite the willingness of NGOs to call on the World Bank to divest from Lonmin just one day after the massacre[55] and the fact that at least a dozen spontaneous protests broke out at SA embassies and consulate offices across the world in subsequent days.

There was, though, the hope that, as another example, the women of Marikana, organizing across the divides of labour and community, could set an example so desperately needed by the broader left. Their organizing efforts ranged beyond Marikana itself, as they briefly helped connect the dots elsewhere in the society, including in nearby terrains ranging from mining villages to land struggles in North West, Limpopo and Gauteng provinces. Yet South African women were as diverse and ethnically divided as the broader society: wives, girl-friends, mothers, daughters, sisters, health workers, educators, sex-workers, cooks, cleaners, salespersons.[56] Moreover, these women had the additional

---

[53] See www.facebook.com/KhanyaCollegeMovementHouse/posts/139762889503120, accessed 5 October 2013.

[54] www.socialistsouthafrica.co.za, accessed 5 October 2013; and see WASP founding statement at www.politicsweb.co.za/politicsweb/view/politicsweb/en/page71654?oid=347787&sn=Detail&pid=71616, accessed 5 October 2013.

[55] Center for International Environmental Law, 'CIEL calls on World Bank to revisit investment in Lonmin', Washington, 17 August 2012, available at http://ciel.org/Law_Communities/Lonmin_17Aug2012.html, accessed 5 October 2013.

[56] In fact, in two cases, the voice were heard even of women serving as super-exploitative mining house managers (Cynthia Carroll of Anglo and Mamphela Ramphele of Goldfields), capitalist ideologues who could provide very little in the way of sister-hood, though at least the former World Bank managing director Ramphele did acknowledge that migrant labour needs a rethink.

burdens of handling trauma counselling for victims of violence, and providing mutual aid to those who were suffering enormously, directly and indirectly, as a result of the wildcat strike wave's reduction of immediate cash in communities. In short, as in other sectors of the society, much political work was needed in order to create a truly coherent oppositional voice amongst women.

The same could be said of 'progressives' more generally. Such people had long been associated with the ANC because of the century-old party's best instincts, but after 1994 many of them continued their determined work of liberation mainly from within civil society. In this political space, one found organizations that jumped into the Marikana political breech with much needed support activities. These included, for example, the Socio-Economic Rights Institute, Sonke Gender Justice, Studies in Poverty and Inequality, Students for Law and Social Justice, the Treatment Action Campaign and Section 27 (which is named with reference to the country's Bill of Rights).[57] Yet, here again, where was the coherence, organizational and ideological, that could render this a cumulative and defining force?

As for the official 'left', here there was, to be brutally frank, absolutely nothing worth salvaging. As *Business Day*'s Peter Bruce wrote four days after the massacre: 'What's scary about Marikana is that, for the first time, for me, the fact that the ANC and its government do not have the handle they once did on the African majority has come home. The party is already losing the middle classes. If they are now also losing the marginal and the dispossessed, what is left? Ah yes, Cosatu and the communists – Zuma's creditors.'[58] It was almost surreal to find COSATU and Communist leaders anxiety-ridden at the prospect of widening worker revolt. It was no wonder that controversy-seeking liberal journalist R. W. Johnson could easily find an SACP ideologue to serve as his 'useful idiot' in making this bizarre case:

> *[T]his time the Left was in favour of the massacre* [emphasis added]. Dominic Tweedie of the Communist University, Johannesburg, commented, 'This was no massacre, this was a battle. The police used their weapons in exactly the way they were supposed to. That's what they have them for. The people they shot didn't look like workers to me. We should be happy. The police were admirable.' The Communist Party's North West section demanded the arrest of ANCWU's Joseph Muthunjwa and his deputy, James Kholelile.[59]

[57] Interestingly, Mark Heywood, formerly a leading AIDS-medicines activist and now leader of this latter very vigorous NGO, was on the one hand a vital supplier of solidarity but at the same time perhaps a victim of his own belief in liberal *muti* (traditional medicine). Thus when speaking to the Marikana workers and community in late September he asserted that 'The Constitution of South Africa is the most important weapon we have. It is more powerful than Jacob Zuma, but it will only give you power if you organise around the Constitution, if you organise around its rights.' Shown this quote, maverick left intellectual Ashwin Desai merely chuckled: 'I don't think the workers won their 22 percent raise with a second thought about the Constitution.'

[58] Bruce, 'Thick End of the Wedge'.

[59] R. W. Johnson, 'Massacre at Marikana', *politicsweb*, 19 August 2012, available at www.politicsweb.co.za/politicsweb/view/politicsweb/en/page72308?oid=320136&s n=Marketingweb+detail&pid=90389, accessed 5 October 2013.

Yet in a context where social protest in the townships had reached very high levels in mid-2012 with no hope of relief, the panic of bosses and their spokespeople – neo-liberals such as Bruce – was also easy to discern. Some commentators apparently feared the potentially uncontrollable contagion of disrespect; thus Frans Cronje of the SA Institute of Race Relations immediately rose to the ANC's defence, declaring in mid-September that 'a myth has taken hold in South Africa that service delivery was a failure.'[60] Cronje's defence of state provision of water, electricity, housing, etc reverberated well with *Business Day* editorialists as well as SACP leader Blade Nzimande, who warmly endorsed the 'research'.[61] Yet when Cronje was asked whether he had determined what percentage of post-1994 communal water taps were still working amongst those the ruling party claim serve more than fifteen million people, he conceded that he had no clue.[62] The last serious audit – a decade earlier by David Hemson, at the behest of then water Minister Ronnie Kasrils – put the share at less than half, using even the most generous definition of what is 'working', and by all accounts the sector's management has degenerated since then.[63]

There was, then, plenty to be frightened about, and in the immediate wake of Marikana, *Business Day* columnist Steven Friedman appealed for a return to a 'social partnership' strategy because such an approach 'has not failed us – it has not been tried'.[64] Meanwhile, the corporatist elites did meet in mid-October 2012, issuing what were soon seen as meaningless statements against wildcat strikes and worker violence against scabs. However, the big-business representatives at that gabfest were apparently loathe to even name themselves publicly.[65] Instead, they turned back to straightforward class struggle. In 2012, for example, Gold Fields Chief Executive Officer Nick Holland was remunerated R45.3 million, a raise of R12.6 million from 2011. As for his employees, however, 'We can't continue giving double-digit increases when productivity is declining. That's not sustainable.'[66]

[60] Nick Hedley, 'Service delivery: Presidency blames apartheid', *Business Day*, 12 September 2012, available at www.bdlive.co.za/national/2012/09/12/service-delivery-presidency-blames-apartheid-denial, accessed 5 October 2013.
[61] Blade Nzimande, 'Transforming University and Society', *politicsweb*, 2 October 2012, available at www.politicsweb.co.za/politicsweb/view/politicsweb/en/page72308?oid=329837&sn=Marketingweb+detail&pid=90389, accessed 5 October 2013.
[62] Frans Cronje, personal correspondence, 13 September 2012.
[63] Hemson, 'Rural Poor Play a Role'.
[64] Steven Friedman, 'We Must Stop Blaming and Start Compromising', *Business Day*, 19 September 2012, available at www.bdlive.co.za/opinion/columnists/2012/09/19/we-must-stop-blaming-and-start-compromising, accessed 5 October 2013.
[65] Tim Cohen, 'Time for a Bold New Idea of what it means to be SA', *Business Day*, 15 October 2012, available at www.bdlive.co.za/opinion/columnists/2012/10/15/time-for-a-bold-new-idea-of-what-it-means-to-be-sa, accessed 5 October 2013.
[66] Martin Creamer, 'Mining Doomed if 'Crazy' Pay Increases Continue – Nick Holland', *Mining Weekly*, 10 May 2013.

Conclusion

The strike wave continued rising through late 2012, no matter narratives about social 'leadership'. Truck drivers received an above-inflation settlement in October 2012 after resorting to sometimes intensely violent methods to disrupt scab drivers, in the process creating shortages of petrol and retail goods in various parts of the country. With Durban's Toyota workers, municipal offices and then the farm workers of the Western Cape all also engaged in wildcat strikes, no one was taking the signals from Pretoria seriously. This was not new, of course, for in September 2012, the World Economic Forum's *Global Competitiveness Report* placed South Africa in the number one position for adverse employee-employer relations (in a survey done prior to Marikana), whereas using the same measure of class struggle in 2011, South African workers were only in seventh place out of the 144 countries surveyed.[67]

Partly as a result of labour militancy, major ratings agencies began downgrading the country's bond rating, for example, to BBB level by Standard & Poor's. The resulting higher interest rates to be paid on the country's prolific foreign borrowings – about five times higher in 2012 in absolute terms than inherited from apartheid in 1994 – created yet more fiscal pressures as well as household and corporate repayment stress. Given Europe's crisis and South Africa's vulnerability, much lower GDP growth rates in 2013 and beyond were anticipated. Instead of countering that prospect with an interest rate cut by the SA Reserve Bank in late 2012, as was projected, the country's shaky financial standing put countervailing upward pressure on rates.

Thus in the period after Marikana, the situation remained fluid, and it was impossible to assess which forces would emerge from the chaos. It was here that contemporary South African narratives from within 'nationalism,' 'populism,' 'Stalinism,' 'Trotskyism,' 'autonomism,' 'Black Consciousness,' 'feminism,' 'corporatism,' 'liberalism' and 'neo-liberalism' all appeared inadequate to the tasks at hand, be it on the platinum belt or so many other workplaces and communities. No ideologues posed a vision that could rescue South Africa from the intense pressures that seem to be growing stronger each week.[68]

---

[67] World Economic Forum, *Global Competitiveness Report 2012–2013*, Davos, September 2012, available at www.weforum.org/reports/global-competitiveness-report-2012-2013, accessed 5 October 2013.

[68] However, after I first made this case in 2012, journalist Kwanele Sosibo rebutted:

> Activists and political leaders organising in the North-West, for the most part, differ with Bond. Trevor Ngwane of the DLF-linked Socialist Group, argues that more emphasis should be on what the workers in the platinum belt, whom 'even for a moment, were the vanguard of the working class struggle in the country ... If Bond is emphasising the weaknesses of the left, I'm saying, he's right, but don't look at what the left did' [...]
> Ultimately, any hope for the left in Marikana depends on the type of union Amcu will be. In his rhetoric, Amcu president Joseph Mathunjwa espouses socialism;

The centrifugal pressures pulling outwards on the ANC were some of the most intense, with a near certain fragmentation in the short-to-medium term, according to William Gumede:

> South Africa is entering the 20-year post-liberation mark when many African liberation governments turned governments, who fail to deliver adequately on promises, either break-up, splinter or fragment when members and supporters leave it for new parties. The tipping point have been reached where the gap between the ANC leadership and the daily grind of ordinary members may have now become such a wide gulf that many ANC members who may have deep affinity with the party may now not be able anymore to identify themselves with both the leaders and the party.[69]

Who would pull the hardest, from the left? The most visionary major force representing workers during this period was the National Union of Metalworkers of South Africa (NUMSA). Its president, Cedric Gina, worked as a shop steward at the huge BHP Billiton smelter in Richards Bay, where he observed the state-corporate revolving door that continues to over-empower the Minerals-Energy Complex. NUMSA stood up not only to BHP Billiton in numerous battles, but to the broader neo-liberal faction promoting the National Development Plan (NDP). Said Gina:

> Inevitably, the rupture in Cosatu is between those who want to see a thoroughgoing implementation of the Freedom Charter, thus a rejection of the GEAR that the NDP is, and those who are consciously or unconsciously defending South African capitalism. Those who want Comrade Zwelinzima Vavi out of Cosatu want a Cosatu which will be a 'toy telephone', a 'labour desk', a pro-capitalist Cosatu, and those who are defending Comrade Vavi want a revolutionary socialist, anti-colonialist and anti-imperialist Cosatu.'[70]

The problem at that point, mid-2013, was in some ways reduced to a personality battle, over whether the sex scandal that engulfed COSATU's general secretary Vavi gave legitimate space for his enemies to argue for a suspension and deepened investigation. Reflecting its militancy, NUMSA's Central Committee issued a statement on 12 August 2013, under the headline, '*The history of all hitherto existing society is the history of class struggles.*'

(cont.) hectoring on about turning the tables on the capitalist class and nationalising the mines for the benefit of posterity. In its trajectory to the top and in its attitude to bargaining infrastructure, however, the union has sought to safeguard the very same status quo that rendered the NUM ventricose and lethargic.

Kwanele Sosibo, 'Why the Left Has Failed to Capitalise on Post-Marikana Massacre Cracks in the ANC Hegemony', *The Con*, 25 June 2013, available at www.theconmag. co.za/2013/06/25/why-the-left-has-failed-to-capitalise-on-post-marikana-massacre-cracks-in-the-anc-hegemony, accessed 5 October 2013.

69 William Gumede, 'ANC fragmentation', *Pambazuka News*, 4 July 2013, available at http://pambazuka.org/en/category/features/88110, accessed 5 October 2013.

70 Greg Nicolson, 'Numsa's Ready to Fight for the Future of the Left', *Daily Maverick*, 13 August 2013.

Capitalism and the failure of the Alliance to pursue consistently a radical National Demo-
cratic Revolution (NDR) are at the heart of the crisis in Cosatu today. In our view, the
struggle for freedom in South Africa cannot be achieved without the popular democratic forces advancing a socialist oriented National Democratic Revolution ...

It is evidently clear that those within Cosatu that has been advocating the idea of
a rupture in Cosatu might be correct. From Numsa's perspective this rupture in
Cosatu is between forces of capitalism and forces of socialism. We make this bold
statement because we have seen how in the CEC some argued why we should not
campaigning against e-tolling, why we must not honour and execute the Cosatu resolution and policy of Nationalisation of the commanding heights of the South African
economy... Those who want Comrade Zwelinzima Vavi out of Cosatu want a Cosatu
which will be a 'toy telephone', a 'labour desk,' a pro capitalist Cosatu and those who
are defending Comrade Vavi want a revolutionary socialist, anti colonialist and anti-
imperialist Cosatu ...

From where we stand, our analytical work confirms that the centre of the crisis in
Cosatu resides in the capitalist trajectory of our post 1994 socio-economic formation. Comrade Zwelinzima Vavi is seen as a threat to the ambitions of the rightwing
capitalist forces, which see a Cosatu under his leadership as obstructing their capitalist
ambitions... For the working class, especially the progressive and socialist workers of
South Africa and the world we say: let history not be written that you stood aside
when Cosatu was imploding, that you did nothing to save the giant revolutionary
shield of the working class and the poor! (emphasis added)[71]

What was definitive, though, was the waning of any remaining illusions that
the forces of 'liberation' led by the ANC would take South Africa to genuine
freedom and a new society. Marikana had that effect, permanently, and
Ramaphosa's December 2012 elevation could do nothing to restore faith in the
ruling party – just the opposite. In coming years, protesters would keep dodging
police bullets and moving the socio-economic and political-ecological questions
to centre stage, from where ANC neo-liberal nationalism could either arrange
a properly fascist backlash or, more likely under Zuma's on-going misrule
through 2019, continue shrinking in confusion with regular doses of necessary humility. That humility, borne of repeated embarrassments we will
continue witnessing in South Africa reminds, in sum, of a tragic temporal
evolution in a geographically concentrated site: from the birth of the hominid
Mrs Ples on the border of North West and Gauteng Provinces; to Mandela's era
when hopes for a new humanity were birthed in Pretoria via full-fledged non-
racial democracy on 11 May 1994; to the death at Marikana of any remaining
hopes for the stability of class apartheid. Looking ahead, something new must
yet be born – so that the present will no longer be the prisoner of history.

[71] National Union of Metalworkers of South Africa, Central Committee Statement,
Johannesburg, 12 August 2013.

7.

Liberating Liberation:
The Struggle against Recolonization in South Africa[1]

JOHN S. SAUL

> Does it sit easily with the millions of ANC supporters here at home, and in the world at large, that during [the organization's] centennial year, the government, led by the ANC, presided over the first post-democracy state massacre ... [For] Marikana is symptomatic of a much deeper malaise ... Over the past eight years we have seen the escalation of local protests over perceived delivery failures and corruption at local government levels. It might well be that many of these protests were fuelled by rising expectations: [Certainly] there can be no doubt that in many instances this has led to ANC councilors losing legitimacy among the people. It is only a matter of time before that loss of legitimacy percolates upwards – to the provincial and national levels ... [Indeed] the credibility of the ANC today is probably the lowest it has been since 1990!
>
> Pallo Jordan, September 7, 2012[2]

From the vantage point of the troubled present, my conclusion highlights within South Africa's history both the rise of the ANC's mission of liberation and the disappointing and anti-climactic outcome that has followed from the ANC's 'victory'. But it also seeks to register the complex cross-currents of the present moment and the still somewhat hesitant signs that some novel brand of post-ANC, counter-hegemonic, political expression may be beginning to emerge in South Africa – one that could in time displace the present ANC government itself and do so for the better. With the echoes of the recent and starkly sobering

---

[1] The South African magazine *Amandla!* in its issue 24 of March/April, 2012, marked the one hundredth anniversary of the founding of the ANC with a symposium entitled 'ANC: 100 Years: Looking Ahead', a symposium to which I was asked to contribute. I have modified, as the first section of the present book's conclusion, parts of the article I then wrote – originally entitled 'A Poisoned Chalice: Liberation, ANC-style'. Then, in two further sections, I have developed a number of additional observations sparked in part by the 'Marikana Massacre' (which occurred during the period that this manuscript was being completed) and by the responses of others to it. It is those killed in this massacre to whom, in addition to Neville Alexander, this book is dedicated. My concluding observations in this chapter therefore seek further to capture the tenor of the politics of the present conjuncture, although these primarily serve here as mere grace-notes to Bond's own chapters (Chapters 4 and 5) on the period running from 1994 to the present which have comprised Section II of this book and as well as a complement to his own concluding chapter (Chapter 6).

[2] I quote from a copy of this speech sent to me by Jordan himself on September 9, 2012.

Marikana massacre still vibrating through the body politic the moment seems a particularly ripe one in which to hazard such speculation. Of course, as we will see, ebbing confidence in the ANC's hold on power has been rife in South Africa for some time, and well before the moment of the massacre. Nonetheless, there are signs that not only has Marikana challenged the self-esteem of some of the more thoughtful of ANC veterans but also has helped further to delegitimate the party itself and to shake its hegemonic grip on South Africa's polity. If this proves to be the case, the grim events that occurred at Marikana may indeed mark the 'decisive turning-point in [SA's] post-apartheid history' that some have deemed it to be.[3]

In this connection, the startling speech from senior ANC notable Pallo Jordan (quoted above, in our epigraph to this conclusion) is worthy of special attention. As reports of this speech have underlined, Jordan also seemed to recognize Marikana as marking a crucial moment.

> The ANC is embroiled in a 'profound crisis', with its credibility at its lowest point in the past 22 years, according to Dr Pallo Jordan, a member of the party's highest decision-making body, who called for a 'dignified and moral' leadership to take over and clear out the corruption. Jordan voiced his disappointment during his address to ... guests on Thursday, attending the 20th commemoration of the Bisho massacre in the town's Good News Christian Centre. [Speaking explicitly of the Marikana massacre he also said:] 'The leadership of the ANC has been stripped of its dignity. The ANC has lost legitimacy.'[4]

'The ANC has lost legitimacy'? What might follow from this? Is there afoot in South Africa a new politics, at once viable and progressive, that might give effective focus and force to the 'rebellion of the poor'[5] that is seen to have been swelling in South Africa's townships for some time.[6] It would take another book to begin to answer such questions properly. Nonetheless I will also here briefly canvass a range of informed opinion that has begun to wrestle with them.

---

[3]   Martin Legassick, 'The Marikana Massacre: a turning point?' *The Bullet: A Socialist Project E-Bulletin*, 689, 31 August 2012, available via info@socialistproject.ca. See also Vishwas Satgar, 'The Marikana Massacre and the South African State's Low Intensity War Against the People', *The Bullet*, 693, 5 September 2012.

[4]   *IOL news*, 'Profound ANC crisis', 8 September 2012, available at www.iol.co.za/news/politics/profound-anc-crisis-1.1378491, accessed 5 October 2013.

[5]   See Peter Alexander, 'Rebellion of the poor: South Africa's service delivery protests – a preliminary analysis', *Review of African Political Economy*, 37, 123 (March, 2010), cited in chapter 2, as well as his updated survey entitled, 'SA protest rates increasingly competitive with world leader China' 23 March 2012, available from www.amandlapublishers.org.za.

[6]   John S. Saul, 'Conclusion: The Struggle Continues? – On Constructing Counter Hegemony in South Africa' in Saul, *A Flawed Freedom: Rethinking Southern African Liberation* (Delhi, London and Toronto: Three Essays Collective, Pluto Press and Between The Lines, forthcoming).

Liberation, ANC-style

As I wrote in *Amandla!*[7] there is good and obvious reason, in 2012, to celebrate the long history of the ANC and that organization's marked dedication over one hundred years to the cause of the betterment of the lot of the oppressed people of South Africa. The ANC has also sustained an honourable commitment to a multi-racial, pan-ethnic outcome to the struggle against the unequivocally racist system that both segregation and apartheid came for so long to represent in South Africa. Not least important, the ANC is now in power.

Not that, as we have seen above, the ANC was alone in this struggle. The Industrial and Commercial Workers' Union (ICU), the Unity movement, the Pan Africanist Congress (PAC) and the Azanian African People's Organization (AZAPO) were significant and diverse players over many years. Then, in the seventies and eighties, the Black Consciousness Movement, the range of unions that would soon become COSATU, and the township insurgency that first burst into flame in Soweto and then, spreading dramatically and helping to fuel the UDF and the MDM, also had vital roles to play. Much more challenging to apartheid power in their import than either the 'guerilla war' or the actions of any 'internal wing' of the ANC, such assertions were based in a wide range of local outbursts and assertions as part of a genuine mass resistance in South Africa, one not always easily identified as 'belonging' to any one or another broader movement.

In short, the surge forward in South Africa was never monopolised by the ANC, despite the longevity of its existence, its persistence in exile, and its occasional quasi-military appearance within SA's borders. Yet the ANC did manage to translate its popular salience (and that of Nelson Mandela), its international resonance (becoming much more credible in this respect with the virtual disappearance from the scene of its own long-time Soviet-bloc allies), its rather spottier presence on the ground inside South Africa, and its increasing and quite dramatic rapprochement with international capital into a winning hand in the on-going bargaining with the apartheid state. It did, needless to say, emerge victorious in 1994. Moreover, the fact that it had by the 1990s abandoned any promise of offering a radical alternative to continued subordination to global capitalism (and to its leaders' own aggrandizement as the new and well-rewarded masters of state power) did not, at first, cost it heavily at the polls. It was the party of 'liberation' after all.[8]

As such it began merely to absorb other centres of recent and significant public dissent.[9] The SACP was already well within the ANC's tent of power, but

---

[7] See footnote 1, above.

[8] The ANC did, at least in the early post-apartheid years, announce its popular presence by retaining some modicum of organization and of mobilizational activity at the branch level; see Tom Lodge, 'The ANC and the Development of Party Politics', *The Journal of Modern African Studies*, 42, 2, 2004, pp. 189–219.

[9] In 2005 it also, startlingly (but significantly) enough, gobbled up the National Party.

soon COSATU felt compelled to yoke itself as junior partner to the political juggernaut that the ANC had become. As for the UDF, many within it undoubtedly did feel the positive pull of ANC legitimacy but the fact is that those who did not were soon sidelined and the UDF itself disappeared, leaving such old comrades as long-time ANC/SACP stalwart Rusty Bernstein to bemoan that fact. Recall the citation in Chapter 2 of the telling statement from Bernstein's 2001 letter that 'The [ANC's] drive towards power has corrupted the political equation in various ways.' As that letter went on to say:

> it [the ANC's drive towards power] ... paved the way to a steady decline of a mass-membership ANC as an organizer of the people, and turned it into a career opening to public sector employment and the administrative 'gravy train.' It has reduced the tripartite ANC-COSATU-CP alliance from the centrifugal centre of national political mobilization to an electoral pact between parties who are constantly constrained to subordinate their constituents' fundamental interests to the overriding purpose of holding on to administrative power.

Recall, too, his conclusion that 'it has impoverished the soil in which ideas leaning towards socialist solutions once flourished and allowed the weed of 'free market' ideology to take hold'.[10]

Here are the costs, to put it bluntly (as Bernstein has done here), of the fact that the ANC had indeed become 'the party of liberation' – which it certainly has in the eyes of most black South Africans. For, on the one hand, it is true that any doubts as to the ANC's actual struggle credentials and the legitimacy of its continued hold upon electoral power have been slow to take any really significant alternative counter-hegemonic form. Yet it is also true (as we will note more fully below) that a remarkable and rising tide of angry protest and highly charged local demonstration against the structures of popular marginalization is now rife in South Africa. Why this paradox? Here it may be worthwhile to recall Biko's thoughtful analysis of the prospects for transformative change in South Africa (in his conversation with Gail Gerhart, as cited in Chapter 2).

True, in proposing the prioritization of 'Black Consciousness' and a politics of racial as opposed to class assertion Biko quite clearly underestimated (as we have seen) the degree to which the system of 'white power' and 'racial capitalism' that drove apartheid could in time be transformed into a system structured 'merely' around a hierarchy of class and corporate power: exploitative but now relatively colour-blind domination would rely less on a formal system of racist rule and, instead and at least as potently, on the informal imperatives of market logic. Ever more forcefully it was to be an indirect, profit-driven, and dependency-deepening mode of global and local capitalist control that would principally determine the life chances of ordinary South Africans – a system locked into place by means of a continuing recruitment, as active partner in power and privilege, of the local, largely black, political elite, notably those within the upper echelons of the ANC.

In other words, the Fanonist nightmare of 'false decolonization' was now to

---

[10] 'Letter from Rusty Bernstein to John S Saul', *Transformation* (South Africa), 64, 2007.

be visited upon South Africa – albeit a nightmare played out on a global capitalist stage of more diverse racial hue than in the days of the almost exclusive hegemony of the White West (even though the latter has also continued to be an active agent of a renewed imperialism, of course). For now corporate and governmental players of Chinese, Korean, Indian and other centres as well were to join up as participant architects of South Africa's (and Africa's) continuing dependency and of the continued pillage of the country's (and the continent's) natural resources. Yet note as well that if recolonization – not by some individual empire but by an Empire of Global Capital itself – is what now confronts ordinary South Africans, the logic of race and racism are still extremely powerful realities. Perhaps they are less prominent amongst whites, many of whom remain firmly ensconced within the ranks of the extremely privileged and in a new firmly capitalist South Africa in any case – although it should be emphasized that racism is scarcely a non-existent cultural prejudice amongst many of them. But if racial power could no longer be plausibly claimed (as Biko, in the 1970s, had suggested to be the case) to dictate outcomes to class and capital, racial awareness and racial sensitivity remain, not surprisingly, still powerful realities amongst South Africa's long subordinated black population: both a resonant historical memory and, in many continuing ways, a lived contemporary reality.

In short, historians and contemporary analysts and activists alike will underestimate this fact at their peril. True, if both race and class had once been virtual co-equals in determining racial capitalism's grim toll on South Africa's black population, this is no longer a convincing way of understanding South African reality. Yet, to repeat, Biko's emphasis upon the scarring and humiliating effects of apartheid's astonishing ugly version of racism upon the psyches of its erstwhile victims still stands. As does – long after the fall of apartheid and despite the 'recolonization' that the ANC has indeed contributed to – the ANC's legitimacy as the party of power. For it is not just the fact that, as referred to above, the ANC has come to be seen as 'the party of liberation' that has protected it from feeling the full force of popular discontent; it is equally the case that it could be seen to be the party of liberation – in the most visceral, resonantly symbolic, yet absolutely real sense – from 'the Boer'. In sum, those on the left who would now encourage the waging of a 'next liberation struggle' (one both necessary and appropriate) along class, gender, environmental and, yes, racial lines in South Africa, will have their work cut out for them in seeking to encourage amongst their presumptive constituency a much clearer sense of what exploitation and oppression had actually meant in South Africa historically, what they continues to mean, and just what it is that freedom could now be used to accomplish.

Not surprisingly, then, renewed and really dramatic resistance – this time, increasingly, to the ANC in power – has taken a few years to jell. But it is also not surprising that a distinct constituency has emerged to drive a radical grass-roots politics that echoes the revolutionary sensibility of the past – but one that, in articulating the grievances of the present, threatens to surge past the illusions of ANC 'victory'. After all, as many have increasingly sensed, liberation must be about more than racial and national assertion. It must, they reason, also be about transcending class, about ensuring gender equality, about evading environmental disaster, and about ensuring the expression of genuinely and effectively democratic voice. It must, in short, be about policies in the spheres of employment strategies, redistribution, education, health, water and electricity supply, and of a more internally-focused and need-driven industrial strategy that would exemplify some real attempt to overcome the great inequalities that existed.

But just how likely is it that a genuinely viable alternative could coalesce sufficiently to focus any attempt to give effective political weight to such possibilities? Not that the ANC has continued to have much to offer. The government's firmly 'free-market' strategy soon helped produce a society in which even as the economic gap between people defined in terms of racial categories (black as distinct from white) has narrowed statistically (as some blacks have become very rich indeed), the gap between rich and poor has widened dramatically. Here was a growing inequality gap that no mere welfarist pay-out such as that attempted by the ANC government in expanding the modest apartheid-era whites/Indian/'Coloured'-only grants to African households could really hope to paper over. After all (and because one of the first moves of Mandela's government, in 1996, was to lower the value of the payouts), these have amounted to no more than 4 per cent of GDP, thus barely scratching the surface of the poverty of some 25 million people. Meanwhile the infrastructure and delivery of various other social services continued to crumble. It seems that it is only in an alternative politics that a fulfilling future for the vast majority of South Africans is most likely to be found – far more likely than it is to be found through the several hundred years of continued ANC hegemony predicted by current South African President Jacob Zuma!

We do know, for example, that the ANC's vaunted and continuing 60–70 per cent share of the overall national electoral support has, given the rapidly falling number of those who these days actually choose to exercise their franchise, shrunk to rather less than 40 per cent of the eligible voters (and in local elections, much less than that). Even more striking, however, is the on-going 'movement of local protests amounting to a rebellion of the poor' as underscored by Peter Alexander, a proto-rebellion that is 'widespread and intense, and reaching insurrectionary proportions in some cases'. True, 'the inter-connections between the local protests (and between the local protests and militant action involving other elements of civil society) are limited'. But this, Alexander suggests, 'is likely to change,' not least because of the strong 'sense of injustice arising from the realities of persistent inequality'.[11]

In South Africa such grim facts are readily apparent, of course. Indeed, they are by now sufficiently self-evident that even some well to the right on the international stage have come to share something of the same recognition of the ANC's transparent failure. Thus, *The Economist* entitled a banner cover story (October 26, 2012) 'Cry, the beloved country: South Africa's sad decline'.

[11] Alexander, 'Rebellion of the poor'.

Underscoring the fact that 'South Africa's [growth] rate for the past few years has slowed to barely 2%', that magazine then set out a daunting list of further sharp-edged observations:

> Rating agencies have just downgraded South Africa's sovereign debt. Mining, once the economy's engine, has been battered by wildcat strikes, causing the biggest companies to shed thousands of jobs in the face of wage demands and spreading violence. In August a confrontation at a platinum mine in Marikana, near Johannesburg, the commercial capital, led to 34 deaths at the hands of the police. Foreign investment is drying up. Protests against the state's failure to provide services are becoming angrier. Education a disgrace: according to the World Economic Forum, South Africa ranks 132nd out of 144 countries for its primary education and 143rd in science and maths. The unemployment rate, officially 25%, is probably nearer 40%; half of South Africans under 24 looking for work have none. Of those who have jobs a third earn less than $2 a day. Inequality has grown since apartheid and the gap between rich and poor is now amongst the world's largest.

The Economist admits that the reasons for this decline arise in part from the fact that South Africa's 'mature economy' is 'linked more tightly to the rich world, and thus to the rich world's problems' than it is the rest of Africa. But, in the end, the magazine baldly asserts that the ANC's 'incompetence and outright corruption are the main causes of South Africa's sad decline'.[12]

Indeed, the magazine further notes of President Jacob Zuma that, under his aegis, the ANC has 'sought to undermine the independence of the courts, the police, the prosecuting authorities and the press. It has conflated the interests of party and state, dishing out contracts for public works as rewards for loyalty – hence the bitter jest that the government is in hock to "tenderpreneurs".' In sum, 'stuck between the impatient masses stirred up by Julius Malema on the one hand, and anxious capitalist and greedy party bigwigs on the other [Zuma] has drifted and dithered offering neither vision nor firm government'. Of course, for *The Economist*, the 'impatient masses' – never capable of either understanding or acting in their own interests – need 'stirring up' to be naughty. It could also never be, in its pages, a case of 'greedy capitalists and anxious party bigwigs', always the reverse. In sum, it is quite simply the ANC and not capitalism that is at fault in South Africa!

For others, as already suggested, the chief question raised by South Africa's present situation concerns just how long will it be before the anger to which such facts can give rise to becomes ever more potent politically. True, there will be many South Africans who see the prospect of a rebirth of principle – rebirth of the goal of justice and equality – as still being most likely to arise from within the ANC fold itself. Moreover, those who long supported through the global anti-apartheid movement the ANC's championing of the cause of 'freedom' can

---

[12] *The Economist*, 20–26 October 2012, notably its editorial (p. 11) entitled 'Cry, the beloved country'; as it notes of the situation of the ANC, 'for nine years it endured Thabo Mbeki's race-tinted prickliness, so different from Mr Mandela's big-hearted inclusiveness', further commenting that, before his ultimate deposition, 'Mbeki's denial of the link between HIV and AIDS cost millions of lives'.

bring themselves to abandon such hopes for the ANC only with great reluctance. We will discuss the case for a sustained faith in the potential good offices of the ANC and of the ANC-SACP-COSATU Alliance in the next section.

However, it is difficult not to feel that what is actually needed is something quite different. We can begin by recognizing, with Neville Alexander, that unfortunately South Africa has 'not ... experienced a social revolution. If anything, the post-apartheid state is more capitalist than its apartheid parent. To deny the continuity between the apartheid capitalist state and the post-apartheid capitalist state, as some people actually do, is a futile and quixotic exercise.'[13] It is small wonder that Alexander can then suggest that South Africans will have to be more creative and more imaginative than they have yet been in consolidating, in the present, the kind of new movement necessary to realize a more just and equitable South Africa. For it is only then that South Africa might become a country in which, another hundred years from now, South Africans could take further pride. In short, the liberation struggle continues.

Marikana: Sharpeville and Soweto revisited

What then of South Africa beyond 2012? It is no doubt far too difficult even to try to predict such outcomes. Certainly, it is quite possible to imagine that things in SA could quite simply get worse. A further crystallization of the barriers of class and privilege that already scar the country seems certain, if not addressed, to become much more marked with time. As noted in Chapter 1, capitalism's purchase in South Africa has been accompanied by a pervasive cultural impact manifest at all levels of the system: the culture of 'possessive individualism' and competitive consumerism that everywhere, globally, registers the ascendancy of capitalism. True this particular strand of history is not the only factor at play: pre-existing African societies were not without hierarchies of their own. Differential access to education, economic opportunity and the like have comple-

---

[13] Neville Alexander, 'South Africa: An Unfinished Revolution?' fourth Strini Moodley Annual Memorial Lecture, held at the University of KwaZulu-Natal on 13 May 2010, posted at *Links International Journal of Socialist Renewal*; equally useful is another of Alexander's talks, 'South Africa Today: The Moral Responsibility of Intellectuals', a lecture delivered at the 10th Anniversary celebration of the Foundation for Human Rights in Pretoria, 29 November 2006, available at www.fhr.org.za/article.php?a_id=27, accessed 5 October 2013. There he suggests that '[e]ver more frequently, those of us who fought consciously and often at great personal cost for the liberation of South Africa from the shackles of apartheid and capitalism are left asking ourselves whether this is the kind of society we had in mind when, like Faust in Scene 2 of Goethe's enduring drama, we dreamt of a country where we would be able to exclaim triumphantly: *Hier bin ich Mensch, hier darf ich's sein!* ... I am [here] tempted to pose the question slightly differently: Why is it that in spite of a constitution that was arrived at in a 20th century model of democratic bargaining and consensus building and in which are enshrined some of the noblest sentiments and insights concerning human rights, we are living in a situation where very few of those rights appear to be realised, or even [to be] realisable, in practice?'

mented and diversified such inequalities and all have added new differentiations and self-interested aspirations to the South African mix.

One need not be surprised, therefore, that the ANC came to oversee a drift (especially among its leadership) ever rightwards, once it had gained power. Such a leadership was unlikely, it now seems clear, to undertake the hard, dangerous work of seeking to focus popular energies for the kind of firmly and popularly democratic struggle against strong and recalcitrant class forces both local and global that would be necessary to establish a fighting chance at genuine development and any very real liberation. For it is also in the yawning class gap between the well-to-do of all races on the one hand and the urban poor and working classes on the other that diverse social malignancies are already showing clear signs of taking root. It is for this reason that Bernstein (as quoted above) charged the ANC with merely casting the South African masses adrift from their moorings within an overall movement for genuine transformation during the transition. Instead, they were to be converted from being active agents in their own on-going liberation to taking the role of mere passive 'voters' in the new, primarily formal and quite narrowly cast, democratic system.

For the fact is that the absence of any clearly imagined collective social purpose inevitably creates a vacuum, one without the promise of real developmental possibility, enlightened social endeavour or genuine democratic empowerment and practice. This is in sharp contrast to the kind of joint purpose attained so notably during the anti-apartheid struggle itself. Now, in such a context, politics tends to curdle into the most unsavoury kinds of particularism. Here the reference is not merely to the brand of selfish individualism that crime has come to represent so markedly in present-day South Africa. People who feel disempowered and deprived of any other more elevated and society-wide socio-economic and political forms of expression are also tempted to turn to various 'militant particularisms' that they may hope will give their lives expanded resonance, meaning and promise. Unbridled xenophobia has been one form that this 'search for meaning' has taken in recent years. But religious sectarianism, rampant and extremely vicious sexism, and non-negotiable ethnic assertions are other malignant expressions of the same broad impulse. For there is now a grim race for the future of South Africa being run, with all of the various malignancies above-mentioned now competing against the possible realization of the kind of benevolent dialectic between committed leaders and active and assertive citizens that was once aspired to by many – and that Rusty Bernstein for one had once hoped to see.

Absence of both a sense of sustained national and of shared purpose, then. But what of the solidarity that collective class assertions from below could bring? It must be emphasized that despite the strength of both capitalist power and capitalist culture, the basis for more progressive possibilities has not, either with respect to the workers or to the poor, evaporated. Take, first, the workers and recall the apparent promise of more radical change offered by the trade unions and especially by COSATU in the late 80s and early-1990s? There was even some momentary prospect of COSATU's playing such an on-going transformative role through the processes of negotiations undertaken with both business and state representatives under the umbrella of the National Economic Development and Labour Council (NEDLAC). Yet this latter soon proved to be, for the unions, a very false prospect indeed.[14]

Thus, on the one hand, many of the unions' own senior cadres were soon defecting to jobs in party, state and the sphere of business. On the other hand, there was also an attrition of COSATU's actual rank and file as the new ANC government's macro-economic policies after 1994 saw both a decline in the number of stable jobs in industry and the emergence of an economy that would become ever more reliant on a part-time casual and insecure labour force. Indeed, it has been estimated that during the post-apartheid period 'full time waged employment was a reality for only less than one third of the economically active African population'.[15] In consequence, there was a growing number of workers found in only very precarious jobs (seasonal, temporary, casual or fixed-term contract work) – up to as much as 30 per cent of the active labour force even in official figures, with Marlea Clarke arguing that 'qualitative and quantitative research in specific sectors suggests that casual work and other forms of precarious employment with uncertain hours, scheduling and pay [continues to grow] more rapidly than what is documented by national statistics'.[16] This latter group of workers would largely remain without trade-union representation, with COSATU itself having as yet shown little vocation for organizing the unorganized. In fact, it was tempting to see COSATU as becoming, in the post-apartheid period, increasingly representative of a 'labour aristocracy' of the organized and better-paid workers.

True, as Eddie Webster has correctly warned me[17] (while conceding that there is 'more evidence for the concept's appropriateness now'), the 'labour aristocracy' label is 'misleading because neoliberal globalisation is actually eroding the core of the labour market, making this "elite" [itself] very precarious'.'[S]econdly, even these core jobs are often below R2000 per month; and,

---

14 For a detailed discussion of the NEDLAC process, and more generally of the challenges facing Cosatu during this period, see Carolyn Bassett, 'Negotiating South Africa's Economic Future: COSATU and Strategic Unionism', a doctoral dissertation submitted to York University, 2000.

15 Franco Barchiesi, '"Schooling Bodies to Hard Work": The South African State's Policy Discourse and its Moral Constructions of Welfare', a paper presented at the North Eastern Workshop on Southern Africa (NEWSA), Vermont, 2007.

16 Marlea Clarke, personal communication. See also, on this subject Marlea Clarke, '"All the Workers?": Labour Market Reform and "Precarious Work" in Post-apartheid South Africa, 1994–2004', a doctoral dissertation submitted to York University, 2006; Bridget Kenny, 'Labour Market Flexibility in the Retail Sector: Possibilities for Resistance' in Franco Barchiesi and Tom Bramble (eds), *Rethinking the Labour Movement in the 'New South Africa'* (Aldershot: Ashgate, 2003); and, more generally, Marlea Clarke and Carolyn Bassett (eds), 'South African Trade Unions and Globalization: Going for the "High Road", Getting Stuck on the "Low Road"', in *Work Organization, Labour and Globalisation*, 2, 1 (2008).

17 Eddie Webster, personal communication, from which I quote in this paragraph with his permission.

thirdly, almost all workers share their income with a household with an average of five members.' True enough, and yet at the same time, it can be affirmed that differences of interest and of practice do indeed exist between the 'settled' proletariat and the more precariously employed (and also between those in both these categories and the urban 'precariat' even more broadly defined[18]). Such differences can also make for quite divergent 'class practices'.[19] Admittedly, COSATU has from time to time sought to assume some role as an active and critical voice for both working class and popular interests both within the Tripartite Alliance and more generally. Moreover, its present leader, Zwelizinama Vavi, has also acted within the Alliance as a sometimes spokesman of protest against what has happened on the ANC/SACP watch to any transformative hopes in South Africa.[20] Nonetheless, the appalling behaviour of National Union of Mineworkers (NUM) in the run-up to the state's shooting of strikers at Marikana in mid-2012 and Vavi's own disappointing dealings with the Angloplats' strikers and others have tended to cast a less favourable light on COSATU as a possible agent of progressive change.

For it seems clear that any potential COSATU might once have been thought to have to further develop itself and its own goals and to hone its possible vocation as a force for on-going radical transformation (through the mounting of some much more assertive counter-hegemonic alternative to capitalism) has waned. Here both the continued dilution of its grounding within the very broadest constituency of South Africa's working peoples as well as the wasting effects of the subordinate role COSATU has chosen to take within the Alliance led by the still hegemonic ANC have had a cumulatively dispiriting impact. In short, much work remains to be done in order to reclaim the organized workers as a force for revolution in contemporary South Africa. At the same time, any promise that the ANC (or, indeed, the Tripartite Alliance between the ANC, SACP and COSATU) might itself once have seemed to offer as an organization with a prospect of further focusing working-class energies towards the realization of a more radical transformation has largely disappeared.

We will have more to say concerning the further implications for this of Marikana and its fall-out presently. Consider here, however, a recent South African headline which reads 'Zuma calls in army, where needed' – and then

---

18 On the concept of the 'precariat' see Chapter 2, above, and my 'What Working-Class? Non-Transformative Global Capitalism and the African Case' in Baris Karagaac and Yasin Kaya (eds), *Capital and Labour in Contemporary Capitalism* (forthcoming).

19 Eddie Webster, personal communication; indeed, as Webster correctly adds, 'to have a job at all in these times may be seen as a privilege rather than a curse' – a source of real differentiations in attitude and in action. Indeed, Clarke (*ibid.*) correctly observes, 'divergences' of interests and actions, as framed concretely with reference to such matters as differential remuneration and job security and differing degrees of effective self-organization, have had real weight.

20 See my 'Conclusion: Portents of Revival – On Liberating Liberation in South/ Southern Africa' which is the concluding chapter to John S. Saul, *A Flawed Freedom: 'Globalization Made Me Do It' versus 'The Struggle Continues'* (Delhi, London and Toronto: Three Essays Collective, Pluto Press and Between The Lines, 2014).

reports in the accompanying article that 'the SA National Defence Force has officially been deployed domestically from 14 September until next year in Marikana and other areas of the country where needed, the presidency said in a statement on Thursday'![21] Can any remnant of the ANC's waning promise hope to survive this and similar indices of failure. But of course the clearest index of the underlying social-structural and political realities in South Africa had already been revealed by the brutal massacre at Marikana itself, followed by the harsh responses in support of it expressed by the ANC, the SACP and COSATU. For the new black elite closed ranks quickly, Blade Nzimande (General Secretary of the SACP) for one striking a particularly fawning and defensive note in a 27 October 2012 speech to a rally in Rustenburg; indeed he there caricatured worker resistance to both Lonmin and to the NUM, loftily proclaiming that 'an attack on the NUM is an attack on COSATU and an attack on COSATU is an attack on the SACP'![22]

Moreover, there was the equally instructive case of Cyril Ramaphosa, once himself, as head of the NUM, the leader of 1987's historic miners' pay strike during the apartheid years and also a key architect, representing the ANC, of the transition negotiations. Now, however, as millionaire businessman and a prominent shareholder and member of the board of directors of Lonmin (the platinum mining company at the centre of the Marikana moment) Ramaphosa (as also quoted in the previous chapter) was to be found, on the day before the shooting, emailing Lonmin's chief commercial officer, Albert Jamison and calling for 'concomitant action' to tackle the strike: 'The terrible events that have unfolded cannot be described as a labour dispute. They are plainly dastardly criminal [acts] and must be characterized as such.' Indeed, he said, the situation needs to be 'stabilized by the police/army' – and other emails from Ramaphosa urged the same position on Mineral Resources Minister Susan Shabangu.[23] Recall, then, this section's title: 'Marikana: Sharpeville and Soweto

---

[21] See on this escalation of state response (September 20,2012): www.news24. com/SouthAfrica/News/Zuma-calls-in-army-where-needed-20120920, accessed 5 October 2013.

[22] See, for Nzimande's speech, *Umsebenzi Online*, 11, 40, 1 (November 2012). Note that this speech is part of a general approach adopted by Nzimande that Mark Heywood epitomized by evoking his (Nzimande's) scandalous 'warning that the Alliance should beware of people campaigning for social justice in education or health, his misleading allegation that non-governmental organizations cherry-pick issues that they can use to damage "the revolution" and the "liberals under the bed" claim that many NGOs "are captured by particular class interests, not least those of their often (imperialist) donors". These serious allegations – baseless but presented as truths – were designed to keep the ordinary Cosatu member suspicious of all but the party.' (Mark Heywood, 'Whose ANC is it anyway?' *Daily Maverick*, 25 September 2012.)

[23] The emails which form part of the official record of the Marikana commission of inquiry in South Africa were obtained by Reuters; see the article by Pascal Fletcher and Jon Herscovitz, '"Hero" Tied to Mine Killings: One-time South African Apartheid Foe Urged Tough Action on Strikers', *Toronto Star*, October 25, 2012, p. A 23.

revisited.' Marikana: by exemplifying the ready use of state violence against popular protest it is, one might suggest, the 'Sharpeville' of the current regime. But it is also quite possibly the 'Soweto' of a new and rising resistance movement, one that may yet reclaim South Africa's liberation on behalf of the working class – and of the people more generally.

For what of that vast mass of the population – both urban and rural and outside the 'proletariat' per se – whom in Chapter 2 we considered best termed as a 'precariat'? These are those of no very fixed employment, no union voice and no real, direct representation in the politics that shapes their lives. Here it bears noting some quite recent evidence as to the cauldron of discontent that is South Africa, evidence registered by Peter Alexander and other recent observers. Moving beyond his 2009 article cited above, Alexander and the impressive team of researchers he heads has continued to record the extent to which a popular surge from below has continued to grow.[24] Thus in 2010/11, there was a record number of crowd management incidents (unrest and peaceful) with the final data for 2011/12 deemed quite likely to show an even higher figure. Indeed, when he wrote, the number of gatherings involving unrest was already higher in 2011/12 than any previous year, with an increase of 40 per cent over the average of incidents per day recorded for 2004–09. True, such statistics are notoriously tricky to compile and difficult to evaluate; nonetheless, they do indicate that any 'rebellion of the poor' has intensified over the past three years.

Indeed, as Peter Alexander summarizes the present situation in this regard:

> The main conclusion we draw from the latest police statistics is that the number of service delivery protests continues unabated. Government attempts to improve service delivery have not been sufficient to assuage the frustration and anger of poor people in South Africa. From press reports and our own research it is clear that while service delivery demands provide the principal focus for unrest incidents, many other issues are being raised, notably lack of jobs. As many commentators and activists now accept, service delivery protests are part of a broader Rebellion of the Poor. This rebellion is massive. I have not yet found any other country where there is a similar level of ongoing urban unrest. South Africa can reasonably be described as the 'protest capital of the world.' It also has the highest levels of inequality and unemployment of any major country, and it is not unreasonable to assume that the rebellion is, to a large degree, a consequence of these phenomena. There is no basis for assuming that the rebellion will subside unless the government is far more effective in channelling resources towards the poor.[25]

Is there, in fact, any likelihood that the ANC could itself recapture this high ground of genuine liberation struggle? Not likely, is the short answer. True, some, like Julius Malema, do seek, however opportunistically, to seduce the mass with more populist, even rather racist, visions of continuing transformative

[24] See Alexander, 'SA Protest Rates Increasingly Competitive with World Leader China', from which the quotations in this section are drawn.

[25] Alexander, 'SA Protest Rates Increasingly Competitive with World Leader China', but see also Peter Alexander et al., *Marikana: A View From the Mountain and a Case to Answer* (Johannesburg: Jacana, 2012).

purpose.[26] But most in the ANC, from Mandela to Mbeki to Manuel to Zuma and to many others throughout the movement, have drifted under the thrall of the prevailing common sense of capitalist compromise and the mere acceptance of marked and growing social disparities.

Of course, it is also true that Peter Alexander's 'rebellion of the poor' has been happening within the frame of the ANC's continuing apparent national electoral dominance. As a result, the main expressions of popular unease with the present dispensation seem to find voice most assertively at the local level – with the ANC still granted primacy as the presumptive god-father of liberation at the national level.[27] Yet there are clear signs that the ANC's hegemony has itself begun to fray. Certainly few among the citizenry actually appear any longer to harbour any very firm belief that the ANC offers developmental answers that will positively affect the quality of their own lives. Indeed, Neville Alexander (one of those to whom we have dedicated this book) has put the case that:

> All the heady hopes which even those who were not in or of the Congress Alliance had in 1994–95 seem to have turned into ash. There are few thinking South Africans today who would be prepared to say that they are happy with how things have turned out.[28]

Meanwhile, Zuma's ANC-in-power presents only a picture of intense and divisive personalized conflict while offering, as we have argued, virtually no reason to hope that any progressive outcome will spring forward from within the party.[29]

Some within the ANC do continue to stand up to be heard, however. Veteran ANC/SACP hand and present-day MP Ben Turok is an example, a person driven to 'the irresistible conclusion ... that the ANC government has lost a great deal of its earlier focus on the fundamental transformation of the inherited social system', and to the assertion that 'much depends on whether enough momentum can be built to overcome the caution that has marked the ANC government since 1994.

[26] The most recent details on Malema's rise and fall (and rise and fall again) are to be found in Bond's preceding chapter, but see also Malema's own sober reflections when recently interviewed in the *City Press* article of 13 January 2013, 'Malema interview – I have learnt from Zuma', available at www.citypress.co.za/politics/malema-interview-i-have-learnt-from-zuma, accessed 5 October 2013. There he also makes the startling statement: 'People should have analysed it ... that capital runs the ANC and South Africa.' But, of course, some people have so 'analysed it' and continue to do so, including the authors of the present book.
[27] Indeed, it is tempting to see in the diverse contestation in the present the slow dawning of a 'next liberation struggle', a continuation of the very popular struggle that, in Chapter 2, we saw the ANC leadership – in the name of neo-liberalism and what we have felt obliged to call 'recolonization' – to have worked so hard to discipline and tame during the transition years (from the mid-1980s to the mid-1990s).
[28] Alexander, 'South Africa: An Unfinished Revolution?'.
[29] William Gumede, *Restless Nation: Making Sense of Troubled Times* (Capetown: Tafelberg, 2012) presents precisely such a picture of the ANC. See too, for a litany of corruption and malfeasance in high places, the feature 'The ANC's naughty executive committee' in *City Press* (13 January 2013) and compare with 'Zuma blessed with 'crème de la crème' NEC: Ramaphosa', SABC (9 January 2013).

This in turn depends on whether the determination to achieve an equitable society can be revived.'[30] Of course it would be quite another thing for long-time ANC loyalists like Turok to agree with me that the ANC, despite its brave history of a hundred years, has slowly but surely become 'yesterday's movement', one very far from articulating any such 'determination' as Turok here evokes.[31] For me, in fact, it has begun to seem ever more imperative to divine some new counter-hegemonic movement, to delineate its possibilities and its prospects, and to make it ever more potent in practice. In Zimbabwe, the Movement for Democratic Change (MDC) seemed, however briefly, to offer just such an alternative there. Only cruel repression by Mugabe and his Zimbabwe African National Union (ZANU) minions worked to deny the MDC its several rightful electoral victories and the chance to realize the promise it initially bore. How intransigent will the ANC be when it becomes apparent that, despite its long service in the cause of national liberation, its rationale for the retention of power has also run its course?[32] Here, of course, Marikana is a particularly dismaying augury of the likely response of those now in power to fresh assertions from below.[33]

It is true, even in advance of Marikana, Canadian journalist Geoffrey York could write of the ANC that, 'fuelled by a dangerous mixture of high unemployment, slow growth, weak leadership and fierce feuding within the governing party', there are 'influential factions' in the ANC itself that are, from a more progressive direction, beginning to push the party.[34] Beyond Turok, the

---

[30] Ben Turok, *From the Freedom Charter to Polokwane: The Evolution of ANC Economic Policy* (Cape Town: New Agenda, 2008), pp. 263–65.

[31] See also the extremely testy and defensive remarks by Turok to my co-author Patrick Bond's own critical take on the ANC's record (in the latter's 'South Africa's Frustrating Decade of Freedom: From Racial to Class Apartheid' in *Monthly Review*, 55, 10, 2004) in Turok's own letter to the *Mail & Guardian* of 25 June 2004; Bond's response to Turok was published subsequently in the same publication on 2 July 2004.

[32] Jeremy Cronin once spoke briefly of the possible 'Zanufication' of the ANC, though his observation caused such a stir in the corridors of power that he very quickly back-tracked on it. This incident is recounted in John S. Saul, *The Next Liberation Struggle* (Toronto, New York, Scottsville, SA, and London: Between The Lines, Monthly Review Press, University of KwaZulu-Natal and Merlin Press, 2005), in Chapter 10, 'Starting from Scratch: A Debate'.

[33] One immediate response to the Marikana events was a police and state cover-up and an elaborate exercise of 'blaming the victim' – the workers themselves! Fortunately, an officially-appointed judicial Marikana Commission of Inquiry soon began to shed much clearer light on what had actually occurred, not least through the able questioning of legendary South African advocate George Bizos who represented the Legal Resource Centre at the hearings. Among other things, Bizos demonstrated that police photographs themselves showed clearly that 'their claims of self-defence don't hold water'. See 'Bizos questions police claim of self-defence at Marikana,' SABC, 19 December 2012.

[34] Geoffrey York, 'ANC's radical voices growing louder: Proposed agenda includes black economic ownership, farm expropriation, nationalization and tighter controls on the courts', *The Globe and Mail* (Toronto), 8 June 2012. See also York's 'South Africa Reels as Death Toll Rises: Number of miners killed by police revised to 34 as President announces probe and analysts compare event to apartheid massacres', *The Globe and Mail*, 18 August 2012.

horrors of Marikana do also seem to have further focused the attention – and dismay – of other ANC veterans. Thus Pallo Jordan and Ronnie Kasrils, both former cabinet ministers, have, to their credit, each been so shaken by the Marikana moment to have spoken out forcefully: Jordan we have quoted above but Kasrils also affirms that the Marikana slayings merely 'grow more sinister' with each passing revelation.

> Our initial horror and outrage does not subside but deepens. Evidence is emerging of a web of possible vengeance and extra-judicial executions. This points to a scenario as sinister and chilling as anything from our horrific colonial apartheid history.

Thus, while focusing on a pursuit of the 'immediate truth' as to what happened, who did what, and why, Kasrils acknowledges that 'we can and must deal with [the] bigger picture because ultimate responsibility lies with our whole exploitative system'. He even goes so far as to confess that 'there is surely a case for [arguing that] the 1994 compromises [are] coming back to bite us and must also be examined'. For it seems clear to Kasrils that

> A national crisis like this requires frank talk by all concerned South Africans. We need to mobilize and demonstrate solidarity with the victims. Our history reverberates with the words: 'Do not blame the victims.'

As for the mining sector itself, Kasrils suggests[35] that what is needed is a 'new deal for our mineworkers and we also need a system based on economic justice for the poor of our land. We need a leadership not distracted by holding on to their positions at all costs, but one focussed night and day on urgently solving our people's problems and serving their needs. We can achieve that, but only through concerted efforts and mass pressure on the powers that be.' In sum, he repeats, as was also intimated by Legassick and Jordan above, that 'Marikana is undoubtedly a turning point in our history'.[36]

Or take Jay Naidoo, the founding General Secretary of COSATU and a former minister in Mandela's first national government; his 'Open Letter to COSATU' warrants quoting at length. As he writes, 'Now is the time for fearless debate.

[35] 'Three mines at a standstill' 12 September 2012, available at www.fin24.com/Companies/Mining/Three-mines-at-a-standstill-20120912-2, accessed 5 October 2013.

[36] Ronnie Kasrils, 'The slayings grow more sinister', *Amandla!* Issue 26/27, September, 2012; indeed this entire issue of *Amandla!* features a number of pertinent articles on Marikana. We might also note here the doubts about the events at Marikana expressed by former President Thabo Mbeki when, in giving a lecture at Fort Hare university in Eastern Cape province in October 2012, he stated '[my] feeling of unease is informed by questions I have not been able to answer about what happened which allowed the eminently avoidable massacre at the Lonmin Marikana mine in the north-west province to happen'. As Mbeki concludes: 'My feeling of unease is also informed by what I sense is a pervasive understanding throughout the nation that there is no certainty about our future with regard to any of our known challenges, and therefore the future of the nation.' (In David Smith, 'Mbeki fears South Africa is "losing sense of direction"', *The Guardian*, 22 October 2012).

Power has to be confronted with the truth. The Marikana massacre shows all the hallmarks of our apartheid past. Violence from any side is inexcusable, but deadly force from a democratic state is a cardinal sin. It strikes at the heart of democracy.' He continues:

> I was part of the leadership that led COSATU into an alliance with the ANC and the SACP. It had a clear objective. We were making a commitment to a profound transformation that struck at the heart of Apartheid – the cheap labour system and its attendant diseases of joblessness, poverty, gender violence and inequality.
>
> But these same diseases remain, and we desperately need a frank, no-holds-barred clinical analysis of our condition. It goes something like this: Inequality has grown. Formal employment has shrunk. A single breadwinner supports up to eight dependants. The content of migrant labour remains as deeply entrenched as ever, as subcontracted labour and casualisation continue to marginalize the workers' families.
>
> The education system hopelessly fails the poorest in our townships as half of our children, mainly of the working poor, are left with almost no skills to speak of even after 12 years of school. They can't get jobs and many of them are unlikely to do so at all in their lifetime. Our schools have become havens to sexual predators: perverted teachers or male pupils robbing our girl children of their innocence. The growing majority of this dispossessed youth cannot see anyone representing their interests.
>
> That's what I've gathered from conversations I've had with young people throughout South Africa: All they see is the arrogance of a 'blue light brigade' that believes it has some divine right to rule. They see a criminal 'Breitling brigade' that grows fat on looting the public coffers, stealing tenders and licences, and pocketing public funds designated for textbooks, toilets and libraries.
>
> This is not the programme of transformation for which our leaders – beacons such as Elijah Barayi and Emma Mashinini – sacrificed so much. This is not the future for which Neil Aggett was murdered by Apartheid police. This is not the future for which Phineas Sibiya, an outstanding ship steward, died a fiery death in a burning car at the hands of Inkatha vigilantes in Howick.[37]

Small wonder that *The Economist* capped its sobering account (cited above) of South Africa's present condition with the thought that the 'best hope' for the country would be 'a real split in the ANC between the populist left and the fat cat right to offer a genuine choice for voters'.[38] Not that (and for all the eloquence of their presently expressed concerns) any such split to the left is something that Jordan, Naidoo or even Kasrils seem set to argue for. Instead, and perhaps in some cases still mired in the vanguardist[39] temptations of their earlier days, they merely canvass transformation that remains too tantalizingly unspecified.

[37] Jay Naidoo, 'An Open Letter to Cosatu', *The Daily Maverick* (South Africa), 4 September 2012. 'Blue lights' are those atop many politicians' cars and represent a police-style command to get out of their way; 'Breitling' is the ultra-expensive watch worn by Julius Malema and many other prominent political 'leaders'. At the same time we should recall that merely two years previously Naidoo in his own autobiography, *Fighting for Justice: A Lifetime of Political and Social Activism* (Johannesburg: Picador Africa, 2010) had fully endorsed GEAR! Naidoo: part of the problem, or part of the solution?

[38] Strikingly, this formulation parallels an assertion made in the mid-1990s by no less a figure than Thabo Mbeki himself as to the apparent inevitability of just such a split.

[39] To 'vanguardist' some might add here the word 'Stalinist'.

All the more reason to think that any hope that a dramatic turn to the left will spring from within the ANC camp itself does seem a faint one.

Or consider the argument of Thabo Mbeki's brother, Moeletsi, also referred to earlier. The best prospect that such an experienced observer seems able to offer South Africans is a 'Tunisia Day' set to arrive, he writes, in 2020. Then 'the South African masses' will 'rise against the powers that be, as happened recently in Tunisia'. For, in Moeletsi's words, 'the ANC inherited a flawed, complex society it barely understood [and] its tinkerings with it are turning it into an explosive cocktail. The ANC leaders are like a group of children playing with a hand grenade. One day one of them will figure out how to pull out the pin and everyone will be killed.'[40] Startling stuff, but it is far from clear just where Moeletsi wants to take us with it. It is fortunate therefore that there are others who are much more sceptical of the ANC, and who even give signs of going much further in conceiving some fresh and novel ways to reactivate the liberation struggle in South Africa.

One example: COSATU chief Zwelizinama Vavi. It is true that he does seem deeply mired within the Tripartite Alliance but it is equally true that he can vacillate from that posture in extremely interesting ways. Thus, one sign of promise lay in his at least momentarily (2011) breathing possibility into a new coalition between proletariat and precariat. Then, and much to the dismay of the ANC (his having consulted with neither the ANC nor the SACP before taking such an initiative), he held his much celebrated meeting with a wide spectrum of the organizations of civil society.[41] At this workshop he stated:

> Inspired by the African proverb that says 'If you want to go quickly, go alone. If you want to go far, go together,' we gather here – as the progressive trade unions, social movements, NGOs, progressive academics, small business and street vendor associations, taxi associations, religious bodies, youth organisations, environmental groups, indigenous peoples' groups and other progressive formations – to say to ourselves that we have the capacity to make a decisive contribution in changing our current situation for the better.
>
> Internationally, globalisation and neoliberalism have launched assaults on the working class, which include, but are not limited to: informalisation, flexibilisation, regionalisation of states, deregulation, marketisation, financialisation, and securitisation. The global governance, commercial and trade system is supported by political and ideological institutions, rules and enforcement mechanisms that only broad civil society coalitions have historically been able to challenge successfully.
>
> In South Africa, the GEAR strategy epitomised the dominance of the neoliberal ideology within the leading sections of the government. The neoliberal logic still continues to be dominant, in spite of some talk about a developmental state. Increasingly though it has taken a more crude political expression and there are some

[40] Moeletsi Mbeki's recent thinking on South Africa's possible future, together with that of Zwelizinama Vavi and of people close of the Democratic Left Forum, is dealt with in my text as referenced in footnote 6.

[41] Here too at least one reader of this text has objected in a private communication to the phrase 'wide spectrum' and suggested that 'independent left and radical social movements outside the ANC fold were entirely ignored'; I am not sure that this is true, however.

emerging elements that tend to perceive the working class and active elements of civil society as merely being a nuisance that must be crushed with the might of the state apparatus.

Today, as we gather here, there is panic in the ranks of the predatory elite, which is a new coalition of the tenderpreneurs. Paranoia elsewhere is deepening with the political elite, convincing itself that any gathering of independent civil society formations to confront our challenges is a threat to them.[42]

Yet there was no indication that such novel and dramatic outreach towards the creation of a broad new constituency of change is to become a permanent feature of either COSATU's or Vavi's political practice. The workshop was a tantalizing initiative nonetheless. It is small wonder, then, that other aspirants to the construction of a new counter-hegemony hold out hopes that COSATU might ultimately step outside the Tripartite Alliance – and into the future.

It is true that both Vavi and COSATU fell in with apparent ease (but see, on this, below and also the previous chapter) behind Zuma and the ANC in the white-washing of the Marikana outrage that has occurred. Nonetheless, Vavi has also continued to excoriate that same ANC for its 'factionalism, patronage and corruption' and for the fact that struggles within the organization are primarily only 'over control of the levers of accumulation.'[43] The many dramatic failures in such spheres as 'service delivery' have also been underscored by Vavi, with these and other failures seen to be 'laying the foundation for growing disillusionment in society'; indeed, Vavi states, questions are even 'being asked about the [very] legitimacy of leadership in the movement and the state'. As he then elaborates:

Opinion polls ... are increasingly showing worrying trends, particularly, but not only, among the youth, which suggest a growing political demobilisation and alienation of

---

[42] Zwelinzima Vavi, 'Keynote address to the Civil Society Conference', 27 October 2010, available at www.cosatu.org.za/show.php?ID=4170, accessed 5 October 2013. See also Bekezela Phakathi, 'Cosatu launches UDF to Rescue Country', *Business Day*, 28 October 2010, in which he writes: 'Warning that SA faced a "national catastrophe," Cosatu yesterday launched a major civil society effort to tackle corruption, poverty and unemployment ... In his address to the Civil Society Conference, [Vavi] evoked the landmark formation of the anti-apartheid United Democratic Front in 1983, but was at pains to stress that it was "not an anti-African National congress and anti-government coalition." "The challenges we face today are different but nonetheless very major and require a similar mobilisation of the democratic forces as we saw in those years," Mr Vavi told the delegates at the launch in Boksberg.'

[43] Indeed he went so far as to observe that 'those challenging [such] abuses find their lives increasingly in danger'! However, it is also true, as Bond has discussed in the previous chapter, that apparently serious mis-steps in Vavi's own personal/sexual politics have weakened him in the in-fighting within COSATU, this in-fighting between more and less progressive member unions already becoming ever more intense in any case. This is an arena within which it is difficult to foretell outcomes – although the on-going politics of organized workers within or without the Tripartite Alliance are of considerable importance. Bond does, however, give us some reason to take the progressive claims of the National Union of Metalworkers quite seriously.

society. This includes suggestions that growing numbers of the electorate don't intend to vote in 2014, and had increasingly negative perceptions of the leadership. Any programme of radical transformation, if it has any hope of succeeding, must rely on mobilisation of the people. Therefore this trend should not be taken lightly, or dismissed as a creation of the media.[44]

Of even more importance, perhaps, is the fact that significant segments of the broader COSATU membership are themselves becoming quite uneasy with the present state of things; thus a report – suppressed by the leadership but based on the findings of a ntional survey of 2,000 COSATU shop stewards – found that 'most of [them] did not support the re-election of President Jacob Zuma as president of the African National Congress (ANC)'.

The survey has found that COSATU shop stewards want nationalization, they have no confidence in the South African Communist Party and they want COSATU to form a labour party.[45]

At the same time, Dale McKinley has, in his recent writings, consistently documented the dispiriting presence in South Africa of what he terms a prevailing 'culture of impunity' – and an almost total 'avoidance of responsibility associated with varying positions and levels of power'.[46] Small wonder too that well-known blogger Helen Moffett, faced with the paltry signs of progress on the front of gender emancipation and equality in South Africa, can simply tell the current regime (in a prose of studied inelegance) that it should, 'in light of its paltry record, take [its] pathetic, meaningless, mind-blowingly expensive and stomach-churningly patronising Women's Day and shove it.'[47] But what does any of this mean in terms of the grounding of any new, coherent and integrated initiatives and programmatic plans? It is difficult to avoid the feeling that in South Africa at the moment there is now quite a lot of smoke but still not too much sign of a meaningful fire.[48]

One specific example of the attempt to begin construction of a new counter-hegemonic project has been the launching of the Democratic Left Front (DLF). The DLF articulates a politics that seeks to be much more firmly democratic, socialist in orientation, gender sensitive and environmentally alert than either the ANC or the SACP give any sign of being remotely interested in advancing. As analysed by one commentator, 'the establishment of the DLF by social movements, community organisations, political parties, labour unions and working-class organisations across the ideological spectrum of anti-capitalist left politics,

---

[44] Vavi and his report are quoted extensively in Matuma Letsoala, 'Cosatu Report Hammers "Self-Serving" ANC', *Mail & Guardian*, 9 August 2012.

[45] Natasha Marrian, 'Cosatu Cans Report Showing Unionists Split on Zuma', *Business Day*, 11 December 2012.

[46] Dale McKinley, 'Power Without Responsibility,' e-report for The South African Civil Society Information Service, dated 10 August 2012.

[47] Helen Moffett, 'Take your Women's Day and Shove it', Books Live, 8 August 2012.

[48] On some such earlier signs of promise see, however, 'Starting from Scratch: A Debate', being Chapter 10 of Saul, *The Next Liberation Struggle*.

is the most positive development in the efforts to creatively and proactively deal with the challenges presented by the neo-apartheid, neoliberal capitalist dispensation'.[49] As its impressive founding document argued:

> Post-apartheid South Africa is experiencing a social crisis due to neoliberal globalisation. The old apartheid pattern of development has continued with a few elites (and now Black elites) benefiting while the majority are enduring profound suffering. Deepening poverty, inequality, hunger, homelessness, unemployment and ecological destruction are affecting the working class and the poor the most. We believe this has to be confronted to ensure our post apartheid democracy works for all. Moreover, we refuse to accept that the workers and the poor of South Africa need to carry the cost for the current global crisis that has come to our shores.
>
> At the same time, the organisations of the working class and the poor have been weakened, divided and have generally found themselves in a state of desperation. An effective transformative politics advancing anti-capitalist alternatives for the country has not been able to come to the fore. This represents a strategic defeat for the South African anti-capitalist left as a whole.
>
> However, through the 1st Conference of the Democratic Left, held from 20-23 January 2011 at Witwatersrand University, Johannesburg, South Africa, we are making a call to the workers, the poor and the anti-capitalist left to draw the line and to fight back. Our conference was an important milestone in a long journey to regroup anti-capitalist forces and to reclaim lost ground.[50]

The document itself was a clear statement of counter-hegemonic intent, something underscored by two of the DLF's key organizers, Mazibuko Jara and Vishwas Satgar, in speaking out strongly in a *Mail & Guardian* article pegged to the DLF launch:

> One conference is merely a milestone in a long journey that has to do with trying to reimagine a left politics through ethical practice. Our ethical compass is about living and inventing democracy inside this process (definitely through heated debates, differences and new ways of thinking about consensus), plurality as strength, collective intellectual practice, self-education and building transformative power through struggles.
>
> This is a process without preconceived outcomes and thus is unique in South Africa. Such a process means abandoning the illusions of a vanguardist left committed to a violent overthrow of capitalism or a reformist left seeking to make capitalism more humane.
>
> More importantly, we are about strengthening and advancing grassroots struggles through opposition but, at the same time, advancing transformative alternatives from below. This is illustrated by the ideas, proposals and campaigns that were adopted as

---

49 Mphutlane wa Bofelo, writing in *Pambazuka News*, 27 January 2011. As Bofelo continued, 'The DLF is envisaged to be a mass political movement that seeks to explore and establish bottom-up, people-driven participatory democratic forms of organisation and people's power beyond elections, the government, the state and the party-political space ... Its focus is connecting and escalating the struggles of the poor and working-class communities and exploring and building together with communities – through action and the culture of 'each-one-teach-one' – sustainable, democratic, and egalitarian, eco-friendly economies and community driven development.'

50 Democratic Left Front, 1st Democratic Left Conference Report 20–23 January 2011, Johannesburg.

part of our common platform of action dealing with ecological resources, unemployment, food sovereignty, education and public services.[51]

The DLF thus seeks to expand its links into the urban townships and with the township-based organizations of the members of precariat and proletariat alike who dwell there. It also speaks pointedly in its founding document and other subsequent public statements of the potential of 'the alliance of workers and the poor' – the distinction made here is quite deliberate – that the DLF is seeking to craft. Yet, even as it strives to lay the basis of a movement that is firmly democratic, socialist in orientation, gender sensitive and environmentally alert its ties to the organized expressions of the working class are still fragile. Perhaps this is why it has been so aware not only of the fleeting promise of Vavi's meeting with the organizations of civil society discussed above but also of the possible implications of the Marikana/Lonmin proletarian moment as well. In consequence, the DLF has called for various forthright actions in solidarity with 'the Marikana workers and communities'. It has done so publicly in assertive symbolic gestures and in strong terms:

> In the aftermath of the barbaric Marikana massacre of 16th August in which 34 Lonmin mineworkers were shot in cold blood by the South African Police Services, South Africa has started burying the murdered workers. Workers are being taken back to their home areas to be buried. In some places a few burials have taken place.
>
> In this moment, the Democratic Left Front working with other social justice organisations call on all South Africans and international friends to say farewell to these workers with the observance of 3 minutes of silence on August 29th, at 1pm (in symbolic reference to the 3 minutes it took the callous South African Police Services to mow down the 34 workers on 16 August 2012).[52]

Nor is the DLF's the only effort both to think and to act radically and, from the left, in potentially counter-hegemonic terms. There is, for example, the effort by Julius Malema and his Economic Freedom Fighters to do just that too. True, there are good reasons to treat Malema's claims to left-leadership with some scepticism in light of his existing track record, but the fact remains that the visible popular distemper afoot in South African society must eventually find more effective popular focus and organizational clout if the activation of more malignant channels (xenophobia, sexual violence, ethnic outrage) for it are to be avoided. In sum, it will be extremely important to monitor the political progress of various organizations as possible claimants to the playing of such a role.

What is to be done, then? Writing exactly one year after Marikana, Andrew Nash of the University of Cape Town, deftly epitomizes the many horrors of Marikana as being 'our first "democratic" massacre – that is, the first time a government has given the go-ahead for the massacre of the black workers who

---

[51] Vishwas Satgar and Mazibuko Jara, 'New times require new democratic left', *Mail & Guardian* online, 7 Feb 2011.

[52] DLF, 'Solidarity Action with the Marikana Workers and Communities!', e-message from democraticleftmedia@gmail.com. See also *Amandla!* Issue 28/27 (September, 2012) with a special feature section of several useful articles on Marikana.

fought for the overthrow of apartheid and voted the ANC into power; the people for whom [the ANC is] supposedly providing a better life.' As Nash continues, the subsequent official foot-dragging in really facing up to the massacre – and instead, in a very real sense, merely ignoring it – may mean 'that we can maintain the illusion of democracy. [But] in the process, real democracy is sacrificed or kept at bay.' True, a careful and serious investigation might offer 'the new ruling elite – the ANC, its allies and the big corporations' the chance 'to turn back from the path that led to this deadly confrontation [at Marikana]. But this is not what is happening. For that new elite, there is no turning back.' For

> Marikana marks a turning point in South African history. It will either lead to growing repression in civil society and the workplace [in order] to recreate an apartheid order now under non-racial rule, or it will lead to the growing realization among the mass of the oppressed and exploited that they can no longer rely on the promises of their rulers and must organize both to defend the political gains they have made since the end of apartheid and to create a social order that embodies the freedom they fought for under the banner of the ANC.[53]

Mangaung and after

For the fact is that, despite the powerful writing of Andrew Nash and others and also the best efforts exerted by organizations like the DLF, the haunting question remains: is Marikana really likely to mark, in any positive way, the 'turning point' that Nash's article invokes? Any definitive break with the prevailing 'common sense' of ANC rule that would be so necessary to establishing a credible, viable, counter-hegemonic challenge to it – a challenge resistant to recolonization, unyielding poverty and popular demobilization – has so far remained an elusive goal. Indeed, in December 2012, we find at the ANC's own elective conference at Mangaung that Jacob Zuma has been re-elected as leader of the party and thus confirmed as President for another four-year term. The same old, same old, then, or so it would seem: the year of the one hundredth anniversary of the ANC, the year of Marikana ... and the year of Zuma's reaffirmation in office.

But the ANC's Congress was noteworthy for something else as well: the re-emergence of Cyril Ramaphosa. Now Zuma's principal deputy, he stands elected as the new Vice President of the ANC with 'some analysts' predicting that Ramaphosa 'will become the unofficial "manager" of the country, leaving Mr Zuma in more of a ceremonial role'![54] Ramaphosa, once a militant labour leader (of the NUM) now turned fabulously wealthy South African capitalist. As noted earlier, he is, among other things, on the board of directors of Lonmin, the corporate perpetrator, alongside the South African state, of Marikana and is

[53] Andrew Nash, 'One year after the Marikana massacre', posted on Z-Net at http://mobile.zcommunications.org/one-year-after-the-marikana-massacre-by-andrew-nash, accessed 6 October 2013.

[54] As reported by Geoffrey York in his article 'Zuma Easily Retains ANC Party Leadership: Wealthy businessman and former union leader Cyril Ramaphosa chosen to be President's deputy leader', *The Globe and Mail*, 19 December 2012.

even known to have urged on the state to play an enforcer's role there – as indeed it soon after did. Of course in the wake of the massacre Ramaphosa donated $250,000 in conscience money to pay for the funerals of the dead protestors. He even 'accepted part of the blame for the disaster', saying that it 'should not have happened ... We are all to blame and there are many stake-holders that should take the blame.'[55] For blame there certainly was.

Note also, however, the broader significance of the ANC's new pairing, in tandem, of Ramaphosa with Zuma. Especially noteworthy here is the ever more forthright marriage of corruption and capitalism that such a tandem exempli-fies. Not that the latter two defining features of the present South African moment ('corruption and capitalism') have been incompatible elsewhere, of course. Nor are they likely to be so in South Africa. Nonetheless Zuma would seem to epitomize a more rough-and-tumble, more right-wing populist, style of high-handed rule whereas Ramaphosa – his role in the events at Marikana notwithstanding – may symbolize a more polite and 'rational' form of the hegemony on the part of a local elite hand-in-glove with capital, global and local. Not that Zuma is any pushover. News reports of Mangaung bear more or less the same imprint on this score: 'Zuma's political coup d'état: Shows leadership and political finesse to purge all adversaries',[56] reads one headline. Global capitalism is less easy to 'finesse' or to 'purge', however. Enter Ramaphosa to handle that side of the equation!

True, the centre may not so easily hold, as William Gumede has recently suggested in evoking the spectre of 'ANC fragmentation'.

> The almost irreversible fragmentation of the ANC, Africa's oldest liberation move-ment has begun. It does appear [that] the ANC does not have the quality leadership at the head of the party, neither does it appear open enough to bring in fresh leader-ship and ideas nor is it willing to genuinely introspect, to be able to reverse the decline. The ANC, the party of liberation, is starting to fragment on the back of the governing party's inability to reduce poverty [or] deliver jobs and effective public services. The ANC may have reached its electoral peak; in future, the ANC may never again secure the two-thirds majorities it grabbed in previous national elections.[57]

In sum, with the further 'splintering' of the ANC itself that Gumede then predicts in some detail, he concludes that

> South Africa is entering a period of realignment of politics where the ANC's majority

---

[55] Geoffrey York, 'Ramaphosa Poised to take ANC job: Businessman, former politician may ascend to party's second highest post without even campaigning', *The Globe and Mail*, 18 December 2012.

[56] Ryk van Niekirk, 'Zuma's Political Coup d'État: Shows leadership and political finesse to purge all adversaries', *Moneyweb*, 21 December 2012, available at www.moneyweb.co.za/moneyweb-mangaung/zumas-political-coup-dtat, accessed 6 October 2013.

[57] William Gumede, 'ANC Fragmentation', *Pambazuka News*, 637, 4 July 2013, available at http://pambazuka.org/en/category/features/88110 accessed 6 October 2013; this article also appeared, on about the same date, in *The Sowetan* (Johannesburg). In this regard, see also Adam Habib, 'Civil Society is our Best Way to Check Misrule', *Mail & Guardian*, 8 August 2013, being an 'edited extract' from his promising new book *South*

is likely going to be dramatically reduced and where we are we are going to see a number of smaller breakaway parties emerge from within the ANC – from the Left, centre and populist wings [of the party]; break-ways from the opposition parties; and entirely new parties from both the Left and centre of SA's politics.

There is also an additional dimension of the possible weakening of the ANC's hold on power to consider. For, difficult as it is to so argue aloud, the death in December 2013 of the great Mandela might also bear a possible silver lining. For, after an initial and fully understandable period of general mourning, one can imagine that the removal from the ANC of the brilliant lustre of Madiba's public image and the halo of his almost supra-historical resonance could well mean there could be a further diminishing of the once seemingly impregnable image that the ANC, at least at the national level, had managed to acquire. And, with this, a further beneficial levelling of the playing field of political contestation.

For, finally, there is the role, present and potential, of the broader South Africa populace to again consider, even as these various shadow waltzes of political intrigue, organizational distemper and corruption, and magical personality play on down the corridors of power. Thus, newspaper accounts suggest that, in addition to all this and, of course, alongside the massacre at Marikana, 'the wave of strikes and violence across South Africa has inflicted heavy damage on the Zuma government, exposing it as disconnected from the workers'.[58] But how then is it best to interpret the present paradox of the ANC's smug and apparently still legitimate hold on power on the one hand and the clear signs of the decay of any such legitimacy on the other? Andrew Beresford, for example, has criticized Bond and myself for 'claim[ing] that we are now witnessing the beginnings of a "post-nationalist" political era in which the "exhausted nationalism" of the ANC is confronted by a new class-based politics which challenges the ANC's claim to a monopoly as to the legitimate representation of South Africa's poor'. Beresford will have none of this, however, suggesting instead that it is too limited

> to understand the longevity of the ANC's nationalist appeal as being solely determined by whether the socio-economic aspirations of its core constituency have been met. A second, interrelated point, is that the strong emotional affinities that workers display with the ANC as the figurehead of the liberation struggle are more deeply rooted than those predicting a 'post nationalist' political era give credit for. We have not, in short, witnessed a moment where such emotive attachments to the party have simply been jettisoned in the face of the ANC's cold economic embrace of a conservative macroeconomic development strategy, as Bond and Saul would suggest.[59]

True, Beresford does concede that

> If in the longer term the party lacks the capacity or political will to pursue this form of

(cont) *Africa's Suspended Revolution: Hopes and Prospects* (Johannesburg: Wits University Press, 2013) which also looks towards a viable 'alternative progressive political agenda' to counter that offered by the ANC.
58 York, 'Zuma Easily Retains ANC party leadership'.
59 Alexander Beresford, 'The Politics of Regenerative Nationalism in South Africa', *Journal of Southern African Studies*, 38, 4, 2012, p. 864.

expansionary nationalist politics, based on racial inclusion and broad-based social transformation, it may well resort to more defensive strategies of nationalist regeneration. These might include jettisoning this racial inclusiveness for a more exclusionary politics, in which a primary strategy of the party rests on regenerating its nationalist appeal through a more racialised politics, whether through discursive appeals to black voters and/or racially discriminatory state patronage. While the ANC can currently employ the resources of its symbolic political capital, the manner in which it responds to the growing challenge offered by leading opposition parties will reveal a great deal about how the party seeks to regenerate its appeal in the longer term.[60]

Our claim however is that in fact the ANC shows little sign of ever using its 'symbolic political capital' as a liberation movement for any transformative purposes such as might, in the long run, meet the bulk of the population's material and emotive needs; and that popular resistance to such a 'post-liberation' outcome must inevitably grow.

At the same time, it must again be admitted that the ANC, as Zuma, Ramaphosa or whoever else, in due course, steps forward to lead it, still has a strong, albeit increasingly wavering, hand in controlling events. Moreover, the forces of discontent, while palpably growing, still desperately need to find a more effective and focused voice. Nonetheless, the South Africa people have, as the history explored in this volume demonstrates, been marginalized and exploited in the past (before, during and after apartheid itself) and they nonetheless sought and found ways to play their own strong hand – as exemplified by the anti-apartheid struggle. Nor is there reason to think that, whatever the present odds against a next liberation struggle, they will not be able to do so again. Indeed, as even Beresford concedes, there are clear indications that the stirrings of the struggle to make such a break – and to recapture the kind of collective trust and breadth of hope and purpose that made the risks of involvement in the anti-apartheid struggle itself worth running – do indeed exist.

Here it is worth noting that some ANC/SACP/MK veterans like former Cabinet Minister Ronnie Kasrils, his most recent analyses having already been quoted been extensively in Chapter 2, has also continued to reflect ruefully on the events at Marikana and to put them ever more probingly into historical context – as we have ourselves attempted to do in this book. Thus even as our book goes to press, we can turn (as, previously, in Chapter 3) to Kasrils and to his present speculations as to 'how South Africa's Faustian pact sold out South Africa's poorest'.[61] For he finds that such gains as had been made by the ANC in power

> have been offset by a breakdown in service delivery, resulting in violent protests by poor and marginalised communities; gross inadequacies and inequities in the educa-

---

[60] Beresford, 'The Politics of Regenerative Nationalism', p. 884.
[61] This is Kasrils' title – 'How the ANC's Faustian Pact Sold out South African's Poorest: In the early 1990s we in the leadership of the ANC made a serious error. Our people are still paying the price' – for the piece he published in *The Guardian*, June 24, 2013 (as previously cited in chapter 3) – this in turn being drawn from the new 'Introduction' to his newly republished autobiography *Armed and Dangerous* (Johannesburg: Jacana, 2013).

tion and health sectors; a ferocious rise in unemployment; endemic police brutality and torture; unseemly power struggles within the ruling party that have grown far worse since the ousting of Mbeki in 2008; an alarming tendency to secrecy and authoritarianism in government; the meddling with the judiciary; and threats to the media and freedom of expression. Even Nelson Mandela's privacy and dignity are violated for the sake of a cheap photo opportunity by the ANC's top echelon.

Most shameful and shocking of all, the events of Bloody Thursday – 16 August 2012 – when police massacred 34 striking miners at Marikana mine, owned by the London-based Lonmin company. The Sharpeville massacre in 1960 prompted me to join the ANC. I found Marikana even more distressing: a democratic South Africa was meant to bring an end to such barbarity. And yet the president and his ministers, locked into a culture of cover-up. Incredibly, the South African Communist party, my party of over 50 years, did not condemn the police either.

Here, of course, is where Kasrils describes the ANC (as quoted in Chapter 3) as having merely 'chickened out'.

Good for Kasrils, one is tempted to say, even though, as we have seen – and rather like Naomi Klein whom we also quoted extensively in Chapter 2 – he tends to see the ANC elite has having been more sinned against than sinning. For he, like Klein, is reluctant to root the present firmly in the ANC's own long history or even in the history of its more recent negotiations (engaged in with both capital and, increasingly, with the white state as well) from the 1980s on. For he still thinks that the ANC holds the key, even if 'a revitalization and renewal from top to bottom is required'. Indeed, he argues, 'the ANC's soul needs to be restored, [and] its traditional values and culture of service reinstated. The pact with the devil needs to be broken.' How likely is that to happen? In fact, in light of what this book has sought to demonstrate, it seems, for now, accurate to say that this must merely be considered a fond and unrealistic hope.

Or take a second recent source, this written by Sampie Terreblanche (who himself has a long and honourable history of dissent from the orthodoxy of diverse established South Africa regimes behind him) and entitled, significantly, *Lost in Transformation* (its subtitle: *South Africa's Search for a New Future Since 1986*).[62] Its preface can be quoted here as clearly epitomizing the book's overall thrust:

> The outstanding characteristic of South Africa, eighteen years after the transition of 1994, is the intensification of the country's social problems of poverty, unemployment and inequality (the PUI problem) among the poorest 50 per cent of the population – in other words, the majority of the black people. The interaction between poverty, unemployment and inequality has not only en-trenched and aggravated the black majority's predicament, but has also intensified the burden of their deprivation. The intensification of the PUI problem can be ascribed partly to the co-option of South Africa as a satellite of the American-led neoliberal empire, and partly to the misguided and myopic policy initiatives of the ANC government.
>
> Ironically enough, the power and wealth of the white-controlled capitalist sector

---

[62] Sampie Terreblanche, *Lost in Transformation: South Africa's Search for a New Future Since 1986* (Johannesburg: KMM Review Publishing Company, 2012); see also Patrick Bond, 'Book review – *Lost in Transformation* by Sampie Terreblanche', *Amandla!* 26/27, 2012.

was enhanced by its integration into the power structures of the American orientated neoliberal global economy. By misgoverning South Africa over the past eighteen
years, the ANC government has become trapped in a 'catch-22'. The PUI problem
that was bequeathed to the ANC government by the apartheid regime in 1994 was
already almost unsolvable. The ANC has proclaimed repeatedly that addressing the
PUI problem is its highest priority. But this is only true in the rhetorical sense of the
word. The policy measures implemented by the government over the past eighteen
years have given strong preference to black elite formation and to promoting the interests of local and foreign corporations while it has shamelessly neglected the impoverished black majority. As a consequence, not only has the PUI problem become more
severe – it is also much more unsolvable.

The ANC government is strongly inclined towards elite formation, towards corruption and towards pampering the interest of the capitalist elite, while it displays a
conspicuous inability to govern South Africa with efficiency and fairness and to alleviate the predicament of the poor. This contradiction gives us reason to suspect that
the downward spiral of the PUI problem will be perpetuated for at least another
decade or two.

To liberate itself from the stranglehold of the 'catch-22' situation, the ANC government will have to become more efficient, less corrupt and orientated in a much friend-
lier way towards the impoverished black majority. But it is doubtful whether the ANC
can liberate itself from its misguided priorities and its glaring inability to govern with
[good] governance and fairness.

* * *

To conclude: it is difficult for us to share Karils' optimism: that the ANC's soul
can be restored and its pact with the devil broken. Easier perhaps to share Terreblanche's pessimism: that, to repeat, 'it is doubtful whether the ANC can liberate
itself from its misguided priorities and its glaring inability to govern with governance and fairness'. But is the 'PUI problem' really to be regarded as being more
or less 'unsolvable'. No, we choose instead to leave our last word to Neville
Alexander who, shortly before his death, stated of the present moment that

> The working and unemployed masses are voting with their feet. Whatever their
> lingering loyalties and ever more feeble hopes in the myth that 'the ANC will deliver',
> however big the gap between political consciousness and material practice, the thou-
> sands of township uprisings, countrywide strikes and serial metropolitan protest
> actions have one simple meaning: we reject your policies and your practices as anti-
> worker and anti-poor. It is, in my view, a misnomer to refer to these stirrings of self-
> organisation of the working class as an expression of 'collective insubordination',
> even though their immediate impulse is usually reactive rather than proactive. They
> are saying very clearly and very loudly that the appeal to nationalist, blood and soil
> rhetoric has lost its power and that we are standing on the threshold of a politics that
> will be shaped by a heightened sense of class struggle.[63]

From Mrs Ples, Silver Lake and the Stone and Iron Ages to Sharpeville,
Durban/Soweto, Boipatong/Bisho, Marikana, and the twentieth anniversary,
in April, 2014, of the ANC's great electoral victory of 1994: the present (and
future) as history. But what history? And even more important: what future?

---

[63] Neville Alexander, 'South Africa: An Unfinished Revolution?'.

Postscript

JOHN S. SAUL AND PATRICK BOND

Since the 2014 edition of *South Africa: The Present as History,* there has been further evidence for our earlier reading of the country's current social, political and economic crises – crises linked to a grotesquely wide (and growing) gap of class differentiation and inequality and to an inordinate deference to the illogic of capitalism, all played out within a political system effectual only in its partial pacification of South Africa's masses. Yet that system – led by an overweening President Jacob Zuma and with Cyril Ramaphosa, thought by many (see p. 228) to have been one of the architects of the Marikana massacre, now installed as Deputy President (and likely to succeed Zuma in 2019) – also continues to generate powerful and creative forms of popular resistance.

What of our reading of such forces of genuine resistance in our final two chapters? Though marked by tensions and contradictions, the growth in their saliency continues: 'unrest'-related (violent) protests rose to a police-record level of 1,907 in 2014, for example, and a further radicalization of large segments of the labour movement saw, by 2014, the break of South Africa's largest union, the National Union of Metalworkers, from affiliation with the ANC and the SACP. The initial signs of electoral success greeting Julius Malema's quite unapologetically populist Economic Freedom Front led to its 2015 disruption of Parliament (in a bid to highlight Zuma's personal corruption), while the promise of resurgent liberatory politics was seen in such actions as 2015's 'RhodesMustFall' campaign in Cape Town. And initial stirrings of a new 'United Front', instigated by the metalworkers, had a broad and promising appeal to many other workers and civil society activists. Indeed, it is just such instances of further struggle that a symposium of articles – published in 2016 by the *Review of African Political Economy* (and online at http://www.africafiles.org) – further elaborates upon.

True, it is far too early to predict that such initiatives will continue to flourish, let alone cohere into a politically viable counter-hegemonic challenge to the ANC's grip on power. For several well-rehearsed negative possibilities also exist in South Africa. Thus, township, small-town and shack-settlement activists may continue to be ideology-free, atomistic and resistant to unifying across space and sector. And if their 'popcorn protests' stay up in the air (before the typical rapid drop) long enough to catch a right-wing wind, xenophobic attacks on fellow township residents typically follow: in 2015 (as in 2008 and 2010) working-class township-dwellers attacked and displaced thousands of their immigrant brothers and sisters.

Other dangers to the left include an overly-centralized and formulaic socialist vanguardism that conflicts with the 'autonomist' instincts of many radical social movements. For the latter sometimes do appear to be unreasonably averse to the birth and nurturing of a unifying left political party and the silo-segregation by ostensibly progressive NGOs has often been debilitating. It is equally the case that there remain negative vestiges of both Stalinist and corporatist traditions within the labour movement's breakaway initiatives. Here the repeated failure of poor and working-class constituencies to cohere in 2014–15 in the interest of common struggle has been sobering – and the masses' residual patriarchy and homophobia, the activists' hesitancy to factor in ecological values (to grapple with climate change, for example), and the capacity of the ANC to divide, conquer and intimidate its opponents all represent other substantial threats to the emergence of a new, democratic left.

That said, however, the game is clearly more advanced than at any other moment since 1994. The time is ripe for a shift from the 'war of position' to a 'war of movement', as the struggle for a free, egalitarian, non-racial, non-sexist South Africa continues slowly but surely along the lines that we had predicted.

Bibliography

Asghar Adelzadeh, 'From the RDP to GEAR: The Gradual Embracing of Neo-Liberalism in Economic policy', *Transformation*, 31, 1996.

Glenn Adler and Jonny Steinberg, *From Comrades to Citizens: The South African Civics Movement and the Transition to Democracy* (Macmillan and St. Martin's Press: London and New York, 2000).

Glenn Adler Eddie Webster (eds), *Trade Unions and Democratization in South Africa, 1985–1997* (London: Macmillan Press, 2000).

African National Congress, *Reconstruction and Development Programme, a policy framework* (Johannesburg: Umanyano, 1994).

African National Congress, 'The State, Property Relations and Social Transformation', *Umrabulo*, 5, 3, 1998.

Neville Alexander, *An Ordinary Country: Issues in the Transition from Apartheid to Democracy in South Africa* (Pietermaritzburg: University of Natal Press, 2002).

——, 'South Africa Today – The Moral Responsibility of Intellectuals', 10th Anniversary celebration of the Foundation for Human Rights in Pretoria, 29 November 2006, available at www.fhr.org.za/article.php?a_id=27, accessed 5 October 2013.

——, 'South Africa: An unfinished revolution?' Fourth Strini Moodley Annual Memorial Lecture, University of KwaZulu-Natal on 13 May 2010.

Peter Alexander, 'Rebellion of the poor: South Africa's service delivery protests – a preliminary analysis,' *Review of African Political Economy*, 37, 123, 2010, available at www.amandlapublishers.org.za, accessed 8 October 2013.

——, 'SA Protest Rates Increasingly Competitive with World Leader China' 23 March 2012, available at www.amandlapublishers.org.za, accessed 8 October 2013.

Peter Alexander, Ruth Hutchinson and Deryck Schreuder (eds), *Africa Today: A Multidisciplinary Snapshot of the Continent in 1995* (Canberra: The Humanities Research Centre, 1995).

Peter Alexander, Thapelo Lekgowa, Botsang Mmope, Luke Sinwell and Bongani Xezwi, *Marikana: A View from the Mountain and a Case to Answer* (Johannesburg, Jacana, 2012).

Sam Ashman, Ben Fine and Susan Newman, 'The Crisis in South Africa: Neoliberalism, Financialization and Uneven and Combined Development', *Socialist Register*, 47 (Pontypool, Wales: Merlin Press, 2011).

Reg Bailey and Chris Buckley, 'Modelling Domestic Water Tariffs', presentation to the University of KwaZulu-Natal Centre for Civil Society, Durban, 7 November 2005.

Franco Barchiesi, 'After the March on the Left', *Khanya Journal*, December 2002.

——, '"Schooling Bodies to Hard Work": The South African State's Policy Discourse and its Moral Constructions of Welfare', North Eastern Workshop on Southern Africa (NEWSA), Vermont, 2007.

Franco Barchiesi and Tom Bramble (eds), *Rethinking the Labour Movement in the 'New South Africa'* (Aldershot: Ashgate, 2003).

Jonathan Barker, *Street-Level Democracy: Political Settings at the Margins of Global Power* (Toronto: Between The Lines, 1999).

Howard Barrell, *MK: The ANC's Armed Struggle* (London: Penguin Books, 1990).

——, *Conscripts to their Age: African National Congress Operational Strategy, 1976–1986* (D.Phil thesis in Politics, Faculty of Social Studies, University of Oxford,. 1993).

Jeremy Baskin, *Striking Back: A History of COSATU* (Johannesburg: Ravan, 1991).

Carolyn Bassett, *Negotiating South Africa's Economic Future: COSATU and Strategic Unionism* (Toronto: York University Press 2000).

Carolyn Bassett and Marlea Clarke, 'South African trade unions and Globalization: Going for the "High-road", Getting Stuck on the "Low-road"', *World Organisation, Labour and Globalisation*, 2, 1, 2008.

Peter Batchelor, 'South Africa: An Irresponsible Arms Trader?' *Global Dialogue*, 4, 2, 1999.

Milford Bateman, 'Microcredit and Marikana: How they are linked', *The Star*, 18 September 2012.

BBC, 'Africa's big plan "disappointing"', London, 22 October 2004.

Bjorn Beckman and Lloyd Sachikonye, *Labour Regimes and Liberalization: The Restructuring of State-Society Relations in Africa* (Harare: University of Zimbabwe Press, 2001).

Bjorn Beckman, Sakhela Buhlungu and Lloyd Sachikonye (eds), *Trade Unions and Party Politics: Labour Movements in Africa* (Cape Town: HSRC Press, 2010).

Terry Bell, *Unfinished Business: South Africa, Apartheid and Truth* (London: Verso, 2003).

——, 'How 'Non Jobs' come to the Aid of Government Election Propaganda', *Sunday Independent*, 15 February 2004.

William Beinart and Saul Dubow (eds), *Segregation and Apartheid in Twentieth Century South Africa* (London: Routledge, 1995).

Alexander Beresford, 'The Politics of Regenerative Nationalism in South Africa', *Journal of Southern African Studies*, 38, 4, 2012.

Ann Bernstein, *Policy-Making in a New Democracy: South Africa's Challenges in the 21st Century* (Johannesburg: Centre for Development and Enterprise, August 1999).

Lionel Bernstein, 'Letter from Rusty Bernstein to John S Saul', *Transformation* (South Africa), 64, 2007.

Haroon Bhorat, 'Economic Inequality Is a Major Obstacle,' *New York Times*, 28 July 2013, available at www.nytimes.com/roomfordebate/2013/07/28/the-future-of-south-africa/economic-inequality-is-a-major-obstacle-to-growth-in-south-africa, accessed 2 October 2013.

Haroon Bhorat, Carlene van der Westhuizen and Toughedah Jacobs, *Income and non-income inequality in post-apartheid South Africa: What are the Drivers and Possible Policy Interventions?* (Capetown: Development Policy Research Unit, 2009).

Patrick Bond, '*What is a Crisis of Overproduction*', 1999, available at www.marxmail.org/faq/overproduction.htm, accessed 6 October 2013.

——, *Cities of Gold, Townships of Coal: Essays on South Africa's New Urban Crisis* (Trenton, NJ: Africa World Press, 2000).

——, *Elite Transition: From Apartheid to Neoliberalism in South Africa* (London: Pluto Press, 2000 and 2014, New Edition).

——, *Against Global Apartheid* (Cape Town: UCT Press, 2001; London: Zed Books, 2003).

——, *Unsustainable South Africa: Environment, Development and Social Protest* (London: Merlin Press, 2002).

——, 'South Africa's Frustrating Decade of Freedom: From Racial to Class Apartheid', *Monthly Review*, 55, 10, 2004.

——, (ed.), *Fanon's Warning* (Trenton, NJ: Africa World Press, 2005).

——, *Talk Left, Walk Right* (Pietermaritzburg: University of KwaZulu-Natal Press, 2006).

——, 'Removing Neocolonialism's APRM Mask: A Critique of the African Peer Review Mechanism', *Review of African Political Economy*, 36: 122, 2009.

——, 'Water, Health and the Commodification Debate' *Review of Radical Political Economics*, 2010, 42, 3, 2010.

——, *Durban's Climate Gamble: Trading Carbon, Betting the Earth* (Pretoria, University of South Africa Press, 2011).

——, *Politics of Climate Justice: Paralysis Above, Movement Below* (Pietermaritzburg: University of KwaZulu-Natal Press, 2012).

——, 'Book review – Lost in Transformation by Sampie Terreblanche', *Amandla!* 26–27, 2012.

——, 'Jim Yong Kim's trip to South Africa was just a PR exercise for the World Bank', *The Guardian Poverty Matters* blog, 12 September 2012, available at www.guardian. co.uk/global-development/poverty-matters/2012/sep/12/jim-yong-kim-world-bank-south-africa, accessed 4 October 2013.

Patrick Bond and Greg Ruiters, 'Failure in the Townships? The Development Bottleneck', *Southern Africa Report*, 11, 3, 1996.

Patrick Bond, Yogan Pillay and David Sanders, 'The Rise of Neo-Liberalism in South Africa: Developments in Economic, Social and Health Policy', *International Journal of Health Services*, 27, 1, 1997.

Patrick Bond and Meshack Khosa (eds), *An RDP Policy Audit* (Pretoria: Human Sciences Research Council Press, 2000).

Patrick Bond and Jackie Dugard, 'The Case of Johannesburg Water: What Really Happened at the Pre-paid "Parish Pump"', *Law, Democracy and Development*, 12, 1, 2008.

Patrick Bond and Simba Manyanya, *Zimbabwe's Plunge: Exhausted Nationalism, Neoliberalism and the Search for Social Justice* (London: Merlin Press, 2003).

Susan Booysen, 'The ANC and the Regeneration of Political Power, 1994–2011', Paper presented at the conference, One Hundred Years of the ANC: Debating Liberation Histories and Democracy Today, Johannesburg, 20–24 September 2011.

Eleria Bornman, R. van Eeden and M. Wentzel (eds), *Violence in South Africa* (Pretoria: Human Sciences and Research Council, 1998).

Alexander Brady, *Democracy in the Dominions: A Comparative Study in Institutions* (Toronto: University of Toronto Press, 1947).

Peter Bruce, 'SA Needs a Market Economy', *Business Day*, 4 June 2003, available at http://allafrica.com/stories/200306040569.html, accessed 4 October 2013.

——, 'Thick End of the Wedge', *Business Day*, 13 February 2012 available at www.bdlive.co.za/opinion/columnists/2012/08/20/the-thick-end-of-the-wedge-the-editors-notebook, accessed 3 October 2013.

——, 'Thick End of the Wedge: Man of Action Ramaphosa Good for Zuma', *Business Day*, 19 December 2012, available at www.bdlive.co.za/opinion/columnists/2012/12/19/thick-end-of-the-wedge-man-of-action-ramaphosa-good-for-zuma, accessed 5 October 2013.

Geoff Budlender, 'A Paper Dog with Real Teeth', *Mail & Guardian*, 12 July 2002.

Sakhela Buhlungu, *A Paradox of Victory: COSATU and the Democratic Transformation in South Africa* (Scottsville, S.A.: University of KwaZulu-Natal Press, 2010).

Colin Bundy, *The Rise and Fall of the South African Peasantry* (London: Heinemann, 1979).

Rulof Burger and Rachel Jafta, 'Affirmative Action in South Africa: An Empirical Assessment of the Impact on Labour Market Outcomes', Working Paper 76 (University of Oxford Centre for Research on Inequality, Human Security, and Ethnicity, March 2010).

John Cell, *The Highest Stage of White Supremacy: The Origins of Segregation in South Africa and the American South* (Cambridge: Cambridge University Press, 1982).Center for International Environmental Law, 'CIEL calls on World Bank to revisit investment in Lonmin', Washington, 17 August 2012, available at http://ciel.org/Law_Communities/Lonmin_17Aug2012.html, accessed 5 October 2013.

Janet Cherry, *Umkhonto weSizwe* (Auckland Park, S. A.: Jacana, 2001).

Laura Citron and Richard Walton, 'International Comparisons of Company Profitability,' *UK National Statistics Publication Hub*, October 2002, available from www. ons.gov.uk/ons/rel/elmr/economic-trends—discontinued-/no—587—september-2002/international-comparisons-of-company-profitability.pdf, accessed on 2 October 2013.

City Press, 'Buffalo Soldier Cyril Loses out', 4 April 2012, available at www.citypress. co.za/news/buffalo-soldier-cyril-loses-out-20120414, accessed 4 October 2013.
——, 'Please take me back, I'll be good – Malema', 17 December 2012, available at www.citypress.co.za/news/buffalo-soldier-cyril-loses-out-20120414, accessed 4 October 2013.
——, 'Malema interview – I have learnt from Zuma', 13 January 2013, available at www.citypress.co.za/politics/malema-interview-i-have-learnt-from-zuma, accessed 5 October 2013.
Tim Cohen, 'Time for a Bold New Idea of what it means to be SA', *Business Day*, 15 October 2012, available at www.bdlive.co.za/opinion/columnists/2012/10/15/time-for-a-bold-new- idea-of-what-it-means-to-be-sa, accessed 5 October 2013.
Marlea Clarke, '"All the Workers?" Labour Market Reform and "Precarious Work" in Post-apartheid South Africa, 1994–2004' (Toronto: York University Press 2006).
Marlea Clarke and Carolyn Bassett, 'South African Trade Unions and Globalization: Going for the "High Road", Getting Stuck on the "Low Road"', in *Work Organization, Labour and Globalisation*, 3, 1 (Spring, 2008).
Coalition against Water Privatization, Press Statement: 'One Step Forward, Two Steps Back'. Johannesburg, 25 March 2009.
Julian Cobbing, 'The Mfecane as Alibi: Thoughts on Dithakong and Mbolompo', *Journal of African History*, 29, 3, 1988.
——, 'Political Mythology and the Making of Natal's Mfecane,' *Canadian Journal of African Studies*, 23, 2, 1989.
Columbia University and Yale University, *Environmental Performance Index 2012*, New York.
Constitutional Court of South Africa, 'Soobramoney Decision', 1997, available at www.escr-net.org/usr_doc/Soobramoney_Decision.pdf, accessed 6 October 2013.
COSATU, 'Strategic Policy Framework, Ten-Year Plan', Pretoria, 2004, available at www.nehawu.org.za/images/Congress_June2004_Book5_SPF.pdf, accessed 2 October 2013.
Eddie Cottle (ed.), *South Africa's World Cup: A Legacy for Whom?* (Pietermaritzburg: University of KwaZulu-Natal Press, 2011).
Council for Development and Social Science Research in Africa, Dakar and Third World Network-Africa, 'Declaration on Africa's Development Challenges', Resolution adopted at the Joint Conference on Africa's Development Challenges in the Millennium, Accra, 23–26 April 2002.
Terry Crawford-Browne, *Eye on the Money: One Man's Crusade against Corruption* (Cape Town: Umuzi, 2007).
Martin Creamer, 'Mining Doomed if "Crazy" Pay Increases Continue – Nick Holland', *Mining Weekly*, 10 May 2013.
Jeremy Cronin, 'The Boat, the Tap and the Leipzig Way', *African Communist*, 130, 1992, pp. 41–54.
——, 'Nothing to Gain from All-or-Nothing Tactics', *Weekly Mail*, 13–19 November 1992.
——, 'How we misread the situation in the mid-1990s', speech to the 12th National congress of the trade union SACTWU, as issued by the SACP, 22 August 2013.
Daily Observer, 'Wade: Nepad has failed', 4 October 2007.
T. R. H. Davenport, *South Africa: A Modern History*, Fourth Edition (Toronto and Buffalo: University of Toronto Press, 1991).
John Daniel, 'The Mbeki Presidency: Lusaka Wins', *South African Yearbook of International Affairs, 2001/2* (Johannesburg: South African Institute of International Affairs, 2002).
Basil Davidson, Joe Slovo and Anthony Wilkinson, *Southern Africa: The New Politics of Revolution* (Harmondsworth: Penguin, 1976).
Robert Davies, Dan O'Meara and Sipho Dlamini, *The Struggle for South Africa: A Refer-*

ence Guide, New Edition (London: Zed Books, 1988).Jan de Lange, 'Archie Palane points finger at NUM failings', *Miningmx*, 10 September 2012, available at www.miningmx.com/page/news/markets/1388854-Archie-Palane-points-finger-at-NUM-failings, accessed 4 October 2013.

Ron Derby, 'Could Debt Costs be Behind Miners' Pay Demands?' *Business Day*, 14 September 2012.

Mandy de Waal, 'Cyril Ramaphosa: ANC deputy, captain of industry', *Daily Maverick*, 20 December 2012, available at http://dailymaverick.co.za/article/2012-12-20-cyril-ramaphosa-anc-deputy-captain-of-industry, accessed 5 October 2013.

Peter Delius, *The Land Belongs to Us: The Pedi polity, the Boers and the British in the Nineteenth Century Transvaal* (Johannesburg: Ravan, 1983).

Democratic Left Front, 'Another South Africa and World is Possible!' 1st Democratic Left Conference Report, 20–23 January 2011, Johannesburg.

Ashwin Desai, *We are the Poors: Community Struggles in Post-Apartheid South Africa* (New York: Monthly Review Press, 2002).

Cosmas Desmond, *The Discarded People: An Account of African Resettlement in South Africa* (Harmondsworth: Penguin, 1971).

Robyn Dixon, 'South African President Jacob Zuma Retains ANC Leadership', *Los Angeles Times*, 18 December 2012, available at www.latimes.com/news/nationworld/world/la-fg-south-africa-zuma-20121219,0,340440.story, accessed 5 October 2013.

Lynley Donnelly, 'Throwing Good Money at EU Troubles', *Mail & Guardian*, 22 June 2012.

Alison Drew, *South Africa's Radical Tradition: A Documentary History* (Cape Town: University of Cape Town Press, 1996/1997).

Saul Dubow, *Racial Segregation and the Origins of Apartheid in South Africa, 1919–36* (Basingstoke: Macmillan, 1989).

——, *The African National Congress* (Stroud: Sutton Publishing, 2000).

Saul Dubow and Alan Jeeves (eds), *South Africa's 1940s: Worlds of Possibilities* (Cape Town: Double Storey, 2005).

Hassen Ebrahim, *The Soul Of A Nation: Constitution-making in South Africa* (Oxford: Oxford University Press, 1998).

Economic Freedom Fighters, *Founding Manifesto*, available at www.politicsweb.co.za/politicsweb/view/politicsweb/en/page71619?oid=393903&sn=Detail&pid=71616, accessed 4 October 2013.

The Economist, 'Cry, the Beloved Country', 20–26 October 2012.

L. Ensor, 'South Africa: Get Down to Brass Tacks – Mbeki', *Business Day*, 18 June 2007.

David Everatt, G. Rapholo, H. Marais and S. Davies, 'Civil Society and Local Governance in the Johannesburg Mega-city', Community Agency for Society Enquiry, Johannesburg, for the United Nations Research Institute for Social Development (Geneva, 1997).

Frantz Fanon, *The Wretched of the Earth* (New York: Grove Press; Harmondsworth: Penguin, 1963, 1967).

Farlam Commission, 'Transcription of the Commission of Inquiry: Marikana – Days 1 to 7, 1 to 31 October 2012', available at www.seri- sa.org/images/stories/marikana_consolidatedtranscript_days1-7.pdf, accessed 4 October 2013.

David Fasenfest, 'Good for Capitalists, Not So Much for Capitalism', *Critical Sociology*, 37, 3, 2011.

Financial Times, 'G8 Vows to "Fully Commit" to Developing African Nations', 2 June 2003.

Alan Fine, 'SA Electorate Repeats 1994's "Perfect Fluke"', *Business Day*, 9 June 1999.

Robert Fine, 'The Workers' Struggle in South Africa', *ROAPE* 9, 24, 1982, pp 95–99.

Ben Fine and Zavareh Rustomjee, *The Political Economy of South Africa: From Minerals-Energy Complex to Industrialization* (Boulder: Westview, 1996).

Louise Flanagan, 'Taxpayers to Subsidise Gautrain', *The Star,* 21 June 2011.

Pascal Fletcher, 'Former-ANC "Bad Boy" Plans Election Bid against the Odds', Reuters, Johannesburg, 24 July 2013.

Pascal Fletcher and Jon Herscovitz, '"Hero" Tied to Mine Killings: One-time South African Apartheid Foe Urged Tough Action on Strikers', *Toronto Star*, October 25, 2012.

Fiona Ford, 'Mbeki link to toxic cure', *The Star,* 15 September 2007.

Dick Forslund, 'Wages, profits and labour productivity in South Africa', *Amandla!* 24 January 2012, available at www.amandla.org.za/special-features/the-wage-and-productivity-debate/1142-wages-profits-and-labour-productivity-in-south-africa-a-reply, accessed on 4 October 2013.

Joe Foster, 'The Workers' Struggle: Where Does FOSATU Stand?' *Review of African Political Economy*, 9, 24, 1982.

Philip Frankel, *Pretoria's Praetorians: Civil Military Relations in South Africa* (Cambridge: Cambridge University Press, 1984).

——, *An Ordinary Atrocity: Sharpeville and Its Massacre* (Johannesburg: Witwatersrand University Press, 2001).

Malcolm Fraser, 'No More Talk. Time to Act', *The Times* (London), 30 June 1986.

Bill Freund, *The Making of Contemporary Africa: The Development of African Society Since 1800*, Second Edition (Boulder: Lynne Rienner, 1998).

Steven Friedman, *Building Tomorrow Today: African Workers in Trade Unions, 1970–1984* (Cape Town: Ravan, 1987).

——, (ed.), *The Long Journey: South Africa's Quest for a Negotiated Settlement* (Johannesburg: Ravan, 1993).

Steven Friedman, 'South Africa's Reluctant Transition', *Journal of Democracy*, 4, 2, 1993.

——, 'We Must Stop Blaming and Start Compromising', *Business Day*, 19 September 2012, available at www.bdlive.co.za/opinion/columnists/2012/09/19/we-must-stop-blaming- and-start-compromising, accessed 5 October 2013.

Steven Friedman and Doreen Atkinson (eds), *The Small Miracle: South Africa's Negotiated Settlement*, South African Review 7 (Braamfontein: Ravan, 1994).

Stephen Gelb, 'Making Sense of the Crisis', *Transformation* 5, 1987.

——, (ed.), *South Africa's Economic Crisis* (Cape Town: David Phillip, 1991).

Mark Gevisser, *A Legacy of Liberation: Thabo Mbeki and the Future of the South African Dream* (New York: Palgrave Macmillan, 2009).

Stephen Gill, 'Globalisation, Market Civilisation, and Disciplinary Neoliberalism', *Millennium*, 24, 3, 1995.

Barry Gills, Joel Rocamora and Richard Wilson (eds), *Low Intensity Democracy: Political Power in the New World Order* (London: Pluto, 1993).

Piero Gleijeses, *Conflicting Missions: Havana, Washington and Africa, 1959–1976* (Chapel Hill, NC and London: University of North Carolina Press, 2002).

——, *Visions of Freedom: Havana, Washington, Pretoria, and the Struggle for Southern Africa, 1976–1991* (Chapel Hill, NC and London: University of North Carolina Press, 2013).

Pravin Gordhan, 'IMFC Statement by Pravin J. Gordhan, Minister of Finance, South Africa', Washington, IMF, 13 October 2012, available at www.imf.org/external/am/2012/imfc/statement/eng/zaf.pdf, accessed 4 October 2013.

Jeremy Gordin and Eugene de Kock, *A long night's Damage: Working for the Apartheid State* (Saxonwold, S.A.: Conta, 1998).

Pippa Green, *Choice, Not Fate: The Life and Times of Trevor Manuel* (Johannesburg: Penguin S.A., 2008).

——, '100 days, 11 issues', *Mail & Guardian*, 17 August 2009.

William Gumede, *Thabo Mbeki and the Battle for the Soul of the ANC* (Cape Town: Zebra Press, 2005).

——, 'Zuma's Victory may Trigger the Break-up of the ANC', *The Guardian*, 19 December 2007.

——, *Restless Nation: Making Sense of Troubled Times* (Capetown: Tafelberg, 2012).

——, 'ANC Fragmentation', *Pambazuka News*, 637 (4 July 2013), available at http://pambazuka.org/en/category/features/88110, accessed 6 October 2013.

Jeff Guy, 'Analysing Pre-capitalist Societies in Southern Africa', *Journal of Southern African Studies*, 14, 1, 1987.

Adam Habib, 'Civil Society is our Best Way to Check Misrule', *Mail & Guardian*, 8 August 2013.

——, *South Africa's Suspended Revolution: Hopes and Prospects* (Johannesburg: Wits University Press, 2013).

B. Hackland, 'The Economic and Political Context of the Growth of the Progressive Federal Party in South Africa, 1959–78', *Journal of Southern African Studies*, 7, 1, 1980.

Carolyn Hamilton (ed.), *The Mfecane Aftermath: Reconstructive Debates in Southern African History* (Johannesburg: Witwatersrand University Press, 1995).

Gavin Hartford, 'The Mining Industry Strike Wave', Manuscript, September 2012, and presentation to the *Amandla! Colloquium*, Magaliesburg, 18 November 2012.

Ray Hartley, 'An Interview with Jacob Zuma', *The Times*, 9 September 2010.

Shireen Hassim, *Identities, Interests and Constituencies: The Politics of the Women's movement in South Africa, 1980–1999*, (Toronto: York University Press, 2002).

——, *Women's Organizations and Democracy in South Africa: Contesting Authority* (Madison: University of Wisconsin Press, 2006).

Ricardo Hausmann, Laura D. Tyson and Saadia Zahidi, 'The Global Gender Gap Report 2011' (Geneva: World Economic Forum, 2012).

Nick Hedley, 'Service delivery: Presidency blames apartheid', *Business Day*, 12 September 2012, available at www.bdlive.co.za/national/2012/09/12/service-delivery-presidency-blames-apartheid-denial, accessed 5 October 2013.

Robert Heilbroner, *The Future as History* (New York: Grove Press, 1959).

David Hemson, 'Rural Poor Play a Role in Water Projects', *Business Day*, 1 July 2003.

Mark Heywood, 'Whose ANC is it anyway?' *Daily Maverick*, 25 September 2012.

Alan Hirsch, *Season of Hope: Economic Reform under Mandela and Mbeki* (Pietermaritzburg: University of KwaZulu-Natal Press, 2005).

Baruch Hirson, *Year of Fire, Year of Ash: The Soweto Revolt – Roots of a Revolution?* (London: Zed Press, 1979).

Gregory Houston, *The National Liberation Struggle in South Africa: A case study of the United Democratic Front, 1983–1987* (Aldershot: Ashgate, 1999).

D. Howarth and A. Norval (eds), *South Africa in Transition: New Theoretical Perspectives* (New York: St Martin's Press, 1998).

Nina Hunter, Julian May and Vishnu Padayachee, *Lessons for PRSP from Poverty Reduction Strategies in South Africa* (Durban: University of KwaZulu-Natal School of Development Studies, 2003).

iAfrica News, 'Why Land Reform is Failing', 6 July 2010, available at http://business.iafrica.com/features/860926.html, accessed 6 October 2013.

John Iliffe, *Africans: The History of a Continent* (Cambridge: Cambridge University Press, 1995).

INet Bridge, AFP, 'Zuma, Mandela Family Assets Seized in Mining Bankruptcy', 16 April 2012.

Duncan Innes,, *Anglo American and the Rise of Modern South Africa* (Johannesburg: Ravan, 1984).

Institute for Industrial Education, *The Durban Strikes, 1973: Human Beings with Souls* (Durban: Institute for Industrial Education and Ravan, 1974).

International Monetary Fund, 'Article IV Consultations', available at www.imf.org, accessed 6 October 2013.

IOL news, 'Profound ANC crisis', news article of September 8 2012 available at www.iol.co.za/news/politics/profound-anc-crisis-1.1378491, accessed 5 October 2013.

Mazibuko Jara, 'The Marikana Massacre and the New Wave of Workers' Struggle', *New Politics*, 14, 3, 2013, available from, http://newpol.org/content/south-africa-marikana-massacre-and-new-wave-workers%E2%80%99-struggle-0, accessed 4 October 2013.

Hilary Joffe, 'Growth has helped richest and poorest', *Business Day*, 5 March 2008.

R. W. Johnson, 'Massacre at Marikana', *politicsweb*, 19 August 2012, available at www.politicsweb.co.za/politicsweb/view/politicsweb/en/page72308?oid=320136&sn=Marketingweb+detail&pid=90389, accessed 5 October 2013.

Fredrick Johnstone, 'White Prosperity and White Supremacy in South Africa Today', *African Affairs*, 69, 2, 1970.

——, *Class, Race and Gold: A Study of Class Relations and Racial Discrimination in South Africa* (London: Routledge and Kegan Paul, 1976).

Athi Mongezeleli Joja, 'White tears cheapening black suffering', available at http://septembernationalimbizo.org/white-tears-cheapening-black-suffering, accessed 5 October 2013.

Pallo Jordan, 'Strategic Debate on the ANC', *Weekly Mail*, 12–19 November 1992.

Pearlie Joubert, 'Grootboom dies Homeless and Penniless', *Mail & Guardian*, 8 August 2008.

John Kane-Berman, *Soweto: Black Revolt, White Reaction* (Johannesburg: Ravan, 1978).

Baris Karagaac and Yasin Kaya (eds), *Capital and Labour in Contemporary Capitalism* (forthcoming).

Thomas Karis, Gwendolen M. Carter, Gail Gerhart (eds), *From Protest to Challenge: A Documentary History of African Politics in South Africa, 1882–1964*, in multiple volumes (Stanford: Hoover Institution Press; Bloomington, IN: Indiana University Press, 1973 onwards).

Ronnie Kasrils, 'Report on Water Cut-offs a Case of Sour Grapes among US Populists', *Sunday Independent*, 8 June 2003.

——, 'The Slayings Grow More Sinister', *Amandla!* Issue 26/27, September 2012.

——, 'How the ANC's Faustian Pact Sold Out South African's Poorest: In the early 1990s we in the leadership of the ANC made a serious error. Our people are still paying the price', *The Guardian*, 24 June 2013.

——, *Armed and Dangerous: From Undercover Struggle to Freedom*, Fourth Edition (Johannesburg: Jacana, 2013).

Tim Keegan, *Colonial South Africa and the Origins of the Racial Order* (Charlottesville: University Press of Virginia. 1996).

Lesetja Kganyago, 'South Africa as a Financial Centre for Africa', speech to the Reuters Economist of the Year Award Ceremony, Johannesburg, 11 August 2004.

Jaspreet Kindra, 'Aids drugs killed Parks, say ANC', *Mail & Guardian*, 22 March 2002.

Naomi Klein, *The Shock Doctrine: The Rise of Disaster Capitalism* (Toronto: Alfred A. Knopf Canada, 2007).

Richard Lapper and Tom Burgis, 'South Africans Urged to Beware Left Turn', *Financial Times*, 27 October 2008.

Martin Legassick, *Armed Struggle and Democracy: The Case of South Africa* (Uppsala: Nordiska Afrikainstitutet, 2002).

——, *Towards Socialist Democracy* (Scottsville, S. A.: University of Kwazulu-Natal Press, 2007).

——, 'The Marikana Massacre: a turning point?' *The Bullet: A Socialist Project E-Bulletin,.* 689, 31 August 2012.

Ted Leggett, 'Is South Africa's Crime Wave a Statistical Illusion?' *SA Crime Quarterly*, 1 July 2002, available at www.issafrica.org/uploads/CQ1Leggett.pdf, accessed 2 October 2013.

Murray Leibbrandt, Ingrid Woolard, Arden Finn and Jonathan Argent, 'Trends In South African Income Distribution and Poverty Since the Fall of Apartheid', OECD Social, Employment and Migration Working Papers 101 (Cape Town: Southern Africa

Labour and Development Research Unit, School of Economics, University of Cape Town, 2010).

W. le Roux and K. van Marle, *Law, Memory and the Legacy of Apartheid: Ten Years after AZAPO v President of South Africa* (Pretoria: University of Pretoria Press, 2007).

Matuma Letsoala, 'Cosatu Report Hammers "Self-Serving" ANC', *Mail & Guardian*, 9 August 2012.

Merle Lipton, *Capitalism and Apartheid: South Africa, 1910–84* (Aldershot: Gower Publishing, 1985).

Tom Lodge, *Black Politics in South Africa since 1945* (New York and London: Longman, 1983).

——, 'The ANC and the Development of Party Politics', *The Journal of Modern African Studies*, 42, 2, 2004, pp. 189–219.

——, *Sharpeville: An Apartheid Massacre and its Consequences* (Oxford: Oxford University Press, 2011).

Michael Lowy, *The Politics of Combined and Uneven Development: The Theory of Permanent Revolution* (London: Verso Editions, 1981).

Lungile Madywabe, 'A Compelling need for African Innovation' (Johannesburg: The Helen Suzman Foundation, 2005), available at http://hsf.org.za/resource-centre/focus/issues-31-40/issue-37-first-quarter-2005/compelling-need-for-african-innovation, accessed 3 October 2013.

Getrude Makhafola, 'Mantashe: Marikana breeds counter-revolution', *Business Report*, 26 August 2012, available at www.iol.co.za/business/business-news/mantashe-marikana-breeds-counter-revolution-1.1369789, accessed 4 October 2013.

Bronwyn Manby, 'African Peer Review Mechanism: Lessons from Kenya', *Pambazuka News*, 362, 15 April 2008.

Ibbo Mandaza, *Zimbabwe: The Political Economy of Transition, 1980–1986* (Dakar: CODESRIA, 1986).

Xolela Mangcu, 'Far Cry From Biko's Political Approach', *The Sowetan*, 25 September 2012, available at www.sowetanlive.co.za/columnists/2012/09/25/far-cry-from-biko-s-political-approach, accessed 4 October 2013.

Trevor Manuel, 'Mobilizing International Investment Flows: The New Global Outlook', speech to the Commonwealth Business Council, Johannesburg, 24 September 2002.

Hein Marais, *South Africa – Limits to Change: The Political Economy of Transition* (London: Zed Books, 1995).

Gerhard Maré, 'Makin' Nice with Buthelezi', *Southern Africa Report*, 14, 3, 1999.

Shula Marks, 'Southern and Central Africa, 1886–1910', in Roland Oliver and G. N. Sanderson (eds), *The Cambridge History of Africa* Volume 8 (Cambridge University Press, 1985).

Shula Marks and Stanley Trapido, 'Lord Milner and the South African State', *History Workshop Journal*, 8, 1, 1979.

Natasha Marrian, 'Cosatu Cans Report Showing Unionists Split on Zuma', *Business Day*, 11 December 2012.

David Masondo, 'BEE has Evolved into a Family Affair', *City Press*, 5 September 2010.

Mzwanele Mayekiso, *Township Politics: Civic Struggles for a New South Africa* (New York, Monthly Review Press, 1996).

Paul Maylam, *A History of the African People of South Africa: From the Early Iron Age to the 1970s* (New York: St. Martin's Press, 1986).

Govan Mbeki, *South Africa: The Peasants Revolt* (Harmondsworth: Penguin, 1964).

——, *The Struggle for Liberation in South Africa: A Short History* (Cape Town: David Philip, 1992).

——, 'South Africa: Only a Matter of Time before the Bomb Explodes', *Leader*, 21 February 2011, available at www.leader.co.za/article.aspx?s=23&f=1&a=2571, accessed 4 October 2013.

Thabo Mbeki, 'The Fatton Thesis: A Rejoinder', *Canadian Journal of African Studies*, 18, 3, 1984.
——, '*Speech of the President of South Africa, Thabo Mbeki, at the Annual National Conference of the Black Management Forum*', Johannesburg, 20 November 1999, available at www.thepresidency.gov.za/pebble.asp?relid=2596&t, accessed 4 October 2013.
——, 'Steps to End the Two Nations Divide', *ANC Today*, 3, 33, 2003.
——, '*Tackling Illicit Capital Flows for Economic Transformation*', Thabo Mbeki Foundation, Johannesburg, 2012, available at www.thabombekifoundation.org.za/Pages/Tackling-Illicit-Capital-Flows-for-Economic-Transformation.aspx, accessed 3 October 2013.
David McDonald, *Environmental Justice in South Africa*, (Columbus OH: Ohio University Press; Cape Town: University of Cape Town Press, 2002).
——, 'Attack the Problem Not the Data', *Sunday Independent*, 15 June 2003.
——, Why Race Matters in South Africa (Cambridge and London: Harvard University Press, 2006).
Dale McKinley, *The ANC and the Liberation Struggle: A Critical Political Biography* (London and Chicago: Pluto Press, 1997).
——, 'Power without Responsibility', e-report for The South African Civil Society Information Service, 10 August 2012.
Dennis McShane, Martin Plaut and David Ward, *Power! Black Workers, their Unions and the Struggle for Freedom in South Africa* (Boston, MA: South End Press, 1984).
Shamim Meer, 'The Demobilisation of Civil Society: Struggling with New Questions', *Development Update*, 3, 1, 1999.
D. Miller, O. Oloyede, R. Saunders, 'South Africa in Africa – African perceptions, African realities', *African Sociological Review*, 12, 1, 2008.
Andrew Minnaar, et al., *The Hidden Hand: Covert Operations in South Africa* (Pretoria: Human Sciences Research Council, 1994).
William Minter, *King Solomon's Mines Revisited: Western Interests and the Burdened History of Southern Africa* (New York: Basic Books, 1986).
Chester Missing, 'SA politics so surreal, we have lawyers named Dali', *City Press*, 29 July 2013.
Thandika Mkandawire, 'Crisis Management and the Making of "Choiceless Democracies" in Africa', in R. Joseph (ed.) *The State, Conflict and Democracy in Africa* (Boulder, CO: Lynne Rienner, 1999).
Naledi Nomalanga Mkhize, 'Why the Mala Mala Case Should Compel us to a Second CODESA ... and Fast', *The Con*, 11 August 2013.
Daniel Mminele, 'South Africa and the G20 – Challenges and Opportunities', presentation to the SA Institute of International Affairs and the University of Pretoria, Pretoria, 31 October 2012.
Helen Moffett, 'Take your Women's Day and shove it', Books Live, 8 August 2012.
Moloko Moloto, 'Even the Fish will Vote for the ANC', *The Mercury*, 1 July 2013.
Moneyweb, 'Special report podcast: Pravin Gordhan, Minister of Finance', 29 September 2011, available at www.moneyweb.co.za/moneyweb-special-report/special-report-podcast-pravin-gordhan—minister-of, accessed 3 October 2013.
T. Dunbar Moodie, *The Rise of Afrikanerdom: Power, Apartheid, and the Afrikaner Civil Religion* (Berkeley, CA and Los Angeles, CA: University of California Press, 1975).
Robert Morrell, 'The Disintegration of the Gold and Maize Alliance in South Africa in the 1920s', *The International Journal of African Historical Studies*, 21, 4 1988.
Mike Muller, 'Turning on the Taps', *Mail & Guardian*, 25 June 2004.
Ranjeni Munusamy, 'Move to Dislodge Vavi may Fire Back at Zuma', *Daily Maverick*, 13 August 2012, available at http://dailymaverick.co.za/article/2012-08-13-move-to-dislodge-vavi-may-fire-back-at-zuma, accessed 4 October 2013.
——, 'Mandla Mandela and the Chamber of Secrets', *Daily Maverick*, 5 July 2013 available at www.dailymaverick.co.za/article/2013-07-05-mandla-mandela-and-the-

chamber-of-secrets/#.Uk7ctq6B0uk, accessed 4 October 2013.
——, 'The George Dubya of Africa', *Sunday Times*, 13 July 2003.
——, 'Concomitance can mean Dancing with the Devil, Mr Ramaphosa', *Daily Maverick*, 22 July 2013.
Sam Mkokeli, 'Ramaphosa e-mail is a gift to his detractors', *Business Day*, 25 October 2012, available at www.bdlive.co.za/national/politics/2012/10/25/news-analysis-ramaphosa-e-mail-is-a-gift-to-his-detractors, accessed 4 October 2013.
Sam Mkokeli and Carol Paton, 'Ramaphosa SA's Prime Minister', *Business Day*, 20 December 2012, available at www.bdlive.co.za/national/politics/2012/12/20/ramaphosa-sas-prime-minister—mantashe, accessed 5 October 2013.
Ronaldo Munck, The Precariat: A View from the South' *Third World Quarterly*, 34, 5, 2013, pp. 747–762.
Martin J. Murray, *South African Capitalism and Black Political Opposition* (Cambridge, MA: Schenkman, 1982).
Jay Naidoo, *Fighting for Justice: A Lifetime of Political and Social Activism* (Johannesburg: Picador Africa, 2010).
——, 'An Open Letter to COSATU', *The Daily Maverick* (South Africa), 4 September 2012.
Andrew Nash, 'One year after the Marikana massacre', posted on Z-Net at http://mobile.zcommunications.org/one-year-after-the-marikana-massacre-by-andrew-nash, accessed 6 October 2013.
Bill Nasson, *The South African War, 1899–1902* (London: Edward Arnold, 1999).
National Credit Regulatory, 'Consumer Credit Market Report', Johannesburg, available from www.ncr.org.za, accessed 5 October 2013.
National Planning Commission, *Diagnostic Report*', Pretoria, July 2011.
National Security Council (USA), *The Kissinger Study of Southern Africa* (Nottingham: Spokesman Books, 1975).
National Union of Metalworkers of South Africa, Central Committee Statement, Johannesburg, 12 August 2013.
Nicoli Nattrass, 'Post-war Profitability in South Africa: A Critique of Regulation Analysis in South Africa', *Transformation*, 9, 1989.
Babalo Ndenze, 'Inequality gap in SA is a "farce" and media spin, says Zuma', *The Star*, 2 November 2012.
Trevor Ngwane, 'Sparks in the Township', Interview, *New Left Review* (22, July–August 2003).
Greg Nicolson, 'Numsa's Ready to Fight for the Future of the Left', *Daily Maverick*, 13 August 2013.
Gugile Nkwinti, 'Speech by the Minister of Rural Development and Land Reform, Mr G Nkwinti, (MP), Debate on the Budget Vote of the Department of Rural Development and Land Reform', National Assembly, Parliament, March 24 2010.
Paul Nugent, *Africa since Independence: A Comparative History* (Basingstoke: Palgrave Macmillan, 2004).
Blade Nzimande, 'Our condolences and sympathies to the Marikana and Pomeroy victims.' Johannesburg, SA Communist Party, 24 August 2012, available at www.sacp.org.za, accessed 4 October 2013.
——, 'Transforming university and society', *Politicsweb*, 2 October 2012, available at www.politicsweb.co.za/politicsweb/view/politicsweb/en/page72308?oid=329837&sn=Marketingweb+detail&pid=90389, accessed 6 October 2013.
Michael C. O'Dowd, *The O'Dowd Thesis and the Triumph of Democratic Capitalism* (Sandton, S. A.: Free Market Foundation of South Africa, 1996).
Padraig O'Malley, *Shades of Difference: Mac Maharaj and the Struggle for South Africa* (London and Johannesburg: Penguin, 2007).
Dan O'Meara, 'The 1946 African Mine Workers Strike and the Political Economy of South Africa', in Murray, *South African Capitalism* (1982).
——, *Volkskapitalisme: Class, Capital and Ideology in the Development of Afrikaner Nation-*

alism, 1934–1948 (Cambridge: Cambridge University Press, 1983).

——, *Forty Lost Years: The Apartheid State and the Politics of the National Party, 1948–1994* (Athens, OH and Randberg, S. A.: Ohio University Press and Ravan, 1996).

J. D. Omer-Cooper, 'Has the Mfecane a Future? A Response to the Cobbing Critique', *Journal of Southern African Studies*, 19, 2, 1993.

——, *History of Southern Africa*, Second Edition (London: James Currey, 1994).

Vishnu Padayachee, *The Development Decade? Social and Economic Change in South Africa 1994–2004* (Pretoria: HSRC Press, 2005).

Leo Panitch, Greg Albo and Vivek Chibber, *The Socialist Register 2014* (London: The Merlin Press, 2013).

Carol Paton, 'SA's upper class "more African – and ever wealthier"', *Business Day*, 29 July 2013.

Jacques Pauw, *Into the Heart of Darkness: Confessions of Apartheid's Assassins* (Johannesburg: Jonathan Ball Publishers, 1997).

Jeff Peires, '"Soft" Believers and "hard" Unbelievers in the Xhosa Cattle-killing', *Journal of African History*, 27, 1986.

——, 'The central beliefs of the Xhosa cattle-killing', *Journal of African History*, 28, 1987.

Ian Phimister 'Unscrambling the Scramble: Africa's Partition Reconsidered', paper presented to the African Studies Institute, University of Witwatersrand, Johannesburg (17 August 1992).

Marius Pieterse, 'Eating Socioeconomic Rights: The Usefulness of Rights Talk in Alleviating Social Hardship Revisited', *Human Rights Quarterly*, 29, 2007.

Devan Pillay, John Daniel, Prishani Naidoo and Roger Southall (eds), *New South African Review 2: New Paths, Old Compromises* (Johannesburg: University of Witwatersrand Press, 2012).

Deborah Posel, *The Making of Apartheid, 1948–1961: Conflict and Compromise* (Oxford: Clarendon Press, 1991).

Ivor Powell, 'Smoke and Mirrors', *Mail & Guardian*, 1 May 2009.

Kalim Rajab, 'Message to Cabinet: It is NOT just a wedding', *Daily Maverick*, 6 May 2013.

Piet Rampedi and Shaun Smillie, 'Get Back to Work', *The Star*, 18 October 2012, available at www.iol.co.za/the-star/get-back-to-work-1.1405430, accessed 4 October 2013.

Malcolm Rees, 'Financially Illiterate Miners Debt Shocker', *Moneyweb*,1 October 2012.

Republic of South Africa, *Constitution of the Republic of South Africa*, Act 108 of 1996, Cape Town.

Jennifer Robinson, *The Power of Apartheid: State, Power and Space in South African cities* (Oxford and Boston: Butterworth-Heinemann, 1996).

Amy Roeder, 'The Cost of South Africa's Misguided AIDS Policies', *Harvard Public Health*, Spring 2009, available at www.hsph.harvard.edu/news/magazine/spr09aids, accessed 2 October 2013.

John Roome, 'Water Pricing and Management: World Bank Presentation to the SA Water Conservation Conference', unpublished paper, South Africa, 2 October 1995.

Rob Rose, 'Companies "Shirking" their Nepad Obligations', *Business Day*, 24 May 2004.

Zachary Rosen, 'Popstars Politics in the New South Africa: A Conversation with Masello Motana', *Africa is a Country*, 28 March 2013, available at http://africasacountry.com/2013/03/29/popstars-politicians-and-personhood-a-conversation-with-masello-motana, accessed 4 October 2013.

Robert Ross, *A Concise History of South Africa* (Cambridge: Cambridge University Press, 1999).

Greg Ruiters, *Development Challenges in the Eastern Cape* (Pietermaritzburg: University of KwaZulu-Natal Press, 2011).

SABC, 'Nzimande Condemns Exploitation of Mine Workers', 28 October 2012, available at www.sabc.co.za/news/a/7fbbfb804d3dc362af9affe570eb4ca2/Nzimande-condemns-exploitation-of-mine-workers—20121028, accessed 4 October 2013.

Sake24, 'SAA Stops Durban, Cape Town Flights', 6 October 2010, available at www.sake24.com, accessed 3 October 2013.

SAPA, 'SA's "Imperialist" Image in Africa', 30 March 2004.

——, 'Nepad losing momentum: Mbeki', 12 December 2008.

——, 'Police Caspir Burnt down in Protest', 23 March 2010.

——, 'ANC backs NUM, Urges Recruitment', 21 July 2013, available at http://news24.com/fin24/Companies/Mining/ANC-backs-NUM-urges-recruitment-20130721, accessed 4 October 2013.

—— 'Land Beneficiaries owed R34 billion', Pretoria, 25 July 2010, available at www.news24.com/SouthAfrica/Politics/Land-beneficiaries-owed-R34bn-Nkwinti-20100705, accessed 3 October 2013.

——, 'Cosatu to Reclaim Rustenburg from "Forces of Counter Revolution"', 20 October 2012, available from www.timeslive.co.za/local/2012/10/20/cosatu-to-reclaim-rustenburg-from-forces-of-counter-revolution, accessed 4 October 2013.

Vishwas Satgar, 'The Marikana Massacre and the South African State's Low Intensity War Against the People,' *The Bullet: A Socialist Project E-Bulletin*, 693, 5 September, 2012.

Vishwas Satgar and Mazibuko Jara, 'New Times Require New Democratic Left', *Mail & Guardian* online, 7 Feb 2011, available at www.mg.co.za/article/2011-02-07-new-times-require-democratic-left, accessed 5 October 2013.

Richard Sandbrook and Robin Cohen (eds), *The Development of an African Working Class: Studies in Class Formation and Action* (London: Longman, 1975).

John S. Saul 'Now for the Hard Part', *Southern Africa Report*, 9, 5 and 10, 1, July, 1994.

——, *Millennial Africa: Capitalism, Socialism and Democracy* (Trenton, NJ: Africa World Press, 2001).

——, *The Next Liberation Struggle: Capitalism, Socialism and Democracy in Southern Africa* (Toronto, New York, Scottsville, S.A., and London: Between The Lines, Monthly Review Press, University of KwaZulu-Natal and Merlin Press, 2005).

——, 'The Strange Death of Liberated Southern Africa', *Transformation*, 64, 1, 2007.

——, *Revolutionary Traveller: Freeze-Frames from a Life* (Winnipeg: Arbeiter Ring, 2009).

——, 'Two fronts of anti-apartheid struggle: South Africa and Canada', *Transformation*, 74, 2010.

——, *Liberation Lite: The Roots of Recolonization in Southern Africa* (Delhi and Trenton, NJ: Three Essays Collective and Africa World Press, 2011).

——, 'On Taming a Revolution: The South African Case', in *The Socialist Register 2014* (London: The Merlin Press, 2013).

——, *What Next in Southern Africa? 'Globalization Made Me Do It' versus 'The Struggle Continues'* (forthcoming).

——, *A Flawed Freedom: Rethinking Southern African Liberation* (Delhi, London and Toronto: Three Essays Collective, Pluto Press and Between The Lines, 2014).

——, John S. Saul, *A Partial Victory: The North American Campaign for Southern African Liberation in Global Perspective* (New York: Monthly Review Press, forthcoming).

John S. Saul and Stephen Gelb, *The Crisis in South Africa* (New York: Monthly Review Press, 1981; revised edition 1986).

James Saunders, *Apartheid's Friends: The Rise and Fall of South Africa's Secret Service* (London: John Murray, 2006).

Kurt Schock, *Unarmed Insurrections: People's Power Movements in Nondemocracies* (Minneapolis: University of Minnesota Press, 2005).

Jeremy Seekings, 'The Decline of South Africa's Civic Organizations, 1990–1996', *Critical Sociology*, 22, 3, 1996, pp. 113–134.

——, *The UDF: A History of the United Democratic Front in South Africa, 1983–1991* (Claremont, S.A.: David Phillip, 2000).

Jeremy Seekings and Nicoli Nattrass, *Class, Race and Inequality in South Africa* (New Haven and London: Yale University Press, 2005).

Shopsteward, 'Banks buckle under public pressure', 5, 3, 1996, available at www.cosatu. org.za/show.php?ID=2080#INTERVIEW, accessed 5 October 2013.Loyiso Sidimba, 'Khulubuse, Others Face Criminal Charges – Liquidators', *City Press*, 27 March 2013, available at www.citypress.co.za/politics/khulubuse-others-face-criminal-charges-liquidators, accessed 4 October 2013.

Timothy D. Sisk, *Democratization in South Africa: The Elusive Social Contract* (Princeton: Princeton University Press, 1995).

No Sizwe, *One Azania, One Nation: The National Question in South Africa* (London: Zed Press, 1979).

Joe Slovo, *The South African Working Class and the National Democratic Revolution* (Umsebenzi Discussion Pamplet, SACP, 1988).

——, *Has Socialism Failed?* (Umsebenzi Discussion Pamphlet, SACP, 1990).

David Smith, 'Mbeki fears South Africa is "losing sense of direction"', *The Guardian*, 22 October 2012.

——, 'Ramaphosa has blood on his hands, say miners', *The Guardian*, 25 October 2012.

Janet Smith and Beauregard Tromp, *Hani: A Life Too Short* (Johannesburg and Cape Town: Jonathan Ball, 2009).

Sam Sole, 'Browsed and Beaten', *Mail & Guardian*, 1 May 2009.

South African Communist Party, 'Central Committee Discussion of Joe Slovo's Presentation', *The African Communist*, 135 (Fourth Quarter, 1993).

South Africa Government Communications and Information System, 'Statement on Cabinet Meeting', Pretoria, 26 June 2002.

——, 'Towards a Ten Year Review', Pretoria, 2003.

——, 'The State of our environment should remain under a watchful eye', Pretoria, 29 June 2007, available at www.info.gov.za/speeches/2007/07062911151001.htm, accessed 2 October 2013.

South African National Civic Organization, *Making People-Driven Development Work* (Johannesburg: SANCO, 1994).

South African Press Association (SAPA), 'Mankahlana Misses Maintenance-court Hearing', 5 September 2000.

South African Reserve Bank, *Quarterly Bulletins*, available at www.resbank. co.za/Lists/News%20and%20Publications/Attachments/5133/01Full% 20Quarterly%20Bulletin.pdf, accessed 2 October 2013.

Roger Southall and Eddie Webster, 'Unions and parties in South Africa: COSATU and the ANC in the wake of Polokwane', in Beckman et al., *Trade Unions and Party Politics*.

Guy Standing, *The Precariat: The New Dangerous Class* (London: Bloomsbury Academic, 2011).

Statistics South Africa, 'The South African Labour Market', Pretoria, 2002.

——, 'State of the World Population 2004', Pretoria, 17 September 2004, available at www.statssa.gov.za/news_archive/17sep2004_1.asp, accessed on 2 October 2013.

——, 'Gender Statistics 2011', available from http://beta2.statssa.gov.za, accessed 6 October 2013.

Kwanele Sosibo, 'Why the Left Has Failed to Capitalise on Post-Marikana Massacre Cracks in the ANC Hegemony', *The Con*, 25 June 2013, available at www.theconmag.co.za/2013/06/25/why-the-left-has-failed-to-capitalise-on-post-marikana-massacre-cracks-in-the-anc-hegemony,_accessed 5 October 2013.

Kwanele Sosibo, 'After Marikana: The Missing 22% and the Return of R12500', *The Con*, 23 August 2013.

Allister Sparks, *Tomorrow is Another Country: The Inside Story of South Africa's Negotiated Revolution* (Sandton, S.A.: Struik, 1994).

——, 'A Shift in the Political Landscape', *Cape Times*, 19 June 2013.

——, 'ANC is Becoming Beatable', *The Mercury*, 14 August 2013.

Lisa Steyn, 'Marikana Miners in Debt Sinkhole,' *Mail & Guardian*, 7 September 2012.

——, 'Measuring the Waves of Migration', *Mail & Guardian* 11 January 2013.

Veronica Strang, *The Meaning of Water* (Oxford: Berg Publishers, 2004).

Raymond Suttner, 'Central Committee discussion of Joe Slovo's presentation', *The African Communist*, 135, Fourth Quarter, 1993.

——, 'Legacies and Meanings of the United Democratic Front (UDF) Period for Contemporary South Africa', *Journal of Southern African Studies*, 30, 3, 2004) pp. 691–702.

——, *The ANC Underground in South Africa* (Auckland Park, S.A.: Jacana, 2008).

Paul Sweezy, *The Present as History* (New York: Monthly Review Press, 1953).

Mark Swilling, 'Deracialised Urbanisation: A Critique of the New Urban Strategies and Some Policy Alternatives from a Democratic Perspective', *Urban Forum*, 1, 2, 1990.

Sampie Terreblanche, *A History of Inequality in South Africa, 1652–2002* (Scottsville: University of Natal Press, 2002).

——, *Lost in Transformation: South Africa's Search for a New Future Since 1986* (Johannesburg: KMM Review Publishing, 2012).

Leonard Thompson, *A History of South Africa* (New Haven and London: Yale University Press, 1990).

Stanley Trapido, 'South Africa in a Comparative Study of Industrialization', *The Journal of Development Studies*, 7, 3, 1971.

Rick Turner, *The Eye of the Needle: Towards Participatory Democracy in South Africa* (Johannesburg: Ravan, 1980).Ben Turok, *From the Freedom Charter to Polokwane: The Evolution of ANC Economic Policy* (Cape Town: New Agenda, 2008).

Rob Turrell, *Capital and Labour on the Kimberley Diamond Fields, 1871–1890* (Cambridge: Cambridge University Press, 1987).

Glynnis Underhill, 'Duduzane Zuma to be Gupta news channel's BEE partner', *Mail & Guardian*, 9 August 2013.

United Nations Development Programme (UNDP), *Human Development Report South Africa* (Pretoria: UNDP South Africa, 2003).

——, *South Africa Human Development Report 2003*, Appendix 12 (New York: UNDP, 2003).

Salim Vally and C. A. Spreen, 'Education Rights, Education Policy and Inequality in South Africa', *International Journal of Educational Development*, 26, 4, 2006.

A. J. van der Walt. *Theories of Social and Economic Justice* (Stellenbosch: Stellenbosch University Press, 2005).

Ineke van Kessel, *'Beyond Our Wildest Dreams': The United Democratic Front and the Transformation of South Africa* (Charlotteville: The University Press of Virginia, 2000).

——, 'Trajectories after liberation in South Africa: mission accomplished or vision betrayed?' *Zuid-Afrika & Leiden* (Leiden: University of Leiden, 2011) available at http://zuidafrikaleiden.nl/onderzoek/trajectories-after-liberation-south-africa, accessed 6 October 2013.

Ryk van Niekirk, 'Zuma's Political Coup d'État: Shows leadership and political finesse to purge all adversaries', *Moneyweb*, 21 December 2012, available at www.moneyweb.co.za/moneyweb-mangaung/zumas-political-coup-dtat, accessed 6 October 2013.

Charles van Onselen, *The Seed is Mine: The Life of Kas Maine, a South African Sharecropper, 1894–1985* (New York: Hill & Wang, 1997).

Andrea van Wyk, 'Take a Chill Pill and Sit Down, Malema tells Defence Minister', *Eyewitness News*, 12 September 2012, available at http://ewn.co.za/2012/09/12/Take-a-chill-pill-Malema-tells-defence-minister, accessed 4 October 2013.

Zwelinzima Vavi, 'Keynote address to the Civil Society Conference', 27 October 2010, available at www.cosatu.org.za/show.php?ID=4170, accessed 5 October 2013.

Cheryl Walker, *Women and Resistance in South Africa* (New York: Monthly Review Press, 1991 – Second Edition; London: Onyx Press, 1982).

Peter Walshe, *Black Nationalism in South Africa* (Johannesburg: Ravan Press, 1973).

P. Warwick, *Black People and the South African War, 1899–1902* (Johannesburg: Ravan, 1983).

Eddie Webster and Glenn Adler, 'Exodus Without a Map: The Labour Movement in a Liberalizing South Africa', in Beckman & Sachikonye, *Labour Regimes and Liberalization*.

White House Press Office, 'Press Release: Remarks by President Bush and President Mbeki of South Africa in Photo Opportunity', Washington, 8 December 2006.

Phumla Williams, 'Celebrating our women's liberation', *The South African Government blog*, 30 July 2013.

Michelle Williams, *The Roots of Participatory Democracy: Democratic Communists in South Africa and Kerala, India* (New York and London: Palgrave MacMillan, 2008).

Michelle Williams and Vishwas Satgar, *Introducing New Approaches to Marxism: Critique and Struggle* (Johannesburg: Wits University Press, 2013).

Lindi Wilson, *Steve Biko* (Auckland Park, S.A.: Jacana, 2011).

Harold Wolpe, 'Capitalism and Cheap Labour Power in South Africa: From Segregation to Apartheid', *Economy and Society*, 1, 4, 1972.

Elisabeth Jean Wood, *Forging Democracy from Below: Insurgent Transitions in South Africa and El Salvador* (Cambridge and New York: Cambridge University Press, 2000).

Nigel Worden, *The Making of Modern South Africa: Conquest, Segregation and Apartheid* (Oxford: Blackwell, 1994 and in later editions – Fourth Edition 2007).

World Bank, *Country Assistance Strategy: South Africa*, Annex C (Washington DC: World Bank, 1999), p. 5.

——, *Sourcebook on Community Driven Development in the Africa Region: Community Action Programs* (Washington DC: World Bank, 2000).

——, *Where is the Wealth of Nations* (Washington DC: World Bank, 2006).

——, *The Changing Wealth of Nations* (Washington DC: World Bank, 2011).

World Economic Forum, *Global Competitiveness Report 2012–2013*, Davos, September 2012, available at www.weforum.org/reports/global-competitiveness-report-2012-2013, accessed 5 October 2013.

John Wright, 'Mfecane Debates', *SARoB*, Double Issue 39–40, 1995.

Geoffrey York, 'South Africa Reels as Death Toll Rises: Number of miners killed by police revised to 34 as President announces probe and analysts compare event to apartheid massacres', *The Globe and Mail*, 18 August 2012.

——, 'Ramaphosa Poised to take ANC job: Businessman, former politician may ascend to party's second highest post without even campaigning', *The Globe and Mail*, 18 December 2012.

——, 'Zuma Easily Retains ANC Party Leadership: Wealthy businessman and former union leader Cyril Ramaphosa chosen to be President's deputy leader', *The Globe and Mail*, 19 December 2012.

Mona Younis, *Liberation and Democratization: The South African and Palestinian National Movements* (Minneapolis: University of Minnesota Press, 2000).

David Yudelman, *The Emergence of Modern South Africa: State, Capital and the Incorporation of Organized Labor on the South African Gold Fields, 1902–1939* (Westport, CT: Greenwood Press, 1983).

Elke Zuern, *The Politics of Necessity: Community Organizing and Democracy in South Africa* (Madison, WI: University of Wisconsin Press, 2011).

Index

Abdurahman, Adullah 49
Absa Bank 150, 184n22, 202
accountability 3, 96, 188
accumulation: capital 185, 223; class
    conflict and 145–75; personal 209;
    sustainable 182
Acid Mine Drainage 168, 223
Act of Union (1910) 31, 35, 36, 47–9
Adcock Ingram 196
Adelzadeh, Asghar 138
Adler, Glenn 70–71, 73, 74, 92
African Bank 219
African National Congress (ANC) 1, 2, 7, 8,
    16, 47, 48–56, 61, 73, 75, 77–8, 85–6,
    88, 90–91, 93–4, 109, 114–15, 120,
    146, 148, 151, 174, 214, 219, 223,
    234, 256, 261–2; accomplishments of
    178; 'African Claims in South Africa' 51;
    anniversary of founding of 243n1, 245;
    and anti-capitalism 108; and armed
    struggle 51, 56, 99; ascension of to
    legitimacy and power 65, 111, 139, 149;
    black elites linked to 63–64; capital as
    ally in deracialization 173; capitulation
    of to capitalism 123; centrifugal
    pressures on 241; Chancellor House
    investment arm 223; collapse of as mass
    political organization 141; concessions
    made by during transition 146, 151;
    counter-elite of 102; cynicism about
    230; and demobilization of mass
    movements 156; and demobilization of
    unions 154; desultory existence of
    between wars 49; disappointing outcome
    of victory of 243, 247; drive to power,
    94–105; effectiveness of 52; electoral
    dominance of 256; elites of 126, 136,
    236; elitism of 52; embrace of liberalism
    by 213; emergence of 48; exiled leaders
    of 124, 147; fall of from grace and
    morality 184; fractured nature of 227–
    32, 265; hegemony of 104, 248, 253,
    256, 265; history of 124; hold of on
    power 244; hostility of to strikes 154–5;
    internal wing of 245; international
    resonance of 245; leadership 'chickening
    out' 125, 127, 269; legitimacy of as

governing party 1, 65, 247; and
    liberation 245–50; loss of legitimacy of
    244; lost promise of as people's
    movement 3; macro-economic policies of
    252; Mangaung conference 176–7,
    209–10, 227 230–31, 235, 265–70;
    and mass movement for democratic
    change 122–3; multi-racial 79; and NP
    132; negotiations with apartheid state
    121; neo-liberalist nationalism of 242;
    neo-liberal wing of 231, 237; new
    leadership of as marriage of corruption
    and capitalism 265; non-African
    membership of 8; non-racial definition
    of South Africa 8; as party of liberation
    246; petty-bourgeois nationalist
    character of 51; political ascendancy of
    15; as political juggernaut 246;
    Polokwane conference 176; popular
    salience of 245; restoring of soul of 270;
    revival of 50; rightward drift of 251; rise
    of mission of liberation of 243; sabotage
    campaign of 56; social and economic
    policy choices of 3, 78; Soviet support for
    94, 97; stabilization of political turmoil
    of 232; symbolic political capital of 268;
    and transition to post-apartheid state
    121, 128–9, 131–7, 141–2, 146, 151;
    transparent failure of 248; Tripartite
    Alliance 68, 70, 74, 76–8, 150–51, 208,
    214, 225–6, 227, 236, 250, 253–4,
    260–1; turn to mass action 51; two-
    stage revolution 94; unbanning of 120,
    121, 123, 147; underground 101;
    weakening of hold on power of 266;
    Women's League 54; as 'yesterday's
    movement' 256; Youth League 52, 209,
    234–5
African Peer Review Mechanism (APRM),
    199, 204
African People's Organization (APO) 49
African Renaissance 199
Africans: apartheid aimed at 43; clawing
    back of political rights of 39; ethnic
    diversity among 20; as ethnic others 59;
    as farm labourers on white land 35; as
    historical actors 17; indirect rule of 27;

289

Printed and bound by CPI Group (UK) Ltd, Croydon, CR0 4YY

09/06/2025

14685710-0005